SUPER STAR DJS

To my late parents,
Gill and Bernard 'Narse' Phillips

SUPER STAR DJS
HERE WE GO!

DOM PHILLIPS

ADDITIONAL RESEARCH DAN PRINCE

EBURY
PRESS

3 5 7 9 10 8 6 4 2

Published in 2009 by Ebury Press, an imprint of Ebury Publishing
A Random House Group Company

The Random House Group Limited Reg. No. 954009

Addresses for companies within the Random House Group
can be found at www.randomhouse.co.uk

A CIP catalogue record for this book is available from the British Library

The Random House Group Limited supports The Forest Stewardship Council (FSC®), the
leading international forest certification organisation. Our books carrying the FSC label are
printed on FSC® certified paper. FSC is the only forest certification scheme endorsed by the
leading environmental organisations, including Greenpeace. Our paper procurement policy
can be found at www.randomhouse.co.uk/environment

MIX
Paper from
responsible sources
FSC® C016897

Designed and set by seagulls.net

Printed in the UK by CPI Group (UK), Croydon, CR0 4YY

ISBN 9780091926939

To buy books by your favourite authors and register for offers visit
www.randomhouse.co.uk

CONTENTS

ACKNOWLEDGEMENTS

Superstar DJs Here We Go would not have been possible without all the DJs, promoters, agents, record company executives, lawyers, managers and former *Mixmag* staff who participated. I am very grateful to all of them for taking the time to talk to me and for being so honest.

I would like to thank my family, Gareth, Sian and Judith Phillips and Derek Price. My agents David Godwin and Sophie Hoult at DGA. Jake Lingwood and Ali Nightingale at Ebury. David Davies for reading the manuscript and making invaluable suggestions. Dan Prince for invaluable research. Lucinda Duxbury for additional research. Ben Rossington at the *Liverpool Echo*. Amy Howard at The Official Charts Company for figures. Miranda Sawyer for writing the foreword. And Nick Decosemo, Jerry Perkins and all at *Mixmag* for letting me trawl their archive for two weeks.

For encouragement with the initial idea I would like to thank Sheryl Garratt and Simon Prosser. For friendship, feedback, help and support in the UK and Brazil I would like to thank in no particular order Henrique Cury, Roxy Abdalla, Luciana Daud, Sylvia Colombo, Raul Juste Lores. Luiz Eurico. Tony Danby and Ana Marcia Lopes. John Rumsey. Jessé Reis Alves, Andy Robbins, Frank Broughton and Imogen Crosby. Michael Cook. Stephanie Collin. John Mitchell. Ruby Evans. Clare Handford. Antoine Robin. Fatima Carvalho. Richard Lapper. Otavio Cury. Fatima Nunes. Dean Belcher for the best superstar DJ photo ever taken. Marek Budzynksi. Paddy Meehan. Ernesto Leal. Marcia Arcuri. Matt Ballard. Andy Horsfield.

... HERE WE GO!

Acid house was the last great British youth movement, the final hooray before I'm-worth-it individualism took hold. Its music was revolutionary, and its legacy changed the face of modern Britain. The Government felt forced to legislate, passing a law to ban "repetitive beats", clamping down on outdoor raves, panicking about ecstasy. All because, back in the late 80s, the UK's cities just couldn't provide what young people wanted: all night shenanigans, no holds barred.

Post-rave, Britain has changed. Everyone goes out now, for as long as they want. Twenty four hour drinking has ensured that the nation's legal drug is always on tap, no way would the breweries ever again allow young people to enjoy themselves without alcohol in their hands. Today, fun has been mainstreamed. Everyone's doing it.

But for a time in the late 80s and early 90s, the underground was the only alternative. Why bother with violent, no-trainers, early-doors nightclubs when there was an all-night warehouse party going on? Acid house took the best bits of hippy and punk – the come-together equality of hippiness, the screw-the-system of punk – and melded it with exuberance, futuristic music and, yes, love.

Like punk, it was as much about the crowd as the stars. DJs were at one with their audience; faceless, unphotographed, unstyled. Humans love their heroes, though, and there was no way that DJs could remain underground forever. Within a matter of a few short months, a select few became, if not famous, then thoroughly notorious. These superstar DJs rolled like international celebrities, jetting between the most beautiful places in the world, partying for days with the most beautiful people in the world. And getting paid for it. And acid house changed. As it grew bigger, as dance music became so all-encompassing that it spawned its own chart, as those dangerously repetitive beats were used to sell everything from make-up to *The Sun*, the scene became very definitely overground. During the mid to late 90s, house music was on top, in all senses. Superclubs pulled in thousands of punters every weekend, dance music CDs squatted in the Top Ten, ecstasy use peaked and some superstar DJs, such as Norman Cook, became bona fide stars. Dance music became so enormous it spiralled off into other areas, becoming both the soundtrack of eco-warrior protests and the victorious New Labour party.

As editor of *Mixmag*, Dom Phillips lived through acid house's big decade, hanging with high-rollers and hangers-on, superstar DJs and those who fell through the loop. From Miami pool parties to a club in a Russian nuclear fallout shelter, wherever dance music took him, Dom was there. And when he wasn't, he's talked to someone who was. In this rollercoaster book, he documents the wild excesses of the house music happy times. He captures the characters and the come-downs. And he also portrays the shift in British consciousness that occurred with house music.

It's easy to dismiss a musical genre that, in the end, became so cheesy, so all-encompassing. But dance music altered the nation's social landscape. Today, the changes brought about by rave are so embedded in the everyday that we forget what life was like before them. Outdoor festivals, cool bars, the idea that everyone is entitled to some form of mad, music-fuelled youth. A youth that stretches on forever. After all, how many superstar DJs actually retired? The comedown for some can be harsh. But for most of us, acid house made life better.

Miranda Sawyer

INTRODUCTION

Other, more famous DJs might choose more dramatic ways to sum up their superstar DJ lives. Norman Cook DJing in front of 360,000 people on the beach in Rio; Sasha being whisked through rush-hour Manila by a police escort; Jeremy Healy haring around New York in a limousine full of supermodels. For Steve Lee it was a Bank Holiday weekend in 1993 that could have been any weekend in the 1990s. Just as Steve Lee could have been any of a hundred star DJs, charging around the country, playing records, having fun, making cash, losing sleep. Birmingham Friday; Venus in Nottingham, Saturday; a private Primal Scream show Sunday in Aylesbury; somehow passing a breathalyser test after a South London gig on Monday. Home safe with money in his pocket. 'Sweet as a nut,' he said. But it was the football he remembered best, on the Sunday morning that Saturday night had gone into, after Venus. 'We all ended in a car park by the River Trent. I was DJing with Justin Robertson, there was a generator and some record decks. There was no one dancing and Justin's gone to me, "Oh, look at this." Behind us they had a game of football going on. They had no ball, so they was passing a lump of air about, right! Ali from Flying was in goal. Some geezer's taken a shot, they've all gone mad. I would have said, "Oh, it's gone over the bar." And Ali's gone running off down there, picked up a lump of air, come back, kicked it out. Funniest thing.' It is a story that says as much about the superstar DJ era as any wilder tales. A real game, with an imaginary ball...

1

ARTHUR DENT MADE for the unlikeliest of heroes. Clad in pyjamas and a dressing gown, he was the hapless, bumbling leading man in Douglas Adams's intergalactic comedy *The Hitchhiker's Guide to the Galaxy*, which began in 1978 as a comedy series on BBC radio and quickly gravitated to television series and book form. Just as the earth is about to be destroyed to make way for an interplanetary bypass, Dent is rescued by his best friend Ford Prefect, who turns out to be an alien and proceeds to hitchhike around the galaxy in a sequence of increasingly bizarre adventures. The book sold a million copies and even became a movie. But more than a comedy sci-fi series, *The Hitchhiker's Guide to the Galaxy* was the *Gulliver's Travels* of its time, a satire on the absurdity of modern life that struck a chord with its millions of fans.

In it Adams described a planet called Golgafrincham, the inhabitants of which decide to get rid of what they consider the most useless third of their population – the middle managers, telephone sanitisers, hairdressers and environmentalists – with an ingenious ploy. In a Noah's Ark parable, they persuade them that the planet is about to be wiped out and the population has to flee on three giant spaceships. One ship will carry all the leaders: politicians, generals, journalists. Another the workers: mechanics, carpenters, doers, etc. All the hairdressers, telephone sanitisers and middle managers will be on the third ship and it is the only one that actually leaves. This ship crashes into prehistoric earth, wipes out a peaceful, yet primitive population and its passengers become our modern ancestors. The rest of Golgafrincham are wiped out by a disease that begins – oh, the irony – with a dirty telephone.

In 1988 a mother ship did land on Planet UK, full of the same sort of people. It was called Acid House and it was to make quite an impact. Powered by hypnotic electronic grooves and class A drugs, but lacking songs to sing along to, performers to look at, or any kind of structure to an evening out apart than dancing wildly, acid house still somehow conjured up enough entertainment out of thin air to bewitch a nation for more than a decade. It was all smoke and mirrors. But acid house transformed Britain. From 1992, when acid house moved into legal venues, until 2000, this was the era of superstar DJs and superclubs. A generation gleefully lost itself in a maelstrom of disco euphoria and house music and clubbing became the defining sound and lifestyle of 1990s Britain.

The people who landed on that acid house mother ship, the DJs and promoters who wrought that transformation, were not the usual harbingers of pop culture revolutions. They didn't yearn to get on a stage and be rock stars like Jimi Hendrix or Noel Gallagher. They didn't want to change the face of fashion, to play situationist pranks like Malcolm McLaren and Vivienne Westwood did with punk. They weren't interested in art or the history of pop music and they didn't sit in their bedrooms like Morrissey, furiously writing letters to the music papers and dreaming of pop stardom. Instead, they were misfits and middlemen, chancers, blaggers and hustlers, party animals and lairy lads. Telephone salesmen and ticket touts. Oh and hairdressers, because a disproportionate amount of the major players in 1990s club land were former hairdressers. Ordinary guys drifting along until, one enchanted evening, they stumbled into a place where acid house was happening, took ecstasy and decided they never wanted to do else anything again.

Incredibly enough, they by and large succeeded, in many cases never having to pick up those hairdressing scissors or put on those mechanics' overalls again. They played football with lumps of air and made fortunes out of it. 'There was a load of us, working-class people who liked playing records, taking ecstasy, sniffing cocaine, that ended up having excess money, notoriety, fame within their own scene,' said

Phil Gifford, a Birmingham hairdresser whose club Wobble made him a DJ star. 'You're a bit of a working-class idiot. You've got some cash. You're doing well. You've got a buzz off it and you're going to live a rock 'n' roll lifestyle.'

Unlike *Hitchhiker's* Arthur Dent, who was a traditionally British hero, confused, socially awkward and forever in search of a good cup of tea, the passengers on the acid house spaceship were cool: leaders of the pack, the most charismatic guys on the block, the lads with the charm, the blag, the patter, the girls. Just as George Clinton's funk mothership and John Travolta's spinning disco moves in *Saturday Night Fever* had transformed 1970s America, these acid house DJs sent the UK into a spin. They made Britain funky. They put one nation under a groove.

Dancing wildly in nightclubs, as anybody who spent time doing so in the 1990s knows, is an experience as intense as it is inane, as emotional as it is ephemeral. Yet these spaceship passengers understood something simple, yet profound – that wild parties make people feel good about themselves, at least until the next morning. That God sometimes hides in the tiniest of details, no matter how frivolous and facile those details might be. And that nothing feels quite like a new haircut.

ACID HOUSE HAD exploded in the UK in 1988, spreading from clubs in London and Manchester to giant, illegal outdoor raves during the so-called Summers of Love, immortalised on tabloid front pages and in that smiley face logo. Then it had slipped from view, under the radar, into smaller, dressier, in-the-know clubs in places like Nottingham and Stoke. In 1992, smartened up and now staged in legal venues, it came back. The superclub era began in the North, with clubs like Renaissance and later Cream in Liverpool. Ministry of Sound had already opened the previous year in London. The superstar DJs became their stars.

Clubs opened across the UK, with names that captured what they were about: Gatecrasher and Love To Be in Sheffield, Slinky in Bournemouth, Colours in Edinburgh, Time Flies in Cardiff, Decadance in Birmingham, Hot To Trot and Goodbye Cruel World in Leicester, Passion in Coalville, Wobble and Fun and Miss Moneypenny's in Birmingham, Pimp in Wolverhampton, Karanga in Bath, Back To Basics, Up Yer Ronson and Vague in Leeds, Hard Times in tiny Todmorden. By the late 1990s, it seemed that every city in the UK had its own club. Including Inverness and little Lerwick, in the Shetland Islands.

An industry grew up around this expanding network of clubs. The DJs who performed in them, the agents who booked the DJs, the promoters who paid the DJs and ran the clubs, the clubbers who partied and danced in them, the drug dealers who supplied them. This wasn't like the 1980s, when only people down South got rich. In the 1990s, suddenly, money was everywhere. Young Britain had cash in its pocket, a new love of designer clothes, a developing taste for drugs and an eye for a party. DJs suddenly found themselves with high-paid careers, hurtling up and down the country playing at three clubs a night, earning thousands of pounds in cash a year, being offered champagne and drugs for free, partying through it all. 'I think to make party music you have to party,' said Norman 'Fatboy Slim' Cook. 'It's unprofessional if you don't, you have to walk the walk.'

DJs like him, Sasha, Paul Oakenfold, Sonique, Pete Tong, Dave Seaman, Judge Jules and Jeremy Healy became rich and famous, living rock-star lives: fans, fame and a life that was a whirlwind of five-star luxury. 'The biggest indulgence is when you spent money on private jets,' observed Pete Tong. The clubs they played in became part of the architecture of British leisure and their owners became rich, famous in clubland. Superclub albums sold hundreds of thousands of copies – in 1996, just one of them, the Ministry of Sound *Annual II* album, mixed by Pete Tong and Boy George, reached number one in the charts and sold 613,000 copies.*

Acid house bounced into politics. After 20,000 gathered for a free, three-day rave at Castlemorton, the Conservative government legislated against it in the infamous 1994 Criminal Justice Act. Yet three years later, New Labour rode to victory on an ecstasy anthem, D:Ream's 'Things Can Only Get Better'. By the end of the 1990s, brands as diverse as PlayStation, the Halifax and Guinness were using dance music and club-related imagery to sell products. Dance music was everywhere – from Pete Tong's *News of the World* column to daytime radio, from high-street stores to high-street discos. And everyone seemed to be taking drugs. According to NHS statistics, by 1998 31.8 per cent of 16–24-year-olds had used an illegal drug in the last year – more than two million people. These were the boom years of fast living and easy money. Acid house was unstoppable. And then it all went spectacularly wrong.

The millennium was the crux point. It was going to be the biggest party of all time and the superclubs were going to stage it. For DJs, it was a bonanza and they were being paid up to £140,000 for a night's work. But clubbers stayed home. The club industry delivered a bitter night of half-empty raves. The superstar DJ and superclub hierarchy suddenly looked like a rip-off, a nasty, cynical business that had left its client base of clubbers out in the cold. An audience that had suddenly realised they too were playing football with a lump of air.

* Figures copyright The Official Charts Company

The comedown was long and bitter. Clubs emptied out and closed. DJs became taxi drivers and computer programmers and club promoters went back to the hairdressing salon. Worst of all, DJs became uncool, a parody of themselves. 'I don't give a fuck what anybody says,' said James Lavelle, a DJ who lived the 1990s high life before it went wrong. 'I reckon that everybody lost it. That's their stories to tell. But I think there was a massive, massive punch in the face for everybody.'

What happened? How and why did something that had such a momentous impact on UK culture – a massive, decade-long party – come to such a screeching halt? Where did it all go Pete Tong?

I also landed in the UK in 1988 after a period spent travelling. Entranced by what I was hearing on pirate radio and in clubs and raves, I started writing about dance music in 1988, on a small Bristol magazine I set up and in magazines like *Soul Underground* and *i-D*. I joined clubbing magazine *Mixmag* in 1991 and stayed until January 1999, swept up, like many, in the acid house wave. As the magazine's editor from 1993 to 1998, I got to know all the DJs and club promoters of the time.

A decade later, I decided to track down these characters, to interview them and find out where they were at now, to see what they thought looking back. I wanted to tell the story of the superstar DJ era through their stories and make some sense of the biggest British pop cultural phenomenon since the birth of rock 'n' roll itself. To get there I had to go back to the beginning: a nowhere northern town, on a blustery spring night in 1992, the night the game without a ball really began.

Dom Phillips
São Paulo, Brazil
August 2008

ONE

THE RESTORATION OF SASHA TO THE NORTH

TUNE: HARDFLOOR – 'HARDTRANCE ACPERIENCE'

Nine minutes of twisting, intoxicating German trance that caused uproar – especially if it wasn't played in its entirety.

JUNE 1999, IBIZA. They called Space the best club in the world. It was certainly the most international, the most glamorously wasted. It didn't even open until noon. Which barely fazed the crowd, winding its way around the car park by 11.30 a.m., waiting expectantly for the doors to open for the first party of the summer. Most of them had already been up all night. None of them looked any the worse for it.

Hours later, out on the terrace, with dusk beginning to fall and jets from the nearby airport thundering just metres overhead, Sasha played his second set, holding the dance floor in the palm of his hand. A German boy in combat trousers roared his approval next to two beaming British club babes. A transvestite so tall s/he looked like s/he was wearing stilts did sema-phore. An Argentinian hippie chick danced with an Italian male stripper and a delighted Red Indian chief shoved his tongue in the mouth of his rubber-clad dominatrix girlfriend. Up in the DJ booth, Sasha brandished a bottle of Jägermeister like a sword in his left hand and played records with his right: swaying to track after track of fiercely uncompromising grooves as the atmosphere on the dance floor climbed higher and higher.

Suddenly, all eyes on him, he froze. With a theatrical slug he drained the bottle and rapidly executed a stop-start on the harsh percussion track he was playing. He paused the music, finger hovering over the record, barely holding it still. The shock of the silence crashed into the crowd like a wave. They began to whistle and cheer and stomp. The power of the DJ, demonstrated by that one finger, holding not just the record, the music, the soundtrack, but the party itself in suspended animation. Seconds passed. Minutes. The crowd's clapping reached a kind of ragged rhythm, the whistles grew louder. With a vicious sneer Sasha lifted his finger, released the bass-line, let the music explode back onto the terrace – and lifted both arms out wide, crucifix-like to acknowledge the congratulatory roar of the crowd. This is what they had come for, the kind of Ibiza moment clubbers get dewy-eyed over in years to come, the famous Sasha magic, the superstar DJ in full flight.

After his set, Sasha was still centre stage, showing off in front of a pool table, surrounded by an audience of smitten club girls. Nearby, trying not to look, was Claire Manumission, the redhead famous for having sex with her boyfriend Mike on the stage of the Ibiza club she'd named herself after. Drunk on Jägermeister, intoxicated by his set, Sasha did a party trick. He put a pool ball in his mouth. The girls giggled in anticipation. He spat the pool ball out, rolled it down his arm into his fist and simultaneously drained another glass of Jägermeister in one theatrical swallow. Then flipped both ball and glass over his shoulder. Crash! A mock-model pose – ta-dah! His audience applauded. Sasha rolled under the pool table, giggling. The girls reached under the table after him, giggling, prodding him with the pool cues.

After that Sasha disappeared. The next morning, Fritz, the brisk German manager of Space, was on the phone demanding of the party *organisers: 'Vere is my DJ?' Shrugs all round. Sasha turned up at 2 p.m. He had woken in a ditch outside DC10, another, even wilder Ibiza club, beside a friend's car. He'd thought, I'll just lie down here. It's dark. No one will see me. All he had on were his Maharashi combat trousers. But his pockets bulged. In one, a fat wad of cash, his fee for the gig. In the other, a cassette of his triumphant set. Beside him in the ditch, one last, half-empty bottle of Jägermeister.*

MANSFIELD IS A TOWN noted for what it doesn't have, rather than what it does. That is, if it gets noticed at all. It's the ninth worst place to live in Britain, according to a programme screened on Channel 4 in 2008. 'That once romantic now utterly disheartening colliery town,' sniffed D.H. Lawrence in *Lady Chatterley's Lover*. He was the famous son of Mansfield's domineering big brother Nottingham, just 12 miles south. It's a nondescript, nowhere sort of place that falls between the gaps.

Yet it's here, in 1992, that one of Britain's biggest pop culture revolutions of the past 40 years began, in Venue 44, a ballroom above a grimy working-men's club that had seen better days. On 14 March a new Saturday night called Renaissance opened with Sasha, a rising DJ star, as resident. There were a thousand punters inside the club already when I arrived with a friend from Bristol, where I lived, and colleagues from a small dance music magazine I had just joined called *Mixmag*. It was 2 a.m., but there were another 2,000 people outside, trying to get in. The club's promoter Geoff Oakes was a harassed figure in a smart black overcoat, bobbing in a sea of desperate clubbers. Rushing on the magic mushrooms I had gobbled down earlier, we squeezed past, up the stairs, through the double doors – and through the looking glass.

Renaissance wasn't like the raves or hip hop shebeens my friend Johnny and I were used to back in the West Country. It was glamorous. The girls were wearing dresses and the boys were wearing shirts. It was heady, delirious and sexy. We dived in.

The mushrooms were exploding in my brain like fireworks on New Year's Eve. The music was a physical force that swept you towards the dancing. There was nowhere else to go, nothing else to do. People were stacked up in layers on the terraced dance floor, there were giant fake Renaissance pillars everywhere. Laser beams sliced through the smoke. A beautiful girl smiled across the room. Out on the dance floor, the atmosphere kept rising. We found ourselves being hugged by strangers. A soul singer called Alison Limerick appeared out of the blue to sing her deliciously uplifting hit of the time, 'Where Love Lives'.

Sasha came on next. Up in the DJ booth, which was high above the stage, he took a second to survey his new empire. 'It was kind of like a pulpit,' he recalled. 'The view from up there was *brilliant*, cause you could see everyone in the club.' Out on the dance floor, everything swirled into a haze of music and smoke and lights. 'Chaos and huge crowds, great atmosphere,' Sasha said.

The local Mansfield beer boys weren't quite so happy. This was their town – but they'd been told they couldn't come in. About 3 a.m. Geoff Oakes, a promoter from Stoke-on-Trent who'd had the temerity to put this night on in their town, was summoned by the head doorman. 'I want a word,' the giant bouncer said, in a tone of voice that indicated this wasn't a request. Oakes followed him down a corridor to the front door – and was brusquely shoved outside. Facing him was a rabble of irate local lads. 'You come into our town, tell us we can't get into our fucking club! Who do you think you are?' they shouted at him. Geoff laughed at the memory. 'It was like the Frankenstein film where all the villagers are there with the torches.'

Afterwards, when the club finally finished, Sasha and Geoff and all their friends went back to a friend's house, where the party carried on. At five the next afternoon, Oakes decided to go home, in no state to handle the new Porsche he was driving. 'Apparently I fell asleep stood up at the door, twice, before I got into the car,' he said. He got into his car, revved up the engine and shot off at 60 mph – straight into the back of a parked car. Oakes wrote off his Porsche yet walked away unscathed.

Perhaps not the most auspicious start. But that weekend the club, the DJ, the promoter, the punters and the party had all come together in one perfect moment. The Superstar DJ era had begun.

ACID HOUSE WASN'T new: it had been around for four years. Nor were hedonistic, glamorous nightclubs. But acid house was baggy-trousered, androgynous and psychedelic; and glamorous discos a thing of 1970s New York. British high-street discos were scruffy, rather desperate places – exactly what acid house replaced. Renaissance put these two opposites together and created something new. Soon enough, lads like the village idiots clamouring outside the Renaissance door would be dressing up and trying to get into the clubs like this that would copy the model and mushroom across the UK. They would use star DJ names like Sasha to fill their dance floors. And this second wave of acid house would become the pop-culture lifestyle that was to dominate the 1990s. A hedonistic, fabulous world of superstar DJs and 'super-clubs' that would turn a drab, famously reserved Britain into one of the world's most famous party destinations. And it all started in Mansfield, the ninth worst place to live in Britain.

Over the next eight years, Britain went crazy for house music and its associated, exuberant style of partying and disco excess. We would become a nation that lived for the weekend, spending Saturday nights dressed up to the nines, taking ecstasy in one the giant superclubs that had spread throughout the UK. By 1998, 7.1 per cent of adults aged between 16 and 59 would have used an illegal drug in the last month, more than 2,400,000 people. By 1993, marketing analysts at the Henley Centre already estimated British ravers were spending £1.8 million a year on entrance fees, illegal drugs and cigarettes.

Britain would export this culture and the DJs that played it across the world. The working-class lads who created and capitalised on this scene would live it up. DJs would become celebrities jet-setting around the globe. From Milan to Miami, Melbourne to Mexico City – from Mansfield, in short, to the world. For nearly a decade, taking ecstasy and dancing to house music would become what weekends were about. And Saturday night would never be the same again.

But in March 1992, all of that seemed highly unlikely. Acid house was already deemed over. It had enjoyed its moment in the sun, four years previously, during the famous 'Summers Of Love' of 1988 and 1989, when the smiley face and cry of '*aciiieeeed!*' and giant, outdoor raves for thousands had seized the public's imagination and tabloid front pages. And just as quickly, as far as most of the UK was concerned, it had disappeared: yesterday's thing, a quick fad, a novelty.

But it hadn't actually disappeared, just moved into smaller, more fashion-conscious clubs in Nottingham, Manchester and London that had begun to form themselves into a busy little network. Nobody, except for the tiny *Mixmag*, had noticed. Like Mansfield, Britain's pop culture in 1992 was a no-man's-land, a place between the gaps. Brit-pop was yet to happen. The Tories were still, endlessly, in power. There was a recession on. These were in-between days. It felt like everybody was waiting for something, that something was about to happen.

Renaissance was to be a big, all-night club playing acid house music. But it wasn't going to be a rave. Its mastermind was Geoff Oakes, a former car mechanic and kung-fu instructor from Stoke-on-Trent. Oakes was typical of the club promoters who would come to dominate this second wave of acid house. He was, as were many, a northern, working-class guy who discovered acid house and decided he wanted to make it his living. Like his contemporaries, he was a man who could handle money and handle himself, who was as good with cold-eyed doormen as he was with flighty club girls. And who could keep a straight head even after days and days of hardcore partying.

I met up with Geoff Oakes in London, where he was lunching and hosting meetings at the private members' club Hospital. He looked exactly the same as he did in 1992 – ageless, good-looking, quietly charming: the consummate superclub survivor. Now, as then, he is both a passionate defender of the British club scene and one of its fiercest critics. At 46, he has finally embraced fatherhood – he and his wife and business partner Joanne, who was his girlfriend in the early Renaissance days, have a young son.

Geoff had a very clear image for Renaissance. He wanted something different. He didn't want pseudo-psychedelic imagery and wide-eyed kids in baggy dungarees and Day-Glo colours gurning like they did at raves. He wanted something beautiful, something more refined. Quietly spoken, with a soft northern burr to his voice, he could switch from friendly to slightly menacing without really altering very much about his face or demeanour. He was a self-confessed 'Jack the Lad' who had never really done very much with his life apart from go to clubs. But he was a dreamer. And he wanted to transform a working-men's club into a sixteenth-century Italian palace. He wanted clouds, pillars and kings. Renaissance the club would recreate the Italian Renaissance of Leonardo da Vinci, Michelango and Cesare Borgia – in Mansfield, with house music. And in a roundabout, wide-eyed, ecstasy-fuelled kind of way, that's exactly what it was: a northern, working-class, clubbing utopia that would spark a whole new era in British nightlife. 'Clubbing had started to come indoors again. People were dressing a little bit better,' Oakes explained. 'We'd just come through the whole rave culture. I just wanted it to be softer and warmer.'

If raving had been democratic, Renaissance was going to be elitist. Oakes ensured he only let the beautiful people in – sharp northern clubbers who had turned their backs on the baggy, casual fashions of rave in order to smarten up. John Richmond shirts and shiny shoes for the boys, for the girls, heels and slinky, tiny, dresses that looked like nighties. The club – uniquely at a time of 2 a.m. finishes – had a 7 a.m. licence. And unlike the other clubs where acid house had thrived, Renaissance had, in the shape of Geoff Oakes's friend Sasha, a star DJ on the bill. Flyers for Renaissance, glossy, opulent, drenched with distressed sixteenth-century imagery, played on this. 'The Long Awaited Restoration Of Sasha To The North Of England', they proclaimed, as if Sasha was some kind of prophet, rather than a DJ and the North some kind of hallowed turf.

Sasha was already becoming the UK's first DJ star. He attracted hysterical reactions wherever he went and, unlike the faceless figures in the DJ box at, say, Manchester's Haçienda, the spotlight seemed to naturally fall upon him. A slightly shy, good-looking boy with a pony-tail and a taste for flowing white shirts, Sasha had bounced off the Haçienda dance floor into a bubbling DJ career. He made his name at a club called Shelley's in Stoke where his euphoric sets mixed up the harder edge of rave and techno with softer, more soulful sounds. In September 1991, Sasha was the first ever DJ to feature on a national magazine cover, albeit the then small circulation *Mixmag*. His stardom was satirised in another club magazine – London fanzine *Boys Own* who nicknamed him 'DJ Big Up North'. But since then Sasha had been neglecting his northern fan base over the past year to play clubs in London. This only increased the hunger for him, as Oakes was only too aware.

Yet that first night, both Geoff Oakes and Sasha were both nervous as they drove up to the club. Had they taken a huge risk? Would anyone go to Mansfield? They turned the corner to the venue, Oakes fretting, 'Have we done the right thing here? I wonder if it will be busy.' They needn't have worried. 'There was so much hype around the opening, people drove up from all corners of the country,' Sasha noted. That night, Renaissance was the hottest ticket in the country. Mansfield, suddenly, was on the map.

The 'Restoration Of Sasha To The North' had worked. In London, 15 years later, Oakes howled with laughter at the memory. 'Tongue in cheek! Guilty as charged! Funny, eh?'

In the late 1980s at the height of the Thatcher years, illegal acid house raves had hit British youth culture like a tsunami. It was the 'me' decade, a time of selfishness and 'yuppies' and looking out for number one. Yet suddenly thousands had found themselves dancing in fields, hugging each other and taking ecstasy at events drenched with hippie imagery: raves like Sunrise and Energy; at clubs like London's Shoom and Manchester's Haçienda. Clubs like the Haçienda changed people's lives: the intensity of the night, soaked in ecstasy, intensely hot, driven by euphoric house music and squashed into an evening that had to finish by 2 a.m., created an unforgettable experience. People who went there talk about it now in hushed tones. Geoff Oakes is one of them.

In 1988, though, the idea that anyone might make a long-term career out of acid house didn't really exist. 'At that point we had no idea that the scene would last more than a year, or two. Everyone thought it was a passing moment,' said Sasha. The scene was still – as one memorable hit from Chicago producer Joe Smooth had it – a 'Promised Land', one hell of a party, its intensity fuelled by the very temporary nature of its existence. That promised land could be an open-air nightclub in balmy Ibiza; a smoke-filled gym in South London; a grubby warehouse in Blackburn with 10,000 people dancing their hearts out before the police came. Or the dance floor of the Haçienda nightclub in Manchester, a place built like a factory, all yellow and black, steel and brick. On that dance floor the energy was white hot. And on that dance floor were many of the key people who would go on to create the superclub boom.

Geoff Oakes arrived in the summer of 1988, when the club was at its peak. Graeme Park and Mike Pickering were DJing. The queue snaked round the block by 8.30 p.m. Inside, the energy was electric. It took Oakes a while to muster up the courage to try ecstasy. When he did, it all suddenly made sense. 'I was terrified, I didn't know what was happening to me. My brain felt like it was on one of those roller-decks, just flipping really fast – someone took me upstairs into that little bar on the balcony there and sat me down and gave me a brandy and I was okay after that.' The Haçienda in those delirious days was a hothouse. 'You'd feel the whole club come up at once, about eleven o'clock,' Geoff said. 'When you got in the place it was like nowhere else in the world mattered, you were part of something, it was our o⟩ best-kept little secret.'

At the same time, another dour northern town had become party central: Blackburn. As illegal raves and warehouse parties sprung up across the North West, clubbers from the Haçienda and Liverpool's the Underground would also travel in convoy to giant warehouse parties in the city. 'You'd have 10,000 people in a warehouse, all dancing on dumper trucks,' said Dave Beer, a Haçienda and Blackburn rave regular who would go on to launch the Leeds club Back To Basics. 'Solicitors and lawyers and coppers and doctors and everything were all just part of this scene. It was so off the rails, it was amazing, you thought you were changing things.'

Blackburn couldn't last. Its parties ran from 1989 until February 1992, when a brutal police raid at Nelson near Burnley closed down a warehouse rave with 10,000 people inside. As the rave scene moved indoors, the biggest characters on those dance floors began turning their nightlife into a living. There in one corner was Sasha, with his college friend Piers Sanderson from Bangor where they lived. Bouncing around the place in an orange jumpsuit was Sparrow, later to become Sasha's best friend and a club promoter in Plymouth. In another was Dave Beer, a former punk and occasional tour manager from Leeds. Geoff Oakes was there, obviously. So was James Barton, a bolshie ginger Scouser, already a major player in the nascent Liverpool dance scene, long before he would go on to create what became perhaps the ultimate superclub, Cream. These people might have looked like wild-eyed ravers, but they were also charismatic, ambitious, driven ravers.

Like many of the people who would go on to dominate super- clubbing in the 1990s, Geoff Oakes had started out with little more than a determination to keep that Haçienda party going. That is how overwhelming acid house, its combination of drugs, music and camaraderie, could prove. Or perhaps Geoff had always been looking for something. He grew up in Stoke with his single mother in a working-class family. His father was a comedian on the northern comedy circuit. 'We moved from place to place within Staffordshire and I went to lots of different schools and never really settled,' he explained. 'So academically that was where it ended for me. I left school and that was it.' At 15, Oakes used to sneak out of his bedroom window, borrow a car from his grandfather's scrapyard – and drive to the Wigan Casino.

The Wigan Casino club was a mecca for the 1970s working-class cult of northern soul: fuelled on speed, thousands would gather to dance wildly all night to fast, pumping, American soul and R 'n' B, spinning in shiny leather shoes, tight jumpers and giant, flapping flares. It was as blueprint, in many ways, for what would become acid house. 'I vividly remember the first night walking in: 15 years old, stood up on the balcony and looked down, it was an old theatre so it had this stage where the DJs were and this massive space and people dancing and spinning and they'd all clap at the same time,' said Oakes. 'And the Haçienda for me was the same feeling.'

The Haçienda opened on Whitworth Street in Manchester on 21 May 1982 – just months after the Wigan Casino had closed (it shut in December 1981). Now immortalised in pop-culture history – not least by the Michael Winterbottom movie *24 Hour Party People* – the Haçienda was opened by New Order's label Factory as a live venue, but by the time Nude Night arrived in 1985 it had become a more DJ-based club that gradually began to introduce house music. In March 1987, the Chicago House Party Tour with Frankie Knuckles and Marshall Jefferson played. In the same year, friends of the Happy Mondays introduced ecstasy to the club. On 13 July 1988 a Wednesday night party called Hot, with a swimming pool in the middle of the dance floor and free ice pops, started. Nude Night was on a Friday. For northerners, the Haçienda was where acid house began.

People walked in, not knowing what the fuss was about. They soon found out. 'The first week I saw people off their heads, I saw this group of scallies, it was probably the Happy Mondays,' remembered Piers Sanderson. 'And they were kind of doing this dance –' he demonstrated a windmill-like arm-waving dance – 'and I was looking at them thinking, "What the fuck are they doing?" Swinging their arms about. And of course two weeks later once I'd had half a pill, I was swinging my arms around in the corner with them. Then you became the circus attraction when people came in and were thinking "What the fuck is he doing?" And it snowballed.'

Acid house was a new, wonderful place where everybody loved each other. And all of these characters – Oakes, Beer, Sasha, Sparrow, Sanderson – were larger than life, people with presence, wit and ideas. They might have been partying away with everyone else, waving their arms around like windmills, hugging strangers. But ideas were beginning to sprout in their heads. Nobody was in this for the money yet – at least, nobody apart from the club owners and the drug dealers. But at the same time, nobody wanted the party to end. 'There was that feeling of being part of something and that's why it changed my life. I felt I'd found this thing that I'd been subconsciously looking for,' said Piers Sanderson. 'All of a sudden everything just kind of slotted in. And that's when I knew I'd make my life out of that.' Dave Beer shared that feeling. 'To be a part of it you found ways, either by being a DJ or throwing parties or designing clothes, or designing flyers, or giving flyers out or becoming a pill dealer, whatever it was to make you become a part of that society.'

But the glory days of the Haçienda couldn't last. Even at its peak in the late eighties, problems with gun-toting gangsters from Manchester's many viciously competing crews began threatening its survival. In a hard-hitting *Mixmag* investigation published in 1997, reporter Oliver Swanton revealed the history of Manchester's battle between clubs and gangs. In 1989 the Cheetham Hill gang, then involved in a war with Moss Side's Doddington crew, waltzed into the Haçienda, flashing their guns. Haçienda management approached Greater Manchester Police with a plan to pay police to man the door but were refused. The club closed in January 1991 after months of ferocious gang violence and intimidation but later reopened with a metal detector on the door. It didn't stop six doormen being stabbed in June 1991: gangsters had avoided the metal detector. Problems spread across the city. Manchester's Most Excellent night was closed in 1992 after gangsters rammed the club's entrance in a stolen car. In 1995 the club Home followed, after a long catalogue of problems and a series of drive-by shootings.

Time was ticking for the Haçienda, which had always suffered financial problems, being funded through bad patches by New Order. In April 1995 Haçienda doorman Terry Farrimond was shot dead near his home in Swinton. In April 1997 three youths opened fire on another club door. On 28 June 1997, Swinton's report revealed, two senior police officers and seven magistrates witnessed a near-fatal assault outside the Haçienda. Eighteen-year-old Andrew Delahunty was hit over the head by what looked like a metal bar and pushed into the path of a speeding car. He survived a fractural skull and spinal damage. But the club's time was up. As directors were declaring bankruptcy, police were moving to revoke the club's licence. This meant the end of a mooted management buyout and also frightened off a potential buyer. The Haçienda closed. Its dance floor was later sold off in blocks – they went like hot cakes – and it is now a luxury flat development.

MARCH 1992 AND a weak, grey dawn bleached its way over an industrial estate in Slough. The *Mixmag* office was actually a corner of a unit occupied by its parent company, DMC (the Disco Mix Club), a DJ organisation that supplied special remixes to a membership of subscribers. Three of us were slogging through the last hours of a bruising deadline that had lasted 36 hours. Red-eyed from lack of sleep and wired on too much instant coffee drank from wobbly plastic cups, we steeled ourselves for the last pile of records to be reviewed. German techno. Oh God. But there was a surprise in store: a remix by the German production duo Jam & Spoon of a record from Frankfurt called 'Age Of Love' and by Age Of Love. It was the beginning of a sound that still today is called 'trance', probably still the most popular electronic music sound in the world. That morning it sounded utterly fantastic.

'Age Of Love' was sleek, futuristic and hypnotic; furiously energetic, economic in its melodies, utterly different. We played it again and again, louder and louder. Sitting there in the grey Slough dawn, we resolved to find out who the hell was making this music. The magazine's then editor David Davies did just that – he went to Frankfurt, tracked down the original proponents of trance and wrote the first feature about it.

Alongside that grubby Slough sunrise, a new age was dawning for dance music. And throughout the nineties British producers were at the forefront, creating some of the most vibrant and original pop music this country has ever produced – music that took sampling and electronic dance music as a starting point, then brought in deconstructed songwriting and techniques associated with rock 'n' roll to create something genuinely new and different. From Underworld, Chemical Brothers and Leftfield to Portishead and Massive Attack and the more abstract sounds of drum 'n' bass, British artists created a new aesthetic, one that moved popular music on from the guitar-bass-drums format that rock 'n' roll had been following for nearly 40 years and which did something new with it.

I joined *Mixmag* in the summer of 1991 as its assistant editor, when it was selling less than 10,000 copies a month. Downstairs on that industrial unit, DMC had three tiny studios. The place thumped with dance music beats. And every weekend, Dan Prince, *Mixmag*'s clubs editor and the son of the company's owners, Tony and Christine Prince, would go clubbing up North. The family were from Oldham. Dan had been a Haçienda regular, but like much of the northern crowd had moved on to Oakes's hometown Stoke and a club called Shelley's. Held in a mainstream, high-street venue, Shelley's had replaced the Haçienda as the hottest night in the North. Its star was Sasha – he had begun to make a name at the Haçienda, at hardcore raves like Coventry's Eclipse and at the Blackburn raves. But it was at Shelley's he found his feet and his audience.

Sasha's mixture of hard-rave anthems and euphoric, piano-based house music instantly connected with the ecstasy experience. He mixed in vocal a cappellas – famously, Whitney Houston's 'I Wanna Dance With Somebody' over Leftfield's proto-Brit house classic 'Not Forgotten'. 'I really did play what my favourite records were that were out that week,' said Sasha. 'A lot of piano anthems and stuff like that.'

Oakes and Sasha met at a Blackburn rave, but got to know each other at Shelley's and the parties afterwards at Geoff's two-bedroom cottage in the nearby village of Biddulph. 'This culture evolved from

Shelley's of crazy parties at my house,' Oakes said. 'Every week after Shelley's a convoy would migrate to my house. We had the main tunes room upstairs, which was the second bedroom. The kitchen was kind of a chill-out room, it was a bit more laid-back, there was a sound system in there. And then the lounge was videos, games and so on. I used to cram about 40 people in there every week and the party would last for four days without stopping. And Sasha would play on the decks for two days without stopping. Shirt off and away we go!'

The parties came to an abrupt end when Oakes's neighbour, driven insane by months of noise and interrupted sleep, turned up at five one morning, thudding on the door with an axe. Three days later a For Sale sign went up next door. It was at one of these parties that Sasha suggested Geoff do something himself. Not a rave, like Sasha had become used to playing. 'I'm sick of going to all these clubs around the country and they're shit,' Sasha told him. The conversation had stuck in Oakes's mind.

Oakes and Sasha weren't conjuring up their glamorous new vision of clubbing out of the ether. What was different about Renaissance was its scale and its impact. Though acid house had finished, according to the London media, the legal raves continued into the nineties, big, messily organised events that served energy drinks with a diet of menacing hardcore and break-beat music to crowds of thousands: it was this scene that would later throw up The Prodigy and drum 'n' bass. In stark contrast, a small network of DJs were beginning to play guest spots at the smaller, dressier clubs like Most Excellent in Manchester, Flying and Boys Own in London, Slam in Glasgow and Venus in Nottingham.

This was home ground for Dan Prince whose unique advantage as clubs editor was that he was a sharply dressed northern clubber, just like the people he was writing for and about. This new scene was his home turf. And the night that Renaissance opened was to be my introduction to northern clubbing. Dan insisted we start at Venus in Nottingham before heading up the road to Renaissance and as soon as Johnny and I walked in, we instantly understood what he was talking about. It was a small club that felt very cool, very glamorous, but which also had a celebratory atmosphere. Beautiful girls danced wildly on the marble bar in long skirts and chunky heels. There were constant outbreaks of cheering. The crowd greeted coolly funky house records with flamenco-style handclapping. And you had to be – in the parlance of the time – 'clued up' to get in.

Clued up meant you knew who the DJs were and why they mattered. You looked right. You knew the right people. You were cool. 'Clued up' signified all the same kind of insider codes as any other youth cult in British pop history – from Teddy boys to punk rockers, northern soul to mods, they were all based on this insider model. And just as importantly, they were based on being exclusive.

Renaissance picked up on this and took it large scale. It had more in common with working-class pop cults like mod and northern soul than it did with the loose, all-welcome, hippie aesthetic of the giant acid house raves. As Oakes, instinctively from his time at the Wigan Casino, understood only too well. 'I wanted to create a sort of cocoon almost. Once everyone got into that space,' he told me, 'they were all there for the same reasons, the people, the environment, I just needed to get all of those things right.'

Oakes realised he wanted to become a promoter. Like his contemporaries on the dance floor, he decided to try and make a go of this new scene. 'In those days,' Geoff explained, 'if you were involved in that inner circle of people in the industry in the north-west, you were either a DJ, a promoter or a drug dealer and I guess I probably tried all three at some point or another. Came out realising that promoting was probably the best way forward for me.'

SASHA CHEWED COMPULSIVELY, his head nodding to the rhythm. He and Geoff Oakes were in Geoff's car, going to see the venue that would become Renaissance, taking time out from a daytime event Oakes was running at The Yard, another Mansfield club owned by the same people. Geoff had already warned Sasha to behave. The pair had been – and here he used the classic 1990s euphemism – 'Partying. We'd done whatever.' They drove along in silence. Just as they were approaching the venue, Oakes glanced in his rear-view mirror. 'I see Sasha, he's chewing his face and his head's going like this' – Oakes mimed the jerky, tense movements of someone on ecstasy getting into a record, nodding along with a beat. But there was no music playing in the car. Oakes pulled up abruptly. 'I was like, "Oh no, quick, get out the car."'

Inside, the club stank of beer and stale cigarettes. They felt their way upstairs in the dark. 'And then,' said Oakes, 'they knocked the light on and it was this cavernous, church-like room with the DJ box almost up in the sky in the corner. We were feeling quite euphoric at the time anyway.' He smiled, knowingly.

For Sasha, Mansfield was as big a sell. 'I really liked the idea of it being in the middle of nowhere cause it meant that people who came to the gig really wanted to hear the music. I was quite into that idea,' Sasha said. 'We felt the quality of the crowd would be better.'

It was a risk that paid off. Eventually. So many people had been turned away that first night that for the next five weeks the club was only half full. Then, slowly, as the reviews hit in magazines like *Mixmag* and word of mouth began to spread, Renaissance filled up again. In

June 1992, Dan Prince profiled the club. 'It's all a bit like an after-club party with all the malarkey with it,' he wrote. 'Jim from Nottingham has a favourite party trick when he hauls the sofa's cushion off and walks around the place with it under his arm doing his *This Is Your Life* stint. Brian from Leicester is often seen on the podiums doing his Vogue show, to say nothing about the usual running races.' Within a couple of months a fanatically loyal audience was crowding in. One gang of 12 guys came every week from South Wales, in two minibuses, a five-hour journey each way. Renaissance quickly became the most famous club in the UK.

Renaissance ran in Mansfield until 26 June 1993. It felt different. It felt grand. It had ambition. There was an irresistible confidence about it. 'It wasn't going to fail. They really believed it,' said Chris Howe, then *Mixmag*'s art director. Howe had designed the club's flyers and visuals. 'It was living it large and being glamorous. Like that football thing when working-class people started wearing posh clothes.'

The idea of a 'door picker', someone who would decide who would and who would not get in, was beginning. In 1992 the idea that you might have driven hours to get to Mansfield and still not get past the picker on the door was radical. Oakes was unrepentant. 'We wanted people to be there because they were clued up,' he explained. Shyer clubbers in the queue would fade into the wall, hoping he wouldn't single them out for a 'chat'. The more flamboyant would jostle in front of him, parading. 'Me and my girlfriends would be crowded around the door in our crazy outfits, frantically trying to catch his eye and in our heads saying, "Pick me, pick me!"' Renaissance regular Kirsty Drury told me. 'He always did.'

Drury was a Nottingham clubber, studying fashion in Newcastle. Later she became *Mixmag*'s fashion editor. She had grown tired of the illegal parties and hardcore raves of the time. 'My first time at Renaissance I was all dressed up and had done pills and trips,' she remembered. 'I floated into the place at about three in the morning. I was so excited. I opened the double doors to the dance floor and was blown away this cavernous space full of smoke, strobes and lasers and shadowy shapes of people on podiums. The sound system just ripped through me. I remember turning to my boyfriend and saying: "Oh my God! I'm in clubbing heaven!"'

Clubbers loved the sixteenth-century pillars and giant distressed Renaissance images projected onto the wall. 'The décor was different,' noted Marianne Tosh, another Renaissance regular. 'The design of it, the decoration, the name, it was just so great. You'd go just for the luxury of it.' Chris Howe had thought hard about his visuals. He had a point to make. 'The imagery was about a reaction to that computer-generated, hard-edged techno thing,' he explained. 'It was like a grand gesture – destroy something that should be pondered, just smash it up and rebuild it. Use the grandness of it and have no respect for it.'

And for the girls the clothes were increasingly glamorous. An idea began at clubs like Renaissance that was to gain increasing currency throughout the 1990s – that anybody could be a star: you could jump on a podium and become famous for a night. 'Me and my friend would make ourselves a new outfit every week, steadily getting more and more outrageous and revealing,' remembered Kirsty Drury. 'It was such a great place to show off. And everyone loved you for it and encouraged you to be more wild, more flamboyant.'

DJs too found themselves becoming celebrities. John Digweed, the son of a family of butchers in Hastings, became one of the club's star DJ names. 'The first night I played, when I came off the decks and went down there was ten people waiting to shake my hand,' he said.

'You didn't get that in a lot of the southern clubs. It was quite a strange experience for me. Really genuine, it was my first experience of a fan base.'

But beyond the superficiality of the disco lifestyle – looking sexy, showing off – something more profound was going on. Release and abandonment – getting lost in the music – was an intrinsic part of acid house. This element of losing yourself was something that reaches back to the underground, mixed-gay, predominantly black clubs in Chicago and New York where house music began in the 1980s. According to Chicago DJ Felix Da Housecat – aka Felix Stallings Junior – dancers in Chicago house clubs of the 1980s used their elbows to obscure their faces. 'Hiding their tears, because they were feeling the music so much,' he said. The social expectations of British superclubs were imported wholesale from those New York and Chicago gay clubs. At Renaissance, abandon, emotion, joy and release were cool. Skulking around the edge of the dance floor was not.

SASHA COLLAPSED ONTO the ratty sofa in Renaissance's grubby back office. He was utterly exhausted. It was 7 a.m. He hadn't slept the night before, he had played what he thought was a great set. 'The club was really peaking,' he said. And he was done. But the crowd kept stomping and cheering for more. They would not give up. For 15 minutes Sasha lay there, but the noise didn't abate. After 20, he gave in and struggled to his feet. 'I almost got carried back up to the decks and did an encore, which lasted another hour,' he said. This was typical of Renaissance. When there was no music, the crowd created its own, recalled DJ Jeremy Healy. 'You could turn the music off and you'd just get people stomping on the floor, they'd just make their own music,' he said. 'That was pretty amazing.'

This was all very un-British. As a nation, we are famous for restraint, not euphoria and delirium. House music was sending a hot, tropical breeze straight through this white north European nation. The mood of euphoria and celebration found in British clubs at their peak was like that in a Rio Carnival street party. It began in Ibiza, Spain, with an Argentinian DJ Alfredo. The name Haçienda is Spanish. The mood was more Latin than Anglo-Saxon.

What possessed white British people to venture out from the bar and beer-stained carpets of the discos of the seventies and eighties, to forget 'copping off' and the 'fuck or fight' routine to dance like Latins or Afro-Caribbeans? Like gay people? Was it the drugs? Clearly they were hugely important. Ecstasy was initially used in therapy and marriage guidance, as a drug to free up emotions and empathy; on the dance floor it was also a way of unlocking your feelings.

But the drugs and the atmosphere of the time also triggered something else: a freedom to be emotional. This was radical stuff, particularly for men that had grown up in northern and Midlands towns – towns like Mansfield, bitter, grey places wound so tight they sometimes felt they might burst at the seams. Towns where 'the lads' drank together and fought together and kept life's ups and downs behind stiff upper lips, only allowing themselves to be moved by the waves of collective emotion that washed over football terraces. Yet here they were at the Renaissance, roaring and screaming, hugging each other, camping it up.

The ethos was about living for the moment, living for the now. Consequently the clubs of the 1990s reverberated with the joy of abandonment and the roar of life being not so much lived as devoured.

British clubbing was inclusive. It was easy to get. And most important of all, it was a hell of a lot of fun. 'I lived for Saturday nights.

Sundays were so depressing on a comedown and having to wait another six days before we could do it all again,' recalled Kirsty Drury.

Ecstasy would feminise society. A new kind of man would emerge, a softer creature – symbolised at the beginning by the way someone like Sasha would dress, with his long hair and flowing white shirts. All this didn't just make men more popular with girls, it also made Saturday night a lot more fun, full of new friends to meet and new adventures to have.

But Mansfield's tenure as the UK's party capital couldn't last long. By the time Renaissance celebrated its third birthday, the club had moved from Mansfield to Derby where it ran for another year. In the beginning Geoff Oakes ran things from his bedroom in Biddulph, scribbling his dates and deals with DJs on bits of paper. Sasha, £500, John Digweed, £300 second Saturday, Paul Oakenfold, £500 for May. By 1994 he had an office. 'We didn't have a file, we were just hopeless, there were just bits of paper everywhere. We'd stop work at 5.30 every day and smoke a couple of spliffs and then leave the office. It was pretty chaotic really. Then we made a big investment – and bought a fax machine.'

Oakes's girlfriend, Joanna – now his wife – gave up her job in Manchester to sort out the workspace. In November 1994, Renaissance capitalised on the fame of the club and its star DJs and released *Renaissance – The Mix Collection*, mixed by Sasha and John Digweed, with Birmingham independent Network Records. It was the first major legal DJ CD – previously clubbers had bought bootleg DJ tapes – and sold 150,000 in its first six weeks. Now Oakes wasn't just a club promoter, he had a record business and he had, in the name Renaissance and the nefarious concept it represented, a 'brand'. Geoff Oakes and his wife still own that brand today and stage Renaissance parties around the world.

IN THE WAKE of Renaissance's glory days in Mansfield clubs proliferated and as they grew in numbers, they all needed something to differentiate themselves from the competition, something to prove that they were for real – not just two guys with a logo, a banner, an empty hall and a couple of heads full of grand ideas. Which, in reality, was often all they were. Hiring a big-name DJ what was gave a new club credibility. It was often the only thing that gave a new club credibility. As a result superstar DJs took off around the country.

This was a new business world in which everybody – DJs, promoters, clubbers – was finding their feet, making it up as they went along. Success demanded complex social skills. You had to be able to charm and network in a very short space of time. 'There's a lot of egos,' said Jon Carter, a name DJ in the late 1990s 'big beat' scene. 'All I want is peace. And if you want to establish peace, you have to learn these skills.' At the beginning of the 1990s, Dave Seaman, later to become a star DJ, had a note to himself written in his black Filofax diary: 'Be nice to everybody.' When we met, Dave smiled at the memory. 'You never know when you need somebody,' he said. It was a very good motto for superclubbing.

Superclubs like Renaissance would go on to provide a stage on which changing sexual politics of 1990s UK were played out. The political correctness that came with pop music in the 1980s was out. Later on, in marched the 'new lad', armed with a bottle of continental lager and a wrap of cocaine, bristling with slogans nicked from new men's magazines like *Loaded* such as 'nice work, fella', unashamedly predatory in his admiration for the female form. Clattering behind him in her heels, hair askew, fag and pint in hand, came the 'ladette'.

Drugs too flowed out from the superclubs and into society as a whole. The price of ecstasy dropped from £15 a tablet in the late 1980s to as low as £3 a tablet by the millennium. Cocaine became so common-place that city centre bars across the UK started rubbing Vaseline on any shiny toilet surface that might be used for chopping out lines.

The boom that followed would have far-reaching implications for British pop music, fashion and lifestyle. Everyone, suddenly, was a disco king or queen. Everybody was cool. 'It was working class and subur-ban. It drew in the upper class. It made celebrities feel small,' observed Dave Dorrell, a London DJ and club runner heavily involved in the early days of superclubs. The social changes of 1990s Britain – afflu-ence, shifting sexual attitudes, changing fashions, the cult of anyone can be a celebrity and drugs – were played out on the superclub dance floors. Much more than a history of music, DJs and discos, the super-star DJ era is the story of a decade.

In 1995, Renaissance staged their third birthday at the Que Club in Birmingham, where Oakes chose a celestial décor. The *Mixmag* team headed up for the night. Andy Pemberton, our deputy editor, was dating a wild, blonde Birmingham club girl called Heidi who led us from one adventure to another. At one point we screamed along to a perform-ance from the group D:Ream with the Coventry DJs Parks & Wilson. At another, Heidi introduced a rapping doctor she'd met on the dance floor who proceeded to rhyme along to the club hits being played.

The magazine ran a news story on the event that concentred on the club's décor. Oakes had moved on from sixteenth-century palaces to a more celestial theme. Hanging from the ceiling there was a statue of a cherub, wearing a crown, floating on a cloud, from which dripped shimmering chains of stars; Oakes's synthetic recreation of heaven on earth. But he was looking stressed, not angelic, as he ran around on the night, taking care of details. For him, this wasn't just a party now. It was business.

TWO
PROMISED LAND

TUNE! FPI PROJECT – 'RICH IN PARADISE (GOING BACK TO MY ROOTS)'

The delirious Italian house anthem had an infectious piano roll and a seductive female moan.

Trannies With Attitude and their entourage arrived in Ibiza in 1993 to find they'd been booked to stay in a nudist resort. Not much opportunity for Nick Raphael and Paul Fryer, two straight DJs who'd made a career out of DJing badly in ill-fitting drag, to get dressed up as women there. One of their entourage, Vaschco, had a way around this: he positioned a pair of sunglasses over his penis, so his organ became a nose and his scrotum a giant, hairy chin. Fryer and Raphael amused themselves watching passing nudists try not to notice – it being frowned upon to look at someone's crotch in a nudist camp. They cheered up more at the first night of Manumission, the new, giant Ibiza fun-palace where they'd been booked to play. They had new outfits to wear: matching orange dresses, fluorescent white belts and brothel creepers. They looked like a pair of traffic cones. Just before they took to the decks, in front of a crowd of 5,500 clubbers, one of their entourage shook a gram of MDMA powder – pure ecstasy, basically – into a plastic cup of Coca-Cola. Each took a careful sip. Then Fryer drained the rest. Hardened drug users all, they still looked at him askance: he had just consumed enough ecstasy to floor an elephant. 'Fuck off, I've done more drugs than you lot,' said Fryer. As the night picked up pace, with dwarves on stilts and performers and wild-eyed ravers, TWA went on to DJ in their orange and white outfits. In the middle of their set, things for Fryer started to get intense as the immense amount of MDMA he'd taken kicked in. He found it difficult to stand because the waves of energy and emotions rushing through him were too powerful. He sat on a girl's lap, clinging on. But he kept DJing, somehow. Every time he put a new record on, the first lush breakdown or a dramatic chord sequence would knock him off his feet again. Raphael, who himself was finding that the record decks seemed to have turned into a squashy, sponge-like material, looked aghast at his partner. Fryer was by now lying on the floor of the DJ booth, holding on for dear life. He could feel the world spinning beneath him and he knew that if he let go, he would simply fall off. Later, he urinated in a record box belonging to the DJ Alfredo who'd played before them, because Alfredo had irritated him. At least, he aimed to, but got it wrong and pissed in TWA's own record box by mistake. Raphael spent the set wiping down wet records, wondering what had happened. 'One of our more enjoyable sets,' they laughed.

THE SUPERCLUB ERA began in a dizzy kind of idealism. Or so legend has it. It's worth revisiting the story. It starts in a swimming pool in Ibiza in August 1987. With four young London DJs – Nicky Holloway, Danny Rampling, Paul Oakenfold and Johnny Walker – high on their first ecstasy tablet and flush with excitement at the beautiful open-air club they'd just been to. They held hands, listened to Art Of Noise's synth-pop symphony 'Moments In Love' and promised to change the world. 'We'd all had the most amazing night of our life, thinking, "This is ground-breaking, we're going to change the world with this stuff",' said Nicky Holloway. '"If everyone has one of these, there'll be no more wars." That's what we really felt. We weren't fucking about.'

The story of their ecstasy epiphany is famous in dance music history. It's been buffed up and polished and turned into legend – one life-changing Ibiza trip that turned them into disco evangelists. The place they discovered house music, an acid house year zero. The land of acid house is a sentimental place that loves myths and legends. The reality is more prosaic. Paul Oakenfold, Danny Rampling, Nicky Holloway and Johnny Walker were already, in their different ways, DJing, running parties and making waves. All had been to Ibiza before. All were 'faces' on the London club scene. Nicky was already a mover and a shaker, running club nights in London. Oakenfold was already beginning to make his way in the music industry. Rampling was Nicky's sidekick, a new DJ face, looking for a chance to make his mark. Walker, too, was a DJ.

At the time, London's club scene primarily concerned itself with soul and funk, the more obscure the better, as this scene's name 'rare groove' suggests. The DJs may have been largely white, but the music they played, like the culture that DJing had emerged from, was black. The first DJs playing exclusive records on big sound systems at dances began in the late 1950s, in Jamaica. The first house crowds in the seventies and eighties were black, gay, American. Inspired by this and the 1970s Southern soul scene, late 1980s London clubs were an insider's world of jazz dancers and black music collectors and Southern soul-boys who met at pubs like the Royal Oak, warehouse parties like Shake 'N' Fingerpop or Nicky's own Do At The Zoo parties in

London Zoo. Many of the DJs who later became stars in the super-clubs, Pete Tong and Judge Jules among them, came from this world too. But there was little house music and no ecstasy.

Paul Oakenfold, now one of the most successful DJs in the world, was a dyslexic former trainee chef who grew up in Gravesend and Thornton Heath. Nicky had met him when the two were working at the Woodhouse menswear shop on Oxford Street. Oakenfold was DJing, working for promotions companies, writing for *Blues & Soul* magazine. He had lived in New York where he got involved in hip hop and went to famous proto-house clubs like the Paradise Garage, plus insider events like David Mancuso's tiny parties at The Loft.

Nicky Holloway is a born charmer and chancer, streetwise and clever, instantly likeable, with a cheeky grin and a way of making you feel complicit. And 20-odd years after his famous Ibiza holiday, he still has the charm, as I found out when we met in a North London pub. He told me he was born in Isleworth, Middlesex, and grew up in assorted parts of Outer London – places like Barnet and Finchley. He couldn't remember how old he was when his father, a car mechanic, disappeared. 'Fuck knows. About 13 or something. Gonna cry next,' he joked. His mother, a secretary, brought him up. He started going to soul nights at the Royalty in Southgate and became obsessed with DJing. 'I can remember me mum would go to work and I would be hiding in the bushes waiting for her to leave, then I crept back indoors.' He improvised a set-up with two 1970s music centres – an all-in-one sideboard-sized stereo system with record player, cassette deck and radio combined. 'With a microphone Sellotaped to a fucking broom handle. Practising DJing at fucking 15.'

Nicky was already running nights all over London, the Special Branch sessions and his Do At The Zoo, at London Zoo, which mixed up everything from soul and hip hop to Latin, when they arrived in Ibiza. He'd already run Special Branch holidays to Ibiza. But he had never taken drugs – until now. 'I'd always been so anti-drugs. When I did Special Branch, I used to throw people out for having a draw,' Nicky explained. 'To me drugs was, "Wooh, Scary Mary".'

That now-legendary night in Ibiza began at the Night Life disco bar in San Antonio. Nicky, Danny, Paul and Johnny met another London DJ, Trevor Fung, who told them about a drug called ecstasy and a club called Amnesia. Paul Oakenfold and Danny Rampling tried the pill first. Nicky and Johnny held back. 'After about half an hour we saw what fun they looked like they were having so I thought, "Oh bollocks, let's have a go",' Nicky said. They wandered around another San Antonio joint called The Star Club. Then they went to Amnesia.

The ecstasy they took was, Nicky Holloway remembered, very pure – a white capsule of MDMA that cost 4,000 pesetas, or £20. Soon enough Nicky was feeling the effects. 'Everything seemed slow and more animated and everything seemed lovely and more beautiful. It was like we'd discovered Narnia for some strange reason,' he recollected. The club was open air and that year an English contingent of 50 to 60 people, including other London DJs and scenesters like Lisa Loud and Nancy Noise, had started going. Many of them had bunked over the wall rather than pay to get in as money was tight. The Argentinian DJ Alfredo Fiorito was playing – not the narrow, exclusive sounds of 1970s funk and soul that the English crowd were used to in London, but a wide-ranging mix of everything from rock artists like U2 to art-school synth pop like Nitzer Ebb. Music the London DJs, high on ecstasy, were hearing as if for the first time. 'We thought we were in heaven, it was just brilliant,' said Nicky. 'No one would have dared play the dance mix of Rick Astley, "Never Gonna Give You Up" in a cool club in England, you'd have been laughed off the floor. But when we heard it out there mixed in with house records it sounded fabulous.'

Back at the villa, holding hands in the swimming pool, something else was mixing in with all that emotion. Something as crucial a part of the clubbing explosion that followed as house music, something as potent as the ecstasy. That something was ambition. 'Nicky, Paul and Johnny, each and every one of us. We each had our own ideas. And we all sat there saying, "Fucking hell, this is amazing. This is going to be huge,"' said Danny Rampling. Rampling had been working as Nicky's right-hand man for years, trying to break into the rare groove scene. But it was a closed shop: there were no openings for a new DJ. 'The door was closed, you're not coming in. Young talent? No. We're the established crowd and we're holding on to our position,' Rampling told me. 'As we heard that music in Ibiza, I just was blown away by it, it was a complete revelation. Immediately, yeah, I certainly knew that a huge change was going to happen. Then it was like, "Here is my opportunity."'

Today, Danny Rampling is a brisk, direct character with almost a military bearing. But he still has the same hint of the esoteric about him that he had in the 1990s – as I found out when we talked in London. It makes for an odd mix. Rampling came from Streatham, South London. His father was a printer and worked nights. 'I didn't get on with my father a great deal. I still haven't spoken to him for years,' he told me when we met. 'My mother brought up four kids. Really looked after us very well, took pride in being a parent and taught us the value of things at a very early age – sense of morals and decency, politeness.' He hated school. 'There was a lot of nasty people around in that school. There still is in South London.' He fought with his brother and sister and for a period lived with his grandparents. His grandfather had been in the army. During the Falklands War, Danny tried to join the Parachute Regiment but was turned down. 'And my world came crashing down, because I was unemployed, like so many people at that time,' he said. Music had offered an escape. There was a DJ he admired who lived on his same street, who had had a full DJ rig with the flashing lights. Danny used to lie under the covers listening to Radio Luxembourg, dreaming of a career in music. Suddenly, in that Ibiza swimming pool, he saw his chance.

BACK IN LONDON, Danny was first off the block. On 5 December 1987 he opened Klub Schoom in a fitness centre on Southwark Bridge Road. He'd seen the venue years before and always wanted to use it. Filled with smoke and strobe lights and trance-dancing ravers, Shoom, as it became known, was the first acid house club in the UK, the one that introduced all the acid house paraphernalia: the smiley face logo, the dry ice, the pseudo-psychedelic imagery. 'Sensation seekers,' proclaimed the flyers, 'let the music take you to the top.' Alcohol was frowned upon. For the first time ecstasy was the drug of choice. It was a success. And Danny was making his mark. 'I was a complete breath of fresh air. New blood had arrived. I was full of energy and spirit to become a professional DJ and then given that opportunity at Shoom. My life was complete,' said Danny. 'After years of struggling and being unbalanced, I had this sense of inner peace and excitement which was infectious to everybody around at that club.'

Paul Oakenfold, who had already been running a smaller club called Future at the Sound Shaft and Ibiza-inspired nights at the Project Club in Streatham, was close behind. He started his Spectrum night with promoter Ian Paul at Heaven on 11 April 1988. Unlike Shoom, which was a more exclusive affair with Rampling's girlfriend

Jenni choosing who could come in and who couldn't, Spectrum was open to all comers. It was a grandiose spectacle, with a laser light show that announced Oakenfold's arrival on the decks. It was there the famous chant of '*acieed!*' took off.

Nicky Holloway was the third of the gang to launch a night. He began his acid house night Trip at the Astoria in London's West End on 4 June 1988. It too was a huge success. Thousands of ravers clogged Charing Cross Road. That summer the big, illegal raves began happening in fields around the M25. There were giant warehouse parties in places like King's Cross. DJ and club face Dave Dorrell had a night called Love at the Wag. Acid house was off. And with it, the promoters, like Nicky Holloway.

'Nicky was always making money,' recalled Dave Dorrell. 'Nicky had been earning money when he was running the Royal Oak down at London Bridge. He was making money when he was doing the Do At The Zoo. This was Thatcher's children, in sloppy shoulders. Taking pills. But still with that –' Dorrell clicked his fingers, to indicate the street-smarts of people like Nicky, like Danny, people who started making good business out of acid house. 'People came out, started to make money. The scene expands. You can do this. You can do that. Suddenly you're in demand. In *demand*.'

CHARLIE CHESTER BECAME one of those people, though you would have found that hard to believe, watching him struggle to put up his market stall one Sunday in 1988, getting all tangled up in the poles and the canopy. Charlie had been to Shoom the night before and frankly, he was struggling. He was still as high as a kite on the E, which was why he'd got his girlfriend's brother to drive the van to where he set up his stall. He was hoping by the time they got there, he would have come down enough to function. But he hadn't. 'I was so out my brain,' he said, 'I couldn't see. Couldn't even work out how to do it. Absolutely ridiculous.'

On Saturdays, Charlie sold girls' clothing on Roman Road, in Hackney, East London. On Sundays like this, he was at Blackbush Market, on a disused airport near Reading. 'Gutter trader. That's what I was, a gutter trader,' he said. 'Selling girls' clobber. Proper frilly denim.' He wasn't going to be selling anything this particular Sunday. The van had clothes worth £30,000 in it. But Charlie left it there and went home.

Charlie is a big, burly guy, with an infectious sense of humour. Sharp, ebullient, larger than life; life and soul, proper geezer, you might say. He probably would. He hasn't changed since the superclub era. Just a little heavier. We hooked up in Ibiza, where Charlie now lives with his wife, the DJ Jo Mills, and talked over dinner. He chose Elephant, one of Ibiza's chicest and most expensive establishments. He put his cutlery down, drank some red wine and looked back to that Sunday in 1988, his fork in the road. He had realised he could carry on with the market stall, standing there all day, rain or shine, hollering his heart out to sell girls' clothes. Or he could have a good time instead. He could live in a promised land. 'I remember saying, "Fuck it." I thought, "You've got to go one way or the other. You've either got to do the markets or do a party."'

Charlie decided to put on a party. And went on to become one of the most recognisable faces in British clubland, with a chequered career that took in running nights and clubs, two different record labels – and innumerable nights out like that one at Shoom. He became famous, simply for being who he was: Charlie Chester, the life and soul. His last big job was running night at Ibiza's notoriously intense and decadent DC10 club. His main business now seems to be sorting out holiday apartments and arranging boat trips in Ibiza, but he does some work for a club in Singapore.

Charlie Chester grew up in Hayes, West London. His parents were Scousers. 'Just working-class people. Me mum was Miss Liverpool, 1959,' he told me. His dad worked for the RSPCA for 25 years. 'Caught Goldie the Eagle that escaped from London Zoo in 1965 and flew round London. Really famous.' In 1986, Charlie spent a year in Tenerife. 'I was just PRing. Dragging people into bars and all that. Gave me a taste for Spain and this malarkey.' Before the market stall, Charlie was a hairdresser and drove a mini-cab. 'Hairdressers did used to put on loads of parties,' he said. He is 44. 'A 44-year-old 15 years ago was a 44-year-old,' he observed. 'I'm still 25, I'm sure I am. I still knock about and can drink and can have the same conversation as 25-year-olds. I totally forget it sometimes.' One of his best friends, an Australian millionaire, calls him 'Big Kid'.

This raving hairdresser had an entrepreneurial bent. And a couple of DJ friends called Dean Thatcher and Brandon Block, out in Hayes where he lived, who wanted to do a party but didn't know how to go about it. Charlie stepped in. He organised a do at a place called Queens in Collbrook, on a Monday night in January 1989 – 700 people came and it went off. Charlie thought, 'Whoa, what is going on here?' Charlie had become a promoter.

By 1990 he and Dean Thatcher started a night called Flying, a wild, intense party full of crazy suburban kids, at the Soho Theatre Club in a back alley behind Tottenham Court Road in Central London. It ran from 1990 to 1992. It was sweaty, intense, delirious, but it was dressy too, it had an urban cool about it. Charlie then found himself opening the Flying record shop, in Kensington Market. 'I'd never run a record shop or even given myself five minutes in one. It was just boring. But we saw it as a centre,' said Charlie. 'It had to be like a social club. We had leather settees in there. We did loads of merchandising. And it was a hang-out, people came in there on a Saturday night off their cake hole. To hang out.' There was a television and a coffee machine and leather settees for girlfriends of record shoppers to hang out because Charlie, with his hairdresser's eye for detail, had noticed normal record shops left them hanging around like spare parts, getting bored.

Flying also had an exclusive supply of the latest dance music sound – the euphoric, piano-led house music pouring out of Italy. They organised a clubbing trip to Rimini in Italy, which had become, briefly, the new Ibiza. A writer from style magazine *The Face* went with them. In December 1990, shortly after the record shop opened, *The Face* ran a four-page spread on them. That was Charlie, cab driver, market stall-holder, hairdresser, hustler, clubber, in a magazine revered around the world as an arbiter of 'cool'. At Elephant, thinking back, he still couldn't believe it. 'Even now I think about it, even at the time thinking, "Fuck me." Literally only been doing it a year and a half and we were there in what had been our bible, since we were kids. Four pages of our bible.'

11.30 A.M. ON A Saturday morning in Wembley in 1990 and the party had started early. It was a boozy, noisy mob of larger-than-life club characters, London's loudest club lads, on their way to Venus in Nottingham. Charlie Chester had organised it as a Flying expedition. Former plumber turned DJ Terry Farley was there. Brandon Block, a DJ with a burgeoning reputation for outlandish behaviour. Phil Perry, another DJ, was there. And so was Dave Dorrell, who was bowled over by the sheer exuberance of the crew. 'These amazing characters who were so larger than life and so full of life energy, by the time we've reached Luton the best part of a gram of E that they've snorted off the back of a coach table. A six-pack of Tennent's or something,' Dorrell grinned. 'I'm that man on that coach trip, going, "This really hurts, guys. 11.30. This really hurts."'

There too was Danny Rampling, who, with his wife Jenni, was by now running a new club called Pure Sexy that had replaced Shoom's loose psychedelia with a smarter, more studied style. You had to look the business to get past Jenni and into Pure Sexy. Which was why Rampling was appalled by how quickly the coach got so messy. 'The coach had barely left London and people were just completely demolished,' Rampling sniffed. He made sure he got another lift back.

Then they got to Venus, this wild, sexy club that was just as fashion-conscious and just as abandoned in its atmosphere as anything in London. 'People dancing on the bar, everybody was really up for it, it was a great friendly mixed crowd,' Danny Rampling told me. 'It was like a home from home.' Dorrell was struggling to keep it together, after the party on the bus. 'I remember getting on the decks. Putting on the first record and having to stop the record, go outside and throw up – *again*!'

The party was a success and many more would follow. It was a watershed moment. Before 1990, DJs did not travel around the country to play other clubs and party. Now they started to. And Charlie Chester, Dorrell argues, was an explorer. 'We've mapped the world. You can't be Scott again or Livingston or Amundsen. Or any of these amazing young people that took off,' Dorrell said. 'Here's Charlie Chester doing it again, with a bag of E and his hairdressing scissors in his top pocket, probably, going and taking this around the country.'

Chester might not have quite been Robert Amundsen – London to Nottingham being a much less arduous journey than one to the

North Pole – but he had broken down a few geographical barriers. In 1990, the only reason people travelled around the country outside of work or family was for football matches. And that could be a dangerous business. At the time, being a cockney in, say, Liverpool meant running a serious risk of being beaten up. But that changed with the advent of superclubbing. The DJs started travelling, forming a network around smaller clubs like Venus in Nottingham, Most Excellent in Manchester, Slam in Glasgow and Flying in London that became known as 'The Balearic Network' – an Ibiza reference.

The Italian house these clubs played was in sharp contrast to more menacing sounds of hardcore techno that dominated the big, legal raves of the time. It was funky, brash, relentlessly cheerful and it came bouncing in like a space hopper, all 'woohs' and 'aahs' and clonking pianos. This was music made to pack a dance floor, pop music in its simplest, deadliest form: few lyrics, no depth, just pure fun. Pete Tong's Radio 1 show aside, new dance music like this was only being played on pirate radio stations like KISS FM in London, Sunrise in Manchester and FTP in Bristol. 'They didn't play house music on the radio. We were running round trying to find mix tapes,' said Suzie Mason, an art student who would go on to co-found the Leeds club Vague.

But clubbing wasn't just about the nights out and the music. As it began to embrace everything from fashion to haircuts, it was becoming a way of life. The clothes were different and the codes were different. It was colourful, multi-racial. And it wasn't to be found in high-street stores, it was hidden away in places like the Liverpool Palace and Kensington Market, alternative shopping malls full of record shops like Charlie Chester's Flying, funky new hairdressers and little clothes stalls. 'Even fashion, there was lots of things happening that the corporates hadn't clicked into,' explained Suzi Mason. 'It's like they missed it. You went into Top Shop and the clothes were just awful and we'd laugh about them.'

In the early 1990s, Britain was in recession. Clubbing was almost a reaction to the economic downturn that had sent many home-owners into negative equity. Nicky Holloway ran a night at his Milk Bar club called the Recession Session. Another London night was called Job Club – which was what unemployed people had to join to keep receiving their benefit. But by the late nineties, with New Labour in power and the economy booming, hundreds of thousands of British youngsters would be following Charlie Chester and his gang, doing something they had never done before – racing up and down the nation's motorways to giant clubs like Cream in Liverpool or Golden in Manchester or Up Yer Ronson in Leeds. Making friends, forming networks. 'A combination of music, popular culture and drugs created these contact points,' said Dave Dorrell. 'And all of the points that had once been individual towns – Liverpool, Manchester, Glasgow, Edinburgh, Bristol, Birmingham – had suddenly become part of a roadmap of hedonism.'

DAVE BEER WAS a man who knew how to make an entrance. But even by his standards, this one was special. It was his birthday and he was being carried into the crowded bar of the most expensive hotel in Cannes on a surfboard as around him his acolytes set off little fireworks. The bar, bustling with music business executives at the annual MIDEM record company showcase, exploded into laughter. Then it went horribly quiet. Behind Beer, two more of his mates were trailing a white line of wet gloss paint behind him, which stretched all the way down the hotel's grand staircase. The choice of a white line was symbolic enough, even though it was by accident. The bill was not.

The hotel wanted £25,000 in damages. 'I ended up paying five or something,' Beer said. 'Expensive birthday.'

Beer put Leeds on that roadmap of hedonism. Short and slight, with an edgy charisma, he was universally liked in 1990s clubland, even though his Yorkshire accent and the way he munched his words made him virtu- ally unintelligible. He was mad, bad and dangerous to know – all of which made him even more popular. No matter how late and how crazy the party went, Beer always kept himself together and everything else as crazy as possible. He went to the limit. He always had done. Back To Basics, the club night he started on 23 November 1991 with his friend, the DJ Ali Cooke, lived by its slogan: 'Two Steps Further Than Any Other Fucker'. Something Beer and his gang generally managed to live up to.

Beer had found acid house at the Haçienda. He did his first ecstasy tablet there. 'I remember going in there, going through the plastic shut- ters and it just being awash with people with smiley faces, everybody just going full on, full on. Like nothing I'd ever seen. It was just like, "What?" It was like it stopped still for a minute when I saw it,' he told me. 'Such an impact. It was like unbelievable. It was like, "Fucking hell, what is this?" It was like, "That's it. This is it. This is what I do, that's where I'm at." I just joined in and became a part of what was going on.' At Back To Basics, which he still runs today, the music preferred was the darker, less commercial side of house music, the club never went in for the out-and-out dance pop that other northern clubs preferred.

The club's imagery set out its stall. Its logo borrowed the cut-out lettering Jamie Reid had used for the Sex Pistols' iconic album covers. One glossy advert featured a photo of a Victorian monk shagging a nun from behind, both habits rolled up to the waist, together with the slogan: 'Back To Basics: No Beating About The Bush.' Another used a photo of The Who's late, hedonistic drummer Keith Moon, at a

1970s orgy with the slogan 'Tales Of Glamour And Excess' and a quote from Hunter S. Thompson: 'There were no rules, fear was unknown and sleep was out of the question.' It was a fairly accurate description of a Saturday night out with Dave Beer and his gang.

Dave Beer still lives in Leeds today, in the upmarket district of Chapel Allerton – the self-styled 'Notting Hill of the North' – where he owns a house in a building that also houses a recording studio. We met there one Saturday afternoon. Looking back to the early 1990s, he remembered how Leeds had become one of the UK's most popular club destinations, not just with Back To Basics, but others like Vague, the New York house night Hard Times, the poppier house night Up Yer Ronson. 'At one point, it was just mobbed here,' he said. 'It was kind of bizarre to think that everywhere was full.'

The stories about Dave Beer are legion and he became famous for them – another accidental celebrity, notorious for being himself, only more so. At one messy Leeds after party, he once gave a broadsheet journalist ketamine. The poor guy, already off his face on his first-ever ecstasy, was barely conscious as Beer forced brandy down his throat. 'Let's kill him!' declared Beer to shocked onlookers. 'Not even the Sex Pistols did that.' No one was sure how serious he was. It's doubtful that Beer was, either.

In the mid-1990s, visitors from clubland's inner circle to Back To Basics were generally ushered into the office where a desk drawer seemed to be permanently open, filled with ready-racked-out lines of cocaine. If the coke had run out, he would offer an E. Even if he didn't want to party, Beer sometimes found that the reputation that preceded him made that impossible. One night, fancying a quiet night in after the club closed, he got into his car to drive home to the village outside Leeds where he lived with his girlfriend and young son. Halfway home he looked in his rear-view mirror and noticed a convoy of cars following him, all of them having reasoned that wherever Beer was going, there was bound to be a party.

Beer grew up in Pontefract, West Yorkshire, about 40 miles from Leeds. Half barrack town, half mining village, Pontefract was rough in the way that only a Yorkshire mining town could be rough in the 1970s. 'Everybody was just fighting in lumps everywhere. You had to be able to learn to scrap pretty quick,' he remembered. 'You took quite a few knockings. You just had to be able to fight your way to school really. Then going out wasn't much easier really, on a night.' His mother, who married four times during his childhood, worked as a barmaid. The Beers grew up on a council estate. It was rough. 'There was a lot of violence and stuff, really, at the time. I was forever calling the coppers and windows going through and stuff,' he said.

Beer embraced punk rock because it meant he could hide his family's poverty. He couldn't afford the high-waisted, giant flares of the late 70s. 'When punk happened it was brilliant, I could just cut up all me clothes,' he said. 'It meant I didn't have to have all these expensive clothes. Just rip up T-shirts and put safety pins in them and put chains everywhere. And it was a really good way of being accepted by being a part of something.'

But being a punk increased his vulnerability to sudden attack, so Beer learnt to surprise assailants with a sudden head butt. 'It totally freaks people out, it scares the living daylights out of them. They just think, "Shit, this case, he's fucking crazy."' At art college in nearby Wakefield he met Ali Cooke and the two became good friends. 'We were in bands together and stuff. We used to go and see Joy Division. Brilliant. We had a common thing.' He followed bands like The Clash around the country, occasionally blagging a ride in the band's van, progressed on to tour managing – by the mid-1980s he was taking indie bands on the road. 'I wasn't the greatest roadie in the world or the greatest tour manager,' he noted. 'The accounts were always up in the air, but the after-show parties were fucking phenomenal. So bands always wanted me about. I was always getting the backstage passes to all the right girls and making sure the right people with the supplies were there.'

Ali and Dave started throwing parties wherever and whenever after the Haçienda. One location included a library. Then the chance to use a legal venue came up and Back To Basics was born. Beer was the promoter; Cooke one of the DJs. In 1992, Back To Basics won the award for best club at a ceremony *Mixmag* and its parent company DMC held at the Albert Hall in London. Beer and Cooke acted blasé, sneering their way through the after party at the Iceni Club. 'We were a little bit too self-assured at that point,' Beer admitted. After all, picking up awards wasn't very punk. But secretly they were thrilled. 'We had done it. We were fucking there. That was the moment we realised we were starting to achieve us dreams then.' Things couldn't have been better for Basics.

Best of all, they were making money. Not that they had time to actually count it, what with all the partying. Instead he and Ali would divide up the week's profits in a more slapdash fashion. They'd split the cash into two house-brick sized piles of cash – with between £4,000 and £5,000 in each one. 'We'd hold it behind us back and go, "Right or left." This was a weekly ritual. "Left. No. Right, no, left." "Make your mind up."' It didn't really matter who got the biggest brick of tenners. They were going to spend it all anyway.

THE MOOD WAS as bubbly as the champagne in the car, that rainy night in March 1993. They were somewhere north of Carlisle on the way to a night at the club Slam in Glasgow. Ali Cooke was driving. Dave, his girlfriend Jill Morris and Jocelyn Higgin, the new girlfriend of Basics DJ Ralph Lawson, who'd been persuaded to come along and 'be a part of it' were in good spirits. Cooke wasn't drinking, but the others were passing around a bottle of champagne.

The car journey had started well. Cooke and Beer had bought supplies for the trip – a couple of 'Henrys' of cocaine. A Henry – or Henry the XVIII – is a serious amount of cocaine: instead of the common gram, it's an eighth of an ounce, or three and a half grams. It's also called an 'Eight Ball'. They had one each. 'We'd had maybe one bump [a small line, snorted off a key or a credit card] of it before we'd left,' said Dave.

The accident happened very fast. Suddenly the car was on the wrong side of the road. The last thing Beer remembered was the truck headlights and Jocelyn's scream of 'Ali!' The last thing she would ever say. It was a notorious accident blackspot, a point where a dual carriageway became a normal, one lane each way A road. Dave Beer came round realising he had gone through the windscreen. Although he didn't know it, he had a punctured lung. The first thing he thought of was to get rid of his cocaine. The second was to get rid of Cooke's cocaine, but despite horrendous injuries, Ali had already done so himself. Beer had his arms around Cooke's body as he died. 'He just stopped moving. Then I had hold of him for a bit.'

There was an awful silence in Dave Beer's kitchen, 14 years later. His voice faltered. His eyes were wet with tears. 'I remember I looked back and I saw Jos.' Dave shuddered suddenly, at a vision he hadn't seen in his mind's eye for all those years, of the horrific injuries that had killed her, of his best friend dead on the side of the wet road. It was an accident that has marked him for the rest of his life, he said. He will never forget it. Even now, he talks to Ali every day. And the fallout of this accident goes on to this day. Beer has refused to change or to modify Back To Basics or to sell it out – as he sees it – in any way. He can't, not without the permission of his late former partner. Since then, he has remained stuck in a groove, the same club, the same behaviour, a law of diminishing returns.

At the inquest, it came out that Cooke had cocaine in his system. 'All the families were there and the families of Jocelyn,' said Beer. He still remembers their faces, their quiet fury. Headlines in local papers screamed 'Death Disco Cocaine Car Crash'. Beer, Back To Basics, that crazy, decadent DJ lifestyle got the blame. Beer refused to accept it. 'If anything, that [the small 'bump' of cocaine] would have helped him, if he was worn out,' argued Beer. 'It's just so wrong.'

Unlikely as this seems, he may have a point. In 1994, as part of a special drugs issue, *Mixmag* printed a feature entitled 'Can You Drive On Drugs?'. The title was deliberately controversial but the intention was serious. Concerned about the number of readers writing to the magazine with stories about criss-crossing the country to club, driving while still high on drugs, we intended to demonstrate how dangerous this was.

Under legal advice, on private land, we conducted a completely unscientific experiment. There was a driving instructor, a dual control car and three volunteers. Each volunteer drove around a slalom course of 25 traffic cones in a Maestro Diesel 200 with the driving instructor, completely sober. Each then took a drug – ecstasy, marijuana and cocaine. The instructor had no idea who was doing what, if anything. Once the drugs kicked in, the driving abilities of the first two drivers rapidly deteriorated. But after one line of cocaine, the third volunteer, our instructor observed, noticeably improved his driving. After a second line of cocaine, he became noticeably reckless and his driving ability then decreased. Our legal advice said we shouldn't reveal his brief improvement after that one line. We altered the article accordingly.

The day after Ali Cooke's death, Back To Basics opened as usual. Dave felt it was what Ali would have wanted. It's been open ever since, through countless ups and downs, changes of venues and assorted club dramas. But the central idea remains the same. 'Ali died,' said Beer. 'I can't ask him and I'm not going to sell the brand or do whatever, it keeps him alive as well and Jos alive.'

Neither did Beer curtail his drinking and drug taking. Instead, he got worse. To the point that *Mixmag* named him number one Party Animal and dance music magazine *Muzik* actually gave him an award for Caner of the Year. 'I didn't care if I lived or died. I'd have been happy to be dead in that period. One way of doing that is by insane amounts of narcotics. *Insane* amounts. And just fucking cracking on and just partying and doing things like jumping out of hotel rooms into swimming pools, setting yourself on fire with toilet paper, all them things that become legendary.'

Meanwhile the money kept piling up. 'I saved some. I had £30,000. I had it in notes,' said Beer. He kept it in a safety deposit box in a bank. 'I'd go and have a look and put another grand in and just have a look. And think, "Fucking hell. Look at all this money." I'd got this tin full of money.'

Then there was a change of notes and he realised he had to either get it changed – or spend it. 'Flapping, trying to get it changed but not being conspicuous, five grand, can you change this into new tenners or new twenties please? It was fucked.' He managed. He put some into the club. And simply spent the rest.

Jacuzzis. Champagne. Automatic guest list status. Swanky hotel suites. Mini bar bills the size of Mexico's GNP. No wonder they call it the Perks Of Living Society.
Mixmag *feature, 1993*

CHESTER AND HIS boys were so excited when they got to the villa. They were used to cheap side of Ibiza, where the apartments are piled high in concrete blocks. This was the real deal. As soon as the owner had closed the door, they looked at each other – and started pogo-ing around the place, amazed and excited at the luxury they had just landed in. Straight away they got in the jacuzzi. 'We'd come from shitty little bedsits, hotels, hostels in San Antonio to we've got a villa.' Straight away the champagne came out, the cocaine. The ecstasy. 'What do you think?' Charlie asked his crew. All the Flying lot were there. Ashley Beedle, Rocky and Scott Braithwaite, a handful of others. 'Shall we hold the pill in this hand, or that hand?'

If the Perks Of Living Society had never existed, it would have been necessary to invent it, if only to capture the spirit of the time. Charlie Chester and his mob came up with the idea, in that jacuzzi in Ibiza in 1992. An organisation to celebrate the good times they were having. 'We're actually saying how lucky we are. We can't believe it and we're taking this on board and saying, "Bingo",' Chester explained. And he was right. The rest of the UK was in a recession. But this motley, disparate gang of promoters, DJs and hustlers were living like rock stars. Dave Beer turned up a few days later and was instantly voted in. 'Bloody miners think they've got problems. The schoolteachers every morning, they moan about this, that and the other,' Beer told me. 'We've got to decide which colour E to have. A white one or a pink one. It's the Perks Of Living.'

The Perks Of Living Society didn't actually do anything, bar that is the odd drug-fuelled, after-club 'meeting' in a hotel somewhere. But then neither did most of its members, apart from organise clubs and DJ. Their working weeks weren't particularly arduous. Which was just as well, as it took until Wednesday for them to come down from the weekend. But they did decide on some activities at a 'meeting' at the Holiday Inn in Leeds. One was called Clubbing – Know Your Body. There weren't enough activities in clubbing to enable people to keep fit, it was decided. Phil Perry came up with Carpet Scuba Diving. Somebody was told to take his clothes off and did. The 'meeting' descended further into chaos.

The membership expanded to include the DJ Brandon Block – already famous as a party animal – Glasgow's Slam DJ duo Stuart McMillan and Orde Meikle and their manager Dave Clarke, and Tim Jeffries from Brighton remix duo The Playboys. Candidates for membership were fairly obvious. They even released a record, eventually, called 'Body And Soul' on Charlie's Cowboy Records. The joke ran and ran. 'I was just pissing myself laughing, realising that we did have a lifestyle that was taking the piss. Covered in Vivienne Westwood, you just spent so much money, so much. All of a sudden, it was like, we had the Perks Of Living,' said Beer. 'We didn't even have to recruit members, everybody knew who was there. Everybody knew who was having it off at that period of time.'

Somewhat inevitably, Charlie Chester and Dave Beer were by now close friends. They were a celebrity odd couple as they partied together through the club magazine gossip columns. The Perks Of Living Society was profiled in *Mixmag* in November 1993, interviewed at an event called Dance Europe that Nicky Holloway staged near Euro Disney in Paris. The magazine had by now graduated to a London office – in effect, a scruffy flat situated above a Chinese herbalist shop in Hammersmith. Andy Pemberton was the new boy, a shaven-headed, fresh-faced clubber with a university degree who was up for anything. He was sent to France to write the piece.

After Beer and Chester had come down enough, Pemberton attempted an interview. Beer had been playing a three-foot trumpet and indulging in his favourite party trick: when things got particularly messy, he liked to sweep the dance floor with a broom, telling people to 'keep it tidy'. Pemberton asked the pair about their friendship. 'We're kindred spirits,' Beer exclaimed. 'He's up for it, 100 per cent trustworthy, top accent, he can stay the pace, dresses like a loony and he's one of my mates,' added Chester. 'If you've got friends,' concluded Beer, 'you'll be all right.'

The 1990s were off. The Perks Of Living Society, Flying and Back To Basics were setting the pace. And Chester and Beer were already, in a way, famous. In Leeds, particularly, Beer and his Basics gang were like local rock stars. 'We were one of the most famous things round here. It was hilarious really,' Beer observed. 'Maybe that's subconsciously a career, it was never meant to be a business plan, but we started to be able to get things from it, go places, buy things.'

Theirs was a very post-modern kind of celebrity. Like modern *Big Brother* winners, they were famous for simply being themselves, only in a pressurised, artificial environment; the glass bubble of clubland's inner circle. Chester noticed that clubbers would come and talk to him at his nights, but they'd be shy, nervous even. 'Then when you spent some time talking to them, they'd go, "Thanks for talking to me. I was really scared to talk to you, I just thought you'd bat me off."' Charlie, stunned, would ask why. The answer would come back. 'You're Charlie Chester.' But whatever the clubbers thought, Beer and

Chester were both small fry. Soon bigger players with bigger ambitions were going to take over. In 1993, the British club scene was still a playground, a fun, silly place to goof about. It was going to get a lot more serious.

At Elephant in Ibiza, dinner was winding down. Chester had enjoyed sharing his stories. The dinner had been interrupted by occasional phone calls from a friend he was arranging a boat party for the next day. He seems to do a lot of that sort of thing. Charlie still likes to party, he said, but not as much. He remembered that that night at the villa in Ibiza, when the party in the jacuzzi had wound down and everybody was relaxing a little bit. His girlfriend Karen was at home, pregnant. 'I remember sitting in the pool on this rubber ring, wondering if that will slow me down.' He took another swig of his expensive wine at one of Ibiza's finest restaurants. 'Clearly hasn't.'

THREE

MAD MANC SPARROW
AND THE SON OF GOD

TUNE! DOP – 'GROOVY BEAT'

A stabbing riff, staccato vocal sample and piano breakdown made up this dance-floor filler from London's Guerrilla Records.

The Raffles L'Ermitage is one of the finest hotels in Los Angeles and Microsoft hadn't skimped on the budget, renting a suite of rooms across the entire top floor for the launch of a new Xbox video game. They'd hired Sasha, by now one of the biggest names in America, to DJ. As usual Sparrow had gone along. They'd arrived at the hotel to discover that Sasha had been upgraded to the top floor penthouse suite. But after playing the Xbox show, he would have to leave straight away for another gig in Las Vegas.

Disappointed, Sasha surveyed the suite. It was lavish beyond what even he, a superstar DJ, was used to, half a floor of this most luxurious of hotels. 'I literally can't believe I've got to leave,' Sasha said. Sparrow was prone on a pile of cushions. 'But what about me? I can't leave,' he said. 'Just stay here,' Sasha told him. 'Yeah, but who's paying the bill?' replied Sparrow, a plan slowly forming in his mind. 'Bill Gates is paying, mate,' said Sasha. 'It's fucking Microsoft.'

Feigning exhaustion and firing off stage yawns, Sparrow helped Sasha load his CDs and equipment into a cab. 'Off you go, our kid, have a good gig,' Sparrow said. He went back upstairs to the suite and promptly got on the phone to everyone he knew in Los Angeles. 'Get down to the L'Ermitage. There's a party on and Bill Gates is paying.' It was 4 a.m. by this point, but for someone like Sparrow, Los Angeles is always full of people ready to party. Soon enough, he had 40-plus people in there and the night was swinging. 'I'm not joking, Mexican midgets, all sorts, it was insane. The whole place was going mad.'

Sparrow called room service. "Yes, yes, it's Mister Coe here [Sasha's surname]. I'd like six Cristal, two more bottles of vodka.' They were like, 'No problem.' 'Magnums,' I was like, 'magnums. Yeah, sweet.' Sparrow's brothers, in LA pushing their new rock band, turned up and ordered bacon and egg sandwiches. The bill for six bacon and egg sandwiches alone came to $485. 'The most expensive bacon and egg butty of all time,' said Sparrow, proudly.

At noon he checked out, the last to leave, and was presented with a bill to sign for. He asked for an itemised version – as a souvenir. Between 4 a.m. and noon Sparrow and his party had run up a bill for $14,000 on room service alone. He mimicked Bill Gates, scrutinising the bill: 'Fucking wankers! Fucking arseholes! We're not booking him again!'

JAMIE 'SPARROW' ORMANDY is a guy with peculiar talents. It's all that stuff about never having any money, but always knowing where the party is. Everybody loves Sparrow, but mention his name and you get a laugh, an exasperated noise, a story. He is a charmer and a rogue. So best man at a superstar DJ wedding is a role he could have been born to. It is a difficult job. One that requires charm, charisma, a sense of occasion, a level of sensitivity for the atmosphere of a gathering, a nose for a party, the wit to measure up and sum up a character and the ability to deliver a good joke. All qualities Sparrow possesses in abundance. Needless to say, at Sasha's sumptuous wedding to his American girlfriend Zoie at a ceremony in Mykonos, Greece, Sparrow played a blinder.

'He started by saying that when he saw the guest list he nearly didn't make it because he realised he owed so many people so much money,' remembered Geoff Oakes. 'Everybody laughed at that, funnily enough.' The guest list included close dance music industry friends like the DJ John Digweed, along with Oakes and his wife Joanne, but was largely a family affair. Many of Zoie's American relatives had little idea of Sasha's past. Sparrow decided to enlighten them. He flashed up a slide of Sasha's first *Mixmag* cover from 1991. In the photo, a skinny Sasha sported a ponytail, a baggy, white shirt and that awkward, sideways grin. He looked every inch the early nineties Manchester raver he was. And he looked like he'd been up for days – which according to Sparrow, he probably had. The headline declared: 'SASHA: THE FIRST DJ PIN-UP.' Audience in the palm of his hand, Sparrow delivered his punchline: 'Obviously Zoie has gone for the looks.' The audience roared. 'Classic Sparrow,' laughed Oakes.

The friendship between Sasha and his best friend Jamie 'Sparrow' Ormandy is emblematic of two of nineties' clubland's most extreme dynamics – ability versus blag. Sasha, with the undeniable talent, the pop-star good looks, the inoffensive charisma; Sparrow, with the knife-edge wit, the chat, the hustle. Sasha was a superstar DJ, famous all over the world, someone who even today enjoys the sort of evangelical following usually reserved for rock stars. He was a quiet, even shy boy from North Wales who became equally famous for his hedonism, for missing as many gigs as he turned up to. Sparrow was a former club promoter, a chancer and a charmer who bounced around clubland like a pinball around an arcade game. His career has been full of ups and downs. Yet he seems to live a charmed life, subsisting purely on his charm and entertainment value. 'When I'm in the shit, that's when I'm at my best,' Sparrow said. 'I've been to the ends of the earth. I was an adopted kid. Overall I know that I'm a nice kid.'

He uses the word 'kid' a lot, though he is 36. And how he makes a living is anybody's guess. Mostly, he doesn't. There is an undefined vague role helping Sasha out on tour. The other, which a friend coined more recently, is 'International Morale Booster'. 'He really is one of a kind,' said Sasha, awed. 'I'm just amazed that he managed to get almost to his late 30s without ever really having a proper job. Still looks good and manages to pull the best-looking women in the room. He's got no stresses, no responsibilities and he seems to have more fun than anyone, without ever having two pennies to rub together.' Everyone who meets him, remembers him. 'And everyone that meets him, he ends up owing 50 quid to,' said Sasha, rumoured to regularly pass brown envelopes of cash over to Sparrow. 'I'm always helping him out, I'm his best friend.'

At the time of writing, Sparrow was dividing his time between various friends' sofas, in Los Angeles, London and New York. He counts as personal friends English socialite Lady Victoria Hervey and upmarket club owner Amy Sacco. He spent one New Year's Eve at Amy Sacco's New York club Bungalow 8 dining with Benicio Del Torro and Scarlet Johansson. He is a good friend of Brazilian supermodel and Victoria's Secret star Alessandra Ambrosio: they spent time clubbing together in New York, Ibiza and Los Angeles. 'The thing is, he's a really nice person. He's a nice guy,' she told me. 'So, like, why wouldn't people want to hang out with him?'

Sparrow wasn't easy to pin down. He failed to show up for our first lunch appointment, at the Limonia restaurant in London's chic Primrose Hill. I tried calling his mobile number. Somebody answered but nobody spoke – I heard the background noise of a bunch of guys buying something in a shop. A few minutes later, my mobile rang. I answered: 'Sparrow. Where are you?' I asked. 'It's not,' said a male voice, sounding amused. 'He's just left his phone here. He was riding around Primrose Hill last night rat-arsed on a moped without a helmet and he got into a bit of trouble. There it is. He's a bit of a wild card, but he's good value. I've no idea where he is but if he does turn up, I've got your number and I'll get him to call you.'

When we finally met for lunch some weeks later, he turned up early. I arrived at another Primrose Hill restaurant to find he'd already ordered an expensive bottle of wine. I realised lunch was going to be costly. He confirmed the moped story and said he'd spent the night in the cells. He charmed the pretty waitress and called her 'darling'. Meal over, he disappeared and I found him outside, chatting to the chef, who he had just bummed a cigarette off. He told me how he got into acid house, and why. 'I was just a little raver that used to go to the Haçienda, I loved the music,' he said. 'There was a little bit of rebellion in there. There was something that was so appealing in it, the sound, the slight cheekiness of it. Ninety per cent of it was illegal. Once you're in it, it's your life.'

WHEN SPARROW MET Sasha, he wasn't the quintessential superstar DJ whose name filled clubs with adoring fans wherever he played, all over the world. He was a long-haired club kid who had just bounced off the Haçienda dance floor into the DJ booth. Yet already his name had an aura around it that others lacked. 'He does have this real magnetism, of people coming around the box and looking at him and him pulling in the focus,' said Piers Sanderson, a close friend since Sasha's youth.

Sasha was the first superstar DJ, the first DJ to become a celebrity, a pop star, to have fans, to make the cover of a magazine. 'There wasn't a blueprint. No other DJ had smashed it,' Sasha told me. 'It was all new really. I was the guinea pig.' Before then, DJs had just been names on a flyer, elusive, shadowy figures, hidden in the DJ booth. Like Graeme Park and Mike Pickering, the two DJ residents during those halcyon Haçienda days. 'I just wanted to be doing what they were doing,' Sasha said. 'They weren't doing magazine covers. They weren't even doing much DJing abroad. It wasn't that global thing that it became and it didn't have the money attached to it either. You spent all the money you made on records.'

Today Sasha lives in New York and continues to tour the world. For 15 years or more, his life as a superstar DJ has been a rollercoaster of first-class flights, heady club nights and glamorous parties. Adoring fans line up to watch him play. There is a classic photo, taken in San Francisco in 1998, that says it all. The awed faces of California clubbers, reaching out to light his cigarette. You can't even smoke in California clubs; you could if you were Sasha. When Madonna wanted someone to remix the title track from her 1997 dance album *Ray of Light* it was Sasha she turned to. When Bruce Willis or Dan Ackroyd went looking for a party in Los Angeles, it was Sasha's club night Fundaçion they went to.

Sasha's Manila story is typical. He arrived on a Friday night for a DJ date, in the middle of the city's legendary rush hour. To get him to the gig on time, promoters arranged a police motorcycle escort. 'From the roundabout at the airport to the front door of the hotel was literally gridlocked,' he recalled. 'But we had four motorcyclists. Two cars, four motorcycles and they were literally swatting cars out of the way. Creating space. We got to the hotel in about 15, 20 minutes.' Sasha was pleased that Zoie, his girlfriend, now wife, was with him. 'It was good for her to experience that,' he joked. This wasn't a unique experience for him.

Yet despite all the glamour, the money, the free drugs, he has also been able to enjoy an anonymity that eludes pop stars and television celebrities. It's the ultimate trick of the superstar DJ. 'In our little world, we are considered to be the rock stars or actors,' explained Sasha. 'But it's not like we get chased down the street, with girls throwing pants at us.'

Sasha is, on the surface, an unassuming, quiet character. 'He's certainly more complicated than just being shy, but there's an element to him that's bashful,' said Dave Dorrell, who was his manager at one time. 'It's kind of quite sweet. And there's a very powerful personality behind that as well.'

Sasha's career was only a couple of years old when he started his residency at Stoke club Shelley's in 1991, where the northern crowd had migrated as its beloved Haçienda was beleaguered by gang problems. It was here his audience propelled him into a kind of stardom. Unlike Graeme Park or Mike Pickering, Sasha was younger and there, in the booth in front of the dance floor at Shelley's or mingling with the crowd afterwards, he was accessible. His audience loved him. He didn't just look like one of them, he actually was. 'People were like, "He's fucking one of us!"' said Sasha. 'I was definitely the first one to come off the floor and I think people were really buzzing on that. The fact that a scally with long hair was actually rocking the house.'

He was also a naturally gifted DJ, willing to take risks yet not shy of delivering the killer big tunes at the right time. His euphoric sets mixed up apparently contradictory styles like techno and soulful house.

'I definitely approached DJing with quite an open, naïve mind. I was like, "Why not mix that with that? Why not drop that over that and see what happens?" And it kind of worked, mixing Sinéad O'Connor or "The Power Of Love" over techno-trance and Whitney Houston over the top of Leftfield, while everyone was E'd out of their faces,' Sasha said. ' I guess that's what made my name in the beginning.'

The songs he played and the way he played them caught the ecstasy experience. He was brilliant on the decks. 'Those records are unabashedly, uplifting, enormous E records. Those big piano breaks used to send crowds off their knackers. And I used to love that," said Sasha. The crowd at Shelley's went wild. People talked about magic. Clubbers got emotional. At the end of his set, queues would form: men who wanted to shake his hand, and who famously wanted him to kiss their girlfriends. 'It used to weird me out completely,' he said. 'It was just odd.'

Yet much as the shy boy balked at the attention, at the same time he sought it out. 'He used to do a royal walkabout,' said Piers Sanderson. 'He loved speaking to people. And I think he probably loved the adulation of it as well. There was this ruck to come and see him. It was like a pop star.'

It was this groundswell of support that *Mixmag* caught when the magazine featured Sasha on that now infamous cover – the same one Sparrow was to brandish, years later, at his wedding. Editor David Davies was an experienced journalist who had given up a successful freelance career in New York to return to England and run what was then a small insider magazine. Davies realised that the magazine's diet of rappers and American soul singers was not going to produce the cover stars the magazine needed. *Mixmag* needed to create its own celebrities. Sasha was the perfect candidate.

The issue, published in December 1991, caused something of a storm. No one had called a DJ a 'pin-up' or a 'star' before. Least of all a long-haired scally barely known outside the North. Piers Sanderson, just back from a spell hustling in Tenerife, was in Wales when he got a phone call from Sasha telling him to go and buy the magazine. 'It was at that point I realised not only how much he'd changed, but how much the scene had changed,' said Piers. 'There was a gear shift from the emphasis on the night to the emphasis to the DJ.' Piers's mother was amazed. 'That scrawny little skinny guy that used to be round the house?' she said. 'That scrawny, little skinny Sasha is considered a pin-up?'

Embarrassed at the piss-taking he immediately began getting from his mates, Sasha had mixed feelings about his new-found celebrity. 'It was just weird,' he said. 'I really wasn't prepared for people coming up to me and knowing who I was and it took me a good few years to actually accept that.' But it didn't do his career any harm. The DJ bookings kept flooding in. And everyone now knew what he looked like. 'My flowing white shirts and long ponytails were a trademark,' he conceded. It also didn't dampen his appetite for a party. As his earnings skyrocketed, his weekends increasingly became a blur of clubs and parties. The rollercoaster was off and Sasha was on board. Superstar DJs, Here We Go.

MAY, 1992: 3 A.M. and the first Universe rave was going right off. Marquees packed full of thousands of delirious ravers, airhorns blowing, shrieks and cheers. As promoter Paul Shurey paced up and down outside his main arena, the noises from the different systems mingled in the crisp spring air. He had every reason to be pleased – this was his first legal rave after years of running illegal parties. But his star DJ,

Sasha, was yet to turn up. Shurey's credibility as a new promoter depended on Sasha: if he didn't make it, ravers would know Shurey couldn't deliver the DJs he promised on his flyers. He fretted, radioed the front gate once again and paced a little more.

He wasn't the first promoter to be put in this position. As clubs sprouted across the UK, Sasha became more and more in demand. But he was becoming as famous for missing his gigs as he was for playing them. One problem was he couldn't drive. Another was that the after-party from one gig often went on too long for Sasha to make the next. 'I only managed to book Sasha on two provisos,' Shurey remembered. The first was that Sasha had a flight to New York the next morning and Shurey had to promise to make sure he got it. The second was that Shurey also had to book an unknown French DJ and chef, also based in Manchester, called Laurent Garnier, because Garnier would drive the two of them down. They had another show earlier – a protest thing U2 were playing on the beach near Sellafield nuclear power station.

An increasingly nervous Shurey began to formulate plan B. There was a lad working for Universe who was a dead ringer for Sasha and who could DJ a bit. Maybe he could put him on and pretend. Perhaps the audience was already too spangled to notice. At 3.45 a.m. he got a call on the radio: Sasha had arrived. 'Thank fuck,' Shurey thought, already running to the gate. But his relief was short-lived. Sasha didn't so much get out of Laurent's car as fall out of it. His eyes were barely open. He could hardly stand. 'He was absolutely fucking legless,' said Shurey. Undeterred, he and his crew manhandled the star DJ round to the back of the stage and carried him onto the stage. They set him to work, fearing the worst.

The thing was, Sasha played a fantastic set. His mixing was seam-less: Shurey still has the tape. 'It's a sign of what a brilliant DJ he was, cause he didn't know what record he was pulling out of the box,' said Shurey. There were just two mini-disasters. The first was when Sasha temporarily lost consciousness and fell across the decks. Ever the pro, he quickly recovered and got back to work. Paul decided everything was going to be okay. He was walking away from the tent when the second occurred. 'I suddenly became aware the music had stopped. I thought, "Oh fuck, what's going on now?"'

He rushed back in, but there was no one behind the decks. Where was Sasha? What now? There was his star attraction, 50 feet into the crowd, chatting up two starry-eyed girls who'd been raving on the dance floor. Shurey hurried over. 'Sasha,' he said, 'you're meant to be DJing.' Sasha looked at him, glassy-eyed. He was still DJing? Somehow, mid-set, onstage, in front of thousands of ravers, he'd forgotten, drifted off, wandered into the crowd towards those welcoming smiles, leaving the record playing to spin off into silence. *Ker-plunk*, *ker-plunk*, went the needle, as the record continued spinning on the run-out groove. The catcalls and whistles from the thousands of ravers, suddenly cut off from the music that had driving them higher, got increasingly louder. Shurey stared angrily at his star DJ and realisation slowly dawned across Sasha's face. 'Oh fuck. Yeah!' said Sasha. He hurried back on stage, slapped on another record to a cheer and the party continued. Shurey's heart started beating again.

There was just one little drama left. Sasha had lost his ticket for his flight to New York the next day. Shurey spent the early hours on the phone to British Airways, trying to get him another ticket. 'Trying to sort out his fucking life for him.' Sasha made the flight.

SASHA VIVIDLY REMEMBERS the first time he met Sparrow. It was early on in his career. He'd got a rare Haçienda slot, when the club was still good, warming up for one of its big names, Jon Dasilva. 'I went on and played every single one of his big records. The place went fucking ballistic,' said Sasha. 'I think he just looked at that night and went, "Oh my God, I've created a monster!" At the end of my set, there was a knock at the door of the DJ booth, I opened the door and there was this raver in a NASA orange jumpsuit and he was like, "You're brilliant!"' Enter Sparrow.

The kid in the orange jumpsuit was born into a working-class family in Rusholme, Manchester and grew up all over the city. His parents split up when he was young. He had five brothers. His mother taught ballet and tap and Sparrow once persuaded her to include him in a routine her girl students were entering into a local competition. They danced to Boney M's 'Rah Rah Rasputin' and came second. Sparrow was a talented footballer and had trials for Manchester City. His nickname came from a team photo in which he resembled an older player with the same nickname.

Sparrow has fond memories of being a kid. 'It being fucking red-hot and having six weeks off and fucking running through a field and kissing a girl for the first time.' There were the teenage gangs – 'Perry Boys', Manchester's own soul-boy crew, with their polo shirts and Adidas trainers; and mods. By the time he met Sasha, he was working, he said. Though he wouldn't say at what. 'Whatever I could to get by. All sorts of different stuff.'

Sparrow discovered ecstasy at a warehouse party in London – he had gone down for a weekend while working on a market stall. Spinning out on his first ecstasy rush, he spent an hour or so talking to a couple of guys he'd met. He slowly realised they were a gay couple. Later in the conversation, he noticed that one had his arm inserted in the anus of his partner and was gently fisting him.

Back in Manchester, Sparrow fell in love with the Haçienda. 'To be able to get away with rewinding [the Italian house hit by Black Box] "Ride On Time" five times, which Mike Pickering did and the crowd still going off its nut,' he smiled. 'It was a really, really, really special time.' He was just as impressed by the first Sasha set he heard. 'The best set I've ever heard in my life,' Sparrow said, with typical under-statement. A few weeks later, Sparrow took a train on his own to Blackpool to see Sasha play again. They partied afterwards. 'We became instant friends. About two weeks later I ended up splitting up from my girlfriend at the time and he ended up moving in, so it was all very quick,' said Sasha. 'I've been trying to get rid of him ever since.'

Sasha, born Alexander Coe, grew up in a very different existence: a middle-class family in the village of Hawarden, near Chester, just inside the North Wales border. He was nicknamed Sasha by his mother, who gave him piano lessons. His parents divorced when he was ten and he moved to Maidenhead to live with his father, who worked in advertising. At 17, he was one of six from 600 entrants to pass the exams to enter Epsom public school. 'It was the worst move I ever made in my life. Public school screwed me up completely,' Sasha told me in an interview in 1993. He had been planning to go to university. 'But public school totally freaked me out and I ended up sacking my A levels.' His father had moved to Bangor in North Wales and Sasha went to live with him. Like many of his acid house contem-poraries, he was already dropping out.

Hating Bangor and its Welsh provincialism, he befriended another English exile, Piers Sanderson, who had just moved back to the town after going to school in Manchester to do his A levels. 'We were new to the area and new to the school, we hadn't got any contacts,' said Piers. 'We were like the only two English kids so we immediately gravitated towards each other.' Piers's mum ran a local disco. Sasha even moved into the Sanderson family house for a short time.

The more confident Piers had already lived in Manchester, where he had discovered the Haçienda. Sasha at the time didn't really have much of an interest in music at all – U2, INXS, The The, pop. 'I never really had inspiring musical taste when I was a kid,' he told me in 1993. 'The first music that really grabbed me was house music.' He didn't even like that at first, when Piers first played him an early Chicago house compilation. 'I don't think I'd buy it, but it's all right,' he sniffed.

That all changed when Piers took him to the Haçienda. He went three times. House music was still yet to break big and he was un-impressed by the club's mix of early house, funk and hip hop. Then he went back – to find that everything had changed. 'Acid house had arrived and the place was like a sweatbox and everybody had smiley faces and it was absolutely mental,' Sasha said. 'I was converted. The energy was just unbelievable and you suddenly felt swept up and part of it.' Yet he approached ecstasy with caution. 'I didn't even do whole Es, it was quarters really. Taking the plunge. I was actually one of the last people to get involved, as it were.' Once he did, the drug had a profound effect. 'I took E and everything took on a new meaning,' he told *Muzik* magazine in 1999. 'I became fascinated by how sounds could split your head when you were in that kind of state. Still am.'

Sasha and Piers became regulars at the Haçienda and started buying house-music compilation albums. 'We absolutely loved it, we thought this is amazing,' Piers said. They decided to spread the word in Bangor. 'We need to put this on in North Wales, we can bring this back here.' Flush with excitement, they booked a room at Bangor University and hired some DJ friends of Sasha's from Windsor. But then the DJs pulled out. 'And I said, "Fuck it, why don't we DJ?"' remembered Piers. 'And he said, "We can't DJ. We don't know how to DJ."' But Piers convinced him. 'And we went to the student union hire company, got them to show us how to use the decks.' They bulked up their nascent record collections with some new compilations: *The House Sound Of London*, singles like M/A/R/R/S 'Pump Up The Volume' and Yazz's 'The Only Way Is Up'. And got ready for their first show.

Piers is now a documentary film-maker, but his earnings from running clubs and, later, bars in Birmingham, bought him the white-painted, stylish West London mews house where we met. He showed me photos and flyers from the time. A very young-looking Sasha, with a floppy fringe, wearing a Harrington jacket. The rough flyers, photocopied in Sasha's dad's office, showing their logo, Partners In Crime, and two cartoon gangster heads. And the entry fee: 75p.

Piers had a blue Volkswagen Beetle his mum bought him for his eighteenth birthday. 'She painted two gangsters' heads, Partners In Crime, on the back, which looked really cool and big musical notes down the side. We called it Miss Melody,' he said, 'after a hip hop artist we liked.' Sasha laughed at the memory. 'It was really cheesy.' Piers's mum also had a fish and chip shop, so they'd raid the till for change. Piers's sister did the door. The night was a success and they put on more. 'I just naturally fell into the promoter's side and he was naturally falling into the DJ side,' said Piers. But Bangor was increasingly too small for the two aspiring club kids. Manchester was calling.

The pair moved into a flat Piers's father had there. They got interviews for a job as telesales salesmen – £200 a week, no experience necessary. 'So we borrowed two of his old suits that were in the cupboard, these ridiculous flared seventies suits which on Sasha were too small and on me absolutely drowned me cause my dad's six foot. So we looked ridiculous – like a pair of tramps.' But they got the job.

They moved on to another job selling space on the television screens that you get in post offices. Piers was good at it. 'I was kind of like Billy Keen and really gobby and like, "I'm going to hit my target this week and make loads of money!"' Soon enough Piers was manager of the telesales floor, earning £600 a week and driving an old Porsche 924 he'd bought. He was 18 when he bought his first flat in Manchester's Cheetham Hill. It cost £16,500. 'I bought into this whole Thatcher dream and kind of lost my way for a little bit.'

But Sasha hated the work. 'I wasn't very good at being an employee,' he explained, 'getting into work on time, listening to some cock telling you what to do. I found the whole experience of phoning people up, trying to cold-call people soul-destroying. It just wasn't for me.' But his DJing was getting better. Sasha was offered a paid weekly warm-up gig – and turned it down. 'Why are you saying no to it?' Piers asked him. 'He said, "I should be that main slot." I remember thinking at the time it was confidence bordering on arrogance, but it was just knowing his self-worth. He knew where he wanted to be.'

Sasha left the telesales job to DJ unpaid on pirate radio station WBLS – it stood for White Black Liaison Station – in Moss Side, doing the graveyard shift. Piers couldn't understand it. 'You're carrying your records up dodgy tower blocks, there was the risk of getting mugged all the time, there was the risk of the DTI coming in and confiscating all your stuff all the time.' But Sasha loved it. He would drive down from the Haçienda to Moss Side, arrive around 2.15 a.m. and DJ until 7 a.m.

Bar the exalted few at places like the Haçienda, the job of a DJ in most clubs still rated only slightly above collecting glasses. Ditching telesales – grim though it was – to DJ for free on a pirate radio station in a tower block in the roughest part of town did not look like a smart career move. 'In our lifetimes there hadn't been something that had come along and lasted and what have you. It was just one of those, "Oh, aren't these records cute and funny. All these house records that were getting in the charts." Everyone just assumed it was not going to last,' said Sasha. But he knew what he wanted to do. 'I loved the music, I was absolutely into it.'

They moved to Piers's new flat in Cheetham Hill and Sparrow came too. It was a messy place. 'Seriously more bothered about partying than anything else ever,' said Sparrow. 'People used to come round just to look at us, to see what state we were in.' Sparrow disappeared to Blackburn, helping to organise the warehouse raves. He took part in setting up 76 parties over 18 months. 'It was so cloak and dagger,' Sparrow said. 'Building your own sound systems every week. Once all the hire companies got wise to the fact we were hiring sound systems for Blackburn raves, they had to block us. We had to make our own. We had a great little team of lads who used to come together. One little team would be over there building the sound system, the other team would be sat in an empty warehouse with a mobile phone, with rats running all over the place, waiting for the police to turn up. If the police turn up they have to run. If not, that's where the party's going to be.'

While Blackburn raves were at their height, bringing in thousands every week to totally illegal events, Sparrow was one of a group of ravers that took part in a television debate against councillors on the show *Upfront*, filmed in a studio in Bolton and presented by the late Tony Wilson. Police took pictures of everyone who arrived. Then the crew staged what would be their last ever rave, at Nelson, near Burnley, on 24 February 1990. 'It got so hot in the warehouse, you had to open the side shutter. As this big shutter opened at the side you could see these rows and rows of police officers, all with riot gear on, all ready. And we're like, "Fuck 'em." I thought it was quite funny,' said Sparrow. The DJ was Danny Spencer from Stoke's Candy Flip, who was playing the group's own hit, 'Strawberry Fields Forever', when a fireman began attacking the decks with a sledgehammer.

The raid at Nelson is a watershed moment in the northern rave scene, not just for Sparrow, but for many other key players who were there. Dave Beer was shocked by the police violence. 'It was ugly, they were coming down the hill like Romans, with the shields and just laying into girls and everything. They charged in and squashed everybody. Everybody was climbing on top of each other and they lost all their shoes and clothes. It was just the most dangerous thing I've ever seen,' said Dave Beer.

Piers Sanderson, wearing a straw hat, was spinning his red Porsche around in circles trying to get out. 'Kids had been taking the piss out of them for ages, out of the police,' Piers said. 'This time they'd had enough. This was an easy crowd, all these loved-up kids. They could steam in with their truncheons and lay into them, have a good day. I remember seeing the coppers happily smashing people up, laughing about it, sticking the boot in. They loved it.'

Before Nelson, vestiges of the late eighties, early nineties idealism had survived among the northern rave crowd. Afterwards, it had gone. 'You were seeing the Berlin Wall coming down and Nelson Mandela and all those things, you really felt that things were changing, we had the power to change the world that we lived in,' remembered Piers. 'It did become political, in that way. And also, what we were doing felt so right and so normal and we didn't feel we were harming anybody and yet the police and the authorities were coming down so hard on it, that you were thinking, "What the fuck is going on?"'

With the Blackburn scene effectively finished, Sparrow moved back to

Manchester, living with Sasha, in Fire Station Square in Salford, ironically, just behind the police station. There were a lot of parties. One time Sparrow fell foul of a tablet known locally as Rentokill. 'It was actually angel dust, PCP. What it does is it deadens every nerve ending,' said Sparrow. He was so out of it, he was convinced that he was strong enough to lift up the entire square that they lived in – and throw it like a shot putter. 'I was paralysed first of all for an hour and a half. Completely paralysed from the head down. Couldn't move, couldn't speak. Freaking out. Thought I was about to die. Deadened every nerve. That was scary.'

'Oh look, another fucking fly – zzzzzzt! Extra death for you!!' He chuckles like a madman as he 'nukes' it with 'Death Spray 2000'.

I'm gawping out into the never-ending desert, the sun lazily eases itself over the horizon, a beautiful sunset, an awesome spectacle. Sasha's journey is coming to its progressive peak. Transglobal Underground classics, sounds of North Africa and the Middle East, folding in phat, gritty guitar motifs and the maddest piano tunes electrically blending into a deep percussive drum-based beat. Beauty, hypnotics and excitement all squeezed in.

The set fades out, total silence, divine. He's standing in the middle of the club dazed, confused, the dance floor is still, the lights go on, heart still pounding and head still swirling. 'Is that it? Turn the fucker up,' he shouts. What a set!

Then I wake with a start, a fly on the end of my nose. I'd fallen asleep with my Walkman on for 10–15 minutes, but for a millisecond I was home on a mad one! Then reality dawns. I'm still in Kuwait, I've been in this fucking place four weeks now, the only thing keeping my head in order is the select tapes I've brought with me!

Where would I be without the music?
Letter to Mixmag *from Jay, Leeds, a Sasha fan serving with the*
British Army in Kuwait, 1995

DECEMBER, 1993. I drove Sasha from London to Wolverhampton for a
gig in my little red Renault 5. He was playing a club called Pimp on a
Friday night. As I carried his record boxes through the club, the crowd
parted. People smiled. Pretty girls said, 'Hello, Sasha.' The club didn't
have a VIP area as such, more an empty area behind the decks where
somebody casually chopped out a line of cocaine. Champagne was
poured. Sasha took to the decks. He DJed effortlessly, without seeming
to notice. The crowd cheered. The atmosphere was ebullient. Behind the
decks, Midlands club insiders stood about nodding their approval.

Sasha had an advantage over a lot of other DJs. He had studied
classical piano as a child. And he could mix 'in key'. Most DJs just
made sure the beats on the record they were spinning were playing at
the same speed as the beats on the one they were about to play next –
that was called 'mixing'. dance music singles were even produced with
simple sections consisting of just bass and drums at the beginning and
end to make this even easier. But as Sasha mixed from one record into
another, he didn't just seamlessly combine the two beats, he also
matched the melodies, which gave his sets a distinctive musical flow. It
made watching Sasha DJ a much more emotional experience. Seven
Webster was his manager at the time – and as a former rock musician,
he was only too aware of his young charge's talents. 'He made a broad
statement. A lot of DJs would go on and play the big piano house
tune. He would strip it down to nothing and then watch all the people
that didn't know what he was doing look at the DJ booth weirdly and
then it would slowly pick up and build and build and build. He realised

to really make an impact you've got to play with an audience and tease it and work it.'

I interviewed Sasha after the Wolverhampton show in the kind of dusty hotel frequented by travelling salesmen. In 1993, this was a much smaller DJ world. Sasha was on just £500 a gig, at that stage the most he ever earned was £2,000. Within a few years he would be up to five figures. He talked about his reputation not turning up to shows – which was only getting worse. 'Probably too much partying. Probably too many responsibilities that I actually wasn't ready to take on, for example remixes. I'd do things like go out for a mad weekend, go out for a party instead of thinking I should go to sleep now,' he said. Looking back today, he shook his head. 'I still felt like I was maybe one of the people on the dance floor. If I missed a set, they'd *understand*. I just didn't really take it that seriously, that professionally,' he told me.

But it just made him more desirable. If Sasha actually did turn up, clubbers felt they'd witnessed something special. 'If anything it just added to this myth! Will Sasha turn up or won't he turn up?' said Piers. 'It just goes to show how myth and legend can grow. It's funny, it's not like he had some Svengali manager who was manipulating this to happen.'

PERHAPS INEVITABLY, SPARROW had also been inching his way into the music business. He'd become friends with Steve Finan, music business manager and son of the seventies comedian Tom O'Connor. In his career, Finan had looked after Madness, Monie Love, Neneh Cherry and All Saints and later married the athlete Denise Lewis. Through Steve, Tom O'Connor rented Sparrow a penthouse apartment near Old Brompton tube for a bargain £80 a week. The arrangement lasted as long as Sparrow's first party, after which Tom O'Connor turned up to find a Rastafarian asleep on his antique rug in which he'd stubbed out a cigarette. Sparrow, meanwhile, in his occasional guise as dance producer had signed to Deconstruction Records under the name Bone – he even released a couple of singles. But it wasn't enough to keep him in London and he moved to his mother's in Devon.

For the first six months of 1995 he did nothing. He then used his DJ connections to set up a club night in nearby Plymouth. Scream opened in 1995 and was an instant success. The club had five rooms and as the only dance club in the South West was quickly pulling in 3,500 people a week. DJs like Paul Oakenfold and Tony de Vit, plus John Digweed, and of course, Sasha, played. All of a sudden Sparrow was a successful club promoter. 'It felt like a European club. Apart from the DJ was DJing in like a mirror-ball egg,' he said.

Clubland was becoming a series of little fiefdoms or kingdoms, much like the sixteenth-century Italy Machiavelli wrote about in *The Prince*. The politics could be ruthless. Other promoters would come and check Sparrow out and hang out with him afterwards. Those inter-actions were typically affable and yet tense, a mix of surface friendliness and ruthless rivalry, business and pleasure that was emblematic of the scene. Back-room chats and after-party blow-outs involved money talk, good times, 'larging it' and front. 'There's so much psychology involved,' said Sparrow. 'You realise what a massive mind-game it really is. Everybody is trying to fuck everybody. Everybody wanted to have this off this person, or this off this person.'

For a promoter like Sparrow, the patronage he had with Sasha and other DJs he'd befriended over the years was crucial. 'If this person can't bring this DJ to the table and you can and you're not even looking after them, then you have the fucking power. It's tit for tat. It's rough and tumble,' Sparrow explained. His social skills were enhancing his work life. And this mix between the professional and the personal would become an increasingly common trait in the 1990s. It worked both ways. Sasha liked playing for promoters who were friends – like Geoff Oakes and Sparrow. In turn, Sparrow's position in the clubland hierarchy was elevated because he could get Sasha.

He lived in a house in the country, with his girlfriend, a giant pool table and two Rottweilers – Dollar and Derby. Derby was named because Sparrow once had a trial for Derby County. Dollar for obvious reasons – Sparrow was earning cash, a lot of it. One day, his brothers helped him count out £318,000, which he stashed in his mother's loft. That was the kind of money he was making. Sparrow would keep a book of his income, but then he'd start to doubt his own figures and get into what he called a 'counting mission'. The family would get called in. 'I'd get my little brothers in as well, they were like 12 and 13. I used to go in and throw bin bags of money and go "count this". Obviously they were nicking tenners all over the gaff.'

Visitors to his house for the after-club parties often witnessed an unusual sight: Sparrow, in the early hours, sneaking off down the garden with a shovel to bury his profits. Paranoia was setting in. 'Even living where I was in the country, with the nice house and the three cars and the two Rottweilers, I *never* relaxed,' he said. 'I have buried money in gardens. I've done all sorts of nonsense. I've put money in the backs of cars. I was a hider. I used to hide things.' The cash went into different gardens: his own, his mother's, or other people's. He didn't hang about. 'Usually when you're digging a hole you're either off your head or wanna get it over quickly,' he explained. The bundles of cash were carefully wrapped up. 'About nine plastic bags and ten rolls of tape round it. No wiggly worm was going to get through and eat through that shit.'

The most he buried? £20,000. Unfortunately, he couldn't always remember where he'd dug the holes. One or two, inevitably, got lost. Somewhere underneath Sparrow's mother's garden is a bundle with about £5,000 in it, which he'd never found. 'She lived in the top of a valley. There was like four or five little holes there. I thought one of them would be safe for ever but then I completely forgot where it was.' Sparrow shrugged philosophically. 'It's one of those. Hopefully it will be found in about 50 years when it's not the currency any more.'

The good times for Scream rolled on. But ultimately the power games and tension of promoting took its toll. 'Ask any promoter. You've got to be fucking paranoid to do the job. It's your business to be fucking paranoid. If you think these are happy days, you're about to get fucking screwed.' He organised a tour for Paul Oakenfold. And the tour for Sasha and John Digweed's first mix album for the Ministry of Sound, *Northern Exposure*. But promoting, said Sparrow, was becoming too corporate, too organised, too 'brand orientated'.

'I didn't want to be a corporate club promoter. I would literally be doing it for the money. And I wasn't motivated by that.' Scream came to an end in 1998. The DJ on the last night was Tony De Vit, one of Sparrow's favourites, a popular figure with a distinctive high-octane techno sound who had emerged from the London gay club Trade to become a star. Tragically De Vit died from complications due to AIDS a week later. Sparrow spent most of his profits – at least, those he could still find – paying off a tax bill. The rest he invested in a band his two brothers had started, in which Sparrow still plays a vague, ill-defined role. He claimed this kept him occupied for the next seven years.

Meanwhile, the parties continued. 'I don't think I caned it more than I'd done already,' he claimed. The biggest bender lasted four days straight, in Ibiza, getting over a relationship break-up. 'Staying awake for four days is not that big a deal, is it? Once you get past your second day, you can just have it,' Sparrow said. 'The thing is, if you don't have the responsibilities of work and you can afford to sleep a lot and eat nice food after partying, then you can party a lot. You can recover by not having the normal stresses and strains of what people have to do. That was just part of our life.'

THE ANTICS OF Sasha and Sparrow were regularly detailed in *Mixmag*'s Club Country gossip column; Sparrow banned for driving for six months even though he never had a licence; Sasha on a train to Plymouth leaving his record boxes to go to the bar, then coming back to find they'd been removed as a bomb threat; or Sasha climbing out of a sixth-floor window in Wolverhampton and leading a bemused gang of revellers onto the roof. Sasha was satirised with a fake DJ tape by Leeds club fanzine *The Herb Garden* as DJ FAMOUS BASTARD.

The burgeoning Sasha legend was also fed by constant rumours of his death. He was supposed to have died many times, at least once from a drugs overdose and spent time on a life-support machine. Sasha had also landed on another *Mixmag* cover, published in February 1994. It had been a difficult shoot. Sasha had been awkward and uncooperative in the studio. The photographs were barely usable. It was my first cover as editor – I'd just been promoted – and we sat around a scruffy new office we'd moved to in Hammersmith, West London above a Chinese herbalist, scratching our heads, wondering what to do. There was only one picture that worked: Sasha with his hands clasped together as if in prayer, looking up towards a circle of light. The pose had been photographer Alexis Maryon's idea and he'd developed the black and white print himself, bringing out this heavenly glow above Sasha. But how on earth could we make use of this angelic shot? Deputy editor Andy Pemberton had a mischievous idea. We can't do that, we said. We could. We did.

'SASHA,' screamed the headline: 'SON OF GOD?' Just like 1991, the impact of this cover was instant and dramatic. More piss-taking, more fame, more gigs. 'That changes how people like DJs think about themselves,' said Dave Dorrell, looking back. 'It changes how people think about DJs. It's a catalyst, isn't it, for change.'

But when Sasha saw himself on the newsstands, his heart sank. 'I was pissed off! I just thought it was ridiculous. I thought I'd been stitched up,' he said. This cover and its fall-out, the rumours of his death, the constant after parties, they all began feeding into the dark side of Sasha's fame. He began to get paranoid. 'I just thought the whole thing that had been created around me was going to collapse around me. I just thought it was a big joke and it was going to be followed up next month by "Who does he think he is?"' As Sasha's fame continued to grow, that fear and paranoia was only going to get worse.

FOUR
STYLE, COMFORT, EXCLUSIVITY

TUNE! JAYDEE – 'PLASTIC DREAMS'

A Belgian house groove wiggled underneath a compulsively funky Hammond solo.

You were ironing your shirt or putting on your dress. Swapping make-up with your girlfriends. Squabbling over the music with your friends. Squeezing into heels. Smoothing the collar on a Paul Smith shirt. Sipping a vodka. Doing a line. Feeling fucking fantastic. Like Liam Gallagher said, 'Tonight I'm a rock 'n' roll star.' Tonight you were. Tonight everybody was a prince or a princess. Into the melee. Somebody had a rush and they were in the corner. They'd be all right. You had a rush and you felt like a waterfall was pouring through you. In the toilets the girls were battling for the mirror, wiping away the mascara smears. Somebody had more coke – that interminable wait in the queue and the wiping down of a filthy toilet seat to chop out of a line, you and the powder sweating together as you trembled to cut it before a bouncer stuck his head over the door. Then it was back into battle. The club was LOUD. There was nowhere else to go but the dance floor, not with that rush. There was nothing else to do. You had to join in. You loved it. You hated it. You wanted to go home. You never wanted to go home. You wanted to be noticed. You wanted to belong. You wanted to disappear. You could bounce into the middle of that floor and start smiling at the best-looking, wildest girl in the middle. And she would throw that smile back at you. Or that shy boy would be your new best friend for ten minutes. You felt so happy when there was a breakdown and you could whip round to face the DJ, throw your hands in the air and scream, 'Let's 'ave it!' You undid one more button, turned round, found your friends, did another pill, bought a drink. Before you knew it, it was 2 a.m. and time to find the after party.

NOTHING ENCAPSULATES the difference between the first acid house clubs of the 1980s and the superclubs of the nineties more than their flyers. Flyers for Danny Rampling's Shoom declared: 'Sensation seekers, let the music take you to the top.' Miss Moneypenny's, the Birmingham club that became a byword for disco glamour, offered: 'Style, comfort and exclusivity.' In contrast to Shoom's ecstasy-drenched idealism, it sounds like an advert for an upmarket spa. Even its name, taken from the prim-yet-sexy secretary James Bond constantly flirts with without ever taking to bed, nods to a certain nudge-nudge sexuality that is quintessentially British. British clubbing had lowered its ambitions: from Danny Rampling's offer of Nirvana, to Miss Moneypenny's saucy office games.

But Miss Moneypenny's and clubs like Fun did achieve something that the city had never achieved before: they made Birmingham sexy. Clubbing had become glamorous. Piers Sanderson noticed the change, moving back to the UK after hustling around Tenerife and Ibiza. 'It had moved into Jean Paul Gaultier and Destroy and everyone was wearing leather waistcoats and strutting about. It had kind of gone from baggy tops and trousers to tight-fitting fashions.' People were drinking alcohol again – expensive, imported foreign beers like Beck's had become de rigueur. Instead of ecstasy, it was 'Beckstasy'. 'There was a change of attitude,' said Piers. 'The idea of status. I remember I saw it first of all when I was in Ibiza. I was at Amnesia and there was this balcony and it had all these gorgeous men and women dancing up there and the promoters were up there and there was this separation. I remember seeing it for the first time and realising there was this two tier of clubbing.'

The party animals who had been bouncing happily around the Haçienda and the Blackburn raves had changed too. 'All these people that I'd seen in Manchester, or in the north, who were just party people, who were just dancing in a house, who you knew from just being out,' Piers said, 'they all seemed to be doing something. "Oh I'm doing this, I've got an agency, or I'm promoting a club."' Charlie Chester in West London called them 'Six O'Clock In The Morning Businesses'. 'All back to mine businesses. So many of those companies: Boys Own, Cowboy Records, ideas from being round somebody's house between six and 12 o'clock on a Sunday morning,' Chester said. 'Talking absolute bollocks. But then somewhere people picked the threads.'

Piers smelt the winds of change. 'I was aware of this gravy train of opportunity of making money in dance music and staying in there, that everybody seemed to be getting on.' He got the Yellow Pages out and started phoning clubs in his area, beginning with A. The former telephone salesman found he still had the patter. 'Yeah, I'm a famous DJ and promoter from Ibiza, I've come back and I want to put a night on,' he told venues. He hit paydirt with 'C', a club called Copacabana, in nearby Chester, though it could have been anywhere. They had a free Wednesday. Soon Piers was promoting four nights a week and the club was full. Soon he too was making money.

For established high-street discos, this looked like a win-win situation. They had been hit by acid house, they understood their clientele had moved on and didn't want to stand around the dance floor swigging pints. But they didn't understand how to cater for this new audience. Promoters like Piers took the risk. They would come, hire the club, pay for all the advertising, book the DJs and keep all the money they made on the door. The club would keep the bar takings and whatever they could get away with charging the promoter as a hire fee. Clubs were full again and everybody was happy. Anyone could be a promoter – as long as you could get the DJs.

'At that time, promoting was great, because there weren't any DJ agencies at that stage. It was all down to your address book. If you had the phone numbers for these people, you could get them,' said Piers. 'It didn't occur to a lot of people you could just go up to the DJ and ask him for his number. It was this hallowed thing. "Apparently you've got Sasha's contact number. Can I get it?" "Can you fuck." That was the thing you held on to.'

Then Cream opened in nearby Liverpool. 'It hit us quite hard on a Saturday night. It was only a little club.' One Sunday, Piers headed down to a Sunday afternoon/evening party being run in a mill in the countryside outside Birmingham called Full Of Beans. He saw a new opportunity – in Birmingham. He could also see a new kind of crowd. Full Of Beans attracted a dressed-up, in-the-know audience. In the telling parlance of the time, they were 'clued up'. 'You still felt this "us and them-ness". There was the rest of society and there was us, who lived to party and who took illegal drugs. You felt part of a subculture.'

Piers joined forces with a record shop in Chester called Global Grooves and together they opened a store in Birmingham. 'It was quite big, it must have been 1,500 square foot, so we put a café in and chairs in there and we did teas and coffees. There was a photo gallery, cause I've always been into photography, put that on the walls as well. And so it became a kind of hub.' Piers noticed that Birmingham's 'clued up' clubbers all headed out of town at the weekend, to places like Nottingham's Venus. 'Birmingham was waiting for something,' he realised.

Piers started his first Birmingham night at a club called The Steering Wheel in 1992, launched with his partner Barney and his partners from the record shop Global Grooves. They called it Fun. Already dance music was splitting into genres. There was a harder, more dubby, instrumental house style dubbed 'progressive house'. 'We felt that was far too serious. Really laddy. So we tried to do a counter to progressive. I wanted something that's going to be light-hearted and fun! So it became Fun. It wasn't taking itself seriously at all.'

The night started badly – three other clubs launched around the same time. Just a hundred people turned up and they lost money. The same thing happened the second and third weeks. 'All our money was running out. We had one more week left on the flyer cause there were four weeks on the flyer. So we thought we'd see it out, we could afford to keep losing money on the last one.' Included on the bill was what was called a live PA from a new pop-dance act called D:Ream. The idea of a 'live PA' came from the rave days – it basically consisted of a band miming their hit of the day to a tape, with perhaps some live vocals.

D:Ream were a live PA with a little bit more – worked and polished into an explosive act, with a euphoric house sound and a charismatic, good-looking singer in Peter Cunnah. The week they were due to play, their single 'UR The Best Thing' was the biggest club hit in the country. 'And it was mobbed. And it lasted five years. If it hadn't been for D:Ream. But that night everybody came down and had a brilliant time.' And Fun was off, pushing that poppier, funkier musical style that became known as 'handbag' because girls liked it.

Now there were clubs all over the country – with hundreds of clubbers in each one. They all wanted a star DJ. And DJs started racing up and down the motorways to play at all of them. It was a gold rush. Birmingham, like Liverpool, like Leeds, was right in the middle, of not just the country, but also the action. Birmingham was happening. 'Jeremy Healy used to DJ with me, we used to DJ a lot in Birmingham at Decadence. On a Wednesday, fucking brilliant,' recalled Dave Dorrell. 'The Brummie kids were super up for it and suddenly super dressed up. Everyone was really cool! They wanted us to be really cool! Cause they didn't want us to be less cool than them, right. They wanted to be bigger than life and that was something that was part of the nineties as well.'

Just to tell three other beautiful babes how much I luv 'em! Life hasn't stopped bubbling since I met Milly, Bobbi and Billy. Nuff cornfields, nuff rabbits and nuff respect to the Clucky, Clicky Barn Gang.

    Hang loose in your wellies, Farmer Babes.
    Milly
PS: I think we've found our Hi-Hi-Hi-Hideaway!
Reader's letter to Mixmag, *October 1995*

IF 'HANDBAG' WAS about anything – and you could well argue that the whole point was that it wasn't – it was about not taking anything too seriously. Clubbing in the nineties was like a giant *Big Brother* house – you were there to meet people, have fun, create adventures. *Mixmag*'s Andy Pemberton was fond of saying, 'When I go to clubs, I check my friends at the door, with my coat.' He would then proceed within half an hour to have made friends with a whole new group of people.

Clubbers were silly. They loved songs like De'Lacy's 1994 soulful house romance 'Hideaway' – the hit referred to in the letter above – with its singalong chorus. Games were in. When East West Records' club promotions chief Jean Branch – a well-known party girl on the scene – got married – at Full Of Beans in Birmingham – to David Gill, a Leeds club face who also ran the irreverent club fanzine *The Herb Garden*, one of the many surprises was the transvestite DJ Jon Pleased Wimmin jumping out of a cake. Later, as it got dark, more games developed. 'We performed out in the field. We had these sparklers. There were three of us. And when it got dark we did this Red Arrow display, running out, back to the middle and stuff like that,' she said.

Fancy dress was common, as was acting the goat. Sometimes literally, as in the case of Gerald Bailey, promoter of Pimp in Wolverhampton, who, in 1994, rode a white goat around a house party in Birmingham, one night after the clubs had shut. In 1995 Bailey hired another goat and a llama, for his birthday party at the Palace Hotel in Birmingham. At 10 p.m. he paraded them through the crowd, walked out the door – and promptly lost them.

These were the golden years of 1990s clubbing, when you could meet anyone and be anyone, when the most unlikely networks of people were formed, criss-crossing the country. Club after club sprouted up in drab northern and Midland cities, little blooms of colour and life. Being a clubber felt special. It was about belonging. And for many clubbers, that sense of identity was a huge part of the lifestyle. We felt it at *Mixmag*. Every weekend, we packed up into one of a couple of Renault 5s we had and headed up North with whatever girlfriends could be persuaded along. Clubbing felt like a big, happy party that went on and on. Even working the following Monday morning, the effect of the weekend's partying making everything just a little bit hazy, didn't feel too arduous. Especially when you had piles of new records to listen to, deranged readers' letters to giggle over and advertising staff to banter with. This wasn't work. This was something else.

In 1994, *Mixmag* moved offices from Hammersmith to the top floor of a mews office in Lancaster Gate, inching further from London's outer suburbs towards London's West End, like acid house itself, closing in on the centre of things. It didn't matter what clubs you'd been to at the weekend, at 10 a.m. Monday morning you were at your desk. Friends, family and partners all came second to the magazine. You lived and breathed it. '*Mixmag über alles*,' as Andy Pemberton liked to explain to new recruits. 'You're either on the bus, or you're off the bus.' If they couldn't take the pace, they were out.

By now 20-odd people worked for the magazine: advertising staff, club promotions, editorial. It was a big, messy space, a zoo out of which a finished issue somehow emerged every month. Parachutes hung from the skylights to keep sunlight off the computer screens and barn doors opened out on to the cobbled street outside. Records covered the room, spilling out over desks and floor space like weeds. Stickers covered every inch of space. *Mixmag* covers filled one wall. The rest were filled with jokes, posters covered in graffiti and comments that Pemberton, stalking furiously around the office, burning up ideas, had come up with that amused his colleagues. One favourite was: 'I am a zeitgeist cypher.'

The magazine had an in-house DJ, Dan 'Stan' Farrow, a raver from Maidstone who did a little bit of anything and everything – including, in the 1997 election, standing for Parliament for an organisation we invented called the All Night Party. By the end of the 1990s, Stan had his own column, 'Challenge Stan', written during summers spent in Ibiza, where he became something of a celebrity.

Between him and reviews editor Frank Tope, who sat buried in piles of records, music was constantly thumping away, battling with the phone calls and noisy, ever-present chatter – arguments over records and clubs, piss-taking, one-upmanship, gossip from the weekend. This racket was the cause of constant complaints from the trucking magazine based in the office underneath.

Unlike most magazines, which have a template of set typefaces and layouts to provide a 'look', the only constant in *Mixmag*'s anarchic design was its logo. Fonts and layouts changed constantly, text was poured onto the page like spilt coffee, photos were captioned with joke after joke. The art director was a dour heavy metal fan called Karla Smith, who'd previously worked on Paul Raymond's top-shelf porn mags. She wasn't given to exuberance. When things were good, they were 'not bad'. When they were amazing, such as, say, a pyrotechnic Prodigy show – who she adored – at Brixton Academy, they were 'quite good'. But she churned out the layouts tirelessly.

At the back of this chaotic space was a small, windowless room used for storing clothes for fashion shoots and marking up proofs. A handwritten sign on the door called it: 'The Room of Doom and quite often, gloom.' In there, his red eyes drooping from late nights laboriously proofing copy and layouts, was the production editor and star writer Alexis Petridis. He had arrived fresh-faced from Cambridge University, where he had interspersed raving with his studies, on work experience. Frank Tope and Andy Pemberton were also former students – Tope DJed while at Exeter University with Radiohead's Thom Yorke and Basement Jaxx's Felix Buxton. Together with Petridis, they made a trio – smart, educated, talented journalists who didn't let their enthusiasm for the world of clubs and dance music stop them regarding it with a critical gaze. They followed each other around the office, exchanging witticisms and *bon mots*.

On the other side of a row of filing cabinets sat clubs editor Dan Prince and a Bournemouth club kid called Paul Potter who ran *Mixmag* club nights. They were on the other side of the world of clubs. Dan and Paul weren't university educated. They probably thought a *bon mot* was a type of doughnut. But they knew their way around clubs and they kept the magazine connected to DJs, promoters and readers. Potter was a good-looking charmer with a taste for glamorous girl-friends. He dated Sara McDonald – now Mrs Noel Gallagher – and later Lee Starkey, daughter of Ringo Starr. There was always a creative tension between these two camps. It was a hot house with a lot of talented people competing for attention. I liked that. I wanted it to feel a bit ragged. Clubland was a broad church and I wanted all these different voices, clamouring at the tops of their voices, tumbling out of the pages of the magazine.

Mixmag was a little bit of each of its contributors. But like any successful magazine, it was really owned by its readers and they were loyal, passionate – and heavily critical. Their letters inspired many of our best features – like one about over-40s clubbers, headlined 'One Foot In The Rave', or another, profiling drug-taking ravers in the armed forces who called themselves 'The Lost It Crew'. *Mixmag* kept doing every-thing a magazine shouldn't do, yet it just kept getting bigger. I remem-ber thinking, what would it be like if one month we sold 40,000 copies?

Then we sold 40,000, opened a bottle of champagne – and went back to work. Sales went to 60,000. Then 80,000. Then 90,000. Like the club scene itself, it seemed unstoppable. The January 1996 issue summed up 1995 with a picture of a euphorically happy club girl, dancing in a sea of twirling lights and the headline: 'You've never had it so good.' In January 1996, that's exactly what it felt like.

FAR AWAY FROM Birmingham, in Hastings on the south coast, Miranda Cook was a wayward teenager when she discovered clubbing. Her parents were both tabloid journalists but their marriage had broken up. At 15, Miranda moved out of home. Her mum gave her some money to live on. She worked at shop jobs – Woolworths, the Our Price record shop. She went to clubs but kept getting barred for being too young. 'But I kept going back so in the end they just let me in,' she said. 'That's when it all started.'

Bright, vivacious, intense at odd moments, yet with a devil-may-care attitude, Miranda was independent enough to survive. But she didn't like school and never went anyway, so she'd never really had a 'gang' of friends to call her own. At 17 she had started hanging out in a Hastings pub called the Cricketers, where a colourful crowd gathered early evening. Coaches would pull up and taken them away. Soon Miranda decided to see where it was they were going: a party called Storm on Hastings Pier, helmed by a rising young DJ star called John Digweed. Later she started going to warehouse parties. At one of these she first tried ecstasy.

'First time someone gave me a pill I was too scared to do it. So I put it in a matchbox and pretended I'd done it. They were like, "You haven't done it, have you?"' she said. 'But when I did finally do one, the whole picture fell into place really. I was at the warehouse party and I'd taken it and I was sitting upstairs on the top floor. I'd found a little tiny cupboard and I was sitting on the floor in there. There was a picture of Simon Le Bon on the wall and a tube of haemorrhoids cream and I just thought it was hilarious. And my friend came up and found me and said, "Oh, you need to go on the dance floor now cause you're coming up on your pill." I was like, "Okay," and I went downstairs and they were playing Dan Hartman, "Relight Me Fire" [a dizzy 1970s disco classic] so that was my first pill tune. That was a night and a half.'

She told me the story in her sunny garden in South London, where Miranda now lives and works as a freelance journalist and PR. She still loves dance music, she said. And she explained how back then, aged 17, it was the first time in her life she'd felt part of a gang. 'I'd been let in on the secret, and that's what I wanted to do for the rest of my life!' she exclaimed. 'It was the first time I had that community around me. And it was really naughty, which appealed to me.' Being in that secret society meant you got all the references. In September 1992, The Shamen hit number one with a song called 'Ebeneezer Goode'. Ostensibly, it was about a mythical, Dickensian character, which the group's frontman, rapper and DJ Mr C, used as a cover for a carefully couched lyric about the joys of ecstasy with a chorus that declared that 'Es' were 'good'.

The song spent four weeks at number one. And though The Shamen consistently denied it was about drugs, every clubber in Britain knew that it was, including Miranda. 'I remember around that time "Ebeneezer Goode" got to number one. And we were sat in the pub listening to the chart countdown and we were in hysterics because it was so blatantly obvious and nobody else knew anything about it,' she said. Miranda decided to become a journalist and studied for an NVQ in Sheffield, where she discovered the club Gatecrasher. She did a placement course at the *Sunday Times* and arrived at *Mixmag* one afternoon, sporting a perm and wearing a suit. In 1996 she was given an assignment for her sins. It was called 'Would You Let This Horse Into Your Club?'

The idea – dreamt up by Andy Pemberton – was to satirise the dress codes that were dividing clubbers. In their rush to make sure their crowds had made enough of an effort, because these were aspirational times, and in the luxury of knowing there were more people arriving than could actually get in, promoters were turning away anyone they felt hadn't made enough of an effort with their outfits. Incensed letters were pouring into the office from readers who'd travelled hours to clubs and been turned back. They would lovingly detail their outfits, as this only intensified the outrage they were feeling. Miranda's mission was to crack the door at Birmingham's most desirable clubs – with a pantomime horse in tow, peopled by two young guys. 'Some say door policies are stupid,' ran the headline. 'But are they *this* stupid?'

First in line was Decadance, a night at Bakers. The manager came down to see what all the fuss was about. 'Oh no, health and safety. I don't think we can allow a horse into the club,' he said. 'It's not a real horse,' argued Miranda. But no go. The feature milked the horse for everything it could. 'The horse jockeys for position at the door, hoping to exude that all important "party attitude",' ran the captions around pictures of the animal – which sported a big, shock-amused smile. 'As the night went on the people in the horse costume got more and more pissed,' Miranda recalled. 'The back end was sick. We went to Moneypenny's and they were really hammered and just chatting up girls. And the girls were really up for it cause it was a chance to have your picture taken. They were all in their fluffy bras and stuff. The guys were loving it.' By the end of the night, having 'pulled' a 'young filly', both 'ends' of the horse were by now completely drunk. So the horse passed out. Thus failing to 'get his oats'. 'So we just took the pictures of him lying down in the suit,' she said. 'That was eventful.'

By this point, the idea of 'handbag' had created a divide in the club scene. On one side there were DJs like Sasha, Nick Warren and John Digweed, who regarded their music as more a serious endeavour – as indeed did their fans. Their music was by now largely instrumental, increasingly involving long, flowing introductions and breakdowns. On the other, the fluffier side – literally in the case of the bra tops some girls wore – was 'handbag'. Originally coined as a derogative – as in, oh, that track's is a bit weak, a bit girlie, a bit 'handbag' – the term had been reclaimed by its fun-loving adherents as a term that represented a more feminine, and also sillier, clubbing style. At its heart was a more serious intent, one that for many DJs is fundamental: if girls dance, the boys will come, the club will be full and everybody will be happy. It rarely failed. Yet it was amazing how many DJs couldn't grasp this.

It wasn't difficult to spot handbag DJs – some of them, like the tranvestite star Jon Pleased Wimmin, actually carried handbags, in his case a Gucci number. Their DJ sets were more about creating a party on the dance floor. At its best, handbag meant unadulterated fun, at its worst, it veered into the worst of pop dance. For Jon Pleased, playing handbag was about variety above all. 'Cause you're not purist. And I find that boyish attitude really nauseating. My whole thing has always been surprise,' he said. 'Mixed in with the right records I think anything can work. I like to be surprised, if it's just seamless, takes you on a journey, I find that so boring. For me, it's more about fun.'

THE MAN IN the glasses and the orange shirt had a party trick up his sleeve. As the dancers around his decks got ever more frenzied, he decided to unleash it. He fiddled among his record boxes and produced a bugle. This was a hunt, the fox in sight, the pace getting faster, everybody's blood up. The DJ let trip with a deafening parp – a big, brassy, fart of happiness. Everybody screamed.

As far as the purist DJs and music fans were concerned, handbag DJs were musical sluts, who would do anything to please the crowd, rather than 'educating' them or in that most overused of DJ clichés, 'taking them on a journey'. They hated Judge Jules more than anybody – especially when he produced that bugle. His flamboyant approach to DJing, his loud shirts and his sense of fun made him a natural star on the handbag scene. He had fun with it, which clubbers loved – or hated. He wasn't scared to act the goat and so began bringing the bugle to his gigs. As the atmosphere climbed higher, Jules would let rip.

'He was crap,' said Miranda Cook firmly and she was one of his biggest fans. 'Just a few blasts. But everyone in their state thought it was the best thing they'd ever heard.' Jules's friend Sonique, later to become a star DJ herself and formerly the singer in eighties acid pop act S'Express, was even more damning. 'It was fucking awful. It was the worst thing he could have done. It was like, "Jules, you can't even play the damn thing. You're killing the party with this. Do you want that much attention that you're going to make a fool of yourself?"' she sniffed. 'If I want to see a clown I go to the circus.'

But by the mid-1990s, the club scene was a circus, one so in awe of its DJ ringmasters that the sight of a man in a loud shirt blasting a few notes on a bugle like a huntsman leading his pack would be greeted by cheers. Then ambition got the better of Jules. The bugle wasn't enough. He attempted to graduate to the trumpet, a significantly more complicated instrument. 'I think I had one lesson,' he said. 'It worked, if you blew it a couple of times, if you blew it people went mad. It was so fucking annoying.' He completely failed to learn it and his trumpet-playing remained horribly out of tune. Yet the clubbers roared their approval even louder, no matter how braying, how discordant, how completely out of place Jules's trumpet-playing was. It was, Miranda Cook explained, more about interaction than performance. It didn't actually matter that he couldn't play it. It was just part of the madness. 'It was funny to see him playing the trumpet and having a laugh as well, when lots of other DJs wouldn't even look up,' she said. 'It was a kind of participation thing.'

The tight nylon shirts, the thick glasses and that brash personality made Judge Jules hard to ignore. He had a radio show on London's KISS FM called Judge And The Jury where 'celebrity' guests would review records. He liked to labour a pun. 'I'm going to whip you up like ice cream,' was one of his many catchphrases. 'The Judge won't budge' was another. Miranda, by now a fully fledged handbag queen, thought he was fantastic. She developed a fixation and began following him around the country. 'He was really different from other DJs. And I really loved the music he was playing, because it was funky and percussive and not rave-like at all. And he was a bit of a goon as well.'

His Day-Glo character served Jules well. Married to Amanda – the couple have two children – he is a rich man and a clever one. Later he became a star on Radio 1, where he still has a show listened to by millions. He hosts another radio show that is syndicated around the world, runs a couple of record labels and also promotes and DJs at Judgement Sunday, his very successful Ibiza night. Like most of the superstar DJs and promoters, he spends a lot of time in Ibiza. Unlike most of them, he also speaks fluent Spanish. The nickname comes from his law degree – though he never practised. Judge Jules may be a joke to many serious dance music aficionados, but he got the last laugh.

When we met at his offices in London, he was buying law books on the Internet and off to a Spanish lesson. He likes to brush up. 'I'm 41 but you can put 39,' he said. 'If you don't mind.' With his bookish demeanour, childish sense of fun and trademark lurid nylon shirts, he could be a children's television presenter. Yet he comes across as an intelligent and likeable guy. As one of Radio 1's most enduring presenters, he is the missing link between long-gone personality DJs like Dave Lee Travis – aka 'The Hairy Cornflake' – and the world of dance music. His sentences are delivered breathlessly, full of mixed metaphors that crash into each other like badly mixed beats. 'A tough battle to counteract,' he said at one point.

Born Julius O'Riordan, he grew up in North London and started out as a DJ on the rare groove scene. He was a law student at the London School of Economics when acid house first began. His legal knowledge came in useful at illegal parties when the police arrived. It was here he got the nickname. 'I was prepared to say everyone at the party was my law student mates,' he said. 'It was such a ridiculous lie that the police were kind of bowled over by it.' When acid house arrived, Jules opportunistically ditched rare groove and started playing house. 'The whole rare groove thing by definition ran out of rare grooves. And house was where my heart lay,' he smiled. He began playing at illegal acid house raves like Sunrise. He left college in 1988 with a 2:2 degree, unsure what to do next.

'Am I going to be a lawyer or am I not?' he asked himself. 'Am I going to earn enough money to be able to subsist or aren't I? At that point I could afford to run my little car, pay for the flat, pay for the tunes and feed myself. I realised I was at that point making a living out of it. I haven't really been out of work since.'

Jo was wearing a white dress made up of little more than a fringe and a bra, white long gloves and a giant furry hat wig combination. The pose, one hand on her hip, head tilted to one side, knowing stare, was pure celebrity. The question she was asked: Is There A God? Her reply: 'Yes, because he created me.'
Mixmag *photo feature, July 1995*

THE DJS HAD started out music fans, mixing records in their bedrooms. By 1995 DJing had become a valid career move. Clubland was a lottery, the winnings there for the taking. Dave Seaman was a typical contender. He became another of the big stars of the 1990s – but he literally won his job in a competition. A quieter character than Jules, he is easy-going, good-looking, with a gently charming manner that disguises a driven personality. He is straight talking and has the pragmatism typical of the Yorkshireman. And he started DJing very young. 'I used to pretend to do radio shows in my bedroom with a tape recorder and a little Tandy deck. Acquired records from every family member's loft in the world,' he said. He nagged and nagged his parents until they bought him a Fowl double deck system and a set of floor lights. That was it. He started playing friends' birthday parties, graduated to local pubs and weddings – and by the time he was 16 was playing four gigs a week and earning money. 'I was kind of the town DJ.'

Dave grew up an only child in Garforth near Leeds, where his mother was a spiritualist medium. By 1986 he was working in an advertising agency in Leeds and had joined a DJ subscription service called DMC – or Disco Mix Club. Set up by the former Radio Luxembourg DJ Tony Prince, DMC provided a membership of DJs with exclusive remixes and ran the World Mixing Finals. In the late eighties, this was a huge event that packed out Wembley Arena and presented stars like

Public Enemy and James Brown. Tony Prince, a former personality DJ from Oldham who had been head of programming at Radio Luxembourg, ran the company with his wife Christine and her sister Susan. In the 1970s, Tony had talked his way into scooping an interview with Elvis Presley for Luxembourg – just before an Elvis show in Las Vegas. He ended up introducing The King on stage. That was the kind of charm and persuasion he is capable of. Tony Prince's picture still hangs in Graceland.

DMC also had a monthly magazine for members – *Mixmag*. The Princes' son, Dan, was for many year's *Mixmag*'s clubs editor. His sister Gabrielle also worked as a designer on the magazine. In its earlier form as a DMC member's newsletter, the magazine ran occasional 'Miss Wet T-shirt' competitions. Radio 1's Bruno Brookes wrote a column, which was delivered by his then girlfriend, Anthea Turner. The company was based on an industrial unit on the edge of Slough – as grim and characterless a location as could be imagined. But DMC was a major player in the early days of dance music. As evidenced by a Christmas issue, which featured a set of record industry movers and shakers on its cover, all dressed in Santa Claus outfits – including a young Pete Tong and an even younger Paul Oakenfold, then still sporting his famous mullet.

Seaman turned up at the 1986 World Mixing Finals at Wembley and entered a competition run by Camel Cigarettes, to join DMC at a music conference in New York: the NMS, or New Music Seminar. He won. In the queue in McDonald's in New York he met a bouncer at Nell's, then the most exclusive club in Manhattan. 'You should come down,' said his new friend. Later that night he did and got drunk. At 2 a.m. Seaman stumbled out, to find outside the club, in among a throng trying to get past its fabled velvet rope entrance, were half a dozen DMC bosses – Tony, his wife Christine, some others – stood on the pavement in a throng of NMS conference delegates. 'Oh Michael,' Seaman said. 'These are all my friends from England.' Michael smiled. The velvet rope parted. Everyone went into the club. 'And they just went, "*Right*, okay."' Back in England, impressed, the company offered him a job: working for *Mixmag*. Dave moved to Slough and started his music industry career.

'It was May '88, properly, right time, right place. DJ revolution just happening. Nicky Holloway, Pete Tong, Paul Oakenfold, just come back from Ibiza, met all these people. It was just about to explode so it couldn't have been any better timing,' said Seaman. He started hanging out with Dan Prince and was invited to the Princes' family villa in Marbella, Spain. They went to a club to celebrate Dan's twenty-first birthday, where he did his first E – and immediately dumped his group of friends who'd also come over from Leeds. 'Don't know what happened. They all went off and got pissed and ended up in the gutter somewhere. And I'd just found this completely life-changing thing.' Soon he was another Haçienda regular. Raving at the big M25 parties. 'I'd left Leeds behind and what that whole thing stood for.'

By 1990, with his DMC connections ensuring a supply of free, bang-up-to-the-minute records, Dave picked up his DJing career again. He landed a slot at Shelley's, playing when Sasha wasn't available. It was the perfect opportunity. 'Learning in front of a load of people looking at you, on drugs. And all the other things that got thrown into the melting pot. It was quite a learning curve. You were thrown into the deep end,' he said And it was a captive audience. 'They were running onto the dance floor as soon as the doors opened.'

We talked in the expansive living room of the converted vicarage where Dave now lives in Newark, near Nottingham. He's a father now, with two children by his wife Jessica, who's a former Sky TV presenter. He is still busy DJing around the world – sometimes he takes the whole family with him – and also runs a small record label, Therapy. Dave dug out his DJing diary – a leather-bound Filofax – and talked about how his DJ career kicked off. Once he'd made his name at Shelley's, other clubs were soon phoning up to book him. 'I knew all the people that were putting the gigs on. I was very lucky to be able to get gigs very, very easily. It just kept on snowballing and snowballing.'

This scruffy Filofax was a microcosm of the 1990s business of being a DJ. It showed a month per double page, yet in those tiny squares Seaman found space to fill out his life. Here were the dates and here were his fees, in between friends' birthdays, parties and other commitments. The club names rolled off his tongue – Naughty But Nice in Hereford, Moneypenny's in Birmingham, Love To Be in Sheffield. 'What I used to do a lot of the time was do one on the Friday and two on the Saturday,' he said The diary mixed up recording commitments with DJ gigs. By 1996, he was paying VAT. I read through the entries. £800 plus VAT for Malibu Stacey. Cream, £675 plus VAT. 'That was a good one, Aberdeen, £1,500 plus VAT. Arches, Glasgow, £1,500,' read Dave.

Every weekend was soon being spent hurtling around the nation's motorways, cramming in as many high-paying gigs as possible. 'We used to be haring down the places and straight on to the decks, if you were on time, maybe be a little bit late. And only play an hour, hour and a half's set at times. Which was just ridiculous. Literally, banging out it and straight off again afterwards. You'd no idea what anybody played before you, what anybody played after you. Trying to fit in three in one night,' Dave said. 'It was non-stop. I didn't have any kind of life whatsoever. I didn't see a TV programme, apart from the odd football game. You're so caught up in it, you're just going from week-end to weekend.'

DJs could do anything, it seemed. And as the country went dance music crazy, the record companies increasingly wanted dance remixes to sprinkle a little club cool on their more mainstream artists. DMC's headquarters on that Slough industrial estate also included three small studios and Seaman began working with a young producer called Steve Anderson. Soon they were producing dance remixes for established, mainstream artists. In 1990 they sampled up an old disco a cappella and scored their first hit as Brothers In Rhythm: 'Peace And Harmony'. Island Records snapped it up for £10,000. 'I was like, "Fucking hell!"' Initially the single was a flop. But another barn-storming club track, 'Such A Good Feeling' followed, tailor-made for the Shelley's dance floor. Island put the two tracks on one single and it went into the Top 20. Brothers In Rhythm made a video that was shown on *Top of the Pops*. Within a few short years Dave Seaman had been catapulted into another serious career: producer.

Chris Lowe from the Pet Shop Boys was a fan. Next thing they knew, Dave Seaman and Steve Anderson were in the plush West London studio Sarm, co-producing with the Pet Shop Boys – then one of the biggest pop acts in the country. Dance remixes were in vogue. Brothers In Rhythm were perfectly placed. 'Bottom line,' said Dave, 'making it up as you went along.' But they quickly learnt to polish tracks, to adapt pop vocals to pumping dance beats. They remixed Go West, Janet Jackson, Sting. Everybody at the studio would down tools to watch *Top of the Pops* every Thursday. 'Watching *Top of the Pops* with the Pet Shop Boys and George Michael, or Boy George. It was very entertaining.'

And remixing was lucrative work. 'We're talking about getting at least a £10,000 fee between me and Steve, on top of £1,000–1,500 expenses a day in Sarm when we were doing remixes for two weeks. I think the Sting remix cost £25,000 grand to the record company. Now you're lucky to get couple of hundred quid for a remix.' In 1994, when Kylie Minogue was, quite literally, revamping her career with a dance music-based album for the Deconstruction label, Brothers In Rhythm were one of the production/writing teams she turned to. By the middle of the decade they were producing for Take That! – the biggest pop stars in the UK. Life for Dave Seaman had been completely taken over by dance music. 'Being in the studio all week and then DJing all weekend,' said Dave. 'It was becoming a game of excesses, it just went from one weekend to the next.'

Also in Birmingham, Fun down at the Steering Wheel saw promoters Barney and Piers both kissing goodbye to their marbles. There was Piers filling all the party balloons with helium, whilst Barney spent half the night circling the club collecting for charity. Quite what he was doing emptying the tin towards the end of the night and spending the lot on champagne is a mystery to us all. Not like Mr Moneybags to be short of a few bob is it now?
Mixmag *Club Country gossip column, February 1996*

1996 MEANT HIGH times at Fun in Birmingham and Piers Sanderson was living it large. Dressed to the nines – a sarong was one of his outfits – he checked the punters outside the club door, where 3,000 might be lined up to get into a club that held 800, walking up and down the queue to see who was going to get in. Their outfits chosen, they might have driven for miles, waited an hour or more. It didn't matter. Right now, their night out was in the hands of the small guy with the long, floppy blond hair. This role of the door picker, the arbiter of taste, became increasingly important as the decade wore on. At Fun, Piers decided, who was good-looking, or sharply dressed enough. Who he knew or recognised and who he didn't. Clubland is a cruel place. Get used to it.

Inside, the trauma in the queue had only heightened the atmosphere for those who got in. The boys wore straight, collar-length hair like curtains and flowing shirts or tight satin-look. The girls were in mesh tops that showed their bras, or showing flesh in a cutesy dress, or maybe little devil's horns and matching hot pants, like the outfits now common on hen nights. The smiles were bright, the skin shiny, the eyes wide. In the midst of all of this was Piers with his flowing locks and his partner Barney, his dreads maybe tied up into a tiny pineapple on the side of his head. They moved through the crowd like they owned it. In a sense, they did. 'There's this kind of whole personality of the promoter, which had started,' said Piers. They even posed for publicity photos, like a band. Piers pouting, Barney standing sideways, wearing sunglasses, an unexplained character sporting a giant afro and voluminous 1970s flares next to them. 'You felt like you were a rock star,' said Piers, 'you really did.' His look was typical of the brasher club peacocks of the time and with his long, girlie hair and the soft, flowing contours of his outfits, characteristic of the feminisation that clubland was bringing to male fashion.

On the dance floor, Piers led from the front. The DJ decks were centre stage, surrounded by a metal rail. Piers used this as his stage, hanging on to a beam from the ceiling, dancing wildly in front of the DJ. 'A cabaret part I chose to take on myself! You were part of the show. You had all the beautiful people as you considered them. At the time I loved that.' The DJ might be the visiting star, but the promoter was king. He – and it was invariably a he – held the power. And everybody wanted to talk to him. 'I would have hundreds of vacuous conversations that would go, "Hello mate, how are you, good to see you, yeah you too, how's it going?" "Yeah, good thanks." "Love what you're wearing." "Yeah thanks." On to the next one,' he explained. 'You knew what it was about, a kind of ritual dance thing you do,' he said.

The clubbers knew the rules of this dance too. Clubbing was a hierarchy and they knew their place in it – but they craved this acknowledgement. It was just a nod, a chat, a smile, a kiss on the cheek or a pat on the back, but it mattered. If they didn't know the game, if they lingered too long, Piers had his escape route planned. 'Barney and I had this little signal. If I had my hand on my head, it meant come and rescue me. Because you'd be with someone that wouldn't be happy with that 30-second sound bite,' he said. 'We called them "norsers" – "I'm fucking stuck with a norse." Barney would come up and go, "Listen mate, you're needed at the back here."' And Piers would glide away.

This was a social shift. In the 1980s, being successful meant behaving like a big shot: being a bastard, or a bitch. In the 1990s, if you were a big shot, you no longer felt the need to show it. Sanderson would greet his crowd – his customers – with a personal touch and then escape without having hurt anybody's feelings, or having damaged anybody else's social standing. Because who you were was tied up with who you knew. Be nice to everybody.

Unlike some promoters, Piers never got involved in dealing drugs in the club. 'Obviously we wanted drugs in there because it made the club, it's what gave it the night, but we had to be seen to be policing. So there would be signs up saying "don't take drugs",' he explained. He was simply too scared of the laws that had just come in that could send promoters found dealing in their clubs to jail. 'But I knew the people who were in there selling drugs and people would say to me, "Can I get some pills?" I'd say, "Yeah, go and see that guy over there." I never had to pay for drugs for five years. Cause the dealers would keep you sweet.'

In a glamorous, dressed-up club like Fun, it wasn't done to be seen sweating. 'The thing with that handbag, glammy scene, it wasn't cool to be really off your face. If you looked around the club, you wouldn't see loads of people sweating with their tops off, gurning. You might get the odd one or two who'd misjudged it a little bit. But most people weren't absolutely losing it,' he said. 'There was nothing worse than sweating.'

For the first year Piers was single and clearly became a target for girls. 'It was a very sexual club. I was taking full advantage of being a promoter in that club, for the first year it opened.' One issue of *Mixmag*'s 'Club Country' carried a gossip piece about him being caught by security cameras 'getting a sneaky blow job in the toilet'. Later he got a girlfriend.

The club's inner sanctum wasn't quite so glamorous. But like all the clubs on the circuit, Fun needed somewhere where DJs and visiting aristocracy – other club promoters, for instance, club personalities, or dance music magazine journalists – could be offered something more than just the customary free champagne. They needed somewhere they could snort a line of cocaine. The drug was seeping into clubland, especially in those backroom inner circles. Visiting DJs and club insiders pretty much expected one racked out as soon as they turned up. 'The punters in the club and everybody involved in the club in a room somewhere,' said Jon Pleased, doing an impression of people jabbering, rapid-fire, cocaine-style. 'The fire exit. Standing in piss, taking lines.'

In Fun, that place was the disabled toilets. 'We had keys to the disabled toilets, so that was one room people could go in for a line. And then we had an office at the back. But we would be counting money in there later on so we didn't want too many people in there. But you had your little backroom section and you would get the drinks in and you would look after them.'

Cocaine began creeping not just into the backroom, but into the crowd as well. Piers remembered one Christmas, 1993, when the club suddenly seemed full of it. 'Because it was Christmas Eve everybody decided to make a special thing of it. Everybody was doing coke. The club was so flat. It was flat. It was moody. And I was aware that it was the coke that made it like that.' He would dabble a little during the night himself. But it was afterwards, at an illegal, late-night warehouse party called Cream (no relation to the Liverpool club), that he would really cut loose. 'Towards the end of the night I would do a little line here and there, just to give me a lift towards the end. Because I didn't want to lose it absolutely when I was in the club. Because I knew I had Cream to go on to afterwards and that's when I would let my hair down literally, because I had long hair then.'

Fun was on the circuit and all the main 'handbag' DJs were playing there. They were charging £7 to get in and getting 700 people every week. A couple of DJs at say £400 each, plus flyer costs and promotion. The rest was profit. 'That's quite a lot of money to be making at 22,' said Piers. 'You didn't intend to but all of a sudden you're making thousands of pounds a week, in cash.'

By 1996, the British 'superclub' scene was exploding. In Leeds, there was Vague, Back To Basics, Hard Times; in Sheffield Gatecrasher and Love To Be. The Renaissance one-off big parties were more and more successful. Sasha was a star DJ. In Liverpool, Cream just kept getting bigger. There were clubs everywhere. There were DJs everywhere. But with money and success comes greed and pride. 'It was a very morally shallow existence, you had all the beautiful people there,' said Piers. He was one of them, welcome at clubs all over the country, with cash in his pocket and girls at his beck and call and phone numbers for all the top DJs in his pocket. He was in the inner circle. He had made it. But it wasn't making him happy.

'The problem is when you mix success with drugs and alcohol and most of your time is spent in that social environment and you are the king of your little castle, everybody knows you. There's not many people around you that are telling you you're being a wanker when you're being a wanker. And you get away with quite a lot.'

In the meantime, the superclub scene was just getting bigger and for now, people like Piers were along for the ride. The bigger it got, the bigger the games they played.

'It was about larging it. It was about pulling out a wad of twenties when you were buying your champagne at the bar. It was about buying your coke in an eight ball. It was about wearing designer clothes. At that top bit, that upper tier of that club scene, it was about giving it loads. And I did that quite well,' he said, laughing. He looked back with a shudder at his younger self. 'Oh, what a tosser! What a wanker! You grow up.'

FIVE
BREAKING DOWN BOUNDARIES AND MESSING UP HEADS

TUNE! GAT DECOR – 'PASSION'

This spaciously funky house classic just had an eerie wail and that glorious piano riff.

Sasha's first management company was DMC, who owned Mixmag *at the time. To celebrate signing the star DJ, they gave him a brand-new car: a maroon Rover 216 Coupe. He ambled into their Slough offices a few days after his first weekend out in it, partying and DJing all over the North of England. 'How did you get on with the new car?' asked Derek, the company accountant, beaming behind his thick spectacles. There was a short, bewildered silence. Sasha scratched his head. He drew a blank. It had been a heavy weekend. He had no idea what had happened to the car. It was out there somewhere, but he couldn't tell them which street it was in. He couldn't even tell them which city it was in. It has never been found.*

CALIFORNIA FIRE FIGHTERS know to fear the Santa Ana winds. Especially in late October and early November, when a combination of high-pressure air over Nevada, northern Arizona and Utah and a low-pressure zone over the southern California coast produces just the kind of conditions they dread. Conditions that send humidity plummeting and hot desert winds whipping from the North West down the Malibu canyons cause devastating fires season after season. On 27 October 1993, those winds started a series of fires that were to blaze through Malibu and Laguna Beach in Orange County. Flames reached 60 feet high. Over ten days, more than 1,000 buildings were destroyed over an area of 300 square miles. At one point, 15,000 fire fighters were battling blazes in five counties. By 2 November the worst was over but the cost of the damage was to run into hundreds of millions of dollars. One victim was Duncan Gibbons, a British film-maker who was severely burned while rescuing a cat and later died. This time the Hollywood drama was for real.

In London, the fires had a radical impact on the careers of two producers. Under the name Leftfield, Paul Daley and Neil Barnes were already rising stars in dance music. On 1 November 1993 they released what was potentially the biggest single of their careers. 'Open Up' featured former Sex Pistol John Lydon and his searing vocals turned a powerful, thumping house track with an ethnic tinge in its soaring melodies into something much, much bigger than the dance floor. And with the unerring sense of timing that has characterised much of his career, Lydon shrieked a chorus of 'Burn Hollywood burn!'

It was one of those pop music accidents, the sort of awful coincidence that can transform a career. America was not amused. Johnny Rotten had upset everyone. And the song was banned. MTV declined to show the video, citing its 'insensitive lyrics', as did ITV's *Chart Show* – which at the time showed everything in the charts. *Top of the Pops* just showed a snippet. The single reached number eleven in the British charts but its shockwaves spread much, much wider.

Fanned by the Hollywood flames and Lydon's scorching vocals, the song was to do more for dance music's mainstream acceptance than a thousand superclub nights would ever do. The mainstream rock establishment suddenly took notice of this burgeoning new music culture. The *NME* scooped a Lydon/Leftfield interview and put them on the cover. 'This is the record that people have always wanted Lydon to do,' the rock weekly declared, making it Punk Rock Single Of The Week.

For acid house, 'Open Up' was a gift. Mainstream rock music had always struggled with something this faceless, this ephemeral. Now there was a record with a face to it. Nor was it the outlandish combination it seemed. Leftfield's Neil Barnes had known Lydon for years. In his Sex Pistols days, John Lydon had spent more time in reggae and soul clubs than he ever did at punk gigs. His post-Pistols group Public Image Ltd, like many post-punk acts, didn't restrict themselves to rock: their 1980 album 'Metal Box' worked the heavy dub and disco basslines of Jah Wobble and the stinging guitars of Keith Levene into something closer to early dance music. It came packaged on a selection of DJ-friendly 12-inch singles in a metal canister – hence the name. When Paul Daley first met Lydon, they instantly connected. 'He was like all my mad mates rolled into one,' said Daley.

Barnes and Daley gave John Lydon a crash course in dance music, playing him track after track, taking him out to clubs. Lydon had replied to an early demo of 'Open Up' with a note saying, 'Where's the fucking chorus?' But in the studio, he nailed his vocal straight away. 'He had a few beers and a curry, went into the booth and pretty much did it in one take. And me and Neil was like, "Shit that's it."' They worked long and hard on the track, with the obsessive attention to detail that had already become their trademark. When it was finished Daley and Barnes celebrated by taking an E, bouncing around the room with glee, tripping out on the studio's many little flashing lights. 'Just to make sure it was working properly. The ultimate road test,' said Daley.

With the single out and the Hollywood fires raging, Paul Daley received a phone call from Lydon, who had a house in Los Angeles. 'Ha, ha, it stopped 150 yards from my house. Ha, ha,' cackled Lydon, who was, in fact, singing about a film role he had failed to get. Indeed the song had been recorded the previous May. But Daley, a one-time punk himself, knew this had played into their hands. 'I was like, "You couldn't have planned this better. This is the bollocks."'

He was right. For rock fans who had always found dance music's soul and funk roots a problem, its fun emphasis trivial, 'Open Up' made it sound urgent, thrilling and rebellious again. Lydon had provided house music with a celebrity endorsement of the very best kind. He put in an explosive performance for the video. Daley turned up to the video edit suite, still tripping on the magic mushroom punch he'd been drinking at a Halloween party. He hadn't slept and was dressed as the devil, with horns.

The 1990s is too often seen as the decade of Britpop – personified by the high-profile battles between Blur and Oasis and their coteries of celebrity girlfriends. But Britpop, despite its vitality, was essentially a derivative sound, one that took classic 1960s guitar pop and updated it. Dance music, meanwhile, was hurtling forward. Groups like Massive Attack, Bjork and Portishead created a new kind of soul music. Acts like Leftfield, Underworld, The Prodigy, Orbital and the Chemical Brothers dispensed with traditional performance as readily as they dispensed with rock's song structure: they replaced choruses with screaming roars of synthesisers, guitar solos with cascades of beats, charismatic singers with visuals and flashing lights. Their sound drew from eighties synth pop, punk rock, disco and hip hop to create a whole new style of music.

What sampling allowed in music was the introduction of a completely random element: opposites could be put together and fused into something new. At its peak, this is where the music came into its own. The label Mo' Wax, led by its bespectacled boss James Lavelle, personified 'trip hop', the lazily funky, downbeat counterpoint to 1990s house music. It was a wildly original idea: up until then, the whole point of hip hop had been the rhymes of rappers. But why not just use the beats and put whatever you like on top? This creative thinking fed electronic music acts like Leftfield – why not get a punk rock singer to vocal a house track? What followed was a musical revolution, wrought by British electronic artists deconstructing pop history to build something fresh and new.

'When I look back at that period, it seems to me it was very forward thinking musically,' James Lavelle said. 'Underworld, Chemical Brothers, DJ Shadow, Portishead, Tricky, Bjork, Leftfield. They're not bands that just conjure up a couple of blokes in a back room, they were like everything was big and bold and the graphics, the artwork, everything about it seemed completely new. It was about taking from the past and making something new out of it.'

People like Leftfield and James Lavelle are the other side of the story of 1990s clubbing, serious musicians in casual T-shirts, trainers and jeans, the opposite of the extravagantly dressed showmen of the superclubs. But they and producers like them brought something alchemic to the party – the music. The transformation that super-clubbing wrought on British nightlife and pop-culture would never have happened without the records they and producers like them made and released. Yet theirs too are emblematic stories of the 1990s, because fame and success sucked them in too, and cocaine, over-ambition and bitter relationship breakdowns spat them out again.

TODAY, IT'S HARD to imagine that dance music was as reviled and unfashionable as it was in 1991. Acts like Leftfield, Underworld, Orbital and the Chemical Brothers and labels like Mo' Wax made it acceptable on a wider stage, in a way that rock fans could understand. These acts made albums. They performed at rock festivals, lighting up what their performances lacked in charismatic frontmen with strangely bewitching, abstract video displays and explosive light shows. And they took this into their sleeve design and videos, building identities with graphics and imagery rather than band photos and personalities. Design was everything in 1990s dance music, just as it was in the clubs.

But as British electronica swept across the world, its studio boffin producers became unlikely – and in many cases, unwilling – pop stars. There were no more unwilling pop stars than Leftfield and they did not handle fame well. 'We all didn't expect to make careers out of it. We didn't know what we were doing. We were just experimenting,' said the act's Neil Barnes. Glamour was not their forte. In May 1996, at the peak of their fame, with their album *Leftism* a multi-million-selling worldwide success, they were invited to perform their live show at a party in the Cannes Film Festival for the movie *Trainspotting*, for which they had contributed music for a crucial scene. Director Danny Boyle had previously worked with the pair when they provided the theme for his breakthrough film *Shallow Grave*.

It was a celebrity-stuffed affair. Roger Moore was there with his fingers in his ears. Noel Gallagher and Damon Albarn – sworn enemies then at the height of their rivalry – were almost persuaded to shake hands in Leftfield's dressing room by Leftfield's tour DJ, an affable bearded Geordie called Uncle Al. Lew Grade, Justine Frischmann and the film's star Ewan McGregor were all at a celebrity lunch beforehand. But Leftfield's Paul Daley sat scowling on another table. And when Daley turned up at the party at which his group were the star attraction, carrying his things in a plastic bag, the bouncers wouldn't let him in. Daley thought this was funny. He wasn't interested in 'showbiz sherbert'. 'Parties, madness, meeting people, everyone wanting to talk to you,' he said. 'I just remember wanting to get out of there really. This is not my scene. It was all too Hollywood.'

Neil Barnes grew up in a left-wing, working-class family in Gospel Oak and went to school in Islington, North London. 'We were obsessed by music in the school from a very early age,' Barnes said. 'Sound and music and influences.' Clever, studious-looking, with big eyes that blink behind his glasses, he is a gentle soul. At 18 he got to know John Gray, one of John Lydon's best friends. The three used to hang out at Lydon's house. 'We used to stay up all weekend, taking speed and listening to reggae. That's all we did,' said Barnes.

He started out as a guitarist in punk bands. By 1982, as new wave had replaced punk and begun to draw in influences from soul, disco and the early hip hop scene, he had become more ambitious in the music he wanted to create. But he couldn't afford the equipment. 'You needed a lot of money to make music then.' He took five years out of music and taught in a playgroup.

I talked to Neil Barnes in the sunny garden of his spacious, West London family house, where he now lives with his wife Perree and their two children. We hadn't met since 1999. His eldest daughter studies at the same Brits School that produced Amy Winehouse. Now 46, Neil does a lot of blinking behind his thick glasses and ruffling of his thinning hair. He had a crumpled piece of paper in his hand on which he'd written things he wanted to remember to talk about. When Neil met Paul Daley in 1988, both were percussionists, playing along to a DJ at the Soho nightspot Fred's. 'I remember thinking he was really trendy. He knew everybody. He had tons of energy. He was different,' said Barnes, who was less sure of himself.

I last met up with Paul Daley in 1999 as well. Now, like Barnes, he has mellowed with age. He's more relaxed, more affable, though he's still got an intensity about him. We spoke in another garden, in the shade of the villa he rents in Ibiza where he spends much of his time with his girlfriend Vanda. He never married and has no children. It is a simple, yet stylishly appointed place, surrounded by an olive grove. Daley sat back, nursing a slight beer gut and stubble and rolled a joint. Under the hot Ibiza summer sun his story emerged.

Paul Daley is beefier than Barnes and cockier too – a complicated, pugnacious character with an affable streak and a sense of wounded pride about him. He grew up in a working-class family in Margate, where his parents ran a clothing 'boutique' – Daley laughed at the word, so quaint now. 'I was exposed to fashion at a very young age. My dad was quite a dude. He wore cool seventies suits. I was brought into that world of flash things.' Daley became a hairdresser. 'My dad wanted me to do a trade and it was the only sort of vaguely creative, cool thing to do in Margate.' It gave him a social confidence that was to help later in clubs. 'Broke down those nerdy, anorak, teenage feelings.'

When recession hit in the 1980s, Daley moved up to London and began working in Kensington Market, then a thriving centre for alternative London. He immersed himself in the London club scene – from illegal warehouse parties like Shake 'N' Fingerpop, to the tail end of the New Romantic scene. And he fell for acid house. At the club Solaris, he took ecstasy – though having been a clubber for years, he was already accustomed to drugs like speed and acid. 'I can remember them playing the music and I can remember thinking, "Fuck me, this is fucking brilliant,"' he said. He started going to Charlie Chester's Flying parties and the Full Circle Sunday afternoon sessions that DJ Phil Perry ran in a pub in Colnbrook. 'It opened up this whole new world, which was meeting new people, everyone coming together,' said Daley. 'Do-it-yourself suburban working class attitude really.'

He was always the confident one in Leftfield. 'You have to be a bit confident to survive,' Daley said. 'Social skills. Night-time social skills. Small-talk expertise.' Daley the street-smart club kid nonetheless clicked with Barnes, over music. They became friends, Neil driving Paul to gigs where they would both play percussion, loading his congas into the back of the car. 'I thought he was a bit of a geek,' Paul laughed. 'But a lovely geek. He's just a really nice guy. But quite shy. Quite anoraky about his music.'

Daley was bored of playing percussion in London 'acid jazz' acts like A Man Called Adam. Barnes had taken out a bank loan, bought some basic studio equipment and had started making tracks in the housing cooperative flat in Marylebone where he lived. 'It came at a point when technology changed in music,' Neil Barnes explained. Suddenly, all the stuff he'd wanted to buy years previously but couldn't afford was within his reach. Daley had noted the change too. 'Technology was allowing you to do things easier, quicker, instant, rather than labouring over things. And plus Neil had done this track.'

There's a new breed of hard but tuneful, banging but thoughtful, uplifting and trancey British house. Progressive House we'll call it. It's simple, it's funky, it's driving. The names are Leftfield, DOP, Soundclash Republic, React 2 Rhythm, Gat Decor and Slam. This

is a new breed and what makes Progressive House different is that the sound is uniquely British.
Mixmag *feature by the author, June 1992*

WHEN NEIL BARNES recorded 'Not Forgotten' at home he could hardly have anticipated its impact. It was a cinematic collage of samples, coupled to a reggae bassline and a minimal, very percussive piano refrain. Completely original – and completely at odds with the jazz-based band stuff Daley was playing. Barnes included some speech from the film *Mississippi Burning.* 'I had it in my head it was an alternative piece of music to the film,' he told me, having retrieved the name from his crumpled piece of paper. The track was finished in a studio and released on the Rhythm King label in 1990.

Daley heard the track in Ibiza and loved it. It was just what he had been looking for. 'It was dance music presented in a different way, more thoughtful, not obvious.' He suggested to Neil that he remix it. And after weeks spent in a basement studio in Covent Garden, cutting up bits of tape, he turned 'Not Forgotten' into something harder, more club friendly. Barnes loved the result and immediately realised the pair could work together. 'We realised we'd hit on something.'

'Not Forgotten' was the beginning of a new wave of domestically produced house records that developed an intrinsically British sound. 'It just shook the floor,' said John Digweed. 'You could tell they made that record to kick everything around it off the dance floor. It's such a powerful record.' Another was Gat Decor's 'Passion', recorded by the DJs Lawrence Nelson, Simon Hanson and Simon Slater from a patchwork of Chicago house samples and a piano line played by a session musician. 'Passion' was a big, confident record that still gets played today, a British house classic. Others flowed from the prolific

London-based independent label Guerilla Records: small production outfits like DOP and React 2 Rhythm. Records like these put the space of reggae into their grooves, while matching the hard energy of the European techno hits of the time with the swing of American house and garage. And they gave British producers confidence in themselves for the first time. 'We were proud to be British,' said Darren Emerson from Underworld.

Before this, British house records had disguised themselves as American, even going so far as to put fake New York record company names on the label. Producer Joey Negro pretended to be a black guy from New York with an afro, when he actually was Dave Lee from Essex. Afterwards, this kind of subterfuge was no longer felt necessary. For Sasha, playing at Renaissance in 1992 and 1993, the new sound arrived at exactly the right time. He wanted to move away from the ultra-dramatic pianos and screaming vocals he'd played at Shelley's. 'It was a brilliant time for music,' Sasha said. 'That's the sound that I wanted to play. I was getting to put whole sets together with this sound.'

Renaissance capitalised on this with their *The Mix Collection* in November 1994, mixed by Sasha and John Digweed. Before then, there were no DJ mix CDs. Just a thriving black market business in DJ cassettes, recorded at shows and sold at record shops, with a cash bung being paid to DJs. This was good business. Two of the most famous DJ bootleggers were Andy Horsfield and James Todd, a couple of Geordie chancers known as 'The Fat Lads', because of the weight they put on munching Ginsters pasties at service stations, while charging up and down the motorways with their DAT machine to record DJs. 'In the early days the DJs were recorded without their knowledge,' said Horsfield. 'But then they realised what we were up to, so we started doing it with their knowledge.' Some DJs got a split, others a £250 cash payment.

But Todd and Horsfield realised they could expand on this, went legit and later paid all the royalties due on their early tapes. 'There was a proper business to be built,' explained Horsfield. They began the international DJ mix series Global Underground, selling more CDs abroad than they ever did in the UK: in 1999, the Newcastle-based independent label sold over a million CDs. Once legit, they hired me to write sleeve-notes for their albums, which I did for many years, travelling to clubs all over the world. I later discovered they had already been printing comments I'd written in the magazine on their bootleg cassette sleeves, along with a *Mixmag* logo.

The Mix Collection wasn't the first legal DJ mix album released – *Mixmag* began selling DJ mix cassettes to readers in 1992, soon followed by the CD mix series Journeys By DJ. But it was the first to make a significant impact. Its success opened up a new market that the major record companies had completely missed, yet which the other superclubs were quick to exploit. By the end of the 1990s, DJ mix albums from 'superclubs' like Cream and the Ministry Of Sound would be selling up to 700,000 copies each. Superclub bosses were no longer just club promoters and runners. They were music-industry moguls.

ZOOM RECORDS, IN North London, in 1993 was a boy's club. The shop was hidden above a leather clothes store in Camden Market. You had to know it was there, to find your way through the racks of brown bomber jackets to the door at the back and up the stairs. Inside it was a bare, minimal space. The woodwork was painted orange, about the only concession to decoration of any kind, bar the odd poster. I had taken to hanging out there on Saturdays with the shop's owner, Dave

Wesson, and counter staff, many of whom were DJs playing the new trance and progressive house sounds, like Billy Nasty.

The music was loud, the clientele completely male, the talk only about records and clubs and in the office there was the constant, sweet, sickly smell of marijuana. This – or so it would have liked to believe – was the 'underground': a mythical place where music was made for pure, aesthetic, altruistic reasons, a land whose codes were complicated and difficult to decipher. The mentality of this very male world of 'trainspotters' (the name a reference to the strange souls who hang around railway stations writing down locomotive numbers) and musical obsessives was detailed beautifully in Nick Hornby's book *High Fidelity* and its subsequent film starring Jon Cusack. *Mixmag* had an in-house 'trainspotter' – reviews editor Frank Tope, an expert whose knowledge of all kinds of music could be alarmingly detailed. Tope was unimpressed when *High Fidelity* was published. 'I can't believe he's given the game away to women,' he huffed, snapping it shut.

Pre-Internet though, DJs couldn't source new music without going to a record shop like this and physically buying vinyl. Zoom Records therefore functioned as a communications centre as well as a boys' club. 'It was the only place you could get that music,' said Daley, 'which also made you really wanted to be involved, which made it more attractive. It had that underground, subversive feel to it. It was top anorak.'

Like Jon Cusack's character in *High Fidelity*, Zoom boss Dave Wesson ruled the roost. He enjoyed throwing visitors with ever more obscure records – the latest Italian or Belgian import single you just had to buy. One Saturday lunchtime, Wesson announced he had one of the very first copies of the new single, 'Song Of Life', by Leftfield. In the small, tight hierarchy of London house music in 1993, Leftfield were stars, though nobody would have been so gauche as to admit it.

Wesson drew the record out of its bag like he was uncovering a rare antique and we all sat and listened very seriously. It was a hard, dubby record, its one concession to anything resembling a melody a short, lovely piano breakdown. There was a short silence after it finished. 'That's really good, do you like it, Dave?' I asked.

'Yeah...' replied Wesson, unsure. He looked concerned. 'Not sure about that piano though. I think I might say something to them about it.' He did, later.

Hornby's trainspotters were troubled, lost characters. But in dance music, many of them became rich, famous DJs. The culture of 'trainspotting' was as celebrated as it was ridiculed. In one famous photo superstar DJ Fatboy Slim aka Norman Cook is pictured reading a British Railways guide. The name of Irvine Welsh's book *Trainspotting* – and Danny Boyle's film of the same name – brought the term into the mainstream. As the T-shirt slogan of the time had: 'The geek shall inherit the earth.' One of the geekiest of all was a kid with big glasses from a middleclass family in Oxford: James Lavelle.

LAVELLE'S IMPRINT MO' Wax was another 1990s phenomenon that helped turn the geekiness of trainspotting cool. He loved Japanese toys, trainers and hip hop. He combined these with the label's distinctive, instrumental hip hop sound and a strong visual aesthetic into something fans around the world aspired to. The label's success made Lavelle rich, successful and famous.

He is an intense, restless character who invented himself out of his bourgeoisie Oxford roots to become the DJ world's equivalent of 1970s puppet superhero Joe 90. A slight, small, bespectacled guy who wore obscure trainers, graffiti T-shirts, and a baseball jacket that someone in New York had made for him. He has tattoos especially designed by graffiti artists. Everything about Lavelle was limited edition and it still is. There is a sharp intelligence that he hides behind the slang and jargon of the perpetual teenager. And he turned being a perpetual teenager into a successful career. Lavelle did everything. He was a DJ, scene-leader, producer, record company executive – but primarily, an effortless networker whose connections spread across the world.

He got to know the Beastie Boys and graffiti artist Future 2000 (who did his tattoos) in New York. In Tokyo he connected with designer Nigo of the clothing label A Bathing Ape and the act Major Force. He befriended Massive Attack in Bristol. He hung out with Oasis and talked Thom Yorke and Jarvis Cocker into guesting on his albums. Mo' Wax became a byword for a certain cool – a global boy's bedroom, filled with all the things James loved. There were his records, his *Star Wars* posters, his rare toys, his trainers. But Mo' Wax was also a creative centre, an axis in that crazy mixed-up world, a Factory Records of the 1990s. 'You had intellectual, working class, everyone was hanging out and everyone just wanted to do these crazy things,' said Lavelle. And for a minute, it seemed anything was possible.'

Lavelle was perfectly suited to the new DJ lifestyle that developed in the nineties, with its electronic studios, jet-setting lifestyle and reliance on what ideas you had and who you knew, rather than what you actually did. Music and popular culture in the 1990s opened up to influences as diverse his. 'It was like we could suddenly do things, we found a voice, all those years of going to these weird clubs and being these underground kids suddenly started seeping in,' he said. 'It was as though the country needed to have this youth culture that could work.'

Lavelle is still only 34, and now owns a house in a leafy square in London's Camden, where we met. His daughter stays half the week. He is a conscientious father, taking her to school, fitting her schedule around the career he still runs as a DJ and a producer. His living room is full of memorabilia: the giant TV, the sofa you keep falling off, the designer Japanese toys, the artefacts of his life in music and teenage dreams.

He was only 14 when he started taking the coach up to London to go to record shops and talked himself into 'Saturday boy' jobs behind the counter, first in Bluebird in Soho and later at Honest Jon's in Ladbroke Grove. It was a good place to be; all the big DJs came to shops like these and Lavelle got to know them all – an eager speccy kid, selling them tunes. He moved to London and went round all the major labels blagging free records. 'Here was this odd geeky kid who was obviously so into it,' he said. 'Maybe you hook certain people up because they're so into it they just spread the word. I suppose I was one of those kids.'

And James was still a teenager when he threw his first party in Oxford. Hundreds turned up. At 16 he first took half an ecstasy tablet, which he mixed with half a tab of acid at a rave. It was a potent mix of psychedelics – he remembered, at one point during the night, trying to push down a building with his bare hands. Sunday lunch with his parents the next day, still tripping, 'rushing off your tits', as he put it, was difficult. He didn't eat much. 'Being completely in a totally different zone, trying to get away with it. I just slid out the house and went to the pub.'

By 1992, at just 18 he was writing reviews for the specialist music magazine *Straight No Chaser*. The DJ Gilles Peterson had started his record label Talkin Loud, a home for acid jazz. Electronic music was thriving all around him. But Lavelle realised that the major record companies were too cumbersome to react to it properly. 'I decided the best thing to do was to set up my own label,' he said. He was hanging out with a gang of movers and shakers – designers, DJs, record company hot-shots, all of them on the make. 'That really summed up what the nineties was about for me, that was the beginning of this crew of people coming together, all doing interesting things and all connected in their own little way. You just met so many people. It just seemed to grow.'

In 1994, Lavelle took a risk and released a record by the obscure San Francisco producer, DJ Shadow – 12 minutes of stoned, loping beats, samples, voices and dreamy melodies called 'In Flux'. It exploded, the perfect counterpoint to all those high-energy house records. 'That record was a moment. It worked. And then it became really cool,' said Lavelle. 'It was the moment my confidence was instilled.' With 'In Flux' Mo' Wax became the harbinger of a new sound that *Mixmag*'s Andy Pemberton labelled 'trip hop' in a 1994 feature. Quickly lumped in were Massive Attack, Portishead, a new duo called the Dust Brothers, who were soon to change their name to the Chemical Brothers, and Mo' Wax's French act La Funk Mob. Any act that favoured stoned beats and psychedelic noises. Throughout the 1990s, this sound, made more commercial by groups like Morcheeba and albums like the Buddha Bar mix series, became the background music staple of designer bars around the world – a new kind of lounge or 'muzak'. But in 1994, it sounded like nothing else.

Mo' Wax's free-wheeling approach allowed it to connect with dance music in its widest aspects. In one corner was drum 'n' bass, which had evolved out of rave and hardcore to become a vibrantly creative style of its own and which would throw up star DJs like Goldie and LTJ Bukem. In another were the producers of Detroit techno – people like Derrick May and Juan Atkins whose futuristic music was influential on British DJs but whose DJ sets where never really commercial enough for the superclubs. Mo' Wax brought these strands together – most especially on a double EP in 1994 by La Funk Mob, on which Detroit techno producer Carl Craig transformed a loping groove by French 'trip hop' act La Funk Mob into eight minutes of thrillingly hypnotic sci-fi funk. It was called 'Breaking Down Boundaries And Messing Up Heads'. For Lavelle, this personified everything he thought his label was about. Even better, he was living in West London, going out every night. Living his dream.

THE MAJOR RECORD companies were struggling to catch up with dance music. 'Records would go into the charts without any radio play. And seemingly for them they came from nowhere,' said Jean Branch, who worked from 1992 to 1999 for East West Records, a dance division of Warner Brothers. As the majors grasped what was going on, they increasingly relied on people like Branch to connect them to the clubs. Her job was to spend weekends clubbing and hanging out with DJs – all expenses paid, of course – in the hope that key DJs would push their new records.

Pre-Internet, the hottest new dance record in the country might only exist on half a dozen especially pressed-up vinyl copies. If key DJs like Sasha or Jeremy Healy played these records, they would appear on specialist club charts that would then help build a 'buzz' on a record that could propel it into the charts. As new DJs and clubs emerged, it was Branch's job to go and visit them. In this process they became roped into the burgeoning dance music network that everybody wanted to belong to. 'There were so few clubs in the beginning. As each new club came up and you started hearing about it, you'd be down there,' Branch explained. 'You'd know who the DJs were. And they'd be chuffed that you'd made the effort to turn up at their club. And you'd be like, "Yeah, this is brilliant, this is really, really kicking down here.'" We spoke over lunch in the garden of her South London house. She now works as a nutritionist and has a family, living a life a million miles away from dance music.

This process worked both ways, Jean explained. DJs got free records. Record companies got DJs playing and in doing so endorsing their latest record. And that could just as easily be a dance remix of a mainstream artist as a new dance hit. One example was an infectiously funky, largely instrumental remix of singer-songwriter Tori Amos's 'Professional Widow (It's Got To Be Big)' by American DJ Armand Van Helden that East West released in 1996. This hit was typical in the way it stripped Amos's vocal back to just a couple of repeated, staccato phrases. 'Honey, bring it close to my lips, yeah,' went one, 'got to be big', another, while a funky bassline thwacked away. It sold 300,000 copies and reached number one. Branch would deliver these exclusive, limited upfront copies personally to DJs in clubs. 'It was better to actually go and see them if you wanted to see it played. You wanted to be there because you wanted to see the record kick off.'

All of this was concentrating more power and influence in the hands of the top DJs. They weren't just making big money playing in clubs, they were increasingly at the centre of the dance music industry – with the power to help break hits. And to make sure they got the records they wanted, there was a record industry gold rush for producers who could remix tracks into something club-friendly. Leftfield, restricted from releasing their own material for a time because of a contract problem, were quick to get on board. Ultra Nate, The Sandals, Adamski, Stereo MCs, If?, React 2 Rhythm, Inner City and Pressure Drop all found themselves being played in house clubs, thanks to radical Leftfield reworks of their singles. 'We were trendy as hell. Everything we did people said was the best thing ever,' said Neil

Barnes. 'I think it was a bit hard to live up to even then, I think we didn't believe it.'

In 1992, Leftfield remixed a new David Bowie single, 'Jump They Say', his first release in some time. Leftfield turned a darker, edgier Bowie track into a spooky club epic – effectively, a Leftfield track with David Bowie on vocals. It became a major club hit. In a telephone interview I did with him at the time for *Mixmag*, Bowie astutely nailed just what it was they had done. 'There is an analogy with craftsmen in terms of church builders and painters. The idea of putting their own names on anything was an anathema. Nobody actually has a clue who built these cathedrals. With music, it's coming to a situation where anonymity is a virtue. I find that really interesting. I'm not sure what staying power it has,' Bowie said.

By 1995 Leftfield had finished toiling over an album. They were perfectionists, nothing was ever quite good enough, but they got there in the end. When *Leftism* was finally finished, it was major label Sony who won a bidding war and signed Leftfield through their own Hard Hands label for a £295,000 advance. They also got a £250,000 publishing deal with Chrysalis. This was big money for two skint producers.

Leftism, released that year, is still perhaps the most complete album 1990s dance music produced – grandiose, forceful, melodic and emotional. Guest vocals from artists as diverse as rock singer Toni Halliday from the indie act Curve, Danny Red and reggae MC Earl Sixteen gave it a unique, multi-layered appeal. Hippies liked it as much as punks and clubbers did. It was dance music's *Dark Side of the Moon* and went on to sell 1.1 million copies around the world. Sasha was just one of its many fans. 'I still pester him [Paul] about how brilliant I think he is and how great that record is,' Sasha told me. 'The first time I really hung out with him, I went back to his house after a gig, we were all drinking ridiculous amounts of neat vodka. I talked him into a corner about how important that record was to me.'

All of a sudden, Leftfield weren't left of field at all any more. They were part of the mainstream record industry – and it is a business that needs pop stars to front its acts. As Bowie had predicted, this was going to be a problem for people like Leftfield. Paul Daley hadn't set out to be a pop star. He talked to Mick Clarke, the A&R man at Sony who signed the deal. 'Can't live in the nightclub all your life, wherever everything is cool, you've got to take some things seriously,' Clarke told him. Clarke defended Leftfield against some of the other Sony executives who struggled to understand this faceless pair of studio boffins and their coterie of guest vocalists. This wasn't pop or rock as they knew it. 'One came up to me and said, "I don't understand what you've done, but I think it's going to be big,"' Daley remembered. In a conversation outside the nightclub Browns, another executive, an American, confronted Paul.

'Are you ready to be a pop star?' the executive asked.

'No,' said Daley.

'What do you mean, no?'

'I said, "no",' Daley replied.

'Oh Paul,' said the record company man, 'you can't be a rebel all your life.'

'No, I can be what I fucking want for as long as I want.'

'You all get reeled in, in the end,' insisted the executive.

'No we don't,' said Paul. 'No, we don't.' He started looking down a long tunnel in front of him, thinking: 'Shit. Right, now, am I going to enjoy this?'

NONE OF THIS worried Leftfield's equally successful contemporaries Underworld. Two of the group, Rick Smith and Karl Hyde, enjoyed a separate source of income from a design agency they owned – they had been through the major label music business mill. The third, Darren Emerson, combined his role in Underworld with a very successful DJing career. All three knew just what they wanted out of this – and they got it.

The group pioneered a very British sound, one that combined cut-up, stream-of-consciousness lyrics and shards of guitar from frontman Hyde with a tough, spacious techno sound. Hyde and producer Rick Smith had spent much of the eighties in their own synth pop acts – one was Freur, another an earlier version of Underworld. Hyde ended up as a session guitarist, playing for Prince and Debbie Harry. Smith ended up in Romford, Essex, where he recruited Darren Emerson, then a rising young DJ star. 'He was teaching me how to work the studio and I was teaching him what was good and what was bad, in my head,' said Emerson. 'And it took us a couple of years to get to know each other.' Hyde returned from Los Angeles, hit upon the idea of cutting up his lyrics and Underworld was born. 'When Rick played me early Underworld stuff, I thought it was awful. But then when his [Karl's] voice was all chopped up it made sense, cause it was with the groove,' said Emerson.

Rick Smith was studious, the engine room of the band. Hyde was flighty, artistic, bubbling with ideas and wild conversational tangents. Emerson was a cheerful Essex lad, smart, quick and a talented DJ who learnt to scratch and cut at an early age. It was a good mix. Emerson was more than a decade younger than Smith and Hyde. His father was a dustman and he left school at 16 to work as a runner in the futures market. By 19, his DJing career had taken off enough for him to leave.

Underworld's first single 'Mmm Skyscraper I Love You', released on that early progressive house wave in 1992, was a barnstorming techno number, with Hyde's whispered vocals echoing in and out of a percussive groove. They developed a clever mix of DJing and live performance, where songs would be reworked and remixed live, but where the focus was as much on the party as it was the stage. And in Karl Hyde, they had something Leftfield would always lack: a frontman. 'Rick and Karl had been in a band, they'd been on stages. But they wanted to get into the dance thing,' said Emerson. 'It wasn't about people looking at us, it was about them experiencing the dance thing.'

Underworld became one of the most consistent dance acts of the 1990s – with a distinct sound and a stylish live show that made good use of visuals. They released their first album *Dubnobasswithmyheadman* in 1993 and followed up with *Second Toughest in the Infants* in 1996. Both were accomplished albums of art house and dramatic, grandiose grooves, with moments of exquisite, down-tempo melancholy. The band had its dramas. Karl Hyde conquered a problem with alcoholism in the late 1990s – ironically enough, considering their biggest hit, 'Born Slippy', featured in 1996 movie *Trainspotting*, had a famous chorus of 'lager, lager, lager'. But Underworld wisely kept within both their limits and their talents. And the design agency Tomato, which Smith and Hyde part-owned, gave them financial freedom. Tomato worked for major clients like Nike but was also an outlet for more art-based projects, like the animated video to their twirling techno epic 'Rez' and a book of abstract typography based on the lyrics to 'Mmm Skyscraper I Love You'.

Underworld's third album *Beaucoup Fish* in 1999 was less of a success and Emerson left in 1999 to pursue his DJing. 'I was tired,' he explained. The group carried on without him. He still has his DJing career and now lives on ten acres of land in Essex with his partner, the television presenter and journalist Kate Thornton. Despite

Thornton's fame – she presented TV's *X Factor*, among other shows – he shies away from the limelight. The couple don't do *Hello!*-type interviews. 'Why do I want to go and tell people about my life with my girlfriend?' he asked. 'I want to go to Tesco's, do my shopping. We're private people.'

COCAINE IS LIKE rust. It corrupts everything it touches. At first, it created a few crumbly red blotches around the edges of James Lavelle's shiny life. Soon it covered it. By 1998, Mo' Wax was part of the Universal major record company group and had achieved everything Lavelle could have wanted. People he had looked up to as a fan – like Massive Attack's rapper, producer and in-house artist Robert '3D' Del Naja – had become collaborators and friends. He had succeeded in establishing DJ Shadow as an internationally credible artist – his album *Endtroducing...* was being played all over the world. As a DJ, he was guesting at superclubs like Cream – even providing one mix for a Cream triple-CD album.

Mo' Wax had an office on Mortimer St in the West End. From its ceiling hung a plastic, 1960s egg-shaped chair that only Lavelle was allowed to sit on. Producer Howie B, who would go on to work with U2, had a studio in the same premises where he was recording Bjork, who was around all day. Lavelle's friend Fraser Clarke had a clothing company working with cooler-than-thou fashion label Pervert. Lavelle had even formed his own 'supergroup', UNKLE, with DJ Shadow, Futura 2000 and an Oxford schoolfriend Tim Goldsworthy. Later Goldsworthy became half of the hip New York production team DFA with James Murphy, who then became LCD Soundsystem.

While supposedly recording the debut UNKLE album in a house they had rented from Meatloaf in Los Angeles, the group went to Las

Vegas to be photographed for *The Face* magazine. Though the amount of partying that went on meant no photos were actually taken. 'I remember [fashion photographer] Norbert [Shoerner] having to superimpose backgrounds of Las Vegas on the pictures that were taken in LA because we were so fucked in Las Vegas that nobody could take a picture,' Lavelle recalled.

And Lavelle had fallen in love with a girl called Janet Fischgrund. Janet knew everybody. She worked in fashion and was friends with Kate Moss. She had been an assistant to Lynn Franks, the legendary fashion diva whose antics inspired the TV comedy series *Absolutely Fabulous*. And she was friends with Meg Mathews, then married to Noel Gallagher and Fran Cutler, manager of DJ Jeremy Healy. Mathews and Cutler were two of the best-connected people in London, lynchpins of a celebrity set that would begin to revolve around the tiny, celebrity-packed bar of London's Metropolitan Hotel – the famous Met Bar – and included supermodels like Kate Moss, rock stars like the Gallaghers, pop vixens like the Appleton sisters from girl group All Saints and a galaxy of 1990s stars. Through his girlfriend, Lavelle joined the A list. 'I walked into that. It was like opening doors. I was like a geek.' He was already partying hard. 'You were out and it was fucking musicians and artists and models and drug dealers and everybody together just getting fucked all of the time.' And now opportunity was everywhere.

'Tables of cocaine everywhere,' he said. 'You'd be in a party and it would be Kate Moss and the Beastie Boys and you'd be in New York. Then you'd be back in London and it would be Oasis and Massive Attack and Richard Ashcroft. In London, suddenly it was the Met Bar and the Saint. Monday nights. Going out every night. Caning it every night.' James and Janet bought an old power station in Kentish Town and remodelled it. They were a power couple, linked on Lavelle's side to music stars like DJ Shadow and on hers to fashion icons like Alexander McQueen who she worked with. 'We were the relationship of the moment,' he said. 'When you're very successful young, you're thrown so many things to deal with that you've no experience of. So obviously you're going to go to the Met Bar, you're going to hang out with people that are in similar positions to you.'

In 1998, the UNKLE album *Psyence Fiction* was released with a fanfare. It was everything Lavelle loved and believed in, combined into one album. Radiohead's Thom Yorke featured, as did The Verve's singer Richard Ashcroft, along with rapper Kool G Rap and Mike D from the Beastie Boys. But instead of a triumphant success, an encapsulation of everything that Lavelle believed forward thinking about late nineties music, the album was perceived as a grand failure. Lavelle's vanity project, his ambitions played out as folly.

'*Psyence Fiction* turns the music business on its head, in that it posits the co-ordinator, Mo' Wax founder James Lavelle, as the creator, intrinsically more interesting than the shiny array of musicians he has summoned to do his bidding,' wrote John Mulvey in a scathing *NME* review. 'The tortuous gestation of UNKLE's debut album is already being mythologised by Lavelle as a kind of wracked, psychotic exploration of the human condition, with himself – a clubbable label boss with good ears, in essence – at the black heart of the project. The reality, perhaps predictably, isn't quite as good as it thinks it is. As a grandiose, bloated, egotistical folly, it says all you ever need to know about the state of the music business in 1998.'

Mulvey had nailed the problem. Apart from that fact that the album wasn't very good – a great record takes more than some celebrity guests and a handful of good ideas – what did someone like

James Lavelle actually do? Join the dots together? Hustle? Perhaps James needed to go back to Golgafrincham. Either way, he was crestfallen. Those reviews hurt. Worse, deep down, he knew they were right. 'I think we were very ambitious. I was so out of my depth,' he admitted. Then everything slowly started to go wrong in the golden world of James Lavelle. He had overreached himself. 'It just became too big and I just couldn't handle it,' said Lavelle. His partner had a baby daughter. 'She wanted to change. I didn't. The madness was starting to really kick in.'

The couple broke up and Lavelle continued his downwards spiral. His cocaine consumption intensified along with an increasing sense that he was drowning. 'It wasn't like there was a fucking problem with drugs, there was a problem with the fact I was doing everything. Coke, every day,' he said. 'It was burnout. Because you were running a label, you're DJing, you're trying to be a dad, but you're fucking that up. In the end, you're just fucking everything up because you can't get your head above water.'

In the past his life had been technicolour: fashion, parties, lauded DJ mates like Gilles Peterson. Now it was black and white – the decreasing circle of friends, the same repetitive behaviour. 'Sitting in a hotel room doing fucking cocaine cause you've just left the Met Bar and you're so fucked that ten of you pile upstairs to hire a suite because you know, to go on to the morning. That's what it became like.'

Yet Lavelle continued partying – blowing £30,000 partying, shopping and buying art on one crazy weekend in Tokyo. He even moved into the Metropolitan Hotel at one point – that bill ran into five figures. Then the money ran out – and with it, the friends. Lavelle ended up sleeping on a friend's floor and looking at £270,000 worth of debts for tax and 'other things'. 'You're spending two grand a week on getting fucked up. For five years. It's got to run out some time, hasn't it?' It was a low point. 'Just ending up in dark places. When everything just becomes unmanageable. But you're unmanageable as a human being. And I went to that place and it's a place I'm never going back to. You don't know that you're there until it's too late. And the thing with it all is, it's just a cliché.'

PAUL DALEY AND Neil Barnes should have been enjoying their jacuzzi session in a plush Brighton hotel. Leftfield's cinematic sound was in demand for television and advertising. They were on the last legs of their first tour, which had been a major success. Their album had sold more than a million copies and made the kind of major league impact nobody ever thought a dance music album would make. And yet they were fretting. Worrying about what they were going to do for their next album. Underworld aside, *Leftism* had arrived out of the blue. But electronic music albums packed with crushing beats and vocals had flooded in its wake – the Chemical Brothers had even had Oasis's Noel Gallagher guesting on their number one single, 'Setting Son', in late 1996. How could they do something different?

'I just said electronic,' Daley told Barnes. 'We got to go more electronic, more futuristic.'

Back in London, they sat in front of a pile of records, nonplussed. The follow-up to *Leftism* was a struggle that dragged on for years. It had taken them a year to get their tour ready – they had rerecorded their whole album to take it live as a mix of reggae-style sound system and live performance. Neil and Paul played percussion. Working out how to do just that on stage had been a marathon in itself. 'What's the best way to mike up a berimbau, which is a Brazilian instrument, without getting feedback,' recalled Daley. 'That took us about a month.'

On the tour's first night at the Paradise, a cavernous converted church in Amsterdam, the pair sat in the dressing room sick with nerves as sweat poured down the banister. They had tested out their high-powered sound system. It had blown all the glasses off the bar. 'Music's got to be loud, man,' said Daley. At Norwich University, during another sound check, the sound system shook free a huge metal grill from the venue's ceiling, which fell on an empty hall. On stage, reggae MC Cheshire Cat and singer Djum Djum provided a focus. The tour rolled to a climax at Brixton Academy in London. 'I remember seeing the queue go right round the block,' said Daley. 'I nearly had tears in my eyes, I was like, "This is fucking unbelievable. This is madness."'

During the show, tour DJ Billy Nasty found plaster falling from the ceiling falling onto his decks, it was so loud. 'Fucking hell!' Nasty declared. 'I thought the roof was coming in.' Daley shrugged. 'Another myth. Let it roll.' At the end of tour party, they presented each member of the road crew with a gram of cocaine. Daley was on a high. 'We had commercial success. We had critical success from all the people we looked up to in the scene.'

But Paul was not enjoying being famous. 'People coming up to you in the street was a really weird concept.' The record company wanted them to go and play America – they were told they could be huge. Daley refused, point-blank. 'Big money, dangling carrots. If you do this you get this, you're going to get this, if you don't do this, you're not going to get this. Got to break America. I was still like, "I don't give a fuck about America."' Leftfield never went.

During this time Neil's father died, but within weeks he was back in the studio. His young family was taking up more time. Paul, mean-while, was playing the single man. He bought a Porsche and a house in Camden. 'Living the rock 'n' roll dream.' A fissure appeared between them. That fissure was to become a chasm. Inexorably, the tight friendship and working relationship that made Leftfield function began to fall apart. 'I felt there wasn't much to come from Neil. I'll be honest. I'll say this now,' said Paul. 'And I felt disappointed that there was not much. And then, that made the rift between us even more.' Both had been handed big tax bills – Paul's alone was £90,000. 'And it was like, we've got to make an album.'

The recording process went on for three years. It became a joke. Hip hop legend Afrika Bambaataa arrived and talked alien conspiracies and the Zulu Nation. Hotshot video director Chris Cunningham was hired to make a shocking promo – a homeless man gradually loses his limbs as they shatter like broken porcelain. 'It was lagging, all the time, lagging for ideas and tired. Not good. Not good. This is not how it was before. So the rot starts to set in,' said Daley. South London rapper Roots Manuva was drafted in to vocal one of the album's most successful tracks, 'Dusted'. The furious electro groove of 'Phat Planet' became a soundtrack to a famous Guinness commercial that featured horses surfing in glorious monochrome. It launched the career of director Jonathan Glaser and was voted best TV ad of all time on a Channel 4 show. Other tracks seemed to go on forever. 'Afrika Shox', the Afrika Bambaataa track for instance, went through at least eight different versions.

'We were not particularly confident about whether we can pull this off,' said Daley. 'What are we? We musicians? We DJs? We producers? What are we? This is a fad? All those things go through your mind.' They had set their own standards so high, they weren't quite sure they could reach them. 'It's a confidence thing,' said Daley. 'We knew we had to come up with the goods. And the three years were spent in that studio trying to do something good.'

The album headed off in a hard, techno direction, which Barnes hated. Meanwhile cocaine had begun to creep into an already stressful studio, particularly for Paul, who by now was living his rock 'n' roll life to the full. 'It was never, ever my thing, although I got involved a bit. But it became a Leftfield thing,' said Barnes. 'We weren't getting on, we weren't communicating. I was a bit lost with what we were doing at stages. We'd spend weeks going round tracks, nothing was happening.'

They sat in sullen silences, coked up, not talking about what was – or rather, wasn't – happening. It was like the breakdown of a marriage. 'Arguments. Ego stuff. Doing drugs and feeling shit afterwards stuff. Taking it out on other people,' said Paul. 'And it was horrible because we'd been such good mates. It gradually got worse.' Neil half-heartedly tried a couple of times to confront the problems; Daley stonewalled him. 'I was being bullied by the atmosphere,' said Neil. 'I found it really difficult to talk to Paul, he wouldn't talk. He wouldn't open up – bit of a pun.'

In the end, Barnes gave in to the stronger character. 'I backed out then. I'd had enough. It nearly didn't get finished. I just thought we were completely losing the plot.' After three years' work, neither was particularly happy with the result. Even in the mastering studio, they had keyboards set up and were making changes. 'By the time we'd finished it and we was cutting it, I wasn't into it. I just didn't think it was very good,' said Daley. 'I wasn't happy with it.'

Neither were their fans. *Rhythm and Stealth* neither connected nor sold in the way that *Leftism* had – though it did sell 675,000 copies worldwide, enough to keep them in business. But it's a producer's record, all sonic perfection, little heart and no soul. 'Emotionally it doesn't engage me at all, like the first one did,' said Barnes.

THERE WAS STILL a tour to do, another year to be spent rerecording the album to take it out on the road. Daley was off DJing every weekend, partying, meeting girls. 'The thing is, when you become famous girls are much more attracted to you, that's the reality of it,' he said. More drugs. More distance. Neil spent more time with his family. Paul spent £150,000 building a completely soundproof recording studio in his house in Camden. They sat at opposite ends of the tour bus on the second tour, barely speaking. Daley wouldn't go on stage without doing cocaine beforehand. 'It chips away at your confidence. Makes you moody, makes you a different person,' Daley said.

On the outside, things couldn't have looked better. They played the main stage at Glastonbury Festival. They recorded the theme tune for Danny Boyle's next movie, his biggest yet, *The Beach*, starring Leonardo DiCaprio (Underworld's Tomato agency provided the opening graphics). On the inside, it was rotten. The last night of the tour was in Blackpool, on a Sunday. Daley made a decision. 'I walked off stage and I went onto the tour bus and I just said to myself, "That's it. I am never setting foot on stage with Leftfield ever again. That's it."'

Daley didn't have the nerve to tell the friend he'd been working with for ten years. He told their manager Lisa Horan instead and she delivered the blow. 'Which was probably not that brave of me really, at the time,' Daley said. 'I blew up the golden duck. Much to everyone's shock horror.' Neil had seen it coming. But it still hurt. 'It was a dreadfully heavy thing to have happened.' Neil suggested they meet up and talk about it. Paul refused.

Seven years later they had still not spoken, nor met. Neither had released a record since, bar the odd remix. In the studio at the bottom of his garden, Neil has worked on pop and rock and even folk-electric mixes, but never quite got to anything he felt happy with. On his laptop in Ibiza, Paul has recorded two albums' worth of intricately produced techno that he almost felt might be ready to be released, after some more tinkering. He DJs once a week at a club in Ibiza called – appropriately enough – the Underground, refusing to play CDs like most DJs today, still lugging boxes of vinyl around. Before each gig, he sits at home, waiting for the gig, unable to settle. He almost has the album ready, he said. Almost.

The royalties, the film earnings, the advertising commissions have provided a good living for Neil Barnes and Paul Daley. They haven't had to work. They've also had a lot of time to think, about music, obviously, and also about the way the relationship between them fell apart. Both, each sitting in his ivory tower, have clearly spent a lot of time dwelling on the past.

'Who's fault was it!' said Daley in the Ibiza sun, letting out a big, wheezing laugh. 'At the time it was my fault, I was an egotistical controlling cunt. I know.'

In leafy North London, as a chill set in and another train rumbled past the end of his garden, Neil paused. He hadn't written this down on his piece of paper. 'I never knew whether Paul went through that type of feeling of suddenly lying in bed and thinking, "God, should I let this go?"' he said. 'Cause you were always a really good friend and that's really what the whole relationship was based on.' Lost in the past, I think he was talking to Paul, not me.

WITH THE RESILIENCE and the thick skin that is the armour of every successful music business survivor, James Lavelle is still in the game. Partly to pay off that £270,000 bill, partly because he didn't know what else to do, he became a house DJ. By 2002 he was headlining the main room at London superclub Fabric and releasing albums for the

Global Underground mix CD series. He still tours the world – he is big in Romania, for some reason. He isn't on the A list, but makes good money and he has found a niche with a more percussive, funkier house sound. UNKLE survived too. It has now slimmed down to just Lavelle and his production partner and singer Richard File. Jarvis Cocker popped up on his last but one album, *Never, Never, Land*, which took an electronic/house direction. UNKLE's latest *War Stories* had a rockier style. Produced in Los Angeles with West Coast producer Chris Goss and featuring vocals from, among others, Queens of the Stone Age's Josh Homme, it was released in 2007.

But life on the star DJ circuit, despite its rewards, is a grind. 'It's just a constant up and down, all the time. One minute you're in this world where everybody fucking loves you and everything's for free and there's no boundaries.' Not like being a rock star, Lavelle mused, cocooned backstage behind security, meeting perhaps 20 people out of the whole audience of your gig, safe behind the crash barriers. 'When you're in a club with thousands of people – you finish and everybody's just there. You're starting at *three* in the morning. I think there's a huge price to pay.'

SIX
RANDOM BIRDS, METROSEXUALS AND TRANNIES

TUNE! UNDERWORLD – 'COWGIRL'

'Everything, everything, everything,' repeated Karl Hyde's voice over a techno groove that buzzed, bothered and bewitched.

Tribal Gathering promoter Paul Shurey had hoped his Maldives holiday with girlfriend Daydream would lead to some kind of clean-up – but they'd taken a big rock of crack and the pipe along with them, for one last blow-out. When that ran out, the resort manager sent the helicopter to Sri Lanka to get more drugs. But whatever it was that the helicopter came back with it certainly wasn't cocaine. It wasn't even something they could cook up into crack. So it got flushed down the toilet and the couple got down to a week of swimming and healthier living, interspersed with bouts of athletic sex on the balcony of their luxury hut, which they suspected the resort manager amused himself by spying upon.

Back in London things began to go wrong almost immediately. At Gatwick, Paul found he'd lost his car keys, so they left the motor in the car park and took a cab back to his luxury flat in Fulham. Getting there he found he'd lost his flat keys as well. A big Rasta guy was just getting out of a BMW nearby so Paul wandered over. 'Sorry, mate, I live just over the road and I've locked myself out. You haven't got any tools I could borrow to break in, have you?' he asked. The Rasta rooted in the back of the car and handed over a couple of screwdrivers. 'Thanks, mate. I'll bring them back,' said Paul. 'Don't worry,' replied the Rasta cheerfully, 'just keep them.'

After breaking into the flat, the couple got straight on the phone to their dealer – after all this stress, they felt they deserved it. The dealer didn't mind: he was getting so much business from the couple, he'd given up his day job. He came straight over with some fresh rocks of crack. The couple got straight back into the same old routine: drugs, obsessive fucking, more drugs, more sex.

Was it four or eight hours later when it happened? Did either of them know? Did either of them care? They were deep, deep into the sex marathon. Both were dressed in their usual rubber fetish outfits. In a carefully choreographed routine, Daydream was about to bring Paul to orgasm with one hand, while proffering the crack pipe with the other; so he would experience an intense double rush as he came at the exact second that a blizzard of crack rushed through his system.

Just then, at that exact second, a policeman walked into the room. And time froze.

Hard-core drug users sometimes display amazing presence of mind, lightning reactions, almost as if they were completely sober, rather than frazzled beyond the edge of sanity through hours of narcotic consumption. So it was with Daydream. Deftly hiding the crack pipe behind her arm, she rose to her feet, splendid and terrifying in her rubber outfit, somehow finding the most cut glass of accents, the most aristocratic of voices. Somehow finding the words. 'Oh officer, how awfully, terribly embarrassing,' she said, all of a fake fluster, edging towards him, keen to explain. 'I'm about to give my boyfriend a blow job and you walk in.' Just as quickly, the *policeman began to back nervously towards the door, away from this terrifying, plummy-voiced dominatrix, all the while explaining the major bank robbery nearby, the stolen getaway car found in their street, the door Daydream had left open when she went out to buy cigarettes.*

Later, when Paul's heart had started beating again, he realised why the Rasta hadn't cared about the screwdrivers: he was the getaway driver. That BMW was the getaway car. He and Daydream sparked up the crack pipe again.

IN THE 1980s, before ecstasy and house music took over Saturday night, the rules of engagement between the sexes in clubs were very simple. Men were men and they only danced to pull women. Otherwise they stood around the dance floor watching girls in pairs stepping around their handbags. Some clubs provided leaning posts with little shelves to put pints on for just this purpose. Dancing for girls involved swishing their forearms from side to side as if they were cleaning windows (this was something else men never did either). It was a routine immortalised by Susan Ann Sulley and Joanne Catherall, the backing singers/dancers in eighties synth-pop band The Human League. Indeed, singer Phil Oakey found the two girls, then just 17 and 18, doing just that dance at the Crazy Daisy nightclub in Sheffield on a Wednesday night.

A man might, if he was feeling strong enough to brave the jeers of his mates and the scorn of her friends, approach a woman and ask her to dance with him, at which point they would both step awkwardly around her handbag until she pointedly turned her back on him to signal the dance was over. 'Copping off', as snogging was called in the North, might happen later on. Club DJs helpfully provided 15 minutes of ballads just before the club shut at 2 a.m., to help potential lovers seal the deal – during these 'slowies' couples danced arms entwined, shuffling awkwardly around the floor. If ever a 'snog' or a sneaky grope of the bottom was ever going to occur, it was now. This ritual was known as the 'erection section', for obvious reasons. It usually prompted a last, desperate rush for the dance floor as lone males endeavoured to sweep up whatever half-pissed, single females were still available before the lights came on, reality bit and the night was over. Bar of course the kebab, the taxi queue and, if you were unlucky – or lucky, depending on your point of view – a fight.

Those were the days, eh?

SITUATED AT THE wrong end of the Dock Road, Bootle was never going to be Liverpool's most salubrious neighbourhood. But by 1990 its Quadrant Park nightclub, with its soundtrack of upbeat, piano-drenched Italian house, had become one of the liveliest nights in the country. In the middle of the dance floor was Jayne Casey, who had bounced around the music scene as singer and scene queen for more than a decade. Tonight she was raving it up on ecstasy. But despite the high, she was nervous. She had invited her friend Paul Rutherford, the moustachioed, openly gay dancer from Frankie Goes To Hollywood. And he was heading to the middle of the dance floor, wearing a white T-shirt emblazoned with the slogan 'QUEER AS FUCK'.

Casey had started raving after her fiancé Chris McCaffrey, bassist in local act the Pale Fountains, died tragically from a brain abscess. She had discovered a magic little pill on a previous night at Quadrant Park. 'Some mad-head from Bootle who cut this big brown thing in half and went, "E ah girl have that,"' she recalled. The sudden death of her partner had turned her world upside down. 'It was the man that I loved more than anyone else in the world. Pain makes you very sensitive to beauty. It makes you very tuned in to how incredible life is. For as low as you get, you get as high in a way, because it's so incredible, that we've got another day to live, you know. And they've gone. So it was in that state of mind that I found dance music.'

As a well-known face on Liverpool's colourful 1980s indie scene Casey had lived her life in Liverpool's most bohemian corners. But this was Bootle – a hard-as-nails, no-nonsense kind of place. Rutherford with his QUEER AS FUCK T-shirt and moustache began dancing wildly. 'Oh my God, how's this going to go down,' she thought. 'And all the scally boys just ran to him. And they were just kissing him and loving him and hugging him. And he was just like, "I'm just in heaven and I don't want to leave, the scally boys are kissing me!"' What happened? 'I think it was ecstasy, wasn't it?' said Jayne.

The 1990s had arrived and the rules had changed on the dance floor. 'People were introduced to more gay and lesbians and transvestites and stuff they'd never seen before. And accepted them as well,' observed Miranda Cook. And where would nineties clubbing have been without its transvestites? There haven't been many moments in pop history when swapping gender, at least for the night, was regarded as a good career move – Boy George and Marilyn in the heady new romantic days of the 1980s being an anomaly. The nineties club scene was one such moment and one of its most famous transvestite DJs was a man called Jon Cooper. Clad in designer gowns by John Galliano, he towered imposingly over the DJ booth, used the name Jon Pleased Wimmin and became one of the most popular DJ stars of the day.

For six years he charged up and down the motorway, shoving thousands of pounds a weekend into his Gucci handbag, spending a fortune on clothes and restaurants. 'Because it was me dressed as somebody else it was great. It was like watching somebody else. It was really like acting,' he said. Cooper made and spent a fortune. Then, just as the scene was getting too big, too commercial, he hung up his dresses and got out. Now 38, he was coming of a BA Honours degree course in Edinburgh when I met him. He doesn't do drag any more. But he still has the charm and the wickedly contagious sense of humour that made him such a popular, albeit unlikely, star.

He was born Jon Cooper in Africa, to missionary parents who were unfazed when they realised their son was gay. 'I was dressing up as Adam Ant I think, about eleven,' he revealed, with his machine-gun cackle. There is a big, rowdy dog in his Edinburgh flat overlooking a graveyard and he smokes roll-ups – something his transvestite DJ alter-ego would never have done. In his bathroom is a fashion spread he did in a Union Jack dress for *Mixmag*, blown up to poster size. He has scrapbooks with every interview and photo shoot he's ever done. 'It was just great fun. We didn't take ourselves seriously at all. It was just a scream-up,' he smiled. 'It was a Carry On film, with music.'

Jon went to the London College of Fashion and had a little shop in London's Kensington Market. He had a drag trio called the Pleased Wimmin who started dancing at Danny and Jenni Rampling's club Glam, held at Nicky Holloway's Milk Bar. They were dancing on podiums and falling off them, bouncing into club kids and the kind of beer boys they would never have normally met. 'People just opened right up and all these real cockney gangsters were like loving us,' said Jon. 'People accepting everyone. Probably due to the Es. It was a strange kind of drag we did because although it was glamorous, we never tried to pass ourselves off as women. We were just dressed up.'

The club's charged atmosphere provided plenty of sexual opportunities for the Pleased Wimmin. 'We ended up getting off with quite a lot of straight men at Glam. There was one guy we always used to get off with and we used to take turns with him in the toilet. He'd just come out of prison. And he'd be right up for it. All night we'd be giving him blow jobs.' He unleashed another contagiously filthy cackle. 'Which was brilliant! He was gorgeous so we didn't mind! We were like gangsters' molls!'

Jon was already obsessed with dance music, so when Danny offered him a stand-in DJ slot while he went on holiday, he jumped at the chance. He was a roaring success. Within a year, he found himself with an agent and a thriving DJ career. He was 22. 'Before I knew it I was literally doing like three gigs on a Saturday and two on a Friday and probably three during the week. That's when I realised, "Shit, this is not a hobby any more, it's a job."'

He had an anything goes approach to DJing that appealed to the 'handbag' crowd – he was a regular at Piers Sanderson's Fun nights in Birmingham, and at Cream. He pulled the biggest crowd ever at Wobble, also in Birmingham. 'You could really mix anything in and people would accept it,' he said. Gay club promoters, said Jon, didn't welcome him in the way the straight club scene did. 'I'd gone on to the straight scene as far as they were concerned,' he noted. 'They were so locked up in the whole sexual identity thing and would have been scared to go to a club that wasn't people just like them.'

He signed a record deal with East West Records – part of Warner Brothers – and released a single, 'Passion'. They bought him a Galliano suit for £1,800. He still has it. The cocaine came for free. 'At that point, any promoter would give you a gram when you turned up. So it wasn't like buying it or anything. It was just kind of on offer, so you would just take it.' His cocaine use never got out of hand. His spending did. He was earning up to £5,000 a weekend, in cash. 'I had this

Jean Paul Gaultier handbag thing that was like a bucket with a zip around it and it just used to be full of money. I remember one of my friends was like, "I can't believe you've earned all that money tonight just from playing records." But you're so used to doing it, you don't really think about it,' he said. 'It just becomes routine, doesn't it?'

The taxman didn't agree and slapped him with a bill for £70,000. 'Unless you were business savvy at the time, it was just like people throwing money at you really and you're like, "Great, yeah, it's more money to go away with or go shopping with or let's go out for dinner and get wrecked." It wasn't like, "Oh, I'm going to put 30 per cent away for that."' Luckily Jon had made money on a house he'd bought in Clapham – enough to pay the bill. But the club scene was beginning to bore him. 'It all went a bit Woolworths and I just thought, "Oh God, this is really egg and chips, I don't like it any more, I want to get out really." So that's what I did,' he said. He retired and moved to Edinburgh. 'Saved my sanity anyway. Nothing more degrading than having to keep going to clubs when they're just dwindling. It's like Disco Dad, trying to keep up with the kids.'

1994, BACK TO BASICS, Leeds. On the dance floor, three Yorkshire lads were dancing with each other, straight boys camping it up, throwing 'vogue' shapes, laughing, play-acting, having fun. The DJ was Ralph Lawson and he was playing one of the biggest club hits of the time, a sleazy, New York house record by Junior Vasquez called 'Get Your Hands Off My Man'. The record consisted of little more than a low-hung, compulsive groove and a screechy bitch queen male voice that repeated: 'Get your hands off my man. You hear me girl?'

House music was sexy. And it wasn't just sexy – it was comfortable being sexy. Acid house was like that from the off – be it the moaning orgasmic breakdown on Lil Louis's 'French Kiss', or S'Express's stupidly groovy 'Theme From S'Express' with the beautiful black girl in dreads saying 'I've got the hots for you'. This was in sharp contrast to the 1980s, when music was resolutely unsexy and obsessed with political correctness. The indie group the Au Pairs inadvertently captured this in their 1981 song 'Come Again (Urgh! A Music War)', in which a couple dissect an uncomfortable sexual experience over a strident indie beat. Boy George famously declared he preferred a cup of tea to sex. In the 1970s, Johnny Rotten described the conjugal act as 'two minutes of squelching noises'.

The low-slung, bass-heavy sensuality of records like 'Get Your Hands Off My Man' came from the gay clubs of New York. Vasquez was king of New York's Sound Factory, a gay club that had become a mecca for British DJs, promoters and clubbers. He was whispered to be the greatest DJ in the world – and having witnessed him in action, when I was stone-cold sober, at 6 a.m. one Sunday, mixing together the a cappella from Madness's 'One Step Beyond' with the funky organ-based house track by Jaydee called 'Plastic Dreams' and bursts of an air-raid siren – I think at that point he probably was. His record was on a New York independent label called Tribal, which released a sequence of equally funky, sleazy, bass-heavy and sexy records. In 1994, it was the coolest sound around. And gay wasn't just acceptable. It was eminently desirable. Every self-respecting superclub wanted a transvestite on the door.

In 1998 I travelled to Chicago with a BBC film crew to interview Frankie Knuckles, regarded by many as the first 'house' DJ. The film was a profile of Frankie and The Warehouse, the late seventies/early eighties underground mixed gay club where he used to DJ. It was the club that gave house music its name, though when we came to film its premises housed a law firm, who were agreeably stunned when we arrived with a large, very gay black man and told them house music started in what was now their boardroom.

In a Chicago hotel, we reunited a gang of the club's old regulars. Fifteen years later, they were a lively, vibrant crew, with respectable jobs, yet still imbued with the spirit that made them such party animals. They bought out photos and laughed over outfits and stories and got misty-eyed with memories. Listening to them reminisce, it seemed to me the codes of their club were the same as the codes governing British superclubs more than a decade later. The point of the night was the music. It didn't matter if you were gay or straight. Wallflowers were frowned on. Everybody was there to dance. At its best, that was what house music was about.

'A GORGEOUS GIRL and nightclubs go together really well, don't they? That's hand in glove. So if somebody's really, really beautiful and she walks into a club she'll get tons of attention and she'll work herself up the ranks within the inner circles and the DJ circles,' said Jayne Casey. 'So there is a level when nightclubs and beauty definitely go together.'

In the 1990s, female glamour came back in a way that hadn't been seen in pop culture for decades. And it wasn't just ditzy club bimbos, all kinds of girls were dressing up. Career girls. Post-feminist girls. These were the sort of girls who didn't only define themselves by how men reacted to them. But they too wanted to be princesses on a podium on Saturday night. They wanted to show off. It was all very different from the androgynous rave days. 'It got sexy again,' noted Dave Beer. 'You started thinking, "Look at her, fucking hell!" She'd been around you for the last few years, but she'd been in a rugby shirt and a pair of jogging bottoms and a Berghaus coat. You never noticed she had a figure.'

Short silky dresses, fluffy bra tops, heels, hot pants, spaghetti straps – was it money, discos, or just fashion? Certainly superclubs provided a sense of occasion that hadn't been there before, that demanded an outfit. And Britain was going out, like never before. Times were changing and everybody wanted to fit in. *Loaded* magazine and the deluge of men's magazines that followed it had made an impact. Launched in 1994, it moved the goalposts in the game between the sexes. Suddenly the word 'glamour' itself didn't mean page three girls, but something sexier, something much more iconic, something much more, well, glamorous.

Loaded successfully persuaded well-known female celebrities of all kinds – from actresses like Elizabeth Hurley to television presenters like Zoë Ball, Melanie Sykes, Sara Cox and Denise Van Outen – to pose provocatively in their underwear. This was no longer exploitative, it was supposedly 'empowering'. Celebrities like these found an expensively shot magazine cover did their careers no harm and played up a laddish image. The 'ladette' was born, girls who partied as hard as the boys and liked football. The superclub was a perfect playground for them.

But at the same time, because music and drugs and adventure and making friends had become the dominant themes of a night out, sex – 'copping off' – was no longer the central goal. The 'erection section' had disappeared into the dry ice. And women found a freedom to dress in a more sexually provocative way without sending out the wrong signals. 'The idea of Saturday night being about copping off probably took a bit of a back seat,' said James Barton. 'Cause Saturday turned into a full-on fucking party. There would be girls around but that wouldn't be your main focus.' Ecstasy made everything seem warm and sexy, but it also desexualised nightclubs. Sex, if it was going to happen, came after. Jayne Casey became PR boss of Liverpool superclub Cream in 1994 and she noticed the shift in sexual mood.

'It was quite a good time for the women,' she said. 'A girl could have loads of fun and dance quite sexy with somebody, or dance madly on the podium, show off and feel her own sexuality, without feeling threatened that she had to give out. They did explore their sexuality, under the influence of drugs, but also in quite safe environments, where the guys were also on the same drugs, also a little bit feminised by it and not that predatory really.'

Clubs are about display and men got on those podiums and showed off too. They became more body conscious, started thinking about they way they looked and dressed. 'The guys became quite fashion conscious,' said Casey. 'All the guys looked great. And they related to being somewhere where there were other guys dressed similar to them.' 'Wearing tighter, better-fitting clothes, swapping fashion tips with other male clubbers – it was the beginning of the personal grooming vogue for men that would later be dubbed "metrosexual",' said Miranda Cook. 'Men were wearing tight tank top things and things that had been stereotypically gay.'

Magazines that followed in *Loaded*'s wake, like *FHM* and a revitalised *GQ* (though it had been launched earlier), went big on male grooming to catch the new audience. But none of them ever matched the verve of *Loaded* at its peak. The magazine was perceptive, irreverent, stylish, witty and ironic. Irvine Welsh and Nick Hornby wrote for it. By 1998 it was selling 450,000 copies a month. It made fun of male foibles while at the same time celebrating them. All of which fitted perfectly into this sexy, fun new clubland. *Mixmag* also featured a high quota of fabulous-looking club girls. They weren't difficult to find. They would follow photographers around clubs, demanding to have their picture taken.

And every club promoter and DJ wanted a babe on their arm.

Jeremy Healy usually dated models. For a long while, this was Birmingham clubber and model Philippa Lett – who later became briefly famous in the Sisters of Murphy's ad campaign. He was linked with Naomi Campbell, though he insisted they were just friends. 'I think I was a model groupie, to be honest with you. It is a powerful elixir, the beauty of stunningly beautiful women like that. I've had some amazing times.'

Feeling the pressure to compete in this moneyed, laddish world, I wasn't the only middle-class, liberal *Mixmag* journalist to cajole a girl-friend into playing the trophy babe role – ironically, of course, darling – for the night with promises of free champagne and all-expenses paid nights out and five-star hotels. Even if those hotels were in Birmingham or Leeds. That night out with your smart, witty, glammed-up girlfriend could be a blast. Or it could go horribly wrong if, for instance, an idiot dismissed her with a sexist flick of his finger and a comment like 'stand over there, darlin', the men are talking', leaving you to deal with her resultant wrath. But in truth, *Loaded* had hit a nerve. It is probably no longer necessary to point out – though it was at the time, coming off the back of the horribly politically correct 1980s – but men love to be around glamorous women. Because of sex and ego, obviously, but also because we are clumsy, grubby oafs and being next to someone lovely and feminine smoothes all our awkward, rough edges and makes us feel special. For a while, softened by ecstasy, policed on the door by trans-vestites, clubs became a safe, neutral zone for games like this to take place.

THE LIMOUSINE PURRED to a halt outside Nottingham club Venus. Immediately the queue of clubbers outside began to buzz with antici-pation. In 1993, limousines were still an unusual sight in the UK: they signified celebrity not, as they do now, a bunch of lairy suburbanites on a stag or hen do. A burly, brilliantly unconvincing transvestite got out brandishing a pistol and started firing blanks into the air, followed by a shorter man also in drag. Enter the Trannies With Attitude. Inside, they began DJing – badly. The big one, called Paul Fryer, shouted and sang over the mike. The little one, Nick Raphael, kept playing records that collided into each other. The crowd went wild. Sasha, due to be DJing in another room, was 90 minutes late for his set. He was too busy dancing on the bar, shouting, 'Go on! Play another one!' Trannies With Attitude, two straight men from Leeds, had taken the transvestite DJ idea one step further. It was now a cabaret. And they became superstar DJs.

The idea came late one night – so late, it was actually early the next morning. They were at the flat where Paul Fryer and his then partner Suzi Mason lived in Leeds. The couple ran a small, mixed gay night in Leeds called the Kit Kat Club at Leeds High Flyers club, which was attracting a glamorous crowd. Nick Raphael, the club's promotions manager, had befriended them. Raphael and Fryer were charged up on brandy and cocaine. And they'd already been to Manchester gay club Flesh dressed up as women.

'If a bloke wears a skirt, he's a puff to a beer-drinking rugby football lad who goes out on a Friday night and has a fight,' said Suzi. 'How about if we announced ladies only night, but it wasn't ladies only? Boys come, but you have to come dressed as a lady?' Fryer and Raphael laughed their heads off. But who was going to DJ? They were. Fryer said: 'Fuck Niggers With Attitude [the gangsta rap group]. We're Trannies With Attitude. TWA.' Nick loved the idea. 'We're doubled up laughing. Half a mouthful of brandy and coke coming out of my nose,' he recalled. 'And I went, "Yeah and I'm Danny Rampant and you're Jeremy Feely."'

They DJed at the Kit Kat Club in Leeds and it went down a storm. Then Raphael got a phone call from James Baillie who was running Nottingham's Venus club down the road. 'I'll give you 600 quid, a limo to drive you down, drugs and girls, free booze all night. You DJ. You do four hours.' Raphael said no but he called Fryer anyway. '600 quid?' said Fryer. 'Fuck it, I'll put a dress on.' That was it. They got an agent, a career and spent the next six years touring the country as star DJ turns, earning hundreds of thousands of pounds along the way and consuming monumental quantities of drink and drugs.

The Kit Kat Club closed in December 1992. In April 1993, Suzi Mason, Paul Fryer and Nick Raphael started a bigger, brasher, bolder night at the Leeds Warehouse – the mixed-gay Leeds club Vague. It was to become a national phenomenon that though it only ran for three years is still celebrated by its regulars today. They even have a Facebook group. 'It was very sexy. It was very hedonistic but it was more about your own personal sexual expression, rather than copping off with somebody,' said Mason. Trannies With Attitude were the DJs.

To get into the club, you had to get past 'door whore' Madame JoJo. Boys were asked to kiss each other – and generally obliged. The queues went round the block. In a 1996 *Mixmag* feature, one clubber, Rob North, remembered being confronted at the door by JoJo brandishing a can of squirty cream. 'Do you spit or swallow?' JoJo asked him. 'If you don't give me right answer you can't come in.' He told her he swallowed. She squirted cream on his tongue. He swallowed – and got in.

It was a club where you might see two lesbians kissing on the bar all night, or a man naked except for a coating of gold spray paint and think nothing of it. But this wasn't cosmopolitan London: this was Leeds, in 1993. 'The barbarians were at the door,' laughed Fryer.

Vague was a sexually charged utopia; Fryer, Mason, Raphael and their gang as wild as their club. 'The Vague gang in Leeds at that time was the arty, creative, nutters who were also sexually ambiguous,' said Fryer. Soon Vague was one of the country's most notorious and most desirable clubs and profiled in a spread in the *Observer* Sunday magazine. Nick's middle-class, North London parents were appalled.

'I was on a double-page spread inside, make-up on, wig off, sweating, with my hairy chest, bra on, mini-skirt on, with a gay guy on one arm and on the other hand, JoJo, in a *thing*,' laughed Nick. 'My mum called and said "Did we pay all that money to send you to school for you to embarrass me like this? Everybody in North London has seen it! We are a laughing stock."'

TWA have long since retired from DJing, but they remain friends. They make an unusual duo. Raphael is Jewish, short, business-minded, clever and charming. Private-school educated, an operator, a hustler. Fryer is big, charismatic, arty, chaotic and from a working-class, Irish background. Now a successful record company executive, Raphael is married to Amanda, a former model and Vague regular. The couple live in a big, white house in St John's Wood in London and have two children. Paul, now an artist, lives in Finsbury Park. I met them together, over dinner, at Nick's home and hear their story.

Raphael comes from a family of entrepreneurs – his father bought the Rubik Cube into the UK. He was a promising footballer and signed a deal with Bradford City Football Club, which enabled him to go to university as well. After eight months he had realised he was never going to be more than a journeyman footballer, slogging out his career in the lower divisions. 'I hit the wall of truth, the honesty factor. You're okay, mate, but you ain't the best,' he said. He was 19. For someone as ambitious as Nick Raphael, average was never going to be good enough.

Paul Fryer is eight years older. His father was an installations engineer who was killed cycling to work when Paul was 16. His mother brought them up. 'I became very rebellious after my father died. Not surprisingly really,' Paul said. 'But I was always a weird kid. I would try and get them to go to Japanese restaurants when I was nine and they would just laugh at me. They must have thought they had Little Lord Fauntleroy.'

Nick Raphael put on his first club when he was still at school. In a school project, he earned £7,000 putting on a school disco. Nick had discovered ecstasy at an orbital M25 rave near London – the archetype E experience. He ended up yabbering to strangers at a service station. 'Every time I heard a house record from that night on, everything in my body had a warm glow.' He took it again in Leeds, with a bunch of mates at a club night at the university, where they discovered the drug's liberating effects on male behaviour. 'Everybody in there thought we were four gay guys. We were at the front of the stage, hugging each other.'

He landed a job at the High Flyers club and started booking London DJs to come and play in Leeds. 'I realised there was a group of us, desperate to see these DJs.' Raphael quickly figured out which buttons to press. Jeremy Healy was one of the first DJs he persuaded up to Leeds. Nick phoned him up and asked him what he was being paid: £120 a gig, two gigs a night, said Healy. 'I tell you what, Jeremy, I'll pay you £350 and I'll pay your travel and I'll put you in a four-star hotel,' said Raphael. 'Instead of doing three gigs running round London, you do one gig, then go and get plastered with us, stay in a hotel and it's all on me.' Healy said: 'Love it.'

Fryer met Suzi Mason at Jacob Kramer Art College in Leeds, where they studied with Damien Hirst: Hirst's brother Bradley would later create the art installations for Vague. Fryer sang in a synth-pop band called Bazooka Joe and when he met Raphael he was designing flyers and living on the dole. Fryer didn't care much about money. 'It was mainly beer and drugs. And buying weird clothes,' said Fryer. Suzi arrived back to Leeds after studying at Goldsmiths in London, shocked at the contrast. 'It was a cultural wilderness,' she said. 'Half of Leeds was boarded up. The recession had really hit. And it was really, really dull and so we just used to invent these places in our heads that didn't exist.'

When they came up with the idea for Vague, Flesh promoter Paul Cons, then one of the most influential promoters in the North, was convinced it wouldn't work. 'You can't have a club that is mixed from the word go,' Cons told them. 'Gay people won't be safe in it. Straight people won't wear it. You're wasting your time.' But Vague ran for three years, regularly packing 800 plus in every Saturday night. The pranks became more absurd. There were art exhibits – a man sitting inside a box. One night they turfed the entire club. Another time the lighting rig caught fire and Fryer hung upside down, still half in drag, with an extinguisher trying to put it out. The crowd cheered and kept dancing, they thought it was part of the show. On another occasion, they filled the club with sand and turned it into a beach.

'Occasionally creative people and hedonism and the right drugs all meet up with some good music and the right moment,' said Fryer. 'We were in the right place at the right time. It was offered to us on a plate. It was like someone saying, "Do you wanna come in here? Here's the door. This is the way, step inside." And we did of course.'

Nick's wife Amanda, then an 18-year-old model, was a club regular. 'To not have to queue at Vague was my goal in life,' she said. Nick wooed her by walking on his hands: she was unimpressed. Later she found out he was the DJ. She loved the freedom of Vague. 'It was the place to go and run around with virtually nothing on and not think twice about it. Not be intimidated. Not being sexual,' she said. 'It fits in with the whole drug culture and everything else, to lose your inhibitions in that way.' The couple consummated their relationship at a Leeds hotel, covered in summer fruit pudding. There were two gay friends also in the room, who went down to reception, wrapped in sheets, to find condoms. 'Love's young dream,' said Fryer. The crew were later banned from the hotel.

For Suzi Mason, whose father was in the rag trade, the club was about freedom from prejudice. 'My father was Jewish and my mum wasn't,' she said. 'I was put in an orthodox Jewish school.' Jews believe the line is carried through the mother: Mason's mother wasn't Jewish, therefore neither was she. 'I wasn't accepted by the Jewish kids cause of my mother. And I wasn't Jewish. I was not one thing nor the other, and I was quite badly bullied. I didn't believe in segregation and I certainly didn't believe that because what your preference was sexually that you had anything more in common with somebody. It was more to do with what was going on in your mind.'

In this abandoned atmosphere, there was plenty of sex happening in the club's darker corners and toilets. But really Vague was about personal sexual expression. 'Boys coming in there in dresses and skirts and make-up. Straight boys. They just wanted to explore something and were given absolute freedom to do it without any prejudices or pressures,' said Suzi. 'For me it was a social club. It was like social work really. The amount of people that used to pour their hearts out to me.' The club celebrated its second birthday with actress Liz Dawn from *Coronation Street* singing a medley of old hits. 'My best night in 50 years of show business,' she later said. On the surface, things at Vague couldn't have been better.

TWA's DJ career took off. 'I wanted to make people listen,' Paul Fryer told *Mixmag* writer Mark White in a feature in 1996. 'I wanted my voice to be heard. Wanted to be famous.' TWA loved publicity and sought it out, regularly phoning up *Mixmag*'s Club Country column with their latest drug-fuelled antics. They knew that stories like these fed their profile as mad-cap guest DJs, albeit novelty ones and club promoters. They joined the superstar DJ circuit, earning up to £6,000 a weekend and spending most of it on drugs, clothes, hotels and parties; whatever they could get their hands on. By this point Vague was turning over £600,000 a year and the DJing career doubling that. 'I remember regularly having £2,000 in cash on a Saturday – and then going back to Leeds with a hundred quid,' said Fryer. 'And I'd spent £1,900 on booze and drugs in two days.' Raphael's business sense saved them from tax nightmares: he registered them for VAT and ensured they paid tax.

They coordinated their outfits: air stewardesses, Hollywood stars, whatever. In the beginning it took 90 minutes to get ready. They got it down to 25 minutes flat. Amanda would help out. 'Amanda would walk in, we'd both be putting our bases on, ourselves,' said Nick. 'And she'd start on one set of eyes. Second set of eyes. One set of lips, second set of lips. We'd put our own false eyelashes on while she was doing the other set.' Paul laughed. 'Which were massive. Like big fucking spiders,' he added.

They might not have looked like women, but at least they looked good – until they got behind the decks. 'I'd look round at Nick, literally after five minutes his wig would be off. His make-up would be all over his face. I'd be still perfect. So I'd take my wig off too and stand there. The make-up would wear off your nose, so it looked like somebody had Copydexed your nose, cause it was the wrong colour,' said

Fryer. Both claimed that while single, dressing up as women did wonders for their sex lives.

'Shagging in drag was the easiest thing in the world,' said Nick.

'A lot of women are curious about what it would be like to fuck the same sex,' added Fryer. 'The next best thing is to find yourself a bloke in drag. Then you can find out what it's like and still get shagged at the end of it. There's also another element, which is, "Are you gay?"'

'They'll turn you,' said Nick.

'You'd say, "Might be, might not,"' Paul insisted. 'Because obviously they want to find out and there's only one real way to find out. They'd then be doubly delighted because if you were and they managed to get it up with you, then that's kind of two very peculiar birds with one stone.'

A SUNNY LEEDS Sunday and the Vague after party was at a hairdresser saloon, which its owner occasionally turned into a post-club café. High as a kite and wearing a black Armani suit that had started the night immaculate, Paul Fryer was idling on the building's roof, leaning on a skylight, observing proceedings. Thirty feet below, 30-odd people were relaxing, drinking tea and beers. All of a sudden Fryer lost his balance and plummeted through the skylight, crashing into a plastic table, which exploded. The café went deadly quiet. Somebody started screaming, 'Get an ambulance!' Nick thought. 'Fryer's killed himself.'

Fryer lay there, still conscious, thinking, 'This really hurts.' But somehow he was not seriously injured. 'I thought I'd got two choices,' he said. 'Lie here and look like a complete cunt. Or get up and pretend that nothing happened. So I just got to my feet. Walked up to the bar and said, "Can I have a cup of tea please?"'

TWA partied on. They would go out on a Thursday with local promoters, DJ somewhere on a Friday, do Vague on a Saturday and finish of at the Faversham pub in Leeds on a Sunday. They might sleep four hours the whole weekend. They were hammered the whole time: cocaine, ecstasy, alcohol, whatever. 'We did ketamine. We didn't care. We were experimenting,' said Raphael. 'And I was young. We were DJing and earning loads of money.'

Vague's last night in Leeds was its third birthday party. There was a food fight with green jelly and flour bombs and a wind machine and glitter. And then the club came to a shuddering halt. It ended messily, like a love affair gone wrong. Which in a way is just what had happened. Paul and Suzi split up in winter 1994. In June 1996, after four months of persuasion, Paul bought the Vague name from Suzi for £25,000. Fryer believed that she was going to leave clubland. Instead she started promoting for rival club I-Spy, at Nato, just down the road. Worse, without her input, club numbers began to fall. The Leeds Warehouse kicked Paul and Vague out and welcomed in Sheffield handbag night Love To Be.

Fryer took it badly. He sent out a series of commemorative cards, based on the cigarette cards of the past, detailing his interests and grievances including 1970s synthesisers and Philip Larkin poems. One card, Number Two in a set that Vague regulars still treasure, pictured a housewife with an iron and was entitled: 'Smoothing things over'. Overlead, it simply read: 'Why bother?' The break-up, the love affairs, the madness and the tawdry business bickering that had ended the night were detailed in Mark White's *Mixmag* feature in 1996, entitled 'Love Changes Everything'. It was club drama writ large, as soap opera.

But the trio had held back one crucial fact from this feature. Paul Fryer and Suzi Mason's relationship had ended when Suzi left him –

for a woman. 'Obviously a direct result of being involved in that environment and that club,' Suzi said now. The libertine politics of the club had blown up in their faces. It was all just too terribly ironic. 'It was almost like somebody had said, "All right, you're doing all this work, come on, you better understand it properly for what it really is,"' she explained. Suzi stayed in Leeds but eventually split up with the woman she left Paul for. Since then she has had a daughter with a male partner. She recently split with him and is now a single mother, but best friends with her former female lover. The lives of the Vague characters are still complicated.

Trannies With Attitude called it a day as well. The cocaine had begun to bore them. Their audiences were getting younger and less discerning. The drag outfits had long since become fancy dress – one night they both went out as celebrity DJ Jimmy Savile. Nick got a job as an A&R man at London Records and stopped taking drugs – he was getting panic attacks. One night he looked out at the crowd he was DJing and realised he hated them. Fryer decided not to carry on alone.

Dinner with the former transvestite DJ stars was drawing to an end. Nick Raphael is now an executive at Sony BMG Records. He signed Charlotte Church. Then he dropped her. Paul Fryer became a successful contemporary artist. He dated the artist Abigail Lane and worked for the fashion house Fendi. Now he exhibits all over the world and his works sell for up to six figures. 'Vague, DJing, singing, working at Fendi, all the things I've done in many respects have been avoidance tactics. Because I knew what was coming up and I had to do it one day,' he said. 'I was born to be an artist.' Vague was just another club in Leeds, but at the same time it wasn't. The people behind the big superclubs – Ministry, Cream, Gatecrasher – were ultimately in it for the money. The people behind Vague were in it for the adventure.

Typically conceptual, Fryer saw Vague as a living artwork, not a disco. And in a sense, he was right.

Since then, Fryer has been the catalyst for Nick's growing art collection. Nick has a number of Banksy originals, as well as some of Paul's works. 'My interest in art has come from Paul,' he said. We were lingering over the last of the wine, with Raphael yawning and fretting about his business meeting in New York the next day. But Fryer couldn't resist a dig at Raphael's involvement in the number one single for *X Factor* winner Chico, 'It's Chico Time'.

'I had a number one record,' said Raphael, defending himself, results-orientated as ever.

'It's like Pol Pot explaining why he suffocated all them fucking people in the killing fields, isn't it?' Fryer shot back. 'They've always got a justification.'

'Pol Pot sold a lot of records this year,' Raphael countered.

'TWA reunion, Nick?' asked Paul mischievously, and the pair collapsed into laughter.

I am becomingly increasingly concerned about promoters insisting that women (babes) are being pushed away from the dance floor by these essentially male promoters and treated as a commodity, by which I mean that a better-looking female crowd induces a greater number of men, more media attention and a hipper status.

I can understand that there does have to be a door policy and why, but to get into a venue we are told to glam it up and to look gorgeous. I like to dress up, it gives you a sense of occasion, but I can't dance in high heels, I need to wear comfortable clothes and just tie my hair back. So far I've had no problems entering clubs, but the way clubland is heading, how much longer?

Is it soon to become a distasteful sight to see a woman (babe)
out of it and saying fuck off to all the men, she's here for herself?
Elizabeth, Hastings, Letter to *Mixmag*, July 1995

AS COCAINE BECAME more and more the club drug *du jour*, the sexual dynamic changed. If ecstasy heightens emotions and feminises men, cocaine has the opposite effect: it brings out ego, arrogance and lust. 'It got a bit predatory,' said Jayne Casey. Sonique, one of the biggest stars of the late nineties, observed this in the club crowds she played to. 'Cocaine is an edgy type of drug. It's very sexual as well. Guys see some girl who's doing all those moves and they feel they need to go over there. It's an aggressive horny. Whereas before it was a lovely, sexual thing.'

Inevitably a sleazier side to what had always been an uneasy alliance between male want and female beauty emerged. Clubs began putting pressure on girls to dress up just to get in. And as the 1990s marched on, the DJ groupie arrived. So much so that a term was coined, 'Jockey Slut', which became the name of a Manchester-based club magazine whose founders still run the club Bugged Out today. While following Judge Jules around the country, Miranda Cook noticed the increasing number of club girls hanging around the DJ booth trying to attract his attention.

'He was too polite to tell them to piss off. So I just called them random birds. It took off,' she said. DJs had become celebrities and celebrities attract girls. 'Everyone faced the DJ when they were out. They just became the focus point. And also they were being written about and they were on Radio 1 and in more people's faces. And they were the star prize for a lot of girls. Like pop stars really.'

The after party became the perfect place for a groupie to strike. 'Whoever the DJs wanted, the DJs could have, really, couldn't they?'

said Jayne Casey. 'You saw girls shag two DJs in a night. That was not that uncommon. And you'd just be like, "Oh, God, get a life." I saw [superstar DJ name deleted] and somebody else share a girl. Literally, one walked out of the room and the other one said, "She's in there if you want her." And the other guy walked in.'

As groupies became more common, everyone in a club's inner circle would know what to do if a DJ's actual girlfriend or wife turned up. It was like the rock 'n' roll adage: what goes on tour stays on tour. 'Occasionally they would have to be got rid of and told that the wife's here,' Miranda said. 'I was always taking the piss out of them. "What are you getting out of this, at the end of the day? You're going to go and tell your mates that you slept with a DJ? Are they going to be impressed by it? If so, what kind of people are they?"'

Birmingham was something of a centre when it came to glamorous club girls who wanted to hang out with DJs and club promoters. Promoter and DJ Phil Gifford, a former hairdresser whose parents were market traders, was one of those who benefited. His club Wobble, run with partner Si Long, was the anti-corporate acid house club, whose flyers featured the club's logo clasped between faceless, naked girls' breasts or buttocks. Wobble helped him build a lucrative DJing career. He wasn't in the top division, but he could still earn £500 a show and do three gigs a weekend. And he got groupies.

'You would be jumping up and down a bit, looking at the crowd. And without a doubt, most places, if you had a decent set and it was a good night, there would be two or three girls within the first few rows, who'd catch your eye. You'd think, "Hmm, that one's the nicest",' Gifford said. 'You'd end up going back to some party or going back to the hotel or going back with one of the girls you'd spotted on the dance floor. Groupies. There were girls who used just to hang around with DJs and club promoters. Girls that used to stand at the side of the decks.'

I was in the VIP room of a club in Scandinavia after one star DJ finished his set. A blonde girl who'd been on the dance floor was led over to meet him by one of the promoters. Everyone left them alone. They lit cigarettes, had a drink and got chatting. The promoter wandered back over to me with a smile on his face. 'That's a load off my mind,' he said. 'I don't have to worry about getting him laid now.' Next morning, the DJ had a smug smile on his face. One female friend dated an American DJ for a while. The relationship ended when she discovered his 'rider' – the provisos acts and DJs insist on when playing a show – included the condition that the promoters arrange a blow job for him.

But the DJ groupie scene wasn't always as well organised. Especially back in the hotel room after party, when cocaine brought out a meaner edge in some of the guys. 'There was an underlying very nasty side to that which I didn't like, cause obviously you get sexual tension and it's how it's dealt with,' said Amos Pizey, the MC, producer and club face who travelled with his friend Jeremy Healy. 'I hated that slightly bullying element you'd get around groupies, I found it really distasteful. I got into quite a few physical altercations. It would always split, there'd be a really level bunch and then there'd be, "All right darling, come here." And that's not what it was about.'

Some DJs and record company executives who travelled a lot got a taste for high-class prostitutes, especially in places like Asia, South American and Eastern Europe, where prostitution is part of the social fabric for many men. Lurid tales abounded of drug-fuelled orgies with beautiful, willing young hookers – the 'willing' part the most likely part of the fantasy, or a convincing acting job on the part of the girls. In druggy, dark, after-club situations 'spit roasting' – where two men share a girl, one at each end, so to speak – became popular with some. Years later, 'spit roasting' became a staple of tabloid speak, after a number of high-profile cases involving professional footballers and girls.

Travelling the world as a superstar DJ, Dave Seaman had plenty of encounters with starry-eyed club girls. But one encounter, with a girl he'd met playing a show in Sydney, Australia, backfired badly. 'It was a girl that I'd slept with, but fully consensual and everything. After a gig,' he said. 'She kind of got the wrong idea.' Seaman had fallen asleep. He woke up to find the girl had gone home, packed up all her clothes, come back and was busily unpacking them into his hotel room wardrobe. 'I'm like, "Oh no, you've got the wrong idea,"' he said. 'Then she went a bit loopy loo, started crying, "Think you can just fuck me and then throw me away?" I was like, "No, no." God, what's happening here?' He managed to calm the situation and got her out of the room and hoped that was the end of it.

Back home in the UK, in the converted church where he lived in Henley, he was sleeping off another heavy, cocaine-fuelled weekend when the phone rang. It was 9 a.m. on a Monday and the Canadian High Commission were phoning to tell him his visa for a short DJ tour he was booked to play in Canada was being denied. The girl in Sydney had filed a rape charge with Sydney police – and then reported the charge to a friend who worked at the Canadian High Commission in Australia. 'She knew from my diary that I was going to Canada,' said Dave. He hired a solicitor in Australia and got the charged dropped. But it was too late for his Canadian tour and he lost £30,000 in fees.

Dave also had a longer affair with Julia, a leggy, beautiful dancer from Moscow's Club 13. He knew no Russian and she spoke very little English: it was the perfect club romance. 'We couldn't talk to each other. That was definitely a drugged-up thing I think. It's where the sex, drugs and acid house comes into it,' he said. 'I managed to get her a visa to come over. And managed to get her to come travelling with me, certain places.' She toured Australia with him and lived at his chapel in Henley for a couple of months, learning English. But she ran into visa problems, which spelt the end of the affair. 'It wasn't working, unless I was going to go to Russia every few minutes which was not where I wanted to be living.'

SUMMER 1998, MANUMISSION in Ibiza in full swing and it wasn't just the dance floor. The club's notorious sex show had surpassed itself. Tonight, for once, it wasn't promoters Mike and Clare Manumission simulating sex on stage. The performance starred a naked, very bendy man on a trapeze, a man so well endowed that he could perform fellatio on himself – which is just what he was doing. DJ Sonique was playing records to soundtrack the show, as she normally did. But this time, her mother Shirley was in the DJ booth with her. 'Son, look, look, look!' she exclaimed to her daughter, jabbing a finger towards the trapeze. Sonique sighed. She'd seen it all before at Manumission. 'Mum,' she said, 'I really don't like looking at things like this.'

It wasn't that Sonique was prudish. 'I like to think that I could handle most situations as long as I don't have to get involved,' she explained. It was just that she was concentrating on what music would fit. DJing to a live sex show in a giant club with 8,000 people in it required a degree of delicacy and pace. 'You just think about how you want to have sex and what you want playing while you're making love – but obviously on a slightly hornier, energetic vibe,' she said. 'I was quite proud of what I was playing.' But you have to admire her mother's resilience given the kind of situation her daughter might throw at her. Just a few years later she would be introduced to Sonique's latest boyfriend, Prince Albert of Monaco. 'Yeah,' smiled Sonique. 'They got on.'

Sonique's is a unique story. She turned the innate sexism of club-land on its head and she became the only female superstar DJ. The 1990s club hierarchy was heavily male-dominated and women had to be tougher than the men to get ahead. A few did, but not many. There were powerful DJ agents like Lynn Cosgrave and Cath Mackenzie. Cosgrave particularly became a major dance industry player. Shelley Boswell, the promoter of Club For Life at London's Gardening Club, often outdid her laddish promoter contemporaries in the hard-partying stakes. She once sent out a metre-long flyer for her club, with a picture of herself naked inside a pink fake fur border. The night was called Centrefold.

In the early days of acid house, the DJs Nancy Noise and Lisa Loud made a name for themselves. Lisa Loud worked at record companies and in promotions and still DJs now. DJ Lotte carved a successful career towards the end of the nineties, even hosting occasional shows on Radio 1. But her most famous role was playing herself in an episode of Channel 4's *Faking It*, coaching a classical cellist how to pass herself off as a DJ. The plummy-voiced cellist succeeded, in just four weeks, in convincing a panel of experts that she was a real DJ. She could mix, talk the lingo, the lot. It was great exposure for DJ Lotte. Not such a great advert for the 'art' of DJing, though.

But Sonique was the only one who made it into the superstar DJ league. She got the money, the high life and the celebrity boyfriend. She first tasted stardom as the singer in late eighties pop-acid act S'Express, remodelled herself as an all-singing, all-dancing star DJ, then made her fortune with one all-conquering pop-dance hit. She has a strong, individualistic style that is glamorous and yet androgynous: an athletic black girl with short hair, a fierce, no-nonsense personality, a lot of warmth and a richly contagious, warm laugh. DJing might have been a man's world but that didn't faze Sonique.

Number one, she could do it. 'Because I was a woman it was very uneasy. You would turn up. You knew they were saying, "Bet you can't fucking mix." I'd go in and blow the roof off the place and they'd stand there in shock. Shake my hand. "Wicked. Never heard anyone mix like that."' Number two, she sang, live, in tune, over the records. And number three, the guys in the DJ booth were scared of her. 'I'm not a small woman. And I do look like I would knock you out if you come near me. I would. I'm in a man's world, I had to have that edge.'

Sonique is clearly not a woman you would want to fall out with. I suspected her Italian boyfriend Alessandro, 15 years her junior with model good looks, might have been aware of this, when we all had dinner in Ibiza. He had been quiet and attentive while we ate and Sonique and I talked. He lit her cigarette. Then he took a call on his mobile, chattering away in voluble Italian, his voice getting gradually louder. Sonique slung him a look that could have curdled cream. 'I'm doing an *interview*,' she purred, 'honey.' Alessandro's voice dropped to a whisper. He knew that look.

Sonique was brought up Sonia Marina Clarke, in Crouch End, North London, by her mother. 'I was the one at school that didn't get any attention. The ugly one. The one that didn't have no clothes, didn't have no money. Wasn't really popular. Always tried to be with the people that were popular but the people that were popular didn't want to be with the people like me, because I'm ugly and no clothes and me mum's a single parent. So I never really had a father image,' she said. Her mostly absent father was not, she explained, any kind of father figure. 'I've never had a male to tell me anything. I've never listened to a man.' She looked at Alessandro and the two shared a knowing chuckle.

Sonia was an athlete. She was 15 and had been training for a pentathlon she was running the next day for the London borough of Haringey when she fell off a wall and injured her leg badly. She still raced, but lost. Her running kit got stolen. And when she approached Daley Thompson, looking for a consolatory autograph, he declined and told her she wasn't pretty enough. A deflated Sonia gave up athletics. 'I decided to get into boys. And I did,' she said. She grew her hair. Shaved her legs and put them on show. 'Once they came out, I got a boyfriend!' She unleashed a throaty chuckle. 'And all this was quite interesting for my life.'

When Sonia's mother went to Trinidad to get married, Sonia declined to go along. In London, she became homeless for a while, sleeping in a YMCA, on friends' floors, even in flat doorways. When her mum came home after the marriage failed, she started singing in a band. DJ Mark Moore spotted her and recruited her to his group S'Express – they made one album. Sonia became Sonique. The band split up and she ended up on the dole. She kept going to clubs. Her first E didn't impress her: she spent the night outside a club massaging two friends' feet who were freaking out because they'd taken too much. 'So my first pill was awful, didn't really feel anything. I felt people's feet.'

She met Judge Jules and started hanging around with him and decided to become a DJ. Mark Moore gave her a record deck; Martin Heath from S'Express's label Rhythm King a second deck and a mixer. Sonique spent two years at home, learning how to mix. At first, her male DJ mates told her: 'They don't have girl DJs.' Sonia was unimpressed. 'That's why I want to do it. They don't have girl DJs? Let me be the first then.'

She was going to sing, as well. And unlike Jules and his bugle, Sonique actually could sing. She did her first gig, in Cardiff, for free, standing in for Jules. She got £25 for her second, £125 for her third, £200 for her fourth. Within a year she was up to £700 a show. In 1998, Sonique appeared on the cover of *Mixmag*: 'Move Over DJ Famous Bastard,' screamed the cover, 'this is Sonique!' She was wearing silver and had a David Bowie-style flash painted on her face. DJ Sonique had arrived.

For four years she was resident at Manumission in Ibiza where she based herself, flying back every weekend to play at clubs like Sheffield's Gatecrasher. She loved living in Ibiza, playing at Manumission until early morning, going back to her villa for a couple of hours, then playing a lunchtime slot at the club's 'Carry On' at the club Space. 'Everybody was just off their trolley. In a nice way. Couldn't ask for more than that. See the sun rise while you're in a club, with 8,000 other people. I think I partied for about four years solid.'

The second time I met her, it was at her converted farmhouse on a vast private estate on the outer fringes of North London, one of those lovely autumn days that feels like winter is being cheated. Just warm enough to sit on her terrace in a T-shirt. In an outhouse studio, a young male engineer was working on music for her. Alessandro was kicking a ball around the lawn with her two Dalmatians – bounding after it like a big puppy, bare-chested, his well-muscled torso squeezing out of his skinny white jeans. She shot him an appreciative look and began to talk about the second part of her career. Just as the world of superclubs was collapsing and DJs were watching their bookings dry up and their fees tumble, Sonique was tasting fame as an international pop star.

In 2000, Sonique had released an album, *Hear My Cry*. One of its singles, 'It Feels So Good', an airy, light pop-dance single that she both wrote and sang, became a huge hit. Not just in the UK, where it was number one for three weeks and won Sonique a Brit Award, but in America too – where it reached number eight on the Billboard Top 100. It earned her enough money not to have to worry too much about having to work again, though she still DJs, here and there.

Being an international pop star and DJ catapulted her into a luxury, superstar lifestyle. She arrived at the Barcelona Grand Prix to DJ in a helicopter. She flew by private plane. She met Prince Albert in 2002 at the World Music Awards, a glitzy pop ceremony held in Monaco and the two fell for each other. 'That was it. Instant. Absolutely instant. Not much of an introduction,' she said. The relationship lasted a year. She refused to ever go into the palace, though the prince invited her. 'I wasn't going anywhere in that relationship. It wasn't going to happen. So why am I going to see what's not going to be mine? No. We were just having fun.'

It was an unreal relationship – the girl from a North London single-parent family and the Mediterranean prince. One night they were in a Monaco club, surrounded by people. She grabbed him and sneaked him out the club, put him at the wheel of his own car and took him off on an adventure for two hours. Without any security, assistants or anything. 'Nobody could find us for about two hours. And they found us eventually. I completely forgot who he was. I completely, completely forgot that he was who he was.' It couldn't last. The relationship ended. 'It's his life. That whole thing around him, it's much bigger than him.' But she still got to live that whole 'Monaco life', as she called it – before and after Prince Albert. 'Friends of mine got boats and stuff. Security. You know, five-star and helicopter pad and presidential suites, I had that for five years. Solid. Everywhere.'

Sonique was also getting over personal tragedy. While recording 'Hear My Cry', she lost a baby boy she was carrying in the eighth month of her pregnancy. She named the child Sky and recorded a song named after him. Her whole body visibly shuddered, even now, when she talked about him. 'It still bothers me. It's something that obviously I'll never get over, I'll carry that till the day I die,' she said. Fame, DJing, break-up and the loss of her son all combined. Sonique had always been a big drinker. But it got out of hand. Brandy was her thing. 'About half a bottle every night, with no mixer, no ice. I still do the same thing.' She would often be carried back to her hotel by security. 'I lost it for a little while. I was gone for about four years. I wasn't here with anybody. I couldn't deal with it any other way. I just drank. DJed and drank,' she said.

It's all much calmer now. She has made a lot of money. The six-bedroom farmhouse. A house in Barbados. There are the cars – a BMW X5 and an Aston Martin DB9. 'And I bought my mum a house. Bought my sister a flat. Paid for my brother's wedding.' Stupid money, six-figure fees for big gigs. Sonique got up. Her engineer was leaving. The sun was going down. It was time for me to leave. Sonique and Alessandro were going to a charity ball, in the Aston Martin DB9. She smiled at Alessandro, who had finished playing football but still hadn't put his shirt on and stroked one of her Dalmatians. 'Now I'm ready. I've healed the wounds. I'm not carrying around this big weight on my back, this big chunk that was taken out of me. I can actually show love again,' she said. Alessandro drove them off to the ball in the Aston, its engine growling like an angry puppy.

SEVEN

(NOTHING'S GOING TO TOUCH YOU IN THESE) GOLDEN YEARS

TUNE! CHEMICAL BROTHERS – 'HEY BOY, HEY GIRL'

The furiously funk beats, the screechy synthesiser wail, the thunderous tension and the chant: 'Hey boy, hey girl, superstar DJs, here we go!'

The long dazed journey into white: for Bleach, it begins with a phone call from his big league DJ buddy Jeremy and a gentle toot to get the neuro-transmitters dancing. Well you can't blame him, with that top weekend stretching out ahead. Follow Bleach now as he's driven northwards with his wedge-dripping mucker Jeremy. By halfway up the motorway they are inter-nally airborne, a pair of cackling über-lads settling into a pill and nearly losing the gak out of the window. The night loves them, the car is snorting white lines off the road and the underworld of the decks, doormen, dilation and dosh feels like it's their very own pharmaceutical oyster...

Roger Morton, from a script by Sean Pertwee, from the sleevenotes to the Jeremy Healy/Amos Pizey album Bleachin'.

CLUBLAND WAS HEATING up like a giant frying pan. And by 1997, this wasn't about the accidental success of groups of lads playing records for an extended group of friends and ending up with a packed club any more. This was big business. And these weren't audiences of 'clued-up clubbers' nodding hello to the DJ any more, the 'early adopters' or 'opinion formers' of marketing theory. These were big, Saturday night pop crowds, facing the front, cheering their DJ gods. They wanted showmen, not introspective DJ trainspotters. The scene now demanded stars that weren't afraid to play to the crowd and for the crowd: showmen, performers, celebrities... the real superstar DJs.

Three men had already stepped into the limelight. The prize was there for the taking. They weren't hairdressers, car mechanics or telephone salesmen but people who had decided that they wanted fame and success long before acid house came along. Superclubbing simply provided the right opportunity. And each was smart, ambitious and tough enough to handle both the relentless gig schedule and the equally relentless partying that went with it. Or so they thought.

Norman Cook, Jeremy Healy and Peter Cunnah all became ringmasters in the superclub circus; they cracked their whips and crowds jumped for them. And they worked hard for the glory they wanted. Norman Cook became internationally famous as Fatboy Slim; Jeremy Healy was the personification of the 'superstar DJ' at its most glamorous; and Peter Cunnah with his act D:Ream become one of the superclub era's biggest pop stars. Norman Cook and Jeremy Healy had already enjoyed success in the pop charts before they even became DJs. Healy was half of the duo Haysi Fantayzee whose fashiony pop single 'John Wayne Is Big Leggy' was a hit in 1982. After playing bass in indie-pop combo The Housemartins and before becoming Fatboy Slim, Cook formed Beats International act and their pop-reggae skank 'Dub Be Good To Me' was number one for four weeks in 1990.

In 1990, Peter Cunnah was just a good-looking Northern Irish club kid hanging around the DJ box of London's Love Ranch club, dreaming about fame. He came to London to become a rock star. Then he fell in love with acid house, discovered ecstasy, met a DJ – and worked out how to do it. His group D:Ream, formed with London DJ Al Mackenzie, would blur the line between full-blown, euphoric ecstasy anthems and the pop charts. Indeed the group's dynamic depended on this tension between two radically different worlds: the smoky world of clubs on one hand, the squeaky clean world of pop on the other. When their euphoric hit 'Things Can Only Get Better' reached number one in January 1994 and then stayed there for four weeks they straddled both. 'It was what I'd always wanted,' said Cunnah. 'We were high in the charts but we were still playing all these really cool clubs.' But that balancing act couldn't last. The tension between those two worlds would tear the group apart and nearly destroy Cunnah. 'It split us,' he said simply.

Peter Cunnah grew up in Derry, Northern Ireland, during the Troubles with British soldiers on the streets. He could remember showing the squaddies his toy gun – and them showing him their real bullets. His father was a navy man from Manchester who'd met and married a local girl and converted to Catholicism. His dad sold insurance. One night his father was held up and robbed by armed bandits. 'He was visibly shook up and you don't see your dad shaken,' said Cunnah. Derry in the 1970s was tough. Kids like him had a lucrative sideline selling rubber bullets to tourists. When Cunnah joined his first band, they learnt to play two national anthems – the British and the Irish.

The smiley, slightly portly father of two I met in a London pub more than a decade later looks very different. Gone is the mid-1990s skinhead look. But he still has a twinkle in his eye and the Irishman's love of a good story. Cunnah has done well in the property business in the last few years – buying and doing up flats to sell on. He remembered his first encounter with the British music business. It was when the Radio 1 Roadshow rolled into Derry and Cunnah was guitarist with a group called Tie The Boy. Cunnah located the hotel where the Radio 1 DJs John Peel and Janice Long were staying and was sneaking down a corridor to deliver a demo tape of his group to them when security grabbed him.

'There's a commotion in the hallway as they're kicking me out. I was flailing around like a beast in a trap. Two heads poke out of their respective rooms – there's John Peel and Janice Long. And said, "What's it about?"' Cunnah recalled. He shouted out: 'Oh Janice, I've got this single, you've got to hear it!' The BBC DJs shooed the security away, invited Cunnah into a room, poured him a drink and listened to his tape. They learnt some Derry slang from Cunnah that they used on the next morning's show; he had learnt how far his charm could get him.

Tie The Boy went to London – they were signed to U2's Dublin label, Mother – but both deal and group fell apart. Undeterred, Cunnah assembled some basic studio equipment and started working on songs. He went to a rave in Elephant and Castle, took ecstasy and was swept away. 'If you'd only had beer and rock, it's all quite aggressive and full on. This stuff. The colours, the sound, the amount of dancing you could do,' he said. 'It was amazing. It had such an impact on me. For six months I never took another one. I was so in awe of it.'

He became a regular at the tiny West End house club The Brain, getting in for free and earning the odd drink for his charms. 'I'm a young kid. Fairly good-looking. Fairly fit then. So you tend to fit in. People like pretty faces being around.' It was at The Brain that he was introduced to the DJ Al Mackenzie, who towered above him and was quite spectacularly wasted. 'He had a real confidence about him,' said Cunnah. 'A lot of balls and attitude. It's very infectious. Made a real impression.' The pair started working together, Mackenzie bringing his DJ sensibilities to Cunnah's raw pop songs. 'He could see there was something there,' said Cunnah. 'He just started stripping it all down.' Mackenzie would arrive with a pile of records and demonstrate where Pete was going wrong. '"Listen to this, what is it they're doing, we should do that." He'd sit in a corner, roll up a couple of big spliffs, polish off a packet of Jammy Dodgers and pontificate while I worked the machinery. It was great.'

In 1991 Love Ranch, held at Maximus on Leicester Square, was one of those proto superclubs pushing the new, anti-rave style – designer clothes, leather trousers, bottled beer, funkier house music. The club's promoter, Sean McLusky, did his best to foster an atmosphere of sexual abandon. 'Some of the characters would go round handcuffing girls to the bar, then walking off, playing some sort of game with them,' said Cunnah. Lawrence Nelson, one of the producers of Gat Decor's 'Passion' hit, was a DJ. Al Mackenzie was another and he began playing early cassette demos of the new duo's songs, road-testing them on the dance floor. One of these was an early instrumental version of 'Things Can Only Get Better'. But they shelved it.

It was a track that was to go through many changes. Cunnah began it with another producer, Jamie Petrie, before meeting Mackenzie, then shelved it. He was temping in an office – a particularly bitchy, gossipy office – when it came back into his head. 'I was being given hell by people for my ambitions, for running round using part of the office to do stuff, taking calls, whatever.' Sitting opposite Peter, as they both snipped newspaper cuttings for corporate clients, was Ragna, sister to pop star Roland Gift of the Fine Young Cannibals. One day the bitching got too much for him. 'Never mind, Pete,' she told him. 'Things can only get better.' That, he thought, is brilliant and he ran into the bathroom to sing it into the Sony Walkman tape recorder he secretly kept for moments just like this. Then, once again, he shelved it.

1993, another late night, another motorway and another fast car eating the miles. D:Ream, as Cunnah and Mackenzie now called them-selves, had become a live club act, a big draw in all the 'handbag' clubs. Mackenzie normally didn't go along. Cunnah did, with a DAT machine to sing along to, two backing singers and a percussionist. The band were zipping their way back from a barnstorming show at Renaissance and the mood in the car was good. Their single 'UR The Best Thing' had become a club hit, thanks to a strung-out Sasha remix. Peter was sober but still buzzing off the show. And just at the point where the M6 meets the M1, where the motorway lit up with orange street lights, Cunnah suddenly cracked the missing lyrics to his shelved pop song. He only had a white plastic carrier bag to write on. But he started scribbling down verses to what would become 'Things Can Only Get Better'. He had it.

'Things Can Only Get Better' became one of the most unavoidable hits of the 1990s. It bubbled with optimism and celebration. Like a lot of pop hits, it also had a vague, ill-defined sense of something profound about it. Week after week, with a huge smile on his face and his big white collars flapping like the sails of a Spanish galleon, Cunnah would sing this song as if his life depended on it. 'Thingssssssss – can only get better!' Out there in superclubland, dressed up to the nines, pilled up to the eyeballs, his audience flung out their hands too, swept up in Saturday night, enraptured in the moment. If the dizzy heights of the 1990s were about anything, they were about the here and now and aren't we great of hedonism. Cunnah had created the song that captured that. It was all about being in the moment, about trying to make that moment last.

For D:Ream things did get better. The song went to number one. The group partied. They found themselves in Texas, on the last day of an American tour, with a massive pile of cocaine – around six grams. 'So we pulled the sideboard into the middle of the room,' said Cunnah. 'We did two lines, with hurdles, going the whole way the length of this sideboard. And we both got a straw each. And the one first to the end of this sideboard was the winner.' He laughed, aghast at the memory. 'I won, needless to say. I was off my fucking trolley,' he recalled. 'I got on the aeroplane and I noticed my left-hand side became paralysed. I must have looked like some fucking casualty. "I can't move."'

But D:Ream couldn't follow up their number one, never equal its transitory glory with another hit. Their album entered the charts at a disappointing Number 40 and singularly failed to sell in the kind of quantities their record company wanted. The record company's solution was to put D:Ream on tour with Take That!, then the biggest boy band in the world. Cunnah didn't want to do it. Warner Brothers put the pressure on, even getting Paul Oakenfold, who was running his East West imprint through the major, to call and suggest he do it. 'This is the point that Alan left. He said, "I don't like it, I'm not doing that."' Mackenzie went back to DJing. Peter Cunnah was left on his own, in charge of his band of session musicians and dancers. And by the end of his lonely Take That! tour, a cocaine habit that was eating him up.

ZZZZZZZZZZZZOWN. ANOTHER RACING car zoomed by, so quickly it was just a blur. I fiddled with my earplugs and grimaced. After what seemed like hours of this, I had realised that what looked like the best seat at the British Formula One Grand Prix at Silverstone

– a private box on the finish line – was actually the worst. Real fans picnicked on the hairpin bends, where the cars slowed down enough for you to actually see them. But this was summer 1996 and what was important was status. Not what you saw, but who saw you, how you were seen. A private box said it all.

It was what was called a 'jolly up', a record company-funded beano to push the jazz-funk act Jamiroquai's new album, which featured a Ferrari logo on the cover. Some of the most powerful people in the British music industry were there – Trevor Dann, the BBC's music boss and his wife – listed on the printed itinerary as 'wife' – and whoever was in charge of ITV's *Chart Show*. Me because Sony's PR wanted singer Jay Kay on another *Mixmag* cover. We had all been flown there in a fleet of helicopters, no expense spared. Jay Kay was one of the biggest stars of the day – he drove a Ferrari, he was flash. It all fitted.

Motor racing was glamorous. It felt like being in a war zone, with all those helicopters and machines making such a God-awful metallic racket, but it was. And the most glamorous spot of all was the pits. That's where the blonde bimbos in the skin-tight red outfits were. That's where the drivers were. That's where the action was. And that's where a hot young politician called Tony Blair was, shaking hands with Jamiroquai frontman Jay Kay, the pop star of the moment, having his photograph taken with him, a photograph that somehow ended up in *Mixmag* – because Mark Allan, the freelance photographer working for Jamiroquai's PR people that day, also worked for us. And because Tony's people were good: they got him in all the right places, where a photograph like that might just happen.

Change was everywhere in Britain in 1996, not just on the dance floor but in the slow dance of politics, which, after years of bottom-groping 'erection section' sleaze and stasis, was picking up pace like a good DJ set. For the first time in more than a decade, Labour looked like they might actually win an election. This was a new party, with a new name, a new logo – that friendly red rose – and a new leader in Tony Blair who felt like a different kind of politician, a person you might actually meet, rather than a chinless Tory pervert. Blair had smelt the mood in the country. He knew that pop music in all its forms was booming. And he was keen to connect.

By 1997, eager to keep their pop momentum going, New Labour had chosen as their anthem a song that they believed captured optimism, hope and energy – a euphoric pop hit that could soundtrack their sweep into power. They selected a hit that was instantly recognisable to the hundreds of thousands of clubbers out raving every weekend, a song brimming with hope and optimism, good times and positive energy. An ecstasy anthem called 'Things Can Only Get Better', by Peter Cunnah's D:Ream. The BBC later described it as 'the daddy of all off-the-peg election ditties'.

Peter Cunnah was in recovery when New Labour first called, having kicked the dangerous coke habit that had developed during his tour with Take That! – we will hear more about those dark days later. He was spending his days walking his dog on Wormwood Scrubs and had found a new manager, Jaz Summers. Summers wanted Cunnah to let Labour use the song as their election anthem. Cunnah was reluctant. He had been busted under the infamous anti-rave Criminal Justice Act a few years earlier. An irate downstairs neighbour had been complaining against the noise Cunnah was constantly making – so he set his music computer on permanent repeat, put his speakers on his floor and went out leaving a beat as repetitive as possible playing endlessly at maximum volume. He returned to find his street full of police and ended up in Westminster Magistrates Court. Peter Cunnah believed in acid house. He didn't want to get into bed with a political party. Summers talked him round.

'This is a really good move. Warners are going to get behind the record again. And Labour are going to be successful and on the back of that you're going to be successful,' Summers told him. Cunnah got caught up in the mood. 'There was a groundswell of opinion. There was definitely a sea change of feeling among everybody,' Cunnah remembered. Yet still he wavered. John Prescott took Cunnah on a tour of the Houses of Parliament, as Labour sweet-talked Cunnah into giving up his hit. Cunnah took the deal. 'So there I am, supporting the political equivalent of Take That!' he said and roared with laughter. Did Alistair Campbell, himself a former alcoholic, know that Cunnah had been in rehab for cocaine addiction? Had somebody, somewhere in the bowels of the Millbank machine prepared a strategy should Cunnah's drug problem come out? We may never know: despite repeated requests, both Campbell and New Labour declined to discuss the song for this book.

But Peter Cunnah felt the force of Tony Blair's charm offensive. When they finally met, Blair talked to him about guitars – Tony's Fender Stratocaster compared to Cunnah's Gibson. Blair wanted to know about 'Things Can Only Get Better'. 'Tony was really cool. He said, "Um, what's the chords?" I gave him the chords. He said, "I'll try that."' A new version of D:Ream was assembled to play Labour Party conferences. At one, John Prescott came in to complain. 'That fooking tune! I'm fooking sick of that fooking tune! I've heard it more than you have, I'll tell you that,' he raged, only half-joking. 'I doubt that,' Cunnah joked back.

Now clean, Peter Cunnah watched the results of the 1997 election coming in from a hotel room, wired on nothing more than coffee.

Crowds of thousands stayed up all night to see Tony Blair claim his crown at Festival Hall – including members of a jubilant *Mixmag* staff. D:Ream played the song one more time for the triumphant Labour faithful. 'I'm glad it was dark cause none of them can dance,' he quipped. Afterwards, Alistair Campbell gave him a bear hug that nearly crushed him. And the lyrics Cunnah had written on the back of a plastic bag, hurtling back from Renaissance in a Previa, were eventually signed by the entire Labour cabinet and auctioned off for the Nordoff Robbins music trust. That plastic bag is now in a frame somewhere.

> *Friday, the 90s, the A list hardcore*
> *We call the hotel and we take the tenth floor*
> *Wire up the sound and we shake down the block*
> *Someone calls for sea breeze, someone calls for rock*
> *Downstairs security's starting to panic*
> *Those who aren't chosen start to get manic*
> *Upstairs with Charlie everyone's speaking*
> *Is this the real life?*
> *Now we are peakin'*
> *Lyrics by Amos Pizey from the Jeremy Healy and Amos Pizey album* Bleachin'

THERE WAS AN avalanche of dance music records throughout the 1990s. Each day, a new postbag full of it would be piled up on *Mixmag* desks. Yet bar the occasional sample, a voice that might whisper 'open your mind' or the sample on the British house hit 'I'm Rushin' by Bump, not one addressed the lifestyle of the superstar DJs or the clubbers – the drugs, the madness, the parties. None, that is, bar one doomed vanity project, the *Bleachin'* album from DJ Jeremy Healy and his MC, producer and sidekick Amos Pizey. Released in 1999, it was the story of a lost weekend the two spent together as Healy chased around the superstar DJ circuit and Amos rode shotgun.

BMG Records spent a vast amount of money on this 'concept' album that aimed to nail the excesses of the 1990s and the superstar DJ lifestyle through a mythical clubland character and cocaine addict called 'Bleach' who happened, like Amos, to do the odd bit of rapping on top of his superstar DJ mate Jeremy's records. Hundreds of thousands of pounds was spent on videos, including one starring Bush singer Gavin Rossdale for the track he sang, called 'Comin' Down'. The project was named after the Afro-Caribbean slang for the sickly pale colour a black man goes after too many drugs. A film was even mooted and Sean Pertwee wrote a script but it never happened.

With dance music so huge, with the knowing nods of the Met Bar elite (Amos helped set up the famous A-list hangout and partly based *Bleachin'* on his experiences there) and rock stars like the Gallaghers being so brazen about drug use, by 1999 it felt like the whole country was doing drugs, a nation on a massive contact high. Statistics bear this out. According to British Crime Survey Statistics in 2000 nearly 625,000 adults had used ecstasy in the last year – up from 580,000 in 1996. The increase for cocaine powder – as opposed to crack – was even higher. For adults who had used it in 1996, the figure was 204,000. In 1998, just two years later, that had doubled to more than 410,000. By 2000 it was up to nearly 700,000 (or nearly 250,000 a month – from 68,000 just four years previously). In terms of its subject matter, *Bleachin'* was right on the money and its lyrics make direct references to drugs being consumed while also mentioning specific clubs. It is the blatancy of these references that says so much about how mainstream club-based drug use had become by the end of the 1990s. Special copies of the album even came in a limited edition box with a straw. There was a CD version with a mirrored cover that came with a banknote, the 'Bank of Bleachin'. The album, recorded over nine months, cost £1.5 million to produce. The two videos cost £200,000 each. It is not a great record – a messy collision of dance and rock. But it is startlingly confessional.

Healy by now was the master of the clubs and dance floors he controlled and Amos was his Greek chorus. The verse quoted above was based on the New Year's Eve 1998 party Amos ran at the In And Out hotel, opposite London's Ritz. It cost £150 a ticket. 'We had a bar and we had service and we had the four corner suites and everybody was at that thing, on that floor. Downstairs, it was like the Tet Offensive, they had barriers, people hurling themselves at the lift. Someone said, "Whose idea was this?" We were like, "It was ours!"' said Amos. Everybody was there, including, of course, Dave Dorrell. 'It was great. And Jeremy came in. It was New Year's Eve and he came in a kilt, from where had he been? Somewhere in Scotland. But he'd made I think 140 grand, he'd done three or four gigs and he had it in bags. It was just like, "Jesus Christ",' Amos added. 'That was a party. That was days.'

We spoke in the smart West London mansion block flat where Amos's ex-partner Lisa I'Anson, the former Radio One 1 and MTV presenter, lives with their two children. The two are separated but remain good friends. Amos is a sparky, sharp, charismatic guy. Honest, friendly, but potentially callow, especially in a club situation. He could probably have done anything he wanted, but he chose music. He was now working on a digital content launch. He relived the story the album *Bleachin'* was based upon, interspersing his recollections with the lyrics he wrote about what, for Healy and Amos, were four days of clubs, drugs and parties, without sleep. Just another weekend in the life of a superstar DJ.

'It starts with going to Sugar Shack, which was our favourite club, in Middlesbrough, which was great,' he said. 'We played there, then we went to Birmingham [superclub] Decadance. It's a long drive, but that whole feeling, *"Back in the motor, we're soaking in sweat, fog coming down, we haven't reached yet."* Amos grinned, remembering the ride. '*"Reach Decadance and the dance is overflowing, our eyes are all black and the love vibe we're showing."* You get out of the car and you're rushing and you see everyone out in the street and it's like, "Yeah!"'

Healy and Amos soldiered on. 'We were in some party. There were loads of people and everyone was in this hotel. And I remember at some point we got back to London and he [Jeremy] was like, "You've got to come to Paris." And I was like, "No, man, no way!"' Amos was becoming excitable. Words spilled out of him, nineties slang, West Indian colloquialisms: he is white but he grew up with West Indian foster brothers in the battered wives' refuge his mother ran and had dreadlocks at an early age.

In Paris there was a show for Healy's friend John Galliano that the DJ was playing at. '*Naomi and Kate, all the girls superfly,*' the lyrics ran – Healy was friends with all of them. Afterwards, there was one more party at Les Bain Douches. 'It *was* the only club in Paris for ages, but it's very *up*. And when we got there: "*Everything we're drinking, everything we're taking, I grip the mike hard to stop my hand from shaking.*"' Amos was lost in reverie again. Galliano was there, bouncing about in front of the decks. The drugs, the insanity, the intensity – it all clicked back into place, with Jeremy Healy on the decks, Amos babbling on the mike and a one-off pressing of the remix of George Michael's 'Star People' – how apt! – they just had to road test. 'We just tore it up. It was an amazing thing to be in that kind of state, you feel it, you pop one and then you get the vibe.'

The track ends, like the weekend's last night, at dawn. "*Six in the morning, the Parisian streets, my head full of heaven and sharp funky beats, face the reality, the truth we repeat, we break to the cost, but we can't get no sleep.*" That's it, we can't do any more.' Amos sat back, exhausted by the memory. 'We didn't sleep every weekend,' he said. 'Friday till Tuesday, for years. You get geared up for it.'

Tonight Healy is dressed in a wicked tartan suit.
Mixmag *feature, March 1995*

WHEN *MIXMAG* SUMMED up 1995 with the headline: 'You've never had it so good', it must have seemed just like that to Jeremy Healy. He could do no wrong. His life was one long glorious road of clubs, parties, adoration. His girlfriend was invariably a model. He was a star, picking up at least £1,500 in cash from every gig he played – and he did up to five or six a week.

In March 1995, *Mixmag* clubs editor Dan Prince elected to spend a weekend on the road with him. 'Jeremy has become the official Mr Showman of Clubland, the people's DJ if you like,' Prince wrote. The weekend was blurry and full of bravado. 'The last hotel I was in I got caught shagging on the stairs by the manager. Didn't know what all the fuss was about really,' said Healy at one point.

Jeremy DJed in Birmingham in the middle of the night. 'Jeremy, just like a triumphant boxer, leads the way out of the club with a towel wrapped round his neck,' wrote Prince. The night finished at dawn at London's Gardening Club.

Another writer once summed up Jeremy Healy as 'someone who

only makes sense in a club'. And when I spent an afternoon with him in his enormous, white loft apartment near London's King's Cross, I found him still a little like that. On his wall is an original Andy Warhol: John Wayne, dressed as a cowboy, a reference to Healy's first pop hit. Talking to him is like being the straight man in a comedy routine, even though we were alone in the room. He is funny and charming, cocky, larger than life and louder than life too. 'I've got very, very good memories of the nineties,' he said and giggled. Did it change his life? 'It did, in quite a profound way.'

I remembered meeting him at some point in 1997 or '98, in Ibiza and being swept up in a conga he suddenly organised in a back room at the club Amnesia. I remembered how it felt to be whirled into that ridiculous dance. Flattered the star DJ had included you, intimidated too. Amos Pizey was there. He remembered the conga. 'That's a Jeremy-ism, a massive conga.' The conga line, on that particular trip, Pizey said, went on for three days. 'We kept finding a different conga line, all over the island. It's a good thing the conga, it unites people and everyone could do it. And it's a ridiculous dance. Jeremy's really funny when he's like that.'

As Prince's feature and later *Bleachin'* revealed, Healy rode the nation's motorways for years as one of the biggest names in the game. His weekends were a blur. At around 7 p.m. on a Friday, his trademark dreadlocks swinging under a leather hat, Healy would set off with an entourage that might include his friend John Galliano and girlfriend, the model Philippa Lett. His driver would arrive with Healy's dinner, which he'd already cooked. 'I'd be literally eating the dinner in the car,' grinned Healy.

From club to club, his enthusiasm never waned. He had a way of playing records that made people dance. There was an enthusiasm to his performances that clubbers found infectious. Healy brought the party with him. He didn't mind playing the biggest hits, the most popular records. 'Tell you the truth, if you see people liking a record, it makes you like it,' he said. 'Because it makes you happy because they're happy.' Amos Pizey was usually along too. 'It was just incredible, this thing of arriving like a bandit, with your boxes and storming the place and having the five-star suite and all the girls, the whole scene around it. And then leaving,' said Amos.

But then Jeremy Healy had decided very early on that he didn't like the idea of normal work. He grew up in South-east London. As a teenager he worked for three weeks with his friend George O'Dowd – later to become Boy George – in an apple-packing factory. Healy was appalled. 'I was horrified,' he said. 'I was like, "If this is working, I'm not sure I'm ready for this."' Since then, he has never had a normal job.

Instead, George and Jeremy went off to live in squats around the Warren Street area of London. It was the late 1970s and they shared with a gang of creative, rebellious people like film-maker John Mayberry, art students, transvestites. It was a colourful place to live. 'It was a really weird mixture of people,' said Jeremy. 'We'd never met anybody from art school or anything like that and suddenly I was going out with this girl, called Maisie. She used to walk round London dressed as Queen Elizabeth I and people used to clap and that was the New Romantic scene.'

There were only 20 people on the scene at that time but Healy knew it was going to be big. Then he and one of his housemates, a photographer called Kate Garner, found themselves in a recording studio. With their colourful leggings and dreadlocks, they became pop act Haysi Fantayzee and Healy and his mates graduated to Hampstead. And he was already the centre of whatever party was going on. 'We used to get in this Transit van and drive round and round Trafalgar Square on acid! Everyone would pile in the van. We'd have *literally* 40 people in the van going to the next party. It was a real hideous thing.' When their novelty single 'John Wayne Is Big Leggy' was a hit – as was Boy George with his band Culture Club – Healy was blasé. 'You completely took it for granted at the time.'

Haysi Fantayzee went to New York and met music business executive Tommy Mottola – later the Svengali behind Mariah Carey – in his tartan-themed office, decorated with stuffed deer heads. They worked with legendary disco producer Giorgio Moroder, who'd made Donna Summer's sexiest records. But Jeremy didn't like the producer's grey leather trousers, so that didn't work out. The band split up: they didn't know what to do and nobody else knew what to do with them. Jeremy had already moved on – he had discovered hip hop and moved to New York to learn how to rap.

And he had met John Galliano, then a struggling designer, but later to become one of the biggest names in haute couture, a creative radical behind not just his own brand but also with names like Givenchy and Christian Dior. Healy began scoring Galliano's shows. He still does, 24 years later. This was Healy's introduction into the world of fashion – and models. In New York, Healy taught himself to scratch and DJ skilfully. Back in London he went to Danny Rampling's club Shoom and was impressed because they wouldn't let him in. So he went back, on acid, because that's what he thought you did with acid house. 'It was really hot and there were really lots of sweaty people in there. It wasn't about clothes or anything, although clothes were involved in it. It was more like the extraordinary music.'

Once again, Healy had found something right at the beginning that he knew was going to be huge. This time, he stayed with it. 'You had a disparate group of people and they weren't used to being with each other. That's what made it good,' he said. 'I just walked into that club with like 200 people in it and I just knew that it was going to be massive. I just knew.'

Healy was in the right place. He could DJ. And he knew people. When Graham Ball, a promoter who had run the Westworld parties in the eighties, opened a weekly night called Choice at a club called Subterrania in London's Ladbroke Grove, he made Jeremy the resident. Choice rapidly became one of the coolest nights in London – Kylie was dancing on the stage, Seal did live PAs, TV presenter Davina McCall was on the door. Healy was mixing up house, hip hop, Michael Jackson records. He would moonwalk to 'Wanna Be Startin' Something' – a crowd-pleasing gimmick that he would later take around the northern clubs.

'I just knew this was it, this was my stage and I could shine,' he said. 'It was funny that DJing, the fame thing, I'd seen it happen with Danny Rampling, people were real fans of his. So I knew it could be done. I just knew that I could do that.' He loved the music too. 'You've got to have a musical perspective and then everything else will come. You've got to have it that way or it's just silly.'

With Choice a success and the northern clubs opening up, Healy soon found himself in demand. He began playing every weekend. A girl he knew offered to be his secretary. Healy accepted. He went on holiday – and came back to find out she had organised a year's worth of gigs. 'I'd never thought more than two weeks ahead in my entire life before then,' he said. 'There was a good club in every town. It was all completely taken for granted. You just walk in, expect everything to be great. It definitely was a golden time.'

Soon Healy was doing five or six gigs a week. 'It was our music and our scene and people really felt a bonding. Obviously they were all on drugs, which helps!' He felt the crowds had a sense of identity. Just as he'd seen with punk – another scene a teenage Jeremy had joined – with New Romantic and with hip hop. 'There was a naïve optimism. All these cults were more than a record or a T-shirt or a night out. They were like a lifestyle thing,' he explained. 'They change people's lives.'

But he was a controversial DJ too. Unlike the monochrome performances more serious DJs put in – the nodding head, the serious, knotted brow – Healy was a performer. He put on a show – scratching, dancing, vibing. He was pure entertainment. 'Wave your arms. Take your hat off. I enjoy showing off. I love dancing. And I've got a feel for music and I can show that,' he grinned, remembering. 'You feed off people, definitely. But I think you can stir people up as well. And I managed to be able to be good at that.'

People either loved Healy or hated him. He appeared on the cover of *Mixmag* dressed in top hat and tails, next to the headline: 'Has Jeremy Healy Got Too Big For His Boots?' The feature tackled the Healy conundrum. 'Some say he is overpaid, over-praised and over-rated. Others reckon he has done wonders to bring fun and life back into clubbing.' But Healy, maddeningly for his critics, didn't seem to give a toss. He played for the gallery. He got paid. When he wasn't starring in northern clubs, he was hanging out with the fashion crowd.

JEREMY HEALY at his fabulous peak. He was in New York in a limousine with four of the world's most famous supermodels: Kate Moss – he'd known her since she was 15 – Naomi Campbell, Christy Turlington and Shalom Harlow. Between them they were wearing £5 million worth of jewels. Healy had his leather rasta hat on and a big diamond choker. 'We were just running into places and just going nuts, going crazy, jumping into the limo and going to the next one. It was fantastic.'

He kept playing, kept earning, kept having fun. Which for him, he explained, lounging on his couch, his voice booming around his enormous white apartment, was what all of this was about. The great parlour game that was 1990s superclubbing. 'I think this set everyone free, didn't it? It let them be the kids in the playground,' he said. 'When you run onto the dance floor and you go, "Yeah!" You're like the kid in the playground and you can be 28 and it's fine. No one's going to look at him and go, "Oh, he's a wanker."'

But if Jeremy Healy only made sense in a disco, he wasn't going to be able to spend his whole life in one. Sooner or later, reality had to intrude. In 1992, a girl he'd had a brief relationship with announced she was pregnant. 'I said, "All right, I'm never going to be with you, I don't get that idea, but if you want to have a kid, it's up to you and I'll support it." Which I did,' Healy explained. Now he had a daughter. But he didn't take naturally to fatherhood. 'I was like an hour a week dad, you know,' he says. 'When kids get older it's easier, when they're babies you're like, "What d'you want? I can't feed you. Here's some money!"'

In 1997 Jeremy's father passed away. Then his daughter's mother, who was just 32, suddenly, horribly, died, of a rare heart condition, leaving him responsible for a six-year-old. And then his girlfriend dumped him. 'I'd sailed by my whole life up to then and I had a triple whammy. And I'm talking in the space of *two months*. And it just knocked me for six, it really did.' Healy saw himself, suddenly, as a ridiculous figure. 'I'd always really thought what I did was good and really a good vibe and I just felt useless after that.' He started getting nightmares while he was still awake. 'I was seeing these dancing skeletons in this club, I was literally going like, "What the fuck's going on?"' He felt trivial. 'Just completely like a clown. Just like an idiot. Just useless. It made me feel crap. Useless. It made me feel really useless. I'd never felt that before, I'd always felt I could do something and I loved it and everyone else loved it,' he said. 'And I don't think I ever felt like a superhero again.'

Fortunately his superstar DJ friends were on hand to help. Alex P, a notorious party animal and DJ who often played with Brandon Block, proffered advice. 'I was looking for sympathy,' Healy explained, 'and he goes, "Well go and buy a fucking Ferrari, then, cheer yourself up." I was like, "Okay, then, I'll do it." And I did it. It worked for about ten minutes.' Incredulous at this unique superstar DJ solution to the terrible emotional trauma he'd been through, I wondered if the Ferrari was still around. It was. All £100,000 worth, in black, sitting in the garage. He had just had the clutch repaired and was planning to take it down to the south coast. Lots of the DJs bought Ferraris, Jeremy explained. 'I think everyone had one at one point.' They even joked about a group photograph, with all the DJs lined up with their Ferraris, like the famous picture of British 1970s comedians with their Rolls-Royce motors.

Jeremy kept DJing. There was a tax bill to be paid. 'All these disco dollars, you have to pay them back after a while.' In 1999, he and Amos featured on a *Vogue* magazine gatefold cover dedicated to Galliano, along with other friends of the designer, like Annabelle Rothschild and Tricia Ronane, the wife of former Clash bassist Paul Simonon. But that year, he was spending time in Ibiza, where his daughter was now living with her mother's best friend – and now Jeremy was finishing a show at 6 a.m. and getting up at ten to 'play dad'. 'So it completely switched for me. And it completely lost its allure. I don't think Ibiza's fun without drugs!' he laughed.

By 2000 Jeremy's bookings were going down as were the number of dates he could do a week. 'It just trickles down. It goes down slowly and gracefully. But I do other stuff. I'm not reliant on that.' Healy's fashion connections saved his career. He no longer just produces the soundtracks for John Galliano's shows, but now does Victoria's Secret and scores shows for stars like Gwen Stefani and Jennifer Lopez. He still DJs – at the upper-class hangout Boujis, where his crowd includes blue-blood celebrities like Prince Harry and everything is finished by 4 a.m. There is never an after party. And the DJ is no longer a super-star. In 1995 he told *Mixmag*, 'I'm famous in a minor, disco way, but not in the real world.' Now not even that is true.

Late afternoon in Jeremy's gigantic apartment and workmen were busy on the canal below. He explained that when he bought the place, back in the 1990s, he had an amazing view of the sunset. Then another apartment block was built on the other side of the water. Jeremy did his mock sad look. He doesn't get those golden sunsets any more.

THIS WAS NOT an ordinary terraced house in Brighton. It was now an Alpine mountain and the party was headed for the summit. Norman Cook cajoled his after-club party guests into action. Everybody was tied together with ropes and they ascended the staircase of the four-storey house, one step at a time, pulling each other up one by one. 'Took about half an hour. And ended up on the top of the wardrobe in my bedroom, which we reckoned was the peak and planted a little flag,' Cook said with a little grin. 'We were all very proud.' This was the House of Love, a terraced house on Robson Road, in Brighton's Preston Park district and if Fatboy Slim began his career anywhere, it was here.

It was often said in the nineties that Norman Cook was the master of reinvention, as if he was some kind of pop Machiavelli, eternally dreaming up new guises with which to wow the pop masses. The reality was less prosaic. Incredibly productive in his home studio, with a showman's sense of style when behind the decks, he was forced to use a variety of aliases for legal reasons – he was signed to Island Records as part of the live band Freak Power, one of his less successful guises. He began releasing records under different names like Pizzaman and Mighty Dub Cats. But Fatboy Slim was the one that stuck.

He was smart enough to run with it. And in the wider pop arena, Fatboy Slim became perhaps the most famous superstar DJ of all – the one that everybody had heard of. Fatboy Slim achieved something no other DJ of the nineties has succeeded in doing: he became a bona fide rock star. 'You have to live up to being a superstar, you have to be a character and you have to be a persona,' he tells me. 'And I've got the bad Hawaiian shirts and the devil may care attitude and not taking it too seriously.'

Norman Cook is a very likeable man with the easy manner that people who have been very successful sometimes have – nothing to prove, time for everyone. He still hangs out with friends who aren't famous. He is a popular figure in Brighton. And he disguises a keen intelligence and ambition behind a matey, jokey persona. For a while in the 1990s, he had something of a cockney accent, which has now all but disappeared. His home is actually two houses knocked into one. In the living room, there are four original Keith Haring pictures on the wall and there is the gentle sound of the sea outside the window. Next door, on the same secluded mews, is the first house he bought – now rented to friends and still home to his studio. DJs like Tiesto and Paul Oakenfold play stadiums. But Fatboy Slim, with his cheeky grin, his loud shirts and his trademark sound, all funky beats and cheeky melodies, is the most recognisable DJ on the planet. 'I put a bit of theatre into it,' he told me, sitting in his lounge. 'Showboating, vaude-ville, call it what you will. Pantomime, at times. Pizzazz.'

He has sold millions of albums. His 1998 album *You've Come A Long Way, Baby* sold 1,173,000 copies in the UK alone. He doesn't need to play clubs any more, just festivals and giant beach parties. The first time he played for free on Brighton Beach, 65,000 people came. 'There was a moment halfway through where I suddenly thought, "Fuck, we've got away with it, it's worked."' The second time he played the beach, quarter of a million showed up and tragically a 25-year-old Australian nurse died after falling off some railings. In Rio de Janeiro, 360,000 watched him play. At the 2006 carnival, in Salvador in Brazil, the second time he had played, it is reckoned that over five hours, 1.2 million people saw his float go by. He is so rich that he never needs to work again. 'I don't do it for the money. I could have retired about five years ago, probably,' he said.

Like Jeremy Healy, Cook had already enjoyed success in the music business. The son of a middle-class family from Reigate in Surrey, he was born Quentin Cook and joined indie-pop act the Housemartins while at college in Hull. But he had DJed since he was a teenager and avidly collected punk records. When the Housemartins split up, he went back to Brighton and started DJing again. In 1990, his number one hit with his group Beats International was a lazily funky cover of the SOS Band's eighties soul standard 'Just Be Good To Me', converted to 'Dub Be Good To Me' with the addition of the bass line from The Clash's 'Guns of Brixton', dub effects and a vocal from Lindy Layton. It was a record very much of its time – the easy mix of dance beats, pop vocal and a punk-reggae flavour.

When he stumbled on acid house, he was completely thrown by it. Suddenly his friends were all wearing bandanas and smiley faces on their T-shirts. 'It was weird, like everybody had joined some strange religion.' For a while he even ran a club called No Acid Zone, until someone gave him an ecstasy tablet and he worked out why so many people had been dancing on chairs all night. It came at a watershed moment in his life: his first marriage had just broken up. 'I was quite depressed, my wife had left me, hadn't been out for ages and someone dragged me out,' he said. Ecstasy tablets were much stronger then. 'Coming up you had to hold on to your seat for 15 minutes. It was like, "*Wooh*! Don't worry, it's just turbulence."'

The ecstasy, he explained, had a dramatic effect: his depression disappeared. It never came back. At a Boys Own party in Bognor Regis, he took ecstasy again, while listening to Darren Emerson play Robert Owens's hit 'I'll Be Your Friend', a percussive house number that featured a haunting, echoing vocal which Emerson's mix kept going for what seemed like for ever. The DJ was cutting between two copies, repeating a vocal phrase that sang 'I'll be your... I'll be your', building up the tension on the dance floor. When Emerson let it go and dropped the verse's punchline 'I'll be your friend', the crowd went wild. 'Everybody just started hugging each other. Having orgasms and things.' Cook learnt something valuable about dance floor dynamics there and then. He calls it 'the money shot'. 'And it was like, "I get it."'

What followed was a period of incredible productivity. Alongside his jazz funk act Freak Power, he began churning out infectiously funky dance records under different aliases. And he found he was particularly good at making crowd-pleasing records, with hooks and whistles and samples that people instantly responded too. Tracks that built and built – and then delivered that 'money shot'. Norman Cook had always wanted to write brilliant songs, but he'd never pulled it off. He realised he had found his forte. 'Grooves were what I did best. In dance music you can just write a groove and use a vocal hook to tie it together. And you've got a record,' Cook explained. 'It's amazing it took me 12 years of faffing around in bands to realise that.'

By this time, he was living in that terraced house – the House of Love. It was party central: every weekend, after clubs shut at 2 a.m., people would pile back there. 'It was a phase in my life when I was young, free and single and discovered ecstasy. And then even when I wasn't single I had partners who were deeply into mucking about,' said Cook.

The House of Love wasn't just an after-party house. It was a playground where surreal party games were played out. There was Astroturf and wallpaper featuring Tahiti beach scenes in the bathroom. The Disco Toilet had mirrors with lights up the side on every wall, creating an infinity effect. 'So when you were having a shit you'd just look and there were millions of you having a shit, which was quite offputting when you were on drugs.' There were smiley faces everywhere – Norman collected the bright, yellow acid house symbol. The living room and kitchen were in the basement, which meant the neighbours couldn't hear anything, even when the parties went on – as they often did – for days. 'How we didn't get busted I don't know. Cause it was fairly common knowledge what was going on there and it was going on every weekend,' he smiled.

All the ingredients that would go to make up Fatboy Slim were here. A sense that Cook, despite the partying, was genuinely a nice bloke: when he discovered the only noise that bothered his neighbours was the slamming of his front door, he muffled it. When people spilt a drink, they generally cleaned it up. 'We'd just invite strangers in and give them pills and things like that. You couldn't get away with that nowadays.' Some of the fun and games resembled the madcap antics of British TV shows that went out on Saturday nights. It was like *Noel's House Party* – on E. One game involved taking the door of his garden shed, nailing a chair on to it and charging toboggan around the lounge. During another session, in a story that has become part of the Norman Cook myth, he and his friends snorted cocaine off a railway line. 'That's about the stupidest thing I've ever done in my life. I think we only did it so we could tell our grandchildren,' he said. Though they took precautions. 'We did actually have someone 30 foot that way and 30 foot that way looking for trains. And we weighed up the odds.'

And on Sundays, too wired to sleep, Norman retired to his studio. 'By Sunday night I wasn't really capable of operating heavy machinery or driving, eating, anything like that. So I'd just go in the studio.' And everything he'd heard, the records, the jokes, the fun, the riffing, the rhythms would all still be ringing around his head and he'd put them all into his records.

OUTSIDE BRIGHTON, THE superclub scene was becoming uniform. Music was increasingly samey, seamlessly mixed by increasingly self-important DJs. Clubs had dress codes. And no longer were superclubs just for the sharp, fashion-conscious working-class kids who originally dominated the scene. Acid house in the UK is unusual in that students came to it late – once DJs started playing university tours. But once a middle-class student audience did get involved, they inevitably chose to do things differently. In London, in 1994, two Medieval Studies graduates from Manchester University called Tom Rowland and Ed Simons started up a small Sunday night session at the Albany pub in London's West End. The DJs, very often, weren't DJs at all, the crowd was scruffy and messy and had often been up all weekend and most important of all, the music policy was 'anything goes'. The Beatles psychedelic groove 'Tomorrow Never Knows' was one of the club's big tunes, alongside hip hop instrumentals played at the wrong speed.

When Norman walked into the Heavenly Sunday Social and met the Chemical Brothers, as Tom and Ed were to become, he immediately felt at home. 'I just walked in and it was like finding a long-lost family,' he said. 'Like finding the rest of your gang.' Back in Brighton he started up the club Big Beat Boutique – the club would give what was becoming a new movement in clubbing its name: Big Beat. For Cook, it was ringing the changes. 'It was a lot of people who had got bored of house, thought back to what went on before, added elements of punk and rap, the devil-may-care attitude of punk and the breakbeats of rap and just mixed the whole lot up,' he said. 'There was a feeling we were tearing things up, ripping up the rule book and getting away with it.'

At the Big Beat Boutique, there were no spangly dresses, no Paul Smith shirts. The crowd wore jeans, T-shirts and Converse pumps. They lined the front, giving Norman 'cheeky halves' of E while he tried out new records. When he first played the Fatboy Slim hit 'The Rockafeller Skank', he pointed at the crowd, to say, 'This is me!' They roared back over the chaos: 'We already knew!' The Chemical Brothers were guests along with another DJ who had been catapulted off the floor of the Heavenly Sunday Social into a career, Jon Carter. 'Go down there and it was just madness,' he said. Carter, who had also been a studio engineer, used to put records on at the after parties. Next thing he knew, he was playing at the Social. 'Suddenly I was a DJ.'

Norman, Carter and the Chemical Brothers were very different to the wily, street-wise former ravers who'd created the northern club scene. They were university educated. They were clever. They had something the mainstream club scene by now patently lacked – a sense of irony, an ability to laugh at themselves. Their records did not take themselves too seriously and they bought a sense of anarchy and fun back to dance music. And like many middle-class university students, who party happily through their degrees and then knuckle down to their final exams, when it came to their careers they were deadly serious. Norman Cook enjoyed joking and laughing when we met up to talk. But when I pressed him, it was clear that when it came to the business of making Fatboy Slim a successful proposition in the music business, he knew exactly what he was doing.

'I've always insisted that the Fatboy Slim logo is always the same,' he said. 'Every album they rough it up with different lettering. I go, "No, that's a brand, that's recognisable."' The cover of his 1998 single 'Let's Hear It' pictured a fat, redneck teenager wearing a T-shirt that read 'I'm number one so why try harder', above the slogan, 'You've come a long way, baby'. It became an image of Fatboy Slim more potent than any DJ portrait. 'The presentation comes from being in the music industry for ten years and you know what works. It's packaging a DJ like you would a band.'

In 1998, other DJs hadn't thought things out in this detail. They didn't have logos. Neither did many of them really make records. Cook put it all together and created an international name for himself and his alter ego. And as he moved from increasingly lucrative club gigs to stadium shows, he developed his DJing into a performance that would captivate those crowds. 'I put that showbiz element into it,' he explained. 'But having played in bands, you learn about stagecraft and how to wind an audience up. Just doing something like walking down to the front of the stage and going –' he mimed a big happy stage smile and nod – '"This is great!" And you just get an enormous cheer. It's cause I've got the bottle to do that.'

Big Beat DJs like Norman Cook, Jon Carter and Derek Dahlarge
– a former photocopy salesman who became another DJ star and also
recorded for the 'big beat' Wall of Sound label – were particularly
popular with the girls who worked at *Mixmag*. Miranda Cook and
Mandy McGarvey, who was the office manager, were friends with both
Norman Cook and Jon Carter and used to hang out at the House of
Love in Brighton. In 1997, McGarvey organised a *Mixmag* trip to the
Brighton Essential Music Festival – on a double-decker bus. The
following year, as the same festival came to an end, the staff convened
at an afternoon party the Wall of Sound label held at Brighton's
Hobgoblin pub. This was big beat at its peak: Derek Dahlarge tearing
up the dance floor with thunderously funky grooves, beer spilling
everywhere, girls dancing on the bar, on tables, on chairs and late afternoon sunshine spilling through the windows from the beer garden.

But Chemical Brothers aside, none of the other DJs got near
Fatboy Slim's status. In 2002, Norman Cook did a three-date arena
tour of Japan, during the World Cup, supported by Jon Carter. A film
crew followed them around for a documentary for BBC Choice.
Before the tour, Carter accidentally received a fax about Cook's
contract. 'Jesus Christ, you want to know what the superstar DJs were
getting paid? That's the shocker,' Carter told me. For three shows
Norman Cook, said Carter, was getting paid £150,000 – a cool
£50,000 per gig. Carter was getting £1,000 a show. Carter mentioned
the fax during the tour. 'Just to say, "Oh by the way, just went to the
wrong office and by the way, you're doing all right, aren't you, really?"'
Cook immediately doubled Carter's fee. But later, via managers, Carter
got a telling off. 'I had it right down the ear hole,' he said. 'It's not an
unwritten rule and it's not like it's vulgar or anything like that, it's just
something you don't really do. He's on a different level.' It was a

revealing glimpse into how the dynamics of success impact on friend-ship. Cook also DJed at Jon Carter's wedding to Sara Cox for free. 'Norman's one of the nicest fellas in the game,' Carter insisted.

But in 1998, when the redneck fat kid picture first appeared, Cook was still on the cusp of two worlds. In dance music, he was known for his party DJ sets and his hard partying. Outside of that, he was just a name, not a face, on records that were landing with increasing frequency in the pop charts. He had the best of both worlds. That July, he arrived in Ibiza for a series of DJ dates and was invited to be a guest on the Radio 1 Breakfast Show, co-hosted by one of the most famous women in Britain at the time, Zoë Ball. Dance music was about to gain its first celebrity couple. Britain was about to meet its first celebrity acid house DJ. And Tony's people would cotton on to this celebrity: Blair used Fatboy Slim's 'Praise You' as his walk-on song for the 1999 Labour Party conference. For some commentators, its lyric 'I have to praise you like I should' represented Blair's increasingly presidential style: a superstar theme for a superstar prime minister. The *Independent*'s Ann McElvoy was appalled. 'It was pure *führermusik*,' she said.

EIGHT
DANCE MUSIC AND THE ESTABLISHMENT PART 1: A TALE OF TWO CITIES

TUNE! GRACE – 'NOT OVER YET'

A combination of haunting vocal and barnstorming trance that was covered a decade later by 'new rave' act The Klaxons.

13 July 1996 was a bright, sunny day and mingling in the heat among the Saturday lunchtime crowds at Liverpool Street Station in London were nearly a thousand hippies, clubbers and the dreadlocked, combat-trousered crew known as 'crusties'. The police were there too – they knew something was up. A sense of expectation crackled in the air, then an air horn sounded and a voice yelled: 'This is it! Go! Go! Go!' Suddenly the crowd moved as one, onto the tube, past a couple of confused Canadian Mounties. There was confusion on the Central Line – the train didn't stop at Holland Park – but somehow the mob spilled out at Shepherd's Bush. Somebody led the way, around the back of some garages, shinning over a fence – up and onto the M41, the busy Westway motorway that flies over West London. The same Westway The Clash sang about. Now there were 6,000 people pouring onto the motorway and the police, realising it was too late to stop this, began diverting traffic away. Two trucks were pulled up on the hard shoulder, protestors clambering all over them. A few of them ripped off the tarpaulin. There on the truck were the big, black speakers of a huge sound system. There was the taut, buzzing sound of an acid techno riff tense with expectation and a beat kicking in. A deadpan voice on the record that said:

> *'London acid city*
> *London acid city*
> *London acid city…*
> *Our time is now.'*

Everybody SCREAMED. And 6,000 people started dancing on a central London motorway.

29 MARCH 1984. 'Maggie! Maggie! Maggie! Out! Out! Out!' The war cry of 1980s protest marches echoed down central Liverpool streets. Giant trade-union banners fluttered, air horns honked. Margaret Thatcher at her height, a country divided, the bitter picket line battles of the miners' strike on the nightly news, sweeping government and council cuts. Liverpool was on the edge of the knife. Unemployment was running at 20 per cent. Among the city's youth, in areas like Croxteth, it was estimated at closer to 90 per cent. Katherine Hamnett's Frankie Goes To Hollywood T-shirts, their stark white slogan reading 'Frankie Say Arm The Unemployed', were a regular sight on city streets.

That day 50,000 people were marching on the town hall to persuade wavering members of a Labour council effectively controlled by the hard-left Militant Tendency to pass an illegal budget in defiance of Conservative government cuts. The whole of Liverpool was on strike – including the buses, we had to walk into town that day. 'I could taste the revolution in the air,' Derek Hatton said later. The sharp-suited deputy leader of the city council, a member of the hard-left Militant Tendency, was the hero of the hour. And it did feel like revolution, as he spoke from a balcony and the crowd roared.

When Toxteth had erupted into days of riots just three years earlier in 1981, left-wing activist Jed Fizpatrick, a friend and later flat-mate, had received a phone call in the middle of the night. His comrades thought the revolution had come. Finally, the glorious day. Fitzpatrick stood on Lark Lane in the middle of burning Toxteth, handing out leaflets to looters busy carrying fridge freezers and tele-visions they'd yanked through broken shop windows. It was this boil-ing discontent the Militant Tendency tried to channel during Hatton's city council revolt three years later. Would Thatcher step in and suspend the council, putting Liverpool under the rule of appointed commissioners? Was this it?

It wasn't. The revolt ultimately failed, though not before Patrick Jenkin, the Conservative Environment minister, had visited the city and made concessions. Ultimately it ended in farce, with the council sending out redundancy notices to 31,000 council workers it could no longer pay in a fleet of taxis and accepting a $90 million rescue pack-age from Swiss banks. Labour party leader Neil Kinnock purged Derek Hatton and the Militant Tendency from its ranks. The revolution was over. 'The feeling was positive against kicking against the government in 1985 and it just died after that,' said Fitzpatrick.

A sort of desperation set in. Violence was an occupational hazard in mid-1980s Liverpool. I grew up on the other side of the River Mersey on the Wirral peninsula and moved to Liverpool in 1984, living on the dole. There were, quite simply, no jobs of any description and so I concentrated on putting together a fanzine. In Kensington, near where I lived, on the edge of Liverpool city centre, mothers pushing prams would be attacked in daylight by muggers wielding Stanley knives for the child benefit in their purses – then slashed even when they'd handed over the cash. I remember being head-butted by a giant, hulking skinhead on the way home from a club one night, walking beside a girl. As the skinhead passed between us, he whacked us both with the same whiplash motion of his head. He was ten yards down the road before the stars stopped spinning and we realised what had happened. He didn't bother to look back. He didn't say a word.

A 1984 survey ranking the economic health and quality of the European Community's 102 cities placed Liverpool in 102nd place. Heroin addiction was endemic. On 29 May 1985, 38 fans of the Italian football team Juventus died after a fight broke out with Liverpool fans before the European Cup final. I'd already fled the city and watched the footage, appalled, from a campsite in Rome. On 15 April 1989, 93 Liverpool fans were crushed to death at Hillsborough stadium. This was a city on its knees. 'I think people don't realise how grim it was,' said James Barton. I think he was right.

But by 1998, Liverpool had changed. It started in the late 1980s, with the opening of a Tate Gallery and the slow transformation of the Albert Dock area. Then the superclub Cream opened. By the mid-nineties, Liverpool was no longer regarded as a violent, unfashionable place where nobody wanted to go – instead it had become one of the most desirable clubbing destinations on earth. Applications to the university had shot up. Clubbers travelled from as far away as New York and Brazil to party there. The knock-on effect Cream had on the economy of the city transformed the grimy, dingy inner-city area around the building it occupied in Bold Street into a buzzing, upmarket district of cool bars and restaurant and shops. Cream made Liverpool cool again.

BEFORE THIS THERE was another place where acid house thrived and it wasn't superclubs. It was open air and it was free. At the turn of the nineties, the New Age travellers, a motley mix of rebel hippies, crusties and anarchists who had a tradition both of living outside society and of their own free festivals, had discovered raving and adopted it to their own purpose. They weren't afraid to break the law – taking on everyone from Glastonbury Festival security to the police. They'd already seen the worst. On 1 July 1985, a convoy of travellers in the converted caravans, trucks and coaches they lived in on its way to the annual Stonehenge Free Festival was brutally attacked by police at the 'Battle of the Beanfield'. Some 537 people were arrested, vehicles trashed and travellers beaten. To the travellers, dodging police to stage a free rave was no big deal.

In 1990, in the West Country, a crew of travellers called Circus Warp were just one of a number of outfits combining circus performance with well-organised, free parties. In May 1992, this loose movement peaked at Castlemorton Common at the base of the Malvern Hills, when the annual New Age travellers' free festival turned into a giant three-day rave: 20,000 revellers turned up. The Conservative government was incensed and in the 1994 Criminal Justice and Public Order Act attempted to legislate against such an event ever happening again.

In its infamous Clause 63 (1) the Act legislated against open-air gatherings with more than 100 people at which 'music that includes sounds wholly or predominantly characterised by the emission of a succession of repetitive beats' would be played. It is perhaps the only time the British government has legislated against a specific form of pop music and remains on the statute books. A attempt by the free rave movement under its umbrella organisation United Systems to defy this and stage not one but two Castlemortons on 7 July 1995 was thwarted by police using the new Criminal Justice Act powers. Bar a few isolated protests, free raving at that level was dead.

Outdoor acid house parties were transformed into licensed, legal events – most successfully at the giant Tribal Gathering raves that Paul Shurey developed out of Universe and the illegal raves he had run in the West Country. Elaborate, high-production dance theme parks like this were expensive, risky events to pull off but Tribal Gathering succeeded – at least for a while. Shurey spent over a year persuading Kraftwerk to play live at his most famous event in 1997. 'Talk about magic moments,' Shurey said. By then though he reckoned the cost of artists and DJs had climbed from 40 per cent of the total budget to 80 per cent. Tribal Gathering was eventually bought out by the giant Mean Fiddler group, which ran Reading Festival and which is now involved in Glastonbury Festival. Shurey ended up running a hippie resort in Mexico, giving up drugs and is now a successful television executive. 'I fully believe that life is all about overcoming your challenges and hurdles,' he said.

But in the mid-nineties another offshoot of free raving briefly emerged as a form of political protest. This time the organisation was a single-issue, anti-car crew of 'crusties', New Age travellers, politically minded ravers and environmentalists called Reclaim the Streets. In September 1995 they took over London's Upper Street and staged a free open-air party that developed into a minor riot. On 13 July 1996, in their boldest move, thousands dodged police and succeeded in stopping London's M41 to stage a free protest party in the scenes described at the beginning of this chapter. Miranda Cook was the *Mixmag* journalist on the spot that day. As the protest continued, fires were lit, drums were played and somebody hiding under the skirts of a stilt walker drilled two holes in the fast lane tarmac to plant two trees. A pink carpet was laid down for the coppers still in line on the roadblock but they declined to sit on it.

On Saturday 12 April 1997 this movement peaked during a large march for social justice in London that developed into a huge free rave in Trafalgar Square. For three hours 7,000 people danced in front of the National Gallery. But it was effectively a swansong. Reclaim the Streets had already shot their political load a year early, in September 1996, when they arrived in Liverpool to help out a long-running strike by sacked dockworkers. Single-issue politics and dramatic, headline-catching road parties were one thing. This Liverpool strike was a significantly more complicated affair and Reclaim the Streets foundered in the political mud.

Though large, anti-capitalist demonstrations continued throughout the late 1990s, dance music no longer played a central part. Instead, Liverpool became the city to embrace a superclub like no other. By 1996, large-scale free acid house parties and the idea of raving as any form of political protest was dead. The field was free for the superclubs to take over. Liverpool was both the place where acid house as protest died and acid house as establishment began.

THE STORY OF how acid house became part of the establishment is the tale of not one city, but two: Liverpool and London. London because it was there that Ministry of Sound became the biggest acid house business of all – an institution all of its own. And Liverpool because it was in this hard northern city that a superclub became an integral part of the city's cultural establishment. London impacted on Ministry of Sound more than Ministry impacted on the capital. But Cream changed Liverpool. Its bosses Darren Hughes and James Barton became famous as its figureheads. Cream put Liverpool back on the map and became an intrinsic part of the city's fabric. Darren Hughes and James Barton both met the Archbishop – later he even came to their millennium party. And they achieved the ultimate Scouser status symbol: their banner at the side of the pitch at Everton Football Club. 'We turned this place into a party town, for many, many years,' said Barton.

Cream's story can't be told without the contrasting tale of London's Ministry of Sound – they are the yin and yang of 1990s clubs. Each in its own way would come to personify the concept of the 'superclub'. Each was run by hard-headed, yet very different businessmen – in both cases such clichés of their own cities and backgrounds that had they been fictional figures, dreamt up for some superclub soap opera by central casting, nobody would have believed in them.

Cream was opened in Liverpool on 12 October 1992 by James Barton, a red-haired, bullish Scouser and former ticket tout and his partner, an intense former waiter and psychology student from nearby Chester named Darren Hughes. Ministry of Sound had started a year earlier and was opened on 21 September 1991 by a bunch of privately educated toffs – James Palumbo, the Eton-educated son of former arts minister Lord Palumbo, Palumbo's Eton-educated friend Humphrey Waterhouse and Justin Berkmann, a former private-school boy turned DJ and clubber.

Seventeen years later, Palumbo is by far and away the richest man in dance music, his fortune estimated by the *Sunday Times* Rich List 2008 (he came in 501st place) at £160 million and his organisation, aside from its club, the most successful independent record company in Europe. Cream is no longer a weekly club but is still a thriving concern. It stages the Creamfields Festival in Liverpool, Portugal, Romania, the Czech Republic, Poland, Peru, Chile, Malta, Argentina and Brazil. Cream still run occasional nights but primarily rent out their venue Nation to younger promoters. And despite the bitter rivalry that once divided them, Ministry now handle Cream's mix CDs.

That rivalry was as famous as that other North-South battle of the 1990s, the Britpop grudge match between working-class Manc lads Oasis and educated Southerners Blur. In both cases, funnily enough, the posh Southerners won. But in both cases, the Northerners still made a shed-load of money. The metropolitan Southerners proved more adaptable, constantly shifting the central proposition they were selling. In the case of Blur, they glided from the chirpy cod cockney of 'Parklife' to the MTV rock of 'Song 2', while Oasis got artistically stuck in years of muddy, if lucrative, pub rock. Likewise the central proposition at Cream is essentially the same: a northern knees-up, exported around the world. Ministry has proved infinitely more flexible. It started out as a purist, New York-style American house club but by the end of the night was flogging everything from gritty London 'garage' to euphoric European trance. Now they also sell car stereos, music systems, vodka and a fragrance.

IN THE 1990s, Barton confronted problems in typical Scouser fashion: head on, like a bull in a ring. He was cocky, fearless and brusque and if he didn't like something, he shouted. I met him at Cream's offices and encountered a more relaxed, sanguine character than the hard-nosed superclub boss of the nineties. Fitter, too: he had lost weight and was working out. He immediately started talking about the darker side of Liverpool culture: crime, wide-boys, the image of the classic 'scally'. 'Some of it's based on crime, some of it's based on not wanting or feeling as though you have to pay for anything. And also a total disregard for other people in any shape or form, whether you're pissing in their hedge or stealing their car.'

Barton knew his way around this world. 'I'm a townie. I was the kid in the tracksuit back in the eighties. I was born in the middle of Liverpool, right on Everton Road and I was brought up on the type of estate you see on [the Channel 4 comedy drama] *Shameless*,' he said. His dad ran a market stall. 'Wheeler-dealer, bit of a market trader, trained as a pipe fitter but never really done that. Sort of a bit of a ducker and diver. We all at some point in our lives spent time getting up at 4.30, loading the van up and driving off to local markets,' he said. Barton's estate was one of the roughest in central Liverpool. Heroin was a major problem. The Bartons stayed clean.

Jayne Casey, who became Cream's PR queen, knew all about violence too. I met her in a designer bar around the corner from Cream. She is still, as she was in the 1990s, hugely charismatic, loud and vampish; keenly intelligent and fiercely loyal to Liverpool. Classic Scouser, just like James Barton. She grew up in children's homes on the Wirral. In the late 1970s she was a wild, outrageously dressed club kid with a shaved head, a 'face' at the legendary punk club Eric's, then the singer in Liverpool post-punk band Pink Military. She has been famous around town since her teens. 'I grew up in public with me pants down,' she joked. Her and a gang of extravagantly dressed gay mates, which included Holly Johnson, later of Frankie Goes To Hollywood and Pete Burns of Dead Or Alive, regularly fought their way out of trouble. 'I'm a fantastic fighter,' she explained. 'So when we used to get in trouble on the street, Holly and Pete Burns would just push me forward and I'd be like that, "Come on then, guys!"'

Jayne remembered the Barton brothers – there were four of them – from her time spent, pre-Cream, as a queen of the 1980s post-punk scene that threw up classic Liverpool acts like Echo and the Bunnymen and Teardrop Explodes. 'The Bartons used to laugh, cause when I had my little vintage clothes store on Matthew Street, they used to come and rob from us. And they battered us a few times on the street,' she recalled. 'Years later, we'd have a row and all this stuff would come out and you'd go, "Okay, you were part of those scallies that used to batter us, weren't you? You were those nasty scally boys before you took drugs."' Violence, crime, heroin and a failed socialist revolt: that was Liverpool. 'If ever a city needed loving up in the eighties, it was Liverpool,' noted Casey. Barton, interviewed separately, said the same thing. 'It was a *really* shitty time. But then dance music hit in 1988 and changed everything. Certainly changed my life.'

James Barton had been hustling since childhood. At school he sold comics and sweets in the playground. A music fan from an early age, he became a ticket tout, following big acts like U2 and Michael Jackson around Europe, selling tickets on the way in and T-shirts on the way out. He was making money and had a car when most of the city was still struggling. 'I just had a fire in my stomach to make money, to make more of myself, I was ambitious even then,' he said. When acid house hit, Barton was entranced. He discovered it at Nicky Holloway's night at London's Astoria, the Trip. 'Obviously the drugs were better back then, because it genuinely was a euphoric wave, that hit,' he smiled. He put on Liverpool's first dance music night, called Daisy, on 12 September 1988 at The State. Nine hundred people turned up and he made £1,800. 'And I thought, "This is great."'

With local DJ John Kelly, he opened up a club called the Underground, which quickly became legendary for its euphoric atmosphere. I had left the city by then, but during a visit back I spent an evening there in 1989. I was astonished – it was full of hard nuts with the classic scally moustache, in shell-suits, smiling and hugging each other. 'All of these guys who from day one were always destined to be either minor thugs or criminals or whatever, suddenly wanting to be your best friend,' said Barton. 'Because they were all doing E.'

With Barton now DJing alongside John Kelly, the Underground had its year or so of glory, even bringing up early rave act Orbital to play. After the club, Barton and Kelly would lead a convoy of hundreds of cars up to the Blackburn raves. He remembered busting through the window to avoid the police who were trying to stop one party in Warrington and getting in. He was at the Nelson rave that was raided. There were free parties all over Liverpool, in parks and warehouses. Acid house had taken over. It couldn't last. The Underground lost its licence and was closed down. 'They actually tried to take some serious proceedings against us,' said Barton. 'Which was knowingly allowing the place to be used for the consumption of drugs. It never went anywhere.'

JAMES RUDOLPH PALUMBO, son of Lord Peter Palumbo, the property developer and former head of the Arts Council, does not do interviews. He went to Eton. 'He was already displaying the kind of entrepreneurial skills that he would have later in life,' said his schoolfriend Humphrey Valdemar Waterhouse, who remembered an expression the Eton headmaster used to use: '"Don't be a cabbage floating down the river of the time." James was the exact opposite of that.'

When Humphrey and James finished school, the pair headed off to California and set up a butler service. They used their Eton morning coats as uniforms and a copy of *Debrett's* as a guide. They had a ball. And their clients included Roger Moore and former president Gerald Ford. The pair went to Oxford University, where Palumbo read History and Waterhouse Law and later English Literature. While at Oxford, a long-running battle began between James Palumbo and his father, who James accused of frittering away the family fortune. In

1994, this came to a head when he and his sister Annabella sued their own father, accusing him of squandering £30 million on extravagances and saying he was not a 'fit and proper person' to run the £64 million family trust. The case was settled in 1997.

When Palumbo met a young, North London DJ called Justin Berkmann in 1990, he was working as a banker. 'He was looking for some great idea to create a new empire. He didn't really have one,' said Berkmann. Raised in Hampstead and schooled at the private Highgate School, Berkmann had started an apprenticeship at his father's wine importing business but his clubbing activities were increasingly interfering with work. 'I was getting fired from my father's company, by my father, on a daily basis,' said Berkmann. 'He basically told me to piss off round the world. "Here's some money, off you go, take a year off. Go and find yourself."' He landed in New York, took a job in a bar and spent the next 18 months clubbing. 'Stumbled across the Paradise Garage and discovered the best club I'd ever seen.'

In many ways, the Paradise Garage was a forerunner of the superclub: a spartan former parking lot whose superstar DJ Larry Levan created euphoric atmospheres on the dance floor and who was adored by his crowd. The sound system, designed by Richard Long, was as famous as the club. There was no alcohol. Berkmann went every week until it closed in 1987. 'I realised what an impact it had had on the New York club scene and also on me and my friends,' he said. He came back to the UK with dreams of opening a London version. Then he met Palumbo. 'He wasn't in the club business, he hadn't been to any clubs *per se*. He obviously understood that there was some potential in this idea,' said Berkmann. Palumbo set Berkmann working on the project with his associate Humphrey Waterhouse. Berkmann's dream was to become a reality.

After 18 months of work, the Ministry of Sound opened on 21 September 1991. 'We opened a 1,500 capacity club with three people and a bunch of builders from Manchester who were sleeping on the floor. It's not just DJs who were disorganised,' said Waterhouse. Working with designer Lynn Davis, Berkmann had created an authentic Paradise Garage lookalike in one of inner London's roughest areas, Elephant and Castle. With its ominous portcullis design, the club came across like a government department – but this clever, portable logo became one of the most recognisable images in dance music. The sound system, designed by associates of Richard Long that Berkmann had sought out, was the best in the UK: people travelled just to hear it. Ministry of Sound was instantly a success, though customers' cars were occasionally robbed outside. And it didn't even have an alcohol licence.

'Within a couple of weeks we had thousands and thousands of people outside the club trying to get in,' said Berkmann. 'The club was very clear in its simplicity. Huge monster sound system in an acoustically perfect room. A bar area for people to chill out and drink. And then a VIP room for people who wanted to hang out and be in that social scene. We were pulling people from every walk of life, from the top all the way to the bottom of London society.'

But the people running it had never run a club before. 'Almost every fucking night when we opened, a fuse would blow and all the lights would go out,' said Humphrey Waterhouse, who was its first manager. 'I was the only person who knew where the fuse box was.' Then there were issues with door staff and bouncer Carlton Leach was brought in to help clean things up. In his book *Muscle* (John Blake, 2003) – subtitled 'I'm the deadliest bastard you'll ever meet' – Leach described the situation. 'It was a clean-up job and I'd got the boys to do it,' he wrote. Leach brought in a new team but then at the club's first birthday party described a tense stand-off between him and his crew and the former door staff. Armed with a sheath knife, Leach stood his ground. The former door crew backed down and walked away.

Berkmann only found out that Leach's new security crew had been employed after the fact. He had personally hand-picked the original door team. 'All of a sudden, we walked in one night and there's a completely new door staff. To be honest, to this day, I never really knew what really happened.' According to Carlton Leach's book, after two years at the Ministry of Sound, he was told he wasn't wanted as sole head of security any more and would be sharing the job. He stormed out. That same night, an armed gang robbed the club. Leach claimed £38,000 was robbed. Waterhouse, who had left for the night by the time the robbery occurred, said much less was stolen. 'There were two or three of them counting money. Guys with masks on came in and held them up at gunpoint.'

After this, the club quickly got organised. Hector Dewar, an experienced club manager who had worked for big club companies like First Leisure, had worked at the Ministry of Sound for a few months when it first opened. In 1994 he was brought back as operations director. 'I don't think anybody expected it to take off the way it did, to be frank, and they just didn't have the infrastructure,' Dewar said. 'But they very quickly learnt.' He later became managing director.

Initially, the Ministry was owned by a company called Dance Studio UK Ltd. Waterhouse was company secretary and Palumbo, described on their annual return as a 'property financier', the only director. Palumbo put in £250,000 of his own money, but he took a back seat. But Dance Studio UK Ltd went into liquidation in 1993. 'Overspend on the opening,' said Waterhouse. 'It was a pretty hairy patch.' A new company, Speed 2787, had already been incorporated in July 1992. It quickly became Danceclub Ltd and later Ministry of Sound Ltd. Palumbo was again a director. Reorganised, Ministry of Sound Danceclub Ltd began making money and kept on making money. By 1997 it was turning over £3,300,000 and making a pre-tax profit of £480,000. But it was the Ministry's record business that really went boom. In 1998 the record business turned over £17.1 million and made £1.4 million profit before tax. In 1999 it turned over £28.7 million and made £4.1 million before tax.

Berkmann continued as artistic director. But though the club had been his idea, he was just an employee. He had had no share of the bankrupt company and no share of the club's new ownership company. 'There was always the discussion going on about how at some point we were going to cut up the pie. Let's see how it goes, let's see how it goes, all this kind of stuff,' he said. It never happened. Berkmann never got a cut of the Ministry millions. 'I suffered from terminal naivety at the time,' he explained. Neither did Waterhouse. 'I had a bit of a golden handshake later, I don't have a problem with any of that,' he said.

Justin Berkmann now lives in Naples with his Italian wife and children. After being estranged from the Ministry and James Palumbo, he went back as a consultant and has just spent a year in Malaysia working on a Ministry franchise club called Euphoria. 'For a few years I was pretty sour about it. It was a difficult thing to get over,' he said. 'But I just took it on the chin basically and got up and carried on. Put it down to experience. It made me a stronger person, it made me wake up a bit.'

BY early 1992, Barton and his partner, a DJ called Andy Carroll who also played at The Underground, had a small office promoting dance music events at venues like The Royal Court and managing the Welsh dance production outfit K-Klass. But he had gone off clubs after a dismal period running things at a short-lived venue called the 051 Club. He had also met Darren Hughes, while DJing at the Liverpool club Quadrant Park. 'He was a Jack the lad, putting on parties, going into managing bands. I had a lot of admiration for him,' said Hughes. Hughes left his native Chester to study a psychology degree in Manchester and went back briefly to work as a waiter – the perfect job to combine with partying at acid house clubs. He had ended up in Liverpool.

Hughes had a long plait, outlandish clothes and an art-student girlfriend. He was an intense, passionate, driven character who now runs a series of parties called We Love at Space in Ibiza. He described himself as a 'control freak. My nature is an obsessive kind of character.' Naturally wary, he had finally discovered ecstasy at Quadrant Park. Or rather, as he put it, 'it discovered me.' He was put to work in Barton and Carroll's scruffy little office in the Liverpool Palace, an alternative 'city centre' mall of clothes shops, record stores and funky hairdressers, filing invoices for pocket money for their little company. Hughes had staged a birthday party at a venue called Nation for his girlfriend with some success. He persuaded Barton and Andy Carroll to try out a night there. It was a risk for Barton. He was doing well anyway: K-Klass had just had an early dance hit with their single 'Rhythm Is A Mystery' reaching number three in the charts in 1991 and the dance shows he was organising at Liverpool's Royal Court were packed. Barton was buzzing. 'You start to think, "Fucking hell. Everything I touch is *working* right now,"' said Barton.

But Hughes was different and a good foil for Barton. 'I was half student, half woolly back [Liverpool slang for a country bumpkin from the Wirral, Wales and Lancashire meaning, literally, a sheep]. Not a Scouser. And James might have grasped that, understood it,' said

Hughes. Hughes won the argument. Barton put up £5,000 for the first night of Cream at Nation. Hughes's art-student mates decorated the place. Four hundred people turned up: a mixture of Underground veterans, scallies, art students and fashionable gay clubbers. Progressive house DJ Fabio Paras was booked but after an hour of DJing they decided they didn't like his music and threw him off. Music sorted, the party went off.

On Boxing Night 1992, they persuaded the leaseholders of Nation – the wily Liverpool club veterans Stuart Davenport and Len Macmillan – to give them some extra space. 'It blew up,' said Hughes. 'That then launched us.' Over 1,000 people turned up. 'I brought all the football terrace element in and Darren's connections brought all these camp fashion students in,' said Barton. He soon had his £5,000 back. Cream was up and running and Darren Hughes found himself earning a thousand pounds a week – or more. 'It just seemed fucking unreal to me,' he said.

By August Bank Holiday 1993, they had done a deal with Davenport and Macmillan to open up yet another room of the Nation venue, to redecorate the club and to form a company between them to run it. But first Hughes wanted to get rid of Andy Carroll, Barton's original, long-lasting partner. 'Cause he just wasn't working hard enough. He didn't have the capacity, in my opinion,' said Hughes. It was a crux point in the history of Cream. James and Andy Carroll had been friends since the eighties. But dance music was changing. This wasn't about mates any more. It was about making money, about seizing the main chance. Barton didn't hesitate. 'This is what's happening and unfortunately you're not going to be a part of it,' he said to his old friend. 'I think, on reflection, Andy or anybody involved in Cream will probably see the significance of that conversation.'

Barton knew Hughes was right. And he knew the combination of the two of them, the sheer drive, would make Cream a success. 'It's difficult for me to say he was as likeable as Andy was,' he said. 'Darren would literally walk through walls to achieve what we set out to achieve and a lot of time left carnage in his wake.' The August Bank Holiday party in 1993 was Cream's biggest yet. The club was becoming a phenomenon. Clubbers began travelling to Cream from all over the country. Liverpool was starting to feel the changes.

SEPTEMBER 1993, THE early hours of a midweek morning. Hiding in a van outside Buckingham Palace were Damian Mould, a hot-shot dance music PR with his own company Slice, and Mark Rodol, a new Ministry boss. Inside the van with them was a giant, high-powered projector, outside a gaggle of expectant press photographers. This was to be the Ministry's most dramatic move yet. They were going to project their logo onto the palace to publicise their first mix album, 'The Ministry Sessions', and grab the front pages. But somebody had tipped off the police and when they opened the van door, coppers appeared from every direction. They talked their way out of the situation and closed the van door.

Undeterred, Mould led the mob on to Westminster Bridge. This time, they managed to project the logo onto the Houses of Parliament for 20 seconds. Again, the police arrived. The van door was still open, the scrum of photographers complaining they hadn't got their shot. 'So I remember shouting to this copper, "Your jacket's on fire!"' said Mould. ''Cause the beam's really powerful. And she moved away. It went on the fucking Houses of Parliament and they all clicked away! And I got it.' It made front-page news. Suddenly everybody had heard of that club in Elephant and Castle. 'We had an album we thought would sell 5 or 6,000. It ended up selling 65,000,' said Rodol. By the end of the 1990s, Ministry albums could sell 600,000-plus a time.

At Ministry HQ, James Palumbo led from the front. He worked in a glass cage suspended over the main office floor. In 1997, I was approached via a headhunting company to edit the magazine they were planning to launch to rival *Mixmag*. It was all very cloak and dagger. There were a number of meetings with a Ministry executive called James Bethel who, with his tweed jackets and cut-glass accent was possibly the poshest man I had ever met. Eventually I went to Ministry to meet Palumbo. Despite the quiet voice, dark suit and impeccable manners, I felt a certain unease, sensing rightly or wrongly a hint of menace under all that gentility. I didn't take the job. *Ministry* magazine was launched in 1997 and was initially a success. It was perhaps the only time the Ministry acknowledged the drug culture that drove dance music. Its final, memorable, fluorescent cover pictured a cartoon monkey and the headline, 'Are You A Pill Monkey?' The magazine folded in 2002.

Palumbo was more interested in politics than acid house. He didn't actually like dance music. 'I don't find it interesting,' he said in one rare interview. 'Now Beethoven, there was an innovator.' He was more interested in politics and was a friend of Peter Mandelson – he lent him a car during the 1997 election. In a London *Evening Standard* feature in February 1999, Palumbo's former girlfriend, writer Anna Pasternak, described his South Kensington flat as having 'a clinical chill which screams emotional deprivation. It is completely devoid of any comfort or clutter; his fastidious tidiness somehow removes him from the reality of life.' He employed an Asian woman to keep house, who he called 'The Cat'.

Palumbo's offices were as neat and as disciplined as his home. He ran a tight ship. Staff started at 8.30 in the morning and worked until

7 p.m. 'It brought a business approach to what was not a very business-like area,' said Matt Jagger, a music business lawyer who had negotiated Sasha's deal with Deconstruction Records and who had joined Ministry of Sound in 1998 as MD of the recordings business. 'Sometimes something had irritated him [Palumbo] and it was action management. We'd all be round the speakerphone and doing conference calls and action points and he'd be taking command. I've never had a boss like James since.'

Ex-employees generally described Palumbo as a fantastically clever businessman. 'James taught me a lot about business and how people operate. Deals. Incredibly tough dealmaker,' Jagger said. 'I've got to say personally he was very kind and generous to me. But he was very competitive. He could be ruthless. He could turn on people. Sometimes could have quite a nasty streak. But I genuinely really liked him.'

IN JUST ONE month, May 1995, eleven people were murdered in a gang war in Liverpool. One of them was Stephen Cole, a bouncer at Cream and former Liverpool FC reserves player, who was brutally killed in a horrific machete attack by around 12 men at the Farmer's Arms in Fazakerley, Liverpool. Cole himself had been acquitted of attempted murder the previous year.

Cream was by now one of the most famous clubs in the country – and it had become a target. 'It became more and more of a drug dealer's paradise,' said Darren Hughes. 'As the gangs in Liverpool become more cottoned on to it, there was more money to be made and the bigger players got involved.' From April 1995 to February 1996, undercover officers from Merseyside Police conducted a ten-month investigation called Operation Top into the ecstasy trade at Liverpool clubs. At Cream the police found organised drug dealing going on within the club. Though there is no suggestion that Cream's management were involved in the dealing, the club was in serious trouble. Jayne Casey had arrived to work there at just the right time.

'I came along at a period where it had problems, where it had a lot of drugs and a door crew that was out of control and that was my entrance,' she said. 'The doormen were allegedly involved in a drug-dealing scam in there. They were scared of going to the police and trying to work it out with the police.' Casey was by now part of the city's cultural establishment. She had run the Bluecoat Arts Centre and Liverpool's Chinese New Year festival and built relations with Liverpool police. 'I'd always been interested in the way that cities can't manage youth culture till it's gone,' she said. She made the case that despite its problems Cream was an asset for Liverpool – that it was bringing in young people to the city who were spending money, that it was improving the city's image, that university applications were going up as a result of the club.

This famous figure about Cream and students was in fact a clever piece of Casey PR. A research report had shown that 80 per cent of students that came to study in Liverpool came for the nightlife. Casey had read this report, tried to get a copy and found out it had been lost. So she tweaked the figures to read that 80 per cent of students came for Cream, rather than the general nightlife, as students are wont to do. 'We did so well with that that we ended up with the vice chancellors of the university quoting it in *The Times* and things!' But it certainly helped a club that was being investigated by the police and looking at potential closure. 'I came in and started the discussions with the police,' she said. 'There was a "trying to make friends" period with Cream, because it was just obvious that it was going to get closed down.'

In February 1996, Alfie Lewis, the head of security at Cream, and 17 other people were arrested and charged. The charges related to the supply and offer to supply of ecstasy. Nine of the charges named Cream. In court, speaking from behind screens, undercover officers described buying ecstasy with ease at Cream. Police alleged that Lewis controlled the trade. Lewis, a former World Kick-Boxing Champion, was a well-known figure in Liverpool's Toxteth area and supported charitable causes throughout the city. According to the *Liverpool Echo*, which covered the case extensively: 'He had symbolised the regeneration of Toxteth in the wake of the riots and worked to rebuild the image of the area where he was born.' The *Liverpool Echo* later reported that he had been charged before with aggressive behaviour although he was not convicted.

Casey played her cards well. She told the newspaper at the time: 'Cream has over the last three years developed into a thriving business, which plays its part in the economic regeneration of the city. In particular, Cream has acted as a catalyst to the regeneration of the Bold Street area. The position of the company is unequivocally anti-drugs. Obviously, we recognise and take very seriously the threat that this widespread practice poses to our business. We are therefore totally in support of the Merseyside Police and the action that they have taken to curb the sale of illegal drugs in and around our premises.'

At a trial in September 1996 the jury failed to reach a verdict. At a second trial in November and December 1998, Lewis and his associate Amir Khorasani were found guilty of plotting to supply ecstasy. In February 1999 Lewis was sentenced to 12 years and Khorasani to seven and a half. In February 2001, after a retrial Lewis walked free. The jury had failed to reach a verdict and the prosecution offered no further evidence.

Meanwhile Cream had employed new door security staff and survived by the skin of its teeth. 'So that's my entrance into Cream,' said Jayne Casey. 'It's just like, "Oh *fucking* hell!"' Both Barton and Hughes believe that she probably saved the club. 'She talked our talk and talked the authorities talk. And was just what we needed and just at the right time,' said Hughes.

The club became increasingly proactive in the area of drugs. Instead of pretending that drugs did not exist in the club, they worked to stop dealing and to look after the health of their clubbers. Cream employed full-time paramedics, installed free water for customers and worked closely with Dr Chris Luke from Royal Liverpool University Hospital's Accident and Emergency department. In 1997, they even staged a conference on club safety at the club at which Luke spoke, sponsored by Cream, Liverpool University and the North West NHS. Luke said that 80 per cent of admissions to hospitals from clubs were caused by drink and violence, 10 per cent from drug-related problems such as ecstasy-related panic attacks. 'In clubs where ecstasy exists the level of violence is appreciably lower. Where drink is the main cultural vehicle, violence is endemic,' he said. Ecstasy brought all kinds of dangers. But thanks to Cream, Liverpool was a noticeably less violent city.

IN FEBRUARY 1999 James Palumbo took his former employee and former lover, dance music executive Lynn Julia Cosgrave, to court for breach of contract. Cosgrave had been a key player at Ministry and one of the most powerful DJ agents in dance music. While working there, she had a nine-month relationship with James Palumbo. Piqued that she had left and then joined a rival record company, Ministry sued saying she had secretly carried on managing other DJs – including C.J. Mackintosh – while working at Ministry and had taken or removed files and documents when she left. And this complicated case was bound up in their personal and business entanglements, even dissecting a verbal deal they were supposed to have made while walking in Hyde Park.

Cosgrave joined Ministry in March 1993 as an employee but was still managing other DJs. In 1995 she became label manager of MOS Recordings and in 1996 a director and was given 30 per cent shares. She resigned on 25 September 1997, taking her assistant with her, apparently to run her own DJ management business, but quickly joined Sony Records as vice-president of dance. Ministry won on the first two claims and Cosgrave on the third. It was a nasty split between two former lovers and business associates. And in finding for Ministry on two claims – that she was doing her own business secretly while working there – and for Cosgrave on the third, the allegation that she took documents and files – Mr Justice Newberger's 82-page summation didn't mince its language.

'It is clear that Miss Cosgrave regarded and still regards Mr Palumbo as an acute and enterprising, if somewhat manipulative, businessman,' his summation said. He added: 'Mr Palumbo attributes much of the success of MOS Recordings during the period of Miss Cosgrave's employment to her hard work and expertise.' He noted that the turnover of MOS Recordings had increased from £1.3 million in the nine months to August 1995 to nearly £4 million for the following 12 months, to August 1996 and to £12 million by August 1997. Cosgrave and her assistant had 'behaved badly, indeed dishonestly, when employed by MOS'. Dance music was big business now and its fat cats were increasingly bickering with each other. Here was the Ministry's dirty laundry, being washed in public. And it was clear James Palumbo was not a man to be messed with.

But Ministry's record business was booming. Not satisfied with club compilations, they had also started releasing hit singles. In 1999, Ministry signed the trance hit '9pm (Till I Come)' by ATB. 'We signed it for £2,500. We found it in Holland,' said Matt Jagger. 'When we put it out in June 1999 it did 272,000 copies in the first week.' The record went on to sell over a million. But as the millennium passed and new genres like rock and R'n'B became more popular, the Ministry made a brief, doomed attempt to become a traditional record company. Jagger believed the company should sign and develop artists – an expensive and risky business.

In 2001, like many, Jagger believed the new 'electro-clash' scene would be the next big thing. 'Electro-clash' was a new sound from New York and Berlin. Dance music with an eighties' synth-pop tinge, heavy on irony and made by more traditional bands with singers. The hottest band in this world was New York's Fischerspooner. Jagger signed them for Ministry, after a bidding war with BMG Records, for $2 million. 'I was smitten,' said Jagger. 'I thought they were the next big thing.'

But despite a hugely expensive London show, Fischerspooner's album *One* failed to sell. Ministry, by now in a deal with the venture capital company 3i, decided it was not, after all, going to move into the expensive and risky business of developing artist albums. Jagger's strategy had failed. He left to join Mercury Records where he proved his point and signed the hit rock act Razorlight. His deputy Lohan Presencer took over his job and still holds it. Presencer managed to get most of their money back when Fischerspooner were shunted onto EMI, who also failed to break them.

'I think that we had a business plan to grow as an international major record company, globally and in reference to artist development, and it didn't work. And we needed to restructure our business accordingly,' Presencer told me. Ministry went back to its 'core values': the club, events, hit dance singles, club compilations. Its success continues today. 'The reason why the MOS is how it is now, you had two people running it who weren't taking drugs,' concluded Humphrey Waterhouse. 'We weren't interested in that side of it. We didn't do clubbing. We weren't club people in that sense. We were just very focused.'

16 AUGUST 1998. The five Brazilian girls held hands and gazed adoringly at the DJ booth at Cream. They were coming up on their pills and their hero, Paul Oakenfold, was about to begin his set. They had organised their holidays to coincide with this pilgrimage to Cream. 'We loved Paul Oakenfold. We had all his CDs. It was our dream to see him,' says one of them, Roxy Abdalla, who was 30. The five, all from São Paulo, had taken a train from London's Euston. In Liverpool, they took a taxi to Abbey Road – though they couldn't understand a word the cabbie said – and recreated the famous Beatles album cover in photographs. 'I always loved Beatles,' Roxy says. When they arrived at Cream, the outside of the club was covered with pictures of Ronaldo, the football hero, wearing a Brazilian shirt with a Cream logo. 'We started to hug each other – we were so happy when we saw this,' said Roxy.

Oakenfold was the new resident at Cream and people were by now coming all over the world to see him – his fame had even reached Brazil. One designer would even make a weekly trip from New York. Oakenfold emerged from behind a curtain and introduced his set with the lush, pretty chords of a track called 'Mystery Lands' by Y-Traxx. An echoing voice wailed. A beat kicked in. The whole of Cream's Annex, where Oakenfold played, started roaring their approval. Oakenfold launched into a high-octane set – he had hit a vein with a new 'psyche-delic trance' sound that had come out of beach parties in Goa, India, and which Oakenfold, ever the trendspotter, had turned into dance music gold. The crowd was going wild, screaming and shouting. 'Everyone looking at him like a god. I'm looking at him like a god. He was like an idol to me,' Roxy said.

Oakenfold's Cream residency took the superstar DJ to new heights. And not just in terms of the adoring crowds, whose glow he basked in for two years. His agent, the notoriously tough David Levy from ITB, had negotiated a 20-page contract. The DJ, a Chelsea FC fan, was to be picked up by a chauffeur-driven car from Stamford Bridge every Saturday after the match, if the team were playing, and driven to Cream. If they couldn't drive him, he flew. If there were no flights, the club had to hire a plane. The DJ got to design his own booth and specify the sound equipment. And the signing of his contract was cele-brated with a photo session at his beloved Stamford Bridge, where James Barton had a Chelsea shirt printed up but initially got the name wrong – he had them write OAKFOLD – and had to get it redone.

In the midst of the madness at Cream, the five Brazilian girls made friends with all kinds of people. There was no sexual pressure. 'Everybody talking to everybody, girls, boys,' said Roxy. 'If you wanted to talk to someone, you just smiled and you could talk to them.' She remembered that in the grubby toilets all the taps were on and the sinks overflowing with water. After Cream shut, some boys showed them an after-hours party. Later they sat shivering at Lime St Station, waiting for the first train back to London. They even hid in the ladies toilet for a while, because it was warmer. On the train they slept happily. Their dream had come true and Oakenfold had delivered. 'It was a magical night,' Roxy smiled.

Oakenfold's story, including his Cream residency, is told in *Paul Oakenfold: The Authorised Biography* by Richard Norris (Bantam Press, 2007). It is a detailed and well-researched book, but not so much biography as hagiography. The DJ was a key figure in acid house history, but nothing as distasteful as drugs or money was ever mentioned – bar the famous Ibiza ecstasy experience. Instead his impressive career is detailed in glowing terms, every twist and turn given as positive a spin as possible – from his Heineken-sponsored world tour to recent sample-heavy recent pop albums like *Bunkka*. One chapter describes him as the 'Minister for Entertainment'. 'Oakie' reveals, 'I've learnt a lot professionally from Madonna.' In classic acid house style, everything and everybody was listed, and nothing was actually said.

Oakenfold was the consummate trendspotter: from acid house, through 'Madchester' – Oakenfold produced the Happy Mondays album *Pills, Thrills and Bellyaches* – to trance. He is a brilliant DJ but also a ruthless careerist whose fees were famously high. He justified these by saying he was not so much a guy that played records as an entertainer. 'Whether it's raising my hands or pointing to someone in the crowd and smiling, it means the world,' Oakenfold once said. In 1999, helped no doubt by his Cream fees, he was judged the most successful DJ in the world by the *Guinness Book of Records*, with earnings of £728,000. He still owns a house in London's Connaught Square – next door to Tony Blair. His biography does not include the story of when he went to the Rio carnival and danced for the samba school Beija Flor, dressed as an angel. Still in his angel outfit, he turned to one of the group, Brazilian club face Henrique Cury, and said: 'For the first time in my life, I don't see myself as a devil.' Oakenfold still DJs and also works extensively in film soundtracks.

The Cream juggernaut rolled on. James Barton worked during the week as an A&R man for Deconstruction Records. It was the forceful, shaven-headed Darren who was there week after week. He was a regular feature on the dance floor and would prowl the backstage areas, handing out pills to people he liked, presumably without Barton's knowledge. 'All of which were given,' said Hughes. 'What the fuck's that all about? I can't even conceive of that now. I guess it just indicates how carried away we were at that time of our life.' After parties at Hughes's house were famously decadent and would spill out into the garden. He was earning up to £200,000 a year. 'It was a rollercoaster. Unbelievable times, unbelievable memories, unbelievable people,' said Hughes. 'Living the dream, the full cliché. Photograph after photograph after photograph of memories that when you look back at them almost seem too good to be true.' When Hughes got married, with Barton as best man, his wedding was a who's who of clubland.

But James Barton was earning even more because of his high-paid Deconstruction job – two or three times that of his partner. He bought an Alfa Romeo Spider one day – writing out a cheque for £25,000 and driving it off the forecourt. It wasn't his most expensive car purchase. 'I bought a Porsche for 65 grand off a friend of mine, in the South of France, wasted. Couldn't work out afterwards why. I was like, "Fuck."' Unlike Ministry, Cream did not file full accounts and so it is impossible to say what their profits were. James Barton point-blank refused to discuss or reveal them.

At their peak, Cream were famously bolshie. If they didn't like a feature or an editorial, they would phone up and shout down the phone. At a panel during the In The City music conference, they came under fire from the dance industry for their arrogance and overwhelming success. 'Cream had just become too much for people to take,' said Barton. 'I think that's when I certainly felt as though the ego had got out of control.' At that point perhaps they believed they could do anything. As it turned out, they couldn't.

PRESSURE WAS BUILDING at Cream. Darren and James had by now split into two rival camps, with two rival groups of friends. Hughes particularly was feeling the strain of running this huge club. He worked obsessively hard. He used to regularly call Jayne Casey at midnight, worrying. 'Darren was always a bit of a nervous wreck and he used to cry a lot,' she said. 'He was getting wound up in too many directions. He had too many people saying to him, "Oh, you're God in this company, you're doing everything and James is off there."'

Meanwhile Barton liked his record-company executive life – a busy record-company office down South, a huge club in Liverpool at week-ends. 'I had a career in London, I genuinely liked being down there. I found Liverpool quite difficult in a lot of ways,' said Barton. 'We'd just come off all of this drama with police outside and drug busts and everything, I just wanted an easy life.' Meanwhile Hughes was in Liverpool, dealing with the day-to-day – the bouncer problems, the police, the nitty gritty.

But the day Hughes announced he was leaving came as a shock. Casey had had dinner with him the night before and he'd said nothing. Since then, she has neither met nor spoken to him. Barton was expect-ing it. But it still went down badly. 'The look on his face when I told him, it was horrible. It was like you would imagine the situation to be if you were leaving your partner,' said Hughes. James Barton was his friend; he had been best man at his wedding and his partner for nearly a decade. Barton told him to get out. Hughes had already cleared his desk. 'He had to go there and then,' said Barton. He was angry, but also relieved. 'It's a little bit like when you've been in a marriage or you've been in a relationship and you know it's over and you stop fighting,' said Barton. 'And then suddenly there's that sort of calmness.'

Hughes's departure came after a long period of complicated deal-making – he had been talking to Ron McCulloch, one of two bosses of the powerful Scottish Big Beat group that owned a chain of clubs, restaurants and bars across Scotland. McCulloch was also an architect who had designed some of them. He had big plans. He wanted to join with Cream and open a Cream superclub in London. He already had a place in Sydney, Australia, he was talking to the people who owned Twilo in New York. He had started negotiations on a big property in Leicester Square. 'We looked at the Cream brand and we felt there was an opportunity to compete with Ministry and do a world music brand,' McCulloch told me from Australia, where he now lives. 'We felt Cream had the potential to do that.'

It became a saga. Darren was seduced. He wanted Cream to do the deal. Barton was initially tempted. 'When someone's saying to you, "We're going to spend 20 million quid and there's going to be a big screen outside and that screen is going to have a big Cream logo on and you're going to be next to these established brands like Hard Rock Café and Planet Hollywood", there was a bit of me thinking, "Well maybe this is the way this is going to go."' But he backed off after a meeting in a hotel at Manchester airport. He didn't like the deal Big Beat was offering. 'I didn't want to do a shit deal, I didn't want to undersell the business. But I think Darren really felt that this was his big opportunity, his deal,' said Barton. He was coming under pressure to leave Deconstruction and return to Liverpool full time. Barton said he would do it if he could become sole MD of Cream. Hughes wanted to share the job. Barton said no. Big Beat made an offer to buy him out. Barton refused to even look at it.

The boardroom battle raged on. Big Beat changed tack. Their plans were going ahead, but the new 'brand' was going to be called home, not Cream. They went after Hughes alone. 'He was the best promoter I'd ever met, without question,' said McCulloch. 'He's anal, in terms of how he goes about things. But in terms of the passion and the detail that Darren went into in every production he put together it was pretty spectacular.' Meanwhile, in the club, Oakenfold's stardom was sucking in numbers from the rest of the club. They were increasingly finding the other rooms empty as the whole club queued in to see the superstar DJ.

Throughout this manoeuvring, Cream were organising a giant rave with live acts called Creamfields – a rival to Tribal Gathering. Barton and Hughes were being filmed by a Channel 4 crew as part of a music programme about Creamfields called *The Chilling Fields*. There were plenty of tense moments between the two in the finished film. 'They filmed me not having a nervous breakdown but a very, very stressful time,' said Hughes. 'Me sitting there, being filmed, thinking about how I'm going to leave. I left one month later.'

The lives of the main Cream protagonists, the DJs they knew, their music business and club friends, their hangers on, were so entwined that they were difficult to separate. Friends split. It ended, like a bad marriage, in court. Barton won. 'I'm a good fighter, I can fight my own corner and I can do things.' But not before Cream's star attraction Paul Oakenfold left too and joined home a few months later. Hughes thought his third of the company, which he owned with Barton and Stuart Davenport, was worth £300,000–£400,000. Cream didn't. Hughes sent spent £96,000 on a legal battle. 'It was a horrible, horrible, horrible time,' he said. 'I thought I was being completely ripped off. Out of £160,000 that my shares were valued at, I got

£66,000. You know what? Meant nothing to me.' Barton had his own side to this. 'What he certainly doesn't realise is I pulled a loan down on my house to put towards buying his shares.'

Hughes went off to London to pursue his ambitions. But home was to prove a disaster. And Cream was left struggling. 'The club never recovered from Oakenfold leaving, frankly,' said Barton. 'We never got back to that level of intensity, that level of audience, that level of capacity. It was roughly around the same time that the whole question marks about dance started to happen.'

Barton and I lunched in a chic, bohemian restaurant near to Cream's HQ in Liverpool's Bold Street area. In 2003, the designer Hope Street Hotel opened just around the corner – an event celebrated in *Tatler* magazine, a publication more accustomed to celebrating the James Palumbos of this world, in an article that coined the word 'Livercool'. If Cream achieved anything, it was to make a city feel good about itself again. But it achieved much more than that and played a key part in the city's regeneration. In 2008, Liverpool became the European Capital of Culture – Jayne Casey, who left Cream after the millennium, organised the opening ceremony from her office in the grandiose old St George's Hall. And dance music's journey to the centre of this city's establishment was complete. Barton is something of a celebrity here in the way that Derek Hatton once was – the local boy made good.

Barton has run into his old friend Darren Hughes just once in nearly a decade. It was at Pacha nightclub in Ibiza, when both found themselves in a men's toilet together. There wasn't much of a conversation – too much bad blood, too much to be said. They both remembered it the same way. 'It's like meeting up with an old girlfriend. Someone you like and you should be friends with and you weren't any more. It was like, 'Oh, fucking hell. Hi mate. How you doing?' Hughes recalled. 'As soon as one of the cubicles become available Darren went and used it,' said Barton, 'and that was the end of that.'

NINE
DANCE MUSIC AND THE ESTABLISHMENT PART 2: LARGIN' IT

TUNE! STARDUST – 'MUSIC SOUNDS BETTER WITH YOU'

The contagiously funky French house hit that Norman Cook used to sing as 'music sounds better with shoe'.

Derek Dahlarge was asleep in a deckchair outside the open-air Bora Bora club. He had his shades on, looking cool. The DJ liked to party hard. But he could keep it together too. He struggled awake as his mate Jon Carter appeared. But he didn't see the large pink dildo Carter was carrying, nor the grinning photographer following behind, until it was too late. 'I sort of curled it onto him, held it down for 30 seconds cause I'd translated the instructions and then put my hand down,' said Carter. 'So he sees two hands but he still feels a third one. He's sort of chasing his head, like a dog chasing his tail. He's got this really electric look on his face.' The photographer was ready: click, click, click. Within days, the photo of Dahlarge with a large pink dildo glued to his head was on the cover of Mixmag's *weekly Ibiza magazine and being giggled at all over the island. Rumour had it Dahlarge was spotted outside the Manumission office, furiously hosing down a large pile of issues. 'Dildogate' only lasted a few seconds but the story would stick with Dahlarge for ever. He had just one comment: 'Very fucking funny.'*

ZOË BALL WAS late. She was off her head. And she was about to be sick. It was 6.25am and the car bounced up the dusty track to the Radio 1 villa in Ibiza. She was due on air in a matter of minutes. As the car pulled up, she could see a worried line of Radio 1 bigwigs. There was Ian Parkinson, Radio 1's second in command. Pat Connor, in charge of the station's Ibiza weekend and her co-presenter Kevin Greening. 'I could see them all standing on the balcony,' Zoë said. 'My producer's going, "Jesus, she's just about to make it."' The car screeched to a halt and Zoë started dry heaving into a bush. 'Everyone says I was sick, I wasn't actually sick. And I went up to do the show.' In the gang with her was Norman Cook, a guest on that morning's show and Shovel, the party-mad percussionist with pop-dance act M People. They had all been up all night. They were all the worse for wear. And Zoë went straight on air.

Ibiza on that morning, 31 July 1998, was at its peak as a clubbing holiday destination. Packed with ravers from all over the world, brimming with clubs, bars and beaches – decadent beyond imagining. I was there that July. The place was so crowded and dominated by dance music that at night it felt like the whole island was bouncing to a house beat. So it was an ambitious plan to move the whole of Radio 1 to Ibiza for a weekend. And broadcast live. They wanted to 'hit the zeitgeist'. Radio 1 had been there before, presenting shows by DJs like Pete Tong. But never on this scale, nothing like this. Not with daytime presenters.

Pat Connor was the Radio 1 executive in charge of the weekend. 'A risk-taking idea. Quite a difficult thing to do, on a big scale, high impact and taking all of these fish out of water,' she said. 'It was like a big school trip. Find accommodation, set up a base for all the broad-casters. It wasn't like turning up at a festival with an OB truck. It was literally moving the station to a different country for three or four days, which was a massive operation.'

The station's schedule was already dance music heavy. But Radio 1's night-time, specialist DJs – 'They were called the Dark Side,' said Connor – were used to negotiating the craziness of Ibiza. The daytime presenters were not. 'In Ibiza,' Connor explained, 'everything is in a slightly parallel universe. The things that you think are going to happen at a certain time just don't. You think that everything is going to be sorted. Actually it's quite different. It's never quite what you expect.' Zoë Ball was going to present her breakfast show with Kevin Greening. Lisa l'Anson was doing her Sunday lunchtime show. 'I said to them all very clearly,' said Pat, 'you need to be here. They were grown-ups. You can't be their mum.'

Zoë's evening started quietly the night before her show, with a drinks reception at the Radio 1 villa, near San Antonio, where they would broadcast. Despite the fact that they had some of the country's biggest DJs along, they didn't have any dance CDs to play as staff and guests mingled around the pool, so Kevin Greening put on some playlist chart stuff. 'We trundled up to the Radio 1 villa. And I remember thinking, "God, everyone's being so boring, no one's drinking, everyone's being really well behaved,"' Zoë remembered. 'And I was like, "This is Ibiza, we're supposed to be doing something really exciting."'

But Greening and her team all said they were planning an early night. 'And I was just like, "You can't come to Ibiza and not go out. We've got to do the show tomorrow. What are we going to talk about? Our villa? You've got to kind of live a bit of a life."' Then she was introduced to Norman Cook, who was to be the guest on her show the next day. 'I said: "Oh, Mr Cook, I presume." And he said, "How would you like to not go to bed with me this evening?" i.e., "Shall we stay up all night and go to the clubs."' Zoë was instantly charmed. 'Come on then,' she told him, 'we won't go to bed, let's go out.'

It is one of the most famous chat-up lines in pop history. And it worked. Zoë piled into a car with Norman and his mates and went out. It was a messy night that took in the KM5 bar and Cream at the Amnesia club. They finished up at the Manumission Motel, as Ibiza nights out in 1998 often did, which was a former brothel that the Manumission club had turned into a party hotel. There were strippers pole dancing in the bar, sex-themed rooms, celebrities, DJs and clubbers roaming the place. The Motel was a surreal, bacchanalian joint. 'It was half fall of the Roman Empire and half Sodom and Gomorrah and half David Lynch film. Obviously Johnny the Dwarf on the door. Just bedlam. Bedlam,' said Norman Cook. And by the time they got to the Motel, Zoë was the worse for wear. 'I remember coming to, somewhere, I had no idea where I was, in a bathroom, with a load of people and thinking, "I don't know who any of these people are,"' she said. 'Staggering out and I was in the Manumission Motel.' Because there were paparazzi swarming about, Norman had persuaded Zoë not to pole dance. But had Zoë been taking drugs? 'No shit Sherlock!' laughed Norman now. And so, without sleep, Zoë went on air.

Luckily Kevin Greening, a solid radio pro, was able to keep control. 'Thank God Kev was doing it cause I was completely off my tits,' Zoë recalled. She fell asleep at one point and Norman took a picture. She jumped in the pool. Norman came on a little after 8 a.m. Although Zoë had a boyfriend waiting back at her hotel, she and Norman flirted outrageously, joking about the fact that neither could remember where they'd actually been the night before. Their voices were slurred. There were random moments. Greening sounded like an exasperated parent, patiently trying to keep his teenage children under control.

Greening began his interview by thanking Norman for coming on. Norman said he could only be there this early if he'd been up all night. Zoë interrupted: 'It's really funny because everyone said make sure you get Norman on the show, make sure you get him here. Who brought who in this morning? You virtually carried me off the street, didn't you?' The show rambled on. Greening asked about the many aliases Norman Cook used in his recording career. The conversation went like this:

NORMAN: The many sides of Norman. All of which were exposed to Zoë Ball last night.

ZOË (quickly): No, not quite all of them. There's still a couple of them to go. There's still a couple of sides we haven't seen yet.

NORMAN: Oh, you're a game old girl, aren't you?

ZOË: Anyway.

NORMAN: The only reason I'm doing this... Zoë said I was fit one day. And all my mates told me and said, 'Zoë thinks you're fit.' And that's why I'm here now.

It was Norman's birthday. Still on air, station staff presented him with a water cannon, which he began playing with noisily. 'We will have people dancing by the end of the show,' Zoë insisted noisily. Listening, it felt like the show was beginning to disintegrate slightly. Greening did his best to keep order.

KEVIN: I think it could be the end of the show that finally gets people dancing actually.

Zoë was by now using an echo unit to distort her voice. '*Screaming with delight!*' she cried. 'You having a nice time, Norm?'

NORM: Oh she's up on the chair now. Steady. Easy girl.

ZOË: Shov's in his wrestling pants.

[In the background Shovel from could be heard saying: 'Bring it on! Bring it on!']

NORM: Easy. It's going to be a long weekend. Like. Simmer down, you know what I mean, simmer down.

And so the great romance of nineties clubland began – at the end of a long, druggy night out in Ibiza's clubs, live on air on BBC radio, with one of Britain's most famous presenters fooling about with a DJ who in the club world was famous for his narcotic consumption, who bragged in interviews about snorting cocaine off a railway line. Underground acid house and mainstream celebrity collided with a bang. 'I just thought, "What a wicked bloke. What a great attitude to life." He was like, "We're just here to have fun." I was thinking, "Yeah, I could buy into this, this is great",' Zoë said. 'He was absolutely charming. It was love at first sight.' In the study of the couple's vast, comfortable, seafront Brighton home, Zoë Ball laughed about it. 'How I was not fired I don't know. But I still meet people now who say, "I never forget that show, cause it was *hysterical*."'

RADIO ONE NEEDED acid house. The music had been at the centre of the revolution wrought by controller Matthew Bannister in the 1990s, as he purged the station of its old-school DJs – the smarmy personality jocks like Dave Lee Travis and Mike Read, so memorably lampooned as 'Smashey and Nicey' in the sketch from the nineties comedy series

The Fast Show. Pete Tong was first in, hired in 1991, where he replaced the presenter Jeff Young. 'When I arrived at Radio 1 it was the beginning of the changing of the regime,' Tong said. Later, Bannister would turn to Tong regularly for advice. Pete Tong was his guide into a cooler world of music. They met over lunch and at London hotels. Tong told them to get Tim Westwood, to get DJs, to do mix shows. Bannister listened. 'I was taken under Matthew Bannister's wing and became a very strong confident of his inner circle. I was right there,' Tong told me. 'It was the beginnings of the next generation.'

A wave of club DJs followed Pete Tong to the station as Radio 1 transformed itself: Danny Rampling, Judge Jules, Seb Fontaine, plus Tim Westwood, the biggest hip hop DJ in the UK. Drum 'n' bass DJs like Fabio and Grooverider followed. Many of the DJs came from London's KISS 100, which had been a pirate station playing dance and black music and then gained a legal licence. By 1998, Radio 1 was a completely new station, its weekend schedule dominated by the same repetitive beats the Conservative government had legislated against. And on Fridays, Pete Tong had the biggest show of all. At 46 he still has it: *The Essential Selection*.

From pirate radio to the BBC is another way that dance music became legitimised. But this was the BBC and unlike independent dance media – magazines like *Mixmag* and *Muzik* – they could not refer, at least directly, to the drugs and decadence that were driving the scene. Instead, Radio 1 dance music shows began inventing their own vernacular. First was 'larging it': soon everyone on Pete Tong's show was 'larging it', a nice, catch-all phrase that sat neatly next to well-established dance music euphemisms like 'caning it' and 'partying hard'. It could mean a big night out to a club with all your friends, as listeners who quickly latched on often bragged. It could also mean a big night out in the context of 1990s clubbing, which meant all of the above, with drugs.

Dave Pearce's *Sunday Night Dance Anthems* was also broadcast from Ibiza that weekend. His was a kind of nationwide comedown session with all the big records of the weekend being requested on recorded messages by slurry-voiced clubbers who had clearly been 'largin' it' the night before and often sounded like they hadn't been to bed yet. Pearce's catchphrase was genius. 'Roll another fat one, Dave,' the callers would insist. Which, as everybody knew, was an exhortation to roll another fat joint – though the show jokingly pretended it meant 'roll out another tune' – just as most of his audience, winding down from its Saturday night, was doubtless doing.

By 1998 it seemed like the whole nation was in on a secret joke – 'largin' it' on Friday night, 'rolling another fat one' by Sunday evening. Drugs had become mainstream and nobody involved in any big organisation, be that Radio 1 or a magazine or a record company, was going to rock the boat by pretending to be against them. Even at Ministry of Sound, new MD of MOS Recordings Matt Jagger could see what was going on. 'The drug culture of the nineties was so open, wasn't it? That was the new thing. Everybody – Sara Cox and Zoë Ball on Radio 1 – going on about being up all night, everyone was hinting at it all of the time, it was very much in the popular culture. We take drugs. Aren't we cool? Business-wise we were never going to rock that.' But Radio 1's weekend in Ibiza had only just begun. They had got through the Norm and Zoë show. When it came to lunchtime DJ Lisa l'Anson, they would not be so lucky.

LISA L'ANSON WAS another of those faces brought in to make Radio 1 funky. And like many faces on the station, she had come from London's

KISS FM. Daughter of a Danish father and Ghanaian mother, she is still the only black daytime DJ the station has ever employed. L'Anson was a private-school girl from West London who started her career in fashion PR before joining KISS when it was still a pirate station. She presented a magazine show called *The Word*. 'I remember Gordon Mac [KISS FM's boss] employing me cause if you listen to any of the early Word tapes I do sort of talk really quite refined, so I think he quite liked the fact I was a posh girl on air on a pirate.'

And Lisa was down. Lisa hung out with Gilles Peterson and Norman Jay and partied on the West London warehouse party scene. She loved black music: soul, funk, hip hop. She went out to dance. Like a lot of people she came out of the late eighties/early nineties dance music scene when it was largely illicit, based around illegal warehouse parties and pirate radio because the establishment – be that the BBC, or legal clubs – at that time largely ignored it. 'I liked the rebellion of pirate radio. I loved it. I loved that attitude of our scene, we'll have our music our way under any terms.' When KISS finally got a legal licence after years of struggle – they lost out first time to Jazz FM – the station celebrated with a show on London's Highbury Fields. 'It was a really joyous summer. A special time – that we can make a difference. Finally get our music heard legally as oppose to illegally. A real exciting time.'

We met at a Pizza Express in West London. She was warm, friendly and surprisingly honest, that famous throaty voice very much in evidence. She brought up Ibiza within minutes. What happened there in 1998 clearly had a dramatic impact on her life. From KISS she went to MTV. At MTV, she was approached by Radio 1 to join the station. They had to ask her three times. 'It wasn't my thing. I thought I'd be a sell-out if I went.' Finally she jumped. Friends from her West London scene told her she would be 'representing' them. She had a lunchtime show, which meant she had to play playlist pop music, but her easy delivery made her a popular presenter. 'I was a black woman but boy, didn't I make them look good? To slot me in the middle of daytime, with white guys either side. Well done them.' Like Zoë, to listeners Lisa came across like one of their funkier friends. She was cool. She sounded like someone you'd want to hang out with, rather than, say, Jo Wiley, who sounded like your mum telling you which records to like. And she loved presenting. 'Really enjoy it. Get paid to sort of talk, get paid to be myself. It's a joy.'

The problem was she had to play mainstream pop. 'I had to fight so goddamn hard to get the music I loved through. Impossible. It was all producer-directed and playlist, with no input from DJs.' But Lisa fought a few battles. She helped get The Prodigy's 'Firestarter' on the playlist, for example. But when she turned up in Ibiza to present two shows, a simmering discontent turned into something more serious. 'That contradiction of being in that environment and having to stick to a really bloody rigid boring dry-arsed un-funky, un-hip playlist, really,' she said.

On Saturday night, 1 August, Lisa went out to the Radio 1 special broadcast from Manumission – the club, which usually ran on Mondays, had put on a special night but without the usual sex show. 'The famous last words were Pete Tong saying to me, "Stay close,"' Lisa giggled. 'And off I went.' As nights like this were wont to happen in Ibiza, Lisa fell in with a bunch of people. She left Manumission without any of the Radio 1 staff. Pat Connor remembered wondering where she had gone. 'We were leaving the club and the OB [outside broadcast] vans were packing up when there was some uncertainty about where she was and who she was with. But it was just very vague.

Everyone goes off in different directions and you think, "It's Ibiza, some people are going home, some people are going to a party, some people are going to a club."' Connor even wandered down a lane outside the club at one point, looking for Lisa.

But Lisa had gone out, big time. She was 'largin' it', just like they said on the Pete Tong show. But then it all went Pete Tong. She too ended up in the Manumission Motel. And there was Derek Dahlarge, though by this time he had at least removed all traces of the pink dildo from his forehead. Dahlarge was staying all summer, DJing at Manumission. He had a room at the motel. He told me it was the most hedonistic summer of his life. 'There was no perception of reality. It was just Fantasy Island all the way, motherfucker,' he said of life at the Motel.

Derek Dahlarge was already famous in Ibiza. He was part of the Wall of Sound record label crew, friends with Jon Carter and Norman Cook. He was already a notorious party animal and when we met still had that dangerous air about him. He had arrived in Ibiza to DJ at Manumission, been offered a residency, and simply not gone home, just stayed on, DJing and partying. 'I was having the time of my life, it was just amazing. One relentless party after another, living in that motel,' said Dahlarge. His 'disappearance' had made headlines. *Muzik* magazine made up a wanted poster with his photo on it and put it up around the island. 'He was a real face of the scene at that time. I think people really did wonder where he'd gone,' said former *Muzik* editor Ben Turner. Pete Tong even talked about it on his Radio 1 show.

It was all a joke. Dahlarge wasn't hard to find. He DJed at Manumission from 5 to 7 a.m. Went back to the Motel and partied on. 'Or go to a villa and shag some bird.' Then he would go to the Bora Bora open-air beach club, where 'Dildogate' happened. Then, often enough, straight through to Miss Moneypenny's on a Tuesday night and right through until Wednesday morning. 'Big Daddy Caned. Like a motherfucker,' as he put it. 'It was just relentless, it was brilliant. Orgies, you name it, it was all going on.'

By now it was next morning and at the Radio 1 villa they began to wonder where Lisa was. 'There was a moment on the Sunday morning where there was some concern about her whereabouts,' said Pat Connor. Lisa was at a party in Derek Dahlarge's room – a hazy, druggy, intimate after-hours party. Norman Cook was there. So was Jon Carter. By now, she was really 'largin' it'. Perhaps somebody 'rolled another fat one'. Either way, this was not the best place for a Radio 1 presenter with a show to do in a few hours to be hanging out – espcially one, like Lisa, with a simmering discontent. Then somebody offered something described as liquid LSD around, though Norman Cook now believes with hindsight that it was GHB. Whatever it was and whether it was that liquid or something else, Lisa took *something*. And any possibility of her presenting a live radio show in a few hours flew out of the window. 'I remember thinking, "You shouldn't do that,"' said Norman Cook.

Lisa didn't want to tell me what she took. She used words like 'incapacitated', 'disorientated state' and said: 'Of course, I was in an altered state.' Either way, hours later, she was sprawled on the bed in that 'altered state'. 'There's her lying in bed, getting the Manumission people around, the dancers, the strippers, all that,' said Carter. 'She's sort of giggling in bed. Not getting up to anything naughty, just sitting there giggling. There's me and my mate Donkey going, "Lisa, you're not that bad."' Carter tried to persuade her to do her show. 'You're not that bad, you can get through this you know,' he said to her. 'She's going, "*No*." She goes, "No, no, no, no." Going, "Come on, you can do it. We can do the Jon and the Donkey and Lisa show." "No." She just pulled the plug, basically, didn't she.' Instead Lisa wanted to organise a protest and get everybody to march up to the Radio 1 villa and hand over a petition. 'I'm not going to work, sign my petition,' she said to me, mock-slurring her voice. 'We had this notion, whoever the "we" were in that gang at that time, to go up the hill and take over the airwaves and play some real music.' She laughed.

The petition didn't happen. L'Anson stayed sprawled on the bed. Sooner or later, she fell asleep. She did not make her show. It became one of the most famous no-shows in broadcasting history. Radio 1's lunchtime presenter simply did not turn up for work because she was off her head in Ibiza. But she insisted that it wasn't just the drugs, that she was pissed off, that she 'pushed the fuck-it button'. Carter agreed. 'She could have done it but she just didn't want it. Just laying there.' Carter believes she took LSD. 'I think acid maybe gives you a little clarity sometimes.'

As Lisa's show got closer, Pat Connor realised Lisa wasn't going to show up. There were tense phone calls. People went out to look for her. But they also focused on the task in hand: getting the show on air. 'I let [Radio 1 boss] Andy Parfitt know. I called him and said, "Something's happened, can't find her,"' said Pat Connor. 'He was worried. But very calm and very considered. And together we made a plan. You do what you do instinctively if you work in radio. You have to be strategic.' Emma B, a perky, respectable, dependable sort of presenter stood in. The show went on air. At the last minute on that Sunday, just as they thought that arduous weekend was all over, they had to move the location of Dave Pearce's show, shifting the whole station across Ibiza in little more than an hour.

Back in London, Lisa was called in to see Radio 1 chief Andy Parfitt. On the way in, she found she was already becoming notorious. 'The number of people going, "Don't worry, Lise, we'll give you a job!" and

"Go on, babe!"' She met Parfitt. 'I sort of mumbled a story. I'm sure he didn't believe a word of it,' she said. 'But it was the beginning of the end.' Rumours flew: somebody had put liquid acid in her eyeballs, there was an orgy, Johnny the famous Manumission Dwarf was involved. None of the stories were true. Pulling a sickie from work after a big night out became known as 'Doing An L'Anson'. Radio 1 went back to doing smaller, one-off broadcasts from Ibiza. 'We never took the whole station back again,' said Pat Connor. 'That was our one hit.'

Afterwards, Lisa l'Anson received a highly publicised warning from Radio 1. BBC news called it a 'severe reprimand' and said: 'If a repeat situation were to occur Lisa would be summarily dismissed from the station.' She also had to apologise to colleagues. By the following February, she had left the station. 'It was just probably not the best thing she could have done,' Connor observed. 'Not the best look in the world.'

In 1999 Lisa began helping her partner Amos Pizey – Jeremy Healy's *Bleachin'* partner – host the VIP Room at home, London's doomed superclub. She was partying at the Met Bar. And she was taking a lot of cocaine. 'I'm sure you can guess the names of the rock stars or bloody supermodels or whoever I was hanging with. And it was there. And that's what we did, as it were. And such was my thing of, "Ooh, I'm invited, I'm in. All right then, I'll have some." Without any consequences to the burnout, the fallout.' Lisa said she became obsessed with the triviality of how famous the people she was hanging out with were. 'It's actually quite a toxic sort of pursuit, to be so obsessed by that whole celebrity culture. It used to *really matter to me*.' She ran into problems with cocaine and sought help. 'When it started going to a place where it was like, "Oh, I don't like this world any more," then I went to get support and do something about it,' she said. 'I'm in recovery. I go to NA [Narcotics Anonymous] meetings, I go to CA [Cocaine Anonymous], I'm in the fellowship. And have been for nearly two and a half years. And that was a choice I made in order to get some support for myself. I'm alive and it didn't become a mess. I've seen enough examples of it going that way.'

Meanwhile Lisa continued presenting and had a show on BBC Radio London for three years. In 2005 she appeared on *Celebrity Big Brother*, coming sixth out of nine. She hasn't been seen much the last few years and was doing some consultancy work with an Internet company, she told me. She and Amos have two children. They are separated but remain friends. 'I'm doing a creative writing course next week,' she said. Lisa l'Anson never presented national radio again. 'The sad thing is I'm still paying for it all these years later,' she concluded. 'There are cleverer ways to leave a job.'

LIKE LISA L'ANSON, Zoë Ball was a new kind of presenter. She had come from children's television, co-presenting the zany, irreverent Saturday morning show *Alive and Kicking* with Jamie Theakston, himself to later experience a tabloid scandal when he was caught at a brothel. Zoë was a girl next door but she was cool, too. And she was a pin-up. She had done shoots for magazines like *Loaded*. 'Obviously I wasn't a real *Loaded* girl, cause I wasn't fancy pants or big tits, or anything like that. I remember doing this shoot with them and feeling really uncomfortable, thinking, "This is a bit weird,"' she said. *Loaded* liked her because she was a 'ladette', a good-looking girl who also liked a drink and a party. Zoë felt the changes in the mood in the country, the way sexual politics were shifting. 'You got people like Denise [Van Outen] and me and Coxy [Sara Cox] and we were like one of the lads, having a bit of a laugh and it was never intentionally supposed to shock, but we just spoke our minds and it was okay to do that,' she said. 'Before then kids' TV presenters had been kids' TV presenters, radio DJs had been radio DJs, I suppose everyone was quite polite, weren't they? Everyone was quite well behaved. I think it all coincided at that time.'

The day of her Radio 1 Ibiza show, Zoë flew home with her boyfriend. Within months, she and Norman were dating. 'It was in the November when we finally got it together. Will they, won't they? I remember his manager Garry [Blackburn] saying to him, "God, is this a good idea? Notorious party animal, pro-sort of drug, club, going to go out with a kids' TV presenter, this can only mean one thing. It's going to be terrible. Doom."' But it happened. Norm and Zoë became a very rare beast – a celebrity couple people actually liked, endearing themselves to the public by not selling their high-profile wedding to *Hello!* magazine. The wedding made front-page news. There were pictures of it all over their downstairs toilet. They were very much in love. The country was in love with the idea of how much in love they were. Or at least the media were.

'We got offered a *Playboy*,' said Norman. 'You are joking, aren't you? Me and Zoë naked in bed in *Playboy*? "Oh yeah, it will be really tasteful and you'll have photo approval. We can airbrush things."' But though they never got on the celebrity media treadmill – turning down *I'm A Celebrity... Get Me Out of Here, Celebrity Big Brother, Richard and Judy* and countless adverts – there was no avoiding fame. This meant the end of Cook's relative anonymity. 'I enjoyed the fact that people knew my name and didn't know what I looked like,' he said. 'But then I met Zo and cocked the whole thing up. If you want to remain anonymous, things not to do – marry the nation's sweetheart breakfast DJ at the peak of your career. And then have a really big showbiz marriage.'

She was Norman's famous wife, wearing a cowboy hat, dancing on the side of the stage. The BBC children's TV girl, now living the decadent life of the nineties superstar DJ, on the road with Norman Cook every weekend. 'It was just a real crowd of crazy, insane party people and I had always thought of myself as a bit of a crazy, party girl,' Zoë said. 'These guys partied seven days a week! When I first started seeing Norm and we would be off to these clubs every weekend, up to Cream and down to Newcastle, here, there and everywhere. And you'd be like, "Wa-hey!" It's like you walk in and everyone's like your mate. But then Mondays, Tuesdays, Wednesdays, through to Friday, I used to go and do my radio show. Half the time I'm sure I was only 100 per cent compos mentis on a *Wednesday*.'

Then Zoë's close friend Sara Cox started dating Norman's friend Jon Carter – a DJ and producer whose appetite for 'partying' equalled that of his friends Norman Cook and Derek Dahlarge. The two women sometimes joined both partners on tour. One time they went to Cream in Liverpool with them. 'Then the next thing I know, Coxy and I are standing up on the side of the decks doing really bad dancing and suddenly everyone was staring at us,' Zoë recalled, wide-eyed. 'I looked at her and we started to panic, going, "We're up here now, now we have to do something." And we started hitting each other over the bum. It was like really crap porn dancing. It was like, "What are we *doing*?" And you could see Norm and Carter with their heads in their hands, going, "Please, go away, both of you."'

On more than one occasion, Zoë did the show having been up all night. Recently she came back for a Radio 1 fortieth anniversary party – by coincidence, with another hangover, much to Sara Cox's amusement. 'I walked into this loo. I was like, God, I remember the amount of mornings, sitting in this loo, going, "Come on, come on [she mimed panicky deep breaths]. Have another coffee. You can get it together. You'll be fine, you'll be fine,"' she said. 'And then it would all kick off again on Thursday, Friday. Wa-hey, off we go again. To the point where I think towards the end Radio 1 did pull me in and say, "Ah, uh-huh, you're not taking this job very seriously, are you?"'

In October 1998, *New of the World* exposed *Blue Peter* presenter Richard Bacon for taking cocaine. Lorraine Heggessey, the head of children's TV, apologised on national television for him. But the tabloids never ran an exposé on Norm and Zoë. The couple believed this was because Cook never hid what he did. 'I remember friends of mine saying, "What will the big surprise be? Who's going to be so surprised? You're going out with Norman Cook,"' said Zoë. The tabloid sting came eventually, but it wasn't about drugs. In 2003, two years after their son Woody was born, Zoë had a well-publicised affair with another DJ from the same 'big beat' scene, Dan Peppe. 'It was all pretty horrendous. The press on the doorstep, for three months, pretty much. Endlessly. Here, in London, outside, our families, phones were tapped, it was properly wrong and horrible.'

The couple got back together. Zoë took a break from presenting and for a while went to film school. But she resurrected her television career by becoming a contestant on the show *Strictly Come Dancing*. Norman Cook and Ed Simons from the Chemical Brothers were both in the audience. It was a far cry from Cream, Amnesia and the Manumission Motel but it made her respectable for both younger and older audiences. 'Another kind of disco, yeah. But disco for slightly older people,' she smiled. 'But you know what, it did me a lot of favours.' The madness of Ibiza forgotten, Zoë Ball today is a more grown-up kind of television presenter. She still has the breathless chatter and easy friendliness, but she looks older, wiser, if anything rather mumsy. She survived the nineties.

It would be Zoë's calm, organised co-presenter Kevin Greening – the one who went to bed early that night in Ibiza – who would go off the rails. On 29 December 2007 Greening, who was 44, died from a drugs overdose after taking part in a gay bondage session. He had been to a nightclub in South London before engaging in a dangerous sex game. According to the *Daily Mail* police sources said that he had taken large amounts of cocaine, ecstasy and GHB. No one outside of his close circle of friends had ever suspected Greening, who was super-professional, was into that sort of thing. But that's the problem with drugs, they get into the most unexpected places.

THE ESSENTIALLY ANARCHIC nature of acid house created a kind of chaos wherever it went. That was all part of the trip. Radio 1 survived its 1998 Ibiza weekend having only lost one presenter and narrowly escaping losing another. But the station's problems weren't over yet. By 1999, they had an impressive roster of superstar DJs who were all finding that having a national radio show did not do their profile, their DJ bookings or presumably their DJ fees any harm at all. Of course they would inform listeners where they might be playing that weekend. Would a club that booked one of these names expect a mention on air? Would that somehow be factored into the fee? It's impossible to say. But these DJs were also hard-headed players in the music business and had their fingers in a number of pies. Just as they had always been: that was the acid house way, right from the beginning. And nobody had more fingers in more pies than Radio 1's big daddy of dance music, Pete Tong.

In 1999, Tong was investigated for corruption by the *Independent*. The fallout would involve Conservative party politicians, the chairman of the BBC and a host of dance music bigwigs. Ministry of Sound got involved. It was symbol of how big acid house had become. 'What should be relevant to your book is how that could happen and how big a deal I allegedly was,' Tong told me pointedly. 'That someone took it so seriously, that I had so much power.'

The son of an alcoholic gambler and bookmaker, Pete Tong is a cautious, steady kind of guy. Unlike his father, he is also an excellent businessman. He grew up in a small village called Hartley, near Gravesend, in Kent and still has vestiges of his Estuary accent. Tong's ex-army father ran five betting shops around the area – Pete used to work in the backrooms as a teenager. Tong senior was something of a tragic character. 'He died quite young,' said Pete. 'At 59. Alcohol-related, really. It's a pretty miserable story. King of his own little world. Lot of cash. Business was getting harder. He starts gambling to try and make up the numbers. Some days he wins, most days he loses.'

His son was a sensible lad, which is what made him such a safe bet for Matthew Bannister when he set out to modernise Radio 1. He is an excellent radio presenter who more than any other DJ has pioneered, represented and pushed dance music into the mainstream. He always played new records and still does. But he was also always interested in money. His parents put him through public school – he started as a boarder and finished as a day boy. He was aware that the bookmaking business had its shady side. 'I think in my father's era, they all fancied themselves as the Kray Twins,' he said. 'You know, you had bouncers. At my first gigs, I used to borrow one of my dad's bouncers as a security guy, to collect the money.' Tong's first DJ outing was entrepreneurial. He hired a church hall in Hartley and put handwritten posters in cellophane bags on trees. He made £100. He loved being a DJ. 'It was a cult. It was a fashion statement. It was a lifestyle statement. It was being a DJ, it was what it was all about.'

At 29 he married Deborah and the couple had three children. He glided from the closed world of the late seventies/early eighties soul scene into acid house, DJing for Nicky Holloway at Trip and Sin. Tong was typically cautious about that 'first E' moment – too wily to say he did or to say he didn't. 'I was never a big E head, to be honest, never have been. So I think that I was being duped during the time of doing the Astoria. I think there was cheeky pills going into my drinks and all sorts of things, but actually consciously taking – I was just too much of a control freak.' Likewise when I asked him about the free drugs available to star DJs in the 1990s. He laughed and said, 'No comment.'

Club characters had always picked up on this. When the *Boys Own* fanzine first coined the phrase 'It's all gone Pete Tong', they used to phone him up late after parties, knowing that unlike them, he'd gone to bed and shout it down the phone. He graduated from a rising star on the soul scene with a column in *Blues & Soul* magazine. He had a show on Capital Radio. He had a senior job at one of dance music's most thrusting young record labels, London ffrr. And when he landed on Radio 1 in 1991, Pete Tong was already hustling on the new DJ circuit, phoning clubs, talking himself into work. 'Don't wait for someone to knock on your door, just get out and do it,' he said.

So from the very beginning, Pete Tong's various interests – radio, club DJing, record company – were all feeding into each other. This made him valuable to Radio 1 because he was on top of everything going on in dance music – and he still is. It also made him a lot of money. By the early to mid-nineties, he was already rich, powerful and positioned right at the centre of dance music with complex and intertwined roles – record company boss, but also influential BBC radio tastemaker.

Mixmag enjoyed a good relationship with Tong – the magazine printed the track listings from his radio shows. There were occasional lunches with him and his staff, which he always paid for and I used to look forward to the moment when he took out his wallet as it always used so seem to fat, the credit cards pinging out in a roll. Literally, the 'money shot'. He was invariably pleasant, intelligent, slightly dry. Mostly he loved to talk about new records. He was like the head prefect of acid house – he knew what all the bad boys were up to, but he was in with the teachers as well. We knew just how rich and influential he was and like naughty schoolboys would occasionally joke about a 'kamikaze' cover in which Tong would appear, holding out a wedge of cash like the Harry Enfield character 'Loadsamoney'. The joke was that the magazine would of course self-destruct afterwards: he was simply too powerful to take on.

Actually he wasn't, it was more that these circles of patronage in dance music went back to its cottage industry beginnings and a feeling that everybody was in this together. Except it wasn't a cottage industry any more, it was a great big bloody factory. Tong was ultimately perceived as a good thing, but he was in the middle of a lot of potentially conflicting interests. So the *Independent* investigation did not come as a surprise.

I interviewed him in Ibiza, where he plays once a week at Pacha during summer. He was relaxing at the chic Blue Marlin beach resort with his second wife, Brazilian former model Carolina. They both have children from their previous marriages. Now they have a young baby together, who was playing with her in the surf. 'It's complicated,' he said, reluctantly. Though easier, because here in Ibiza Tong and his wife seem to have adopted the middle-class Brazilian way of parenting, which involves a full-time nanny and maid.

Tong's new family all piled into his vast black SUV to head back to his villa and I followed in a tiny red Hyundai I had hired. As we pulled up a dauntingly steep country track I could see why he had the four-wheel drive. As my tinny little motor whined in protest I desperately hoped the Hyundai wouldn't fail me. Please God, not in front of Pete Tong. At the top of a hill, with stunning views over the island, they pulled into a narrow parking lot. Tong got out and surveyed my motor with barely disguised scorn. He explained the difficult reverse manoeuvre needed to get out of the narrow parking bay. 'Then again,' he sniffed, 'that thing's so tiny you could probably just spin it round.'

The villa was beautifully, simply decorated and surrounded by an olive grove. In a giant kitchen, a Brazilian maid was cooking dinner. We sat outside and drank a beer.

In 1999, when the *Independent* began its investigation, Pete Tong had just been judged the Most Powerful Man in Dance Music in a *Muzik* magazine special – above multimillionaire Ministry of Sound boss James Palumbo, who was at number three. Pete Tong's own jingles played on this. 'Who's got the power?' said a powerful black female voice (actually recorded by his signings Salt 'n' Pepa when he was a DJ at Capital Radio), 'Pete Tong's got the power.' His Essential Selection Friday night show had an impressive reach of 1.3 million people and a 12.6 per cent audience share in 1999. The show had the power to break records and create a groundswell that could make a hit – especially if he made a new track Essential New Tune. 'Your killer would be if you could have Pete Tong have it as Essential New Tune on a Friday night,' said Jean Branch of East West Records. Consequently Tong was continuously coming under pressure. 'It was such big business, that you do get people that think it was corrupt and you get people that think you can turn water into wine,' Tong told me. 'I used to get a terrible time from some of the labels, begging me to make their record Essential New Tune. And I would be like, "It's no good."'

Independent reporter Paul Lashmar centred his enquiries on the web of business interests Tong had built up. In addition to his show, Tong also ran ffrr Records, part of London 90 Records and one of the most important imprints in dance music. Tong started ffrr in 1988 – scoring his biggest hit with Shakespear's Sister. By 1992 he was also a director. Tong also introduced Radio 1's *Essential Mix* show, which showcased new DJs and often came from clubs around the country. The recognition of an *Essential Mix* show from a new club was judged vital to its importance. If the show came from a club, Tong might DJ too, earning a DJ fee. 'Starting to take the *Essential Mix* out to live venues, suddenly you had queues around the block,' Tong said. 'Suddenly the whole thing exploded. Booking Pete Tong became a big thing. Booking Pete Tong with the *Essential Mix* became an even bigger thing. I wouldn't say we ran things, but we made a huge impact. I don't think people really thought they'd graduated until they'd had a live *Essential Mix* from their club.'

Pete Tong's *Essential Selection* show was initially produced by the independent production company Wise Buddha, owned by another Radio 1 DJ, Mark Goodier. The *Essential Mix* show was produced by another independent company, West End, owned by Tong's manager Eddie Gordon. Tong was also a director of West End. 'That was the way they [Radio 1] wanted me to do it,' he said. Lashmar thought this convergence of mutually beneficial financial interests looked suspect. 'I thought it was interesting how BBC and Radio 1 were coming under commercial pressures that were moving them away from a public broadcasting remit,' Paul Lashmar told me.

Up until 1997, Pete Tong also mixed 'The Annual' albums for the

Ministry of Sound, with Boy George. Until, Tong said, Roger Ames, his boss at London 90 Records, told him he should be doing these mix CDs for his own label. 'London Records didn't necessarily want me selling 800,000 records for James Palumbo.' Ministry's *Annual III* sold 519,000 (figures copyright The Official Charts Company). A typical deal of the time would mean that Pete Tong could well have got a royalty of as much as 4 per cent and an advance of £25,000.

As the millennium approached, Radio 1 planned a One World 24-hour broadcast from clubs around the world. Ministry of Sound were unhappy that they weren't among them. Darren Hughes's new club home was. So was Kelly's in Portrush, Northern Ireland. 'It related to the most blatant exploitation of the combination of someone having production rights and management rights, at least in our view. This is ridiculous. This is not a level playing field,' Mark Rodol, then at Ministry of Sound, told me.

A fax was sent to Paul Lashmar from the Ministry. 'The London part of the broadcast is coming from a club that hasn't even opened yet run by a promoter that has close links with the production team behind Pete Tong's show,' it read. That promoter was Darren Hughes – who certainly did know Tong and Eddie Gordon, because Tong had played at Cream and the *Essential Mix* show had also broadcast from Cream. 'We're happy to join the party if asked,' the Ministry fax went on. 'It's definitely One World all right although it looks like whoever's controlling Radio 1's airwaves are clearly on a different planet.'

The *Independent* ran Lashmar's story on page three on 24 May 1999. It alleged that Tong played more of his own records than any other Radio 1 DJ. 'Neither is there another comparable radio DJ with such extensive commercial interests as Tong,' it claimed. 'Power in the dance industry is concentrated in a small number of hands. Eddie

Gordon, Tong's manager, agent and co-director used to head A&R at Polygram's Manifesto Record label. He now runs the Neo label. Tong has frequently played both Manifesto and Neo records on his show. Tong's Radio 1 stablemate and heir apparent Judge Jules remains a consultant to Manifesto.' Lashmar had done his sums. 'For 83 weeks over the last two years he played 243 tracks from ffrr and London 90 Records – three records a week,' Lashmar wrote. He stated that Tong's income as a director from ffrr alone was 'at least £200,000'.

Radio 1's defence was to counter with some maths of their own. 'It has been estimated that ffrr/London has approximately a 10 per cent share of the dance music market. Pete Tong plays on average three ffrr/London records out of 40 each week (7.5 per cent),' said a fax to Lashmar from Paul Simpson, press and publicity manager for Radio 1 and music entertainment. 'ffrr/London is widely recognised as an important dance label and therefore it is not inappropriate for Pete Tong to play some records from that label on his programme.' His scripts and running orders were, said the BBC, all approved before broadcast. 'Radio 1 commissions an unmatched line-up of the best specialist music presenters… Many of these DJs have legitimate connections with record companies, with clubs, with artists and with promoters.'

If Pete Tong was DJing during an *Essential Mix* live broadcast, would the price of his fee be influenced by the fact it was going out live on Radio 1? The BBC's reply was nonsensical. 'Although the BBC is not party to these negotiations, Radio 1 are satisfied that Pete Tong's DJ fees are not affected by whether a club night is broadcast or not.' Radio 1 was happy his fee wouldn't be influenced even though they weren't involved in the deal-making that would set that fee. So how would they know?

Pete Tong found the investigation traumatic. 'Horrible. Horrible.

I always feel horrible when anybody doesn't like me. It took a while to get some perspective on it.' But the story made national news. Peter Ainsworth, Conservative party Shadow Secretary of State for Culture, Media and Sport even wrote to BBC chairman Sir Christopher Bland. Ainsworth admitted dance music was a concentrated and specialist area but said: 'I'm sure you would agree that listeners are entitled to be made aware of any financial relationship between a presenter and the music he or she presents,' he wrote. 'It's difficult to imagine that disclosure would not be required in the independently regulated commercial radio sector.'

The BBC disagreed. They got behind Tong. 'The wagons circled around me. The Radio 1 lawyers worked in conjunction with my lawyers,' said Tong. Sir Christopher replied with the official line. He added: 'As a result of this and other follow-up articles, BBC Radio 1 has had discussions of all the issues with Jenny Abramsky, Director of Radio, and Philip Harding, Controller of Editorial Policy. Although they agree with BBC Radio 1 that declaring interests on-air is not the best way of avoiding any conflicts of interest, they have agreed to consider further safeguards in due course. These include analysing all specialist programme playlists over time to examine trends of percentage play of different labels and a more active approval by the network music team before a DJ can play a track from a label in which he or she has a financial interest.'

And that was it. The storm died down. The record company Tong worked for was later sold. The newspaper printed a follow-up story on 8 June but ultimately the *Independent* had nothing on Pete Tong because he had done nothing Radio 1 didn't already know about – he had been a record-company man years before he even joined the station. More importantly, the BBC had rallied around an acid house

DJ to protect him. This was a long, long way from the outlaw days of acid house. Dance music now was the establishment. And if Radio 1 wanted to stay ahead in acid house they needed Pete Tong who was, after all, only doing the acid house thing just as DJs had done since the very beginning; a little bit of everything. Pete Tong really did have the power but it was power in a vacuum because there was then, as there is now, nobody to replace him. The acid house old guard never changed.

Even now, Tong can't seem to see what the problem was. 'I always thought they were good records. That's why I signed them,' he laughed. Indeed if he has regrets about the 1990s they seem more about the break-up of his marriage and the time he was unable to spend with his children while he was keeping all these plates spinning. All those different jobs took up a lot of time. You don't become a millionaire if you don't put the hours in.

All week he worked at ffrr. Thursday night after dinner he was preparing his show until the early hours. Friday he was leaving work early to present it, then charging up North to DJ. Saturday his then-wife might take the kids to the park so he could sleep. 'But quite often I'd be torn with guilt and want to be there, so I'd be going round with sunglasses, trying to make sense to the kids. And then by seven o'clock at night, the process was all about getting your head around the night ahead. It was all about the journey again.'

When his marriage broke up after 13 years, Tong didn't do what many divorced men do and go off the rails. It never went Pete Tong for Pete Tong. Instead, he stopped drinking for six months. 'I just went into this Zen kind of focus of sobriety, not the 12 steps perspective but just absolutely making sure you're happy with all the decisions you're making,' he said. He lived with a friend who was in Alcoholics

Anonymous and even went to a couple of meetings. 'It was a good bunch of people to be around when you're trying to make such a big decision about your life,' he told me. But he found he got recognised – people started shouting, 'Oi, Tongy!' across the room. Then he met Carolina. 'Pretty quickly went into another relationship, so. And pretty quickly got married again and then had a kid, so there wasn't much time to go mad.' Outside his Ibiza villa, crickets twittering in the olive grove, he came back to the subject of his children from the first marriage, now quickly growing up. 'Would life have been different if I'd been around more for them? I'm very close to them. I feel I saw them a lot, but I certainly wasn't the best example of every single thing at their school, every single session of homework. It's how far you can go.'

Money kept pouring into acid house. With his company Slice, Damian Mould was one of a number of players making a fortune acting as an interface between the confusing world of clubs and the shiny world of big corporations. 'I had brands phoning me up in the mid-nineties cause they wanted access to this culture and would fuck it up themselves. So then I started saying, "Well, let me represent you. Rather than go through your big agency that's going to piss all my DJs off," Mould said. 'Pepsi, Levi's, drink brands, Ericsson mobile, energy drink brands, all those ones.'

Mould also for many years acted as Tong's personal PR adviser. He negotiated a fortnightly column in the *News of the World* for his client. Tong was initially unsure. Mould told him to do it. 'If you want to be a household name, yes. But it is what it is, it's the *News of the World*. But you will be like HP Sauce. People will know who you are. That's it. That's the deal.' Tong took it and wrote his column from June 1998 to June 2000. 'Pete would do the bare bones – mention this, mention that. Then I'd whack it together,' said Mould. 'Then when it got really busy we'd have a ghost-writer to do it.' Mould later sold his Slice agency but kept his job. Like Tong, he is now a millionaire.

In November 1996, concerned at the increasing commercialisation of clubland and the growing obsession with profits, *Mixmag* ran a cover special. It wasn't the Pete Tong 'kamikaze' issue, but it was 'Loadsamoney'. The magazine too had become big business, selling 90,000-odd a month: in August 1996, one issue sold 100,000 copies, the most it has ever sold without a free CD. The November 1996 cover featured a shower of £10 notes that we'd had to get special permission from the Bank of England to reproduce. 'Money, money, money,' ran the headline, 'is clubland too commercial?' As this issue went to press, unbeknown to editorial staff, the magazine was being sold by DMC, the family company that owned it, to multinational magazine publishers Emap. Once again, oh the irony.

The deal went through in January 1997. Having funded the magazine through years of loss-making in the 1980s, DMC boss Tony Prince netted £8.5 million. He gave bonuses to all his staff and went to live in New York as a tax exile for a year. The magazine had finally arrived in the centre of London's West End: on Oxford Street. We found ourselves in a major magazine company, looking bewilderedly at pie charts that told us what percentage of the readership liked drum 'n' bass (16 per cent, apparently). I left two years later, in January 1999. I had already been doing the job far too long. Acid house was edging further from the people who were paying for it: the clubbers. And the millennium was yet to come.

TEN
POST-TRAUMATIC SET DISORDER

TUNE! THE FACE – 'NEEDIN' U'

Muscular beats pumped up this delirious Ibiza piano anthem from New York DJ star David Morales.

'I've got friends in LA that are meth heads, you know,' Sasha told me. 'One of them told me with great satisfaction that he'd stayed up for two weeks straight.' Crystal meth, a potent pharmaceutical speed that can keep the user up for days, is one of the most dangerous and addictive drugs there is. And its users? 'Just the sketchiest fuckers I've ever, ever met in my life,' Sasha said. He witnessed the dark side of crystal meth use on the last night of his Delta Heavy tour of America in 2001 at a party in a loft in Los Angeles. Although it was somebody's home, this loft had been done out like a club with a great sound system, black walls – and a crowd of LA meth heads. 'I remember DJing for like four or five hours and nobody in this room communicated with me at all. And I knew a couple of these people.' But they were in a crystal meth zone, congregated in a corner, all furtively, busily working on something that Sasha couldn't see. Pissed off, he finished his impromptu set and began packing away his things. 'This bunch of fucking rude bastards,' he thought, 'I'm going back to the hotel.'

The meth heads were horrified and quickly hurried over with this thing they'd been working doggedly on for the past hours while he DJed – a gift of love for their DJ hero, which they presented with pride. 'It was a picture they'd painted. In the middle was me and I was the sun and then there was pictures of them all dancing around the sun. And they gave it to me with these cracked-out smiles on their faces as I left.' What did he do? 'I was like, "Thanks, so much." Then they all scurried off to their dark corners. Weird. That's a dangerous drug, that is.'

SASHA WAS BEING elusive. Again. Playing hard to get. Sometimes it seemed he had been playing hard to get for the whole of his career, toying with the jealous heart of British clubland. I had been trying to interview him for nine months for this book. We got close. Then it didn't happen. He sent me a text at one point: 'I don't know how to deal with all that nineties' nuttiness,' it said. The closest I had got, sitting in a pub near the West London apartment he was renting for six months, had resulted in a no-show. Normally he cancelled on the day of the interview. This time he didn't bother. He was flying back to New York the next day for six months. I went to his house. He was asleep. He was sick, he said. He sent me a text later on. 'I am so sorry I spaced today.'

I first met Sasha in 1991. Since then, I'd written a lot about him – interviews for *Mixmag*, sleevenotes for his mix albums for Global Underground, sequences filmed in Ibiza for a documentary I produced on DJs for Channel 4 in 2000 called *Getting Away With It*. We had our ups and downs. One night in 1994 we got into a drunken argument about the *Mixmag* 'Son of God' cover, which had just come out, at a Ministry of Sound party. He hated it. I defended it. The argument spilled out of the club and into a slapstick, inconclusive wrestling march on the pavement. After another interview with him and John Digweed in 1997 in New York during their triumphant Twilo residency, the night Princess Diana died, I partied with him. The night finished at dawn, in an apartment near Battery Park, bright sunlight pouring through the window.

In the end, I got two interviews. The first was on the phone from New York. His American wife Zoie had just had their first child, a son, Luca. Sasha was spending a lot of time down at the gym. He was trying to lose his beer belly, he said, because he was off to the annual Miami Music Conference in a month or so and wanted to look his best. Then he came to Brazil, where I was living while writing this book, to DJ. We met on a wet holiday Sunday at a new designer hotel in a resort called Guarujá, about an hour outside São Paulo. It looked like the gym had worked. The hair was very short now, hiding the incipient baldness. Thinking about the Son of God cover, he was philosophical. 'Now I look back at it and it's hilarious. I think it's funny. I guess it's another thing which massively helped my career,' he said.

In 1994, as his career kicked into overdrive, Sasha was in the studio. DJs were the new pop stars. Crowds loved them. They weren't just going to play great records, they were going to make them too. And why not? Sasha hit the ground running. Having studied piano as a child, he had a musical ear. Pete Hadfield was on to Sasha early on, tipped off by Mike Pickering, one of the DJs who ruled that heady Haçienda dance floor. Hadfield was one of two owners of Deconstruction Records, an independent run through major record company BMG and one of 1990s dance music's most dynamic labels. Pickering's own act, the pop-dance ensemble M People who would enjoy a string of hit singles and albums in the nineties, was signed to Deconstruction.

Hadfield went to see Sasha weaving his magic on the crowd at Renaissance. 'He had musical talent and a different take on life,' said Hadfield, 'an artistic flair that a lot of DJs didn't.' He commissioned a remix of M People's 'How Can I Love You More'.

Sasha's then-manager Seven Webster had teamed him up with producer Tom Frederickse. But Sasha's recording career was to prove as haphazard as his DJing. The mix was late. 'It was delayed and delayed and delayed,' said Hadfield. 'At that point I wasn't used to being held up by remixers or anyone else who was going to hold up the advance of the glorious Decon as I saw it.' Sasha delivered not just one remix, but a whole string of them – glorious, spacious reworks that turned a simple soulful pop groove into something utterly different. The remix came in way over budget. But Sasha didn't ask for any more money. Pete Hadfield was impressed. 'I thought, "Why don't we do an album?"'

It made sense. Why shouldn't a superstar DJ make a great album? And Sasha was in the midst of a period of productivity. Together with Frederickse and the French programmer Gaétan, he formed a prolific production team. In one year, they produced eleven top 40 remixes, frequently working through the night. From pop dance singles like D:Ream's 'UR The Best Thing' to straight-up vocal house acts like Urban Soul. One of the best of these was a magical, seven-minute, 14-second version of the Pet Shop Boys' 'West End Girls' – a slow-burning, atmospheric remake of the classic pop hit. Seven Webster regularly popped into the studio. The team was working like clockwork. 'They might not even need to speak to each other, they'd just be understanding and working on remixing something,' he said. 'It was a brilliant marriage.'

Why not an album? Every major record company wanted a remix by an in-demand DJ like Sasha. His remixes stretched songs out into melodic soundscapes, full of ups and downs, peaks of melodic euphoria, valleys of deep bass. Frequently they bore little relationship to the original track, bar a trace of the vocal. But they did the job, sprinkling Sasha's club glamour on to more mainstream artists. And he'd already made singles. In January 1993, he released 'Apollonia'/'Feel The Drop', under the alias B.M. EX.

Why not an album? 'I thought he would make a fantastic producer,' said Hadfield. Singles promote artists. Albums make money. In 1993 Matt Jagger, acting as Sasha's lawyer who was also Seven Webster's partner in the management company 7pm, negotiated a ground-breaking deal for Sasha with Deconstruction Records. An advance reckoned at £200,000 for three albums and a publishing deal with Polygram reckoned at another £100,000. This was big money for a DJ. 'He was very clearly a bright guy, he was very musically talented,' said Jagger. Not that Sasha paid much attention to the business side of the deal. 'He wasn't terribly interested in it.' But already doubt was creeping in. Hadfield's partner in Deconstruction, lawyer Keith Blackhurst, wasn't sure that Sasha wanted to be a producer. 'Is this what he wants to do or are you shoving him?' he said to Hadfield.

Deconstruction wanted that album. But its painful, endless gestation was to become a standing joke. Characteristic of what happened when superstar DJs attempted to reproduce the glories of their club shows in album form while simultaneously juggling hectic, hedonistic and lucrative DJing careers. 'The continual tension of the immediate economic value of DJing and that of putting their talent on records,' said Hadfield. 'One just got used to it. One got used to editing the chaos that came out of those recording sessions.'

In 1994, there was no sign of an album. So Deconstruction packaged together a couple of singles and remixes as a 'mini-album' called

The Qat Collection in 1994 to get something out. In May 1996 Sasha's collaboration with singer Maria Naylor, 'Be As One', topped the club charts. He followed up with the double A-Side 'Arkham Asylum'/ 'Ohmna'. Yet still, no album. Hadfield firmly believed in his talent. But he also felt that star DJs were often intimidated by their own success. 'I almost got the impression they thought that making a record might harm their career. They weren't sure they were going to make a good enough record to justify their superstar DJ status.'

This seemed true of Sasha. 'This is the confidence in his own ability,' said Seven Webster. 'Getting something out and actually making something.' Webster still has a number of tracks Sasha recorded. There were, he said, two songs with Shakespear's Sister singer Marcella Detroit, two with Chicago house vocalist Ce Ce Rogers, three tracks with New York producers David Morales and Satoshi Tomiie. There was, said Seven, a beautiful 'chill out' track with Irish folk musician Davey Spillane he described as an 'amazing, sonically wonderful masterpiece'. Sasha was never happy enough with any of these tracks to release them. He didn't like the way his remixing career was going either. 'I ended up turning down some big name artists, quite a few back to back,' he told me, 'and Tom [Frederickse] got quite pissed off with this, so our relationship fell apart.'

But Sashas's DJ earnings were going through the roof, said Seven Webster, basically doubling year on year. As a DJ, Sasha continued to deliver. He was effortless, a maestro, continuously in demand. He wasn't so much a crowd pleaser; he was prepared to take risks. Watching Sasha DJ was all about tension and release – a long build-up, then the reward of the big tracks – the 'hands in the air moments' as they were called – at the end. 'I consider it an art. I consider what I do very sacred to me and I'm really totally obsessed with it,' Sasha told me in his *Mixmag* interview in December 1993. 'That buzz in a club when everyone's really into what you're doing and they're buzzing on the records, nothing can beat that. It's like total adrenalin, hairs standing up on the back of your neck.'

The lure of the crowd and the circus that increasingly surrounded his DJing career didn't leave much room for studio time. In 1994 Sasha was in San Francisco, with Geoff Oakes, who shaved both their heads on a night out. The next morning, the whole of British clubland was already chattering about Sasha's new look. Turning up to his own gig at San Francisco's Sound Factory club with his new bald bonce, Sasha found bouncers refused to let him in. They didn't recognise him. His fame was spreading – but not everybody knew what he looked like. While he was in San Francisco, an imposter exploited this. The imposter had booked a gig as 'Sasha' at a club in Northern Ireland. 'I knew nothing about it,' said Sasha. But his imposter was informed: he turned up at the club, with a shaved head to match, and DJed. 'About an hour into his set, people realised something was up. I think he got out the club with the money and did one. I think he got away with about three grand,' said Sasha.

In Denver, later on, Sasha was DJing in a pulpit-like DJ booth. 'The promoter had been saying there was this girl and she wanted to meet me,' said Sasha. As he descended the booth to meet his fan her face fell and she began to cry. Through the tears, she explained about the passionate night she'd shared with someone she believed was superstar DJ Sasha. Confronted with the real thing, she realised she'd been duped. 'I had to console her a little bit,' said Sasha, 'she didn't stick around for long. She was mortified.' He grinned. The Manchester lad in him liked this story. 'Just glad my name's got enough to pull cute girls. That's fine with me. I felt really sorry for the girl but I was secretly like pissing myself. Poor girl. That would scar you, wouldn't it? Women don't trust men as it is.'

Being the star DJ meant everyone wanted a piece of him. And everything was free. Sasha's appetite – not just for the party, but for the inevitable after-party as well – was becoming legendary. 'Sasha couldn't walk into a club without that temptation being offered and was one of the people that certainly participated,' said Seven. Guest DJs were generally expected to indulge in whatever was on offer, to party with the club promoter and insiders. 'Feelings were hurt if you didn't get stuck in, basically. And we all quite often did,' said Sasha. 'I was usually the last man standing.' Crazy times. 'Yeah, I definitely got my money's worth.'

Seven Webster got a call one morning from Sasha after one of the decadent Chuff Chuff parties, held in a mansion near Manchester. His star DJ had woken up in an empty dining room, a cleaner vacuuming around him. He had lost his shoes. 'He ended up getting a cab from Manchester to London and having to pigeon hop down the drive way at both ends,' said Seven. 'He always lost items of clothing. Always. It was a continual process. Wherever he went he'd leave bits and pieces behind.' In July 1994 *Mixmag* reported him turning up for a show in Birmingham minus shoes – having lost them in Manchester the night before.

Seven Webster described him as 'The Keith Moon of dance music'. But Sasha didn't want to talk about drugs. 'I don't know how to discuss it in any classy way,' he explained. 'I don't know how to talk about it without it sounding horrible. Cause people have their opinions on drugs and it's black and white.' Instead, he talked about drink. And Sasha loved to drink. 'My metabolism's so high that I could process a bottle of vodka within hours. You know. I could *drink*,' he said. 'My family have always been drinkers, my father's a legendary drinker, there's always been alcohol around and I think I've just got the constitution of an ox, really.'

Binges on alcohol were most likely to happen after he finished DJing. 'I've come up with a name for it, it's called "Post-Traumatic Set Disorder",' Sasha said. 'It's that thing that happens when you're DJing where you can drink as much as you want, you have no idea how drunk you are. And you can probably time it to the second. And literally you sit down after finishing DJing at seven or eight in the morning and within about five, ten minutes it's like watching a tree fall.'

Post-Traumatic Set Disorder struck after he'd DJed at a Homelands rave. He was drinking on the way up, drinking during the show, drinking afterwards. 'I basically drank myself absolutely stupid. Bottle of champagne. Bottle of vodka,' he said. 'I just really, really overdid it.' Sasha came to, somewhere on the grass outside of the marquees. The sun had come up and it was hot. He was surrounded by a handful of ravers. They'd made a little ceremonial circle around the comatose superstar DJ and were sitting around him, skinning up joints. 'They were like, "Are you Sasha?" I'm like, "Yeah." And they're like, "Told yer! Told yer!"' Sasha struggled to his feet and went off to find his friends. 'Where the fuck have you been?' 'Oh, just had to have a little lie-down."

DECEMBER 1993, ST PETERSBURG, Russia. We were in a nuclear fallout shelter converted into a club, a metal bunker buried in the snow. Noise pollution wasn't a problem with walls a metre thick and so it went on all night. Not that anyone was going to argue with the bouncer anyway – an off-duty soldier with a machine gun and a giant Alsatian. Bristol's Nick Warren was DJing, playing the Paul Oakenfold remix of U2's 'Lemon', while jamming along on a keyboard. The guy operating the lights was wearing laser goggles pilfered from the military storeroom in the bunker. Nick and I were later presented with a pair. Was it 8 a.m.? 4 a.m.? A small crowd were still dancing like mad. Nick left the decks and went out to join them. Everybody cheered and surrounded him.

There was no ecstasy in Russia then, but the club's mix of mafia men, off-duty hookers and bohemian artists in sunglasses partied on anyway. This was acid house on the front line, infiltrating its way around the world. An adventure organised after I briefly met a Russian princess called Katya Galitzine at a BBC radio station. She was looking for a DJ for her friend's club: I sold the idea to Warren. Nobody got paid but flights were covered and we slept in the promoter's, Alexei's, apartment. Russia was reeling from perestroika, changing fast. Trabant taxis bouncing over giant potholes in the road. We drank insane amounts of vodka. One night, Nick was the guest DJ on a radio station that was broadcasting to Latvia. We arrived mid-show. Our hosts wired up the decks, Warren went straight on air. By the end of the decade Nick Warren was playing exotic DJ dates all over the world but they weren't for free and he was sleeping in five-star hotels. He was one of a league of British DJs, Dave Seaman, Darren Emerson and Carl Cox among then, who had joined a lucrative world circuit. Like Sasha and John Digweed.

The two began in Florida, which had a nascent 'progressive house' scene in Orlando, run by promoter Stace Bass, a gothic blonde and her DJ Kimball Collins. They ran a night at the Beacham Theater for an enthusiastic crowd of club kids who loved the British sound. The club opened at 3 a.m. and went on well into the morning. Sasha loved walking out afterwards into the Florida sunshine. 'Blue sky. Like, this is brilliant. We immediately had a buzz around us. And I was thinking, "If it's going to work here, it's going to work in the rest of America."'

It did. Over the 1990s, both he and Digweed steadily built a whole new career in the States. America was falling for acid house – this was the new frontier. But if Florida fell for Sasha straight away, New York was a different story.

The British club contingent arrived in force in New York in July 1994 for the annual, now defunct New Music Seminar record industry conference. Vast quantities of cocaine were purchased and consumed – much of it by Dave Beer and his Back To Basics crew. The highlight was to be a night at the Sound Factory where its famous DJ Junior Vasquez was to go head to head with Sasha, the British golden boy. 'Junior was at the height of his powers and added to that all the British were there to see their boy. The place was fucking heaving,' said Sasha. But when Sasha took to the decks, the Sound Factory's world-famous sound system was unnervingly quiet. He could hardly be heard above the chatter of the crowd. Sasha ploughed on through his set, wondering when he would get to meet Junior, who had just remixed one of his tracks.

As Sasha finished his set, two bouncers came in and announced Junior had arrived. 'Oh great,' said Sasha. 'Can you clear the booth,' said the bouncers. 'Move your stuff out. We need to get Junior's stuff on.' Junior Vasquez's record booth was a two-storey cottage at the back of the club, with a room full of amplifiers. Sasha slunk in there to sort out his records. 'The sound guy walks in and switches on all the amps in front of me, like that. Click. Click. Click. Click. Click.' Sasha realised he hadn't been playing on even a tenth of the sound system's power. 'And I'm like, "Oh, you fucking arsehole."' Junior put his first record on. The club's awesome sound system kicked in. Everybody cheered. Crestfallen and furious, Sasha picked up his records, struggled out into the crowd and went back to his hotel. Junior later sniffily apologised. 'I'm very close to this place and I can't bear to see other DJs play this room,' he said.

But Sasha was to conquer New York too, with a residency with John Digweed at the city's club Twilo. From 1996 to 2001 they played every month. It made their name in America. Sasha might have been unreliable, but he never played the diva. His down-to-earth, slightly shy approach endeared him to the Americans. Junior Vasquez still DJs but Sasha is by far the bigger name on a worldwide scale. Even today, Sasha can still sell out a New York club.

But he always took it down to the wire. On another occasion, he was DJing live on Pete Tong's Radio 1 show, from Brighton. Tong began counting down and playing records from that week's Cool Cuts chart, a list of the hot new records. Sasha was on next but he had disappeared. The countdown started at number 20. 'Seven, where's Sasha? Where's Sasha?' asked Tong, worried. Seven shrugged. The countdown went on to number 13. 'Seven, where's Sasha? He's on in a minute,' asked Tong, beginning to panic. As was Seven. 'It's like, "Oh no." Five. "Where's *Sasha*?" Three. "*Where the fuck's Sasha?* Is he here?" And then of course he'd walk in, like one minute before, because he'd get nervous if he hung around, so he used to leave it till the last moment,' said Seven.

Sasha didn't just cause panic in those around him. He also suffered from it himself. He became paranoid going into clubs, convinced the crowd was laughing at him. 'I was having a panic attack in the club and it was all linked to the music.' If Sasha dropped a dramatic tune, this would make it worse. 'The bigger the records that I played the more intense the panic attacks. They would last my entire set,' he said. 'I used to get really pissed off because the crowd were just looking at the DJ booth. I used to sit down between records. And I'm sure my lifestyle didn't help. I was using that as an escape.' The records he was playing were intensifying his fear: the higher the record took the crowd, the deeper the paranoia he suffered. As the panic attacks got worse he became unable to sleep. 'As soon as it got dark all my senses were like hyper. I would be awake until the sun came up and then fall asleep. You're pumped full of adrenalin, it's the fight or flight thing. So your senses are completely heightened.' He would lie there, listening to every creak in the house. 'I thought I was going mad. I thought this is what happens when you hear about people losing their minds and butchering families! I thought I was going to be in a straitjacket in a mental home. It was horrible.'

Sasha never considered seeing a psychiatrist though. 'I would have been put on anti-depressants and stuff like that – it was around the time that Prozac was coming out, I just didn't think that was the way to do it. I self-medicated by drinking a lot of alcohol. Which helped. It definitely took the edge off things when I was feeling a little jittery.' Eventually he met someone who'd had a similar experience. And Sasha reasoned his way out of the problem. 'I just dealt with it. Once I found out what they are, when I felt one coming on I would tell myself this is just a panic attack, you're spazzing out again.' Since then, he's been able to cope with the occasional relapse. 'I've had little twinges of it every now and again,' he said. 'It's like a wave comes up and it was just about controlling that, learning what it was and dealing with it. And I think the fact that I did it myself has helped me move on from it. 'Cause it could have crippled me.'

BY 1996 THE panic attacks had been conquered. But Sasha's album still wasn't happening. Keith Blackhurst would call Jagger on a regular basis, asking: 'Where's the Boy Wonder's album?' Instead, his new project was a double-mix CD for Ministry of Sound with John Digweed, under the name *Northern Exposure*, which was released in 1997. Since Renaissance, the two had built a close friendship and working partnership. 'We connected as two people,' said John Digweed. 'We had a lot in common musically. Personality-wise we were very different but I think that's what made the partnership so unique.'

The accompanying tour hit headlines as one of the most expensive in dance music's history – venues were paying up to £9,000 for both DJs and a live act. An American tour was arranged to promote the album. But though Sasha had sorted out his paranoia, he still hadn't got to grips with his time-keeping. This was causing his management endless headaches. 'I had five or six people working for me. Basically their job was to get Sasha on a plane, pretty much week in, week out,' said Seven Webster. 'And he would always miss the flight. Every flight would get missed.'

John Digweed already knew about Sasha's unreliability – pre-Renaissance, he had booked him twice for south coast gigs and he'd failed to turn up for either. Digweed was organised. He didn't take drugs. He would go to bed early to make sure he was ready for his show the next day. He was in this for the long haul. Throughout this American tour, he was at times the only one of the two who would turn up.

'When people pay money to see a double act, they want to see a double act. It puts stress on me but it also puts stress on the promoters because they're trying to explain that I'm sorry, Sasha can't make it tonight,' Digweed said. One New Year's Eve Sasha missed a crucial flight, leaving his manager to hire a private jet to get him across America. Bang went Seven's commission. There was a press launch in New York for the American release of the *Northern Exposure* album.

Sasha missed the flight and Seven had to face the press and record company bigwigs alone. It was getting worse. In 1996, Seven Webster and Sasha parted company: Webster had had enough, he said. Who was going to pick up the gauntlet next?

DAVE DORRELL HAD seen Sasha play at Shelley's. They had shared the DJ decks at another after party, during a lost weekend spent at a dance event at a holiday camp in Wales. The party took place in a caravan, into which someone had managed to smuggle a sound system. Somebody else had a bottle of poppers – amyl nitrate, a powerful stimulant used on heart attack patients which is popular in gay clubs for the sudden chest-busting rush it gives anyone who sniffs a good lungful. The heart rate increases, the body is virtually immobilised, then within minutes, it's over. Poppers are normally sold in sex shops as a sexual enhancement. But they cropped up on the dance floor too.

An entire bottle of poppers was accidentally poured down a guy's sweatshirt. Rather than waste it, he clamped his mouth over his sleeve and inhaled the lot. Not a good idea. The guy's heart stopped and he lost consciousness. People started freaking out. Dorrell and other guests performed CPR. 'Suddenly he just coughed back to life. And we got up and started DJing again, as you do,' shrugged Dorrell. The sound system they were using had a special effects unit, so they blasted out an ambulance siren noise, to celebrate. 'You end up in a fucking caravan at nine in the morning reviving a dead body, playing with the sound effects of the ambulance siren on the mixer and barging Sasha out the way to get the next record on,' said Dorrell. 'Cause there's not a lot of space. In a caravan.' This was how friendships and business relationships were formed in 1990s clubland. Like Dorrell and Sasha, at another party in a house in North London, tobogganing down a carpeted staircase on tea trays. 'Somebody walked round with a tray of sliced bread going, "Use your loaf." And me and Sasha, tobogganing down the staircase.'

Sasha and his then girlfriend Marie were regular visitors to the Hampstead home Dorrell shared with his then wife Claudia. Dorrell had given up DJing and moved into management, looking after the rock band Bush. He was living in Dublin with Claudia when he got a call from Sasha. 'He phoned me and said, "Can I come and see you?"' said Dorrell. 'Sasha came over and things were kind of a bit difficult for him. I think he came for a kind of cuddle, really.'

Dorrell was in rock music, but he still kept in touch with all the DJs and major players on the club scene. He knew exactly what was going on. 'It was just all so big and awesome and crazy,' said Dorrell. 'The roundabout was going faster and faster and faster. There was more money than anyone knew what to do with, but everybody seemed to know what to do with it, which was all of the wrong things to do with it. And that was life. It was a seven-day-a-week bacchanalia. I think it was unique. I don't think it was like that for the Rolling Stones even at the height of the sixties.'

So it was settled. Dave Dorrell would be Sasha's new manager. 'It was great. Sasha had his own momentum.' Not that he was an easy DJ to manage. 'Like any other DJ I worked with, including myself. Liable to falling asleep in the first-class lounge at JFK [airport, New York] and missing the plane that would get him to the connection that would get him to Japan. You know. Shit happens.'

In 1998, Dorrell got Sasha his biggest studio gig to date – a Madonna remix. 'When I was asked to do "Ray Of Light" I was so excited I was jumping around the room. I got flown out to LA to do it,' Sasha told *Mixmag* in 1999. The Queen of Pop hadn't released an album of original material since 1994's *Bedtime Stories*. Now she had discovered British-style dance music and was working on an album of the same name, with William Orbit, a producer who had started out on that influential early nineties progressive house label: Guerrilla Records. Sasha also remixed the singles 'Drowned World' and 'Sky Fits Heaven'. But he didn't get to meet Madonna.

'Suddenly we were doing Madonna remixes,' said Dorrell. 'Gigs everywhere. If anything, that kind of catapulted him to another place.' But if Seven Webster hadn't been able to get Sasha's album out of him, neither could Dave Dorrell. 'No one could, not even Sasha. There was a huge pressure on him,' said Dorrell. 'He never finished anything. He'd do stuff and play it out and then decide it wasn't quite doing it. And in between he was DJing around the world.' Dorrell understood pop music. He could see what the problem was. 'It's not like he was Jean-Michel Jarre, who he loved, for instance. Who would just sit in a studio and do the record,' he said. 'DJing is like a live act. Doesn't always work. It's not always the best gig ever. It's not always the gig of your career. Can't be. There's magic moments all the time. And I guess for Sasha those acts of creation really took place *live*. Trying to replicate that in a studio, on a laptop screen or whatever. It's sterile.'

The partnership with Dorrell didn't last. 'I worked with him for about a year. It didn't work out,' said Sasha. The roundabout was still spinning. But first of all he had a giant tax bill to contend with. 'I got a call from the tax man saying you owe this much money. And I didn't have any money. It was a bad time, a bad time and Dave tried to help me out but eventually it took a lot of me going back out on the road and being much more professional about my career,' said Sasha. Meanwhile in 1999 he was still talking up the missing album. 'I'm convinced I'm going to make a great album,' he told *Mixmag*. 'I'll be wanting to compete with [Leftfield's] *Leftism*, or maybe even an Underworld album. I'm beginning to think that I can combine everything. I must have listened to *Leftism* a thousand times and that's what I want to achieve.'

But Sasha had also presented himself with another problem – he wanted to make his album himself. It's one thing being a rock musician, learning to play the guitar and sing, then recording your songs with a producer. Dance music is made on complicated computer programmes and studio equipment that take years to learn. There is no guitar to pick up and strum a few chords with. It's all or nothing. Many DJs just hired an engineer to do all the work, gave him a pile of records, sat at the back of the studio with a pile of records to sample, rolled a large spliff and said, 'Can you make it sound like that?' Sasha set out to learn how to produce and engineer his own album. 'I just felt like I had to learn how to make records on my own,' he said.

It wasn't going to be easy. 'I spent a good three years with my head buried in manuals trying to make music on my own.' He almost got there. But he was much slower than a professional. 'Eventually I'd learnt the language but it would take me a good two or three weeks to finish a tune on my own. And by that time you hate the fucking thing. A lot of the stuff I did finish in that time never got released cause it had taken me so long and it was so painful.'

ONE NIGHT AFTER their gig at Twilo in New York Sasha and Sparrow travelled by helicopter to the Hamptons mansion of photographer and artist Peter Beard, famous for his African photographs and artworks. They flew out in beautiful sunshine and landed in the grounds of his stunning house. 'I didn't really know who he was, but he had a lot of interesting, intelligent people around him,' said Sasha. Sparrow loved the experience. 'A massive mansion with fucking amazing pieces of art all over the place.' Still no album; still more madness.

In the summer of 1999 Sasha hired an immense Ibiza villa and flew out 22 friends. He took his mother and father to the club Space. A few months later, *Muzik* magazine went over to New York to interview him. Sasha proved elusive. The magazine's writer and photographer spent days chasing Sasha about, trying to get their interviews and photographs. The eventual feature was entitled 'The Lost Weekend'. After a night DJing at Twilo, he went on to a house party and DJed from midday to 5 p.m. 'Fucked up, but still sharp and generous – this too is Sasha's zone,' the article wrote. 'Last time *Muzik* sees him in New York, he's half underneath his bed at the Soho Grand Hotel, waving a two-litre bottle of vodka in one hand and a bin in the other. Mad Manc Sparrow is standing on the other side of the room, trying to gob into the bin. On the floor, there's a bottle of champagne, which a stewardess nicked for Sasha on the way over. On the table there's his ticket home. Sasha won't be needing that. At the last minute, he'll decide to go to Miami, to live it up with Sparrow for a week.'

Photographer Vincent Macdonald was furious at being messed around. He took a picture of a clearly wasted Sasha on a chair, which editor Ben Turner printed. 'He said, "Look, Ben, that picture is a reflection of what that whole trip was about." And Sasha sat on that chair looking on another planet was Vincent's vision or reflection of what was going on,' Turner recalled. Sasha told the magazine that he loved his lifestyle. 'Having a wicked time and meeting new mates is what's most important.' In the same interview, Sasha revealed that his long-awaited album was now, finally, going to happen. 'People used to take the piss out of me and my missing album. Now I don't care,' he said. It was going to be ready the next year and feature guest vocalists, including Iggy Pop and Dot Allison, formerly of the act One Dove.

But this time, it really did seem like it might actually happen. He had begun working with a new collaborator, Charlie May, from the early 1990s progressive house act Spooky – another of the acts on Guerilla Records. They had already put out something called *Ride* in 1998 as 2 Phat Cunts. In 1999 he finally released a track called 'Xpander' that had suddenly convinced everyone – including Deconstruction – that the talent was back. 'Xpander' is still regarded as a trance classic and is perhaps the best thing Sasha ever did. It is a bold, confident record, built around a gorgeous, shivering keyboard refrain. Pete Hadfield was convinced. 'What a great record. It was a landmark record,' he said.

Like *Qat*, *Xpander* was actually released as a mini-album, stretched out into a slew of remixes. It even charted in the album charts, for one week, and sold 20,000 in the UK. It appeared on an acclaimed mix album for Global Underground, based on an Ibiza show at Space. Sasha was back in force as a recording artist. Now, perhaps, his album would finally arrive. Hadfield had begun visiting Sasha in his country house near Henley. 'In that room, he must have made 60 tracks,' said Hadfield. None of them ever came out. 'He was never satisfied with anything, he always had a criticism of it. I never knew whether he enjoyed so much being the superstar DJ and that was more fun and more profitable than making records.'

IT WAS JUST a fender bender, a screech of brakes, a crash, nothing too serious. Sasha was in the back – he still can't drive, even today – and was being driven to the gym that day in March 2001. 'I didn't have my seat belt on,' he told me. 'Who needs seat belts in the back?' It was the black eye he noticed more afterwards, after he nailed the metal attachment for the front seat belt. There were a couple of stitches and the nurse told him not to get them wet. But after four days he needed a shower and so, careful not to get any water on his face, Sasha washed his hair. 'Then the next minute I could taste soap in my mouth. I was like, hang on a minute, that's a bit weird. Then of course I went to clear my ears and I could feel the water kind of shooting through my ear. I was like, 'Oh shit. That is not good.''

He had a perforated eardrum. For a DJ, this was definitely a major problem. He could hear, though there was a ringing, but the medical advice was pretty clear. Loud music was out. Sasha was confined to his new Henley house. 'I was just not living a healthy lifestyle in London. I'd moved out there,' he'd told *Muzik*. Out in Henley, he took stock. 'The first time probably in ten years when I'd been forced to stop riding this mental acid house wave around the world, wherever it took me. I didn't think anything of just going on the road for six to nine months some years.' His accident inadvertently provided director Michael Dowse with his central plot line for the movie *It's All Gone Pete Tong*. 'Mike just thought that was so funny,' Pete Tong told me. 'That was what he locked on to, it was one of the first stories he heard and he never forgot it. What if a DJ went deaf?'

Sasha took it as an opportunity. 'So the looming monkey on my back, this album that I was supposed to have been recording. Suddenly it was like, "Okay, maybe now's a good time to sit down and write some music."' He began to face his fears. 'I'd been scared of making that album,' Sasha said. 'I set myself almost impossible boundaries.' He set up an electric piano in the living room and put his laptop on top and started sketching out some ideas. Living with him at the house was producer Charlie May. The studio was connected to the kitchen and Sasha was also learning to cook. 'On the phone to my father saying,

"Right, I've got a chicken, what do I do with it?" So I basically spent my entire day going between the kitchen and the studio,' he said. 'I'd always get the timing of my recipes wrong. I'd try something really ambitious and we'd always end up eating some ridiculous meal at four o'clock in the morning that had taken me eight hours to prepare. I always think big. I can't just grill a piece of fish and make a salad. I always have to try something complicated that takes hours and hours of preparation.'

Sasha the chef struggled in the kitchen because he was so over-ambitious with his recipes, just as he did with his records. Then somebody intervened. In September 2001 Dutch producer Junkie XL – aka Tom Holkenberg – was flown to Sasha's Henley house to spend a day working on a track. The two had met a few years earlier when Sasha was playing at Amsterdam's Milky Way club. He'd included a Junkie XL track on his 'Ibiza' mix for Global Underground. The session went well. Holkenberg was soon back to do another. This time he had a radical proposal for the superstar DJ: move to Amsterdam and let's finally finish that album. Sasha agreed. And the quiet, industrious Dutch producer finally achieved what nobody else had been able to do. He got Sasha's album out of him.

Holkenberg was disciplined. 'I think it was really important that he surrounded himself with people that made him stick to the original idea. The plan was to finish an album,' he told me. There was a rigid schedule. They worked from 9 a.m. until 10.30, 11 at night, then had a couple of beers. The tracks Sasha had done at home in Henley were really only rough ideas. 'It's very hard to say that there were actually really tracks there before we started,' said Tom. 'It was just a bunch of samples. A bunch of loops.' They redid all of them. This time there was a team and an engine room. Simon Wright engineered. Charlie May produced and played in synthesiser melodies. Sasha sat in the lounge area. 'He would sit out there with his laptop just jamming with the loops and the sounds that we all provided for him.' Holkenberg mixed the album, giving it a 'sound' and played some guitars. But mainly he provided structure. 'That was my biggest role in that whole process. Creating a discipline that got the album done.'

Suddenly they were knocking tracks out. 'I was like, "This is great, this is good." And then the whole record got a vibe to it, got a sound to it,' said Sasha. *Airdrawndagger* is a polished album of sophisticated armchair trance – with no singing and no big dance floor tracks. Not what BMG Records, who by now had bought out Deconstruction, were hoping for. 'No fucking vocals?' they said to Sasha. They wanted it changed. 'He got a lot of heat from his record company just before the album came out to do stuff with vocals,' Holkenberg said. I met Sasha in London in spring 2002 as he was about to record a vocal track with female pop trio the Sugababes. The session never made it onto the album.

'We ended up sending round all these tracks to all these writers and people started sending back vocal versions of these songs which we'd finished as instrumentals,' said Sasha. 'It was awful. They wanted me to change it into a pop album. It was a soundscape album. It wasn't about to break down the pop charts.' Holkenberg told him to stand firm. 'Sasha, this is not what you wanted initially and you shouldn't be doing it now either,' he said.

Sasha won. *Airdrawndagger* finally came out in September 2002. But Deconstruction never got to see it. In 2000 its parent company BMG bought out the independent and its bosses Pete Hadfield and Keith Blackhurst had moved on. *Q* magazine, in September 2002, judged that 'as a cohesive armchair trance soundtrack, *Airdrawndagger* is a clear success'. But though it was pretty and well produced, the fierce intensity of his early remixes was nowhere to be seen, nor was the euphoric trance melodrama of 'Xpander'. Instead there was a track called 'Mr Tiddles'. Pete Hadfield liked one track. But that was all. 'I don't think it's the greatest artistic statement he ever made,' he sniffed.

It was too little, too late. *Airdrawndagger* arrived nine years after Sasha first broke through, long after the nineties clubbing bubble had burst. He had missed his chance. To date, *Airdrawndagger* has sold just 20,000 copies in the UK in the six years since it was released and 80,000 worldwide. Compared to, say, the 150,000 copies Sasha and John Digweed's *The Mix Collection* for Renaissance sold in just six weeks in 1994. Or the 250,000 the Global Underground mix album *Ibiza* has sold around the world – 47,000 of them in the UK. Still, Sasha likes *Airdrawndagger*, even if nobody else does. He is proud of it. 'I know it polarised opinion but it's part of my life,' he said. 'Sometimes I think if I'd just made an album of "Xpander"-sized tracks everyone would have been happy.' At the very least, he might have sold some records. As it was, BMG Records dropped him.

THE PERFORATED EARDRUM finally slowed Sasha down. 'I'd just come out of my twenties. In your twenties you don't think you're going to get sick. You're just invincible, you know. It was definitely something that made me sit down and grounded me. "Right, you're not invincible. You can hurt yourself."' If the British club scene had all but expired by 2002, America still wanted Sasha. That year he began hosting club nights at the Crowbar in New York and at Avalon in Los Angeles under the name Fundaçion that further boosted his career in America. Sparrow was back, hosting his VIP room, another job he could have been born to. 'Basically get absolutely smashed and make sure everybody's all right,' grinned Sparrow. 'Wicked.'

Celebrities flooded in. Colin Farrell hung out at a show in Las Vegas. Even David Bowie showed up with wife Iman, perhaps finding one DJ craftsman who did achieve celebrity. Sparrow saw their presence as a 'super compliment'. 'Dan Ackroyd came up to the side of the VIP. I clocked him straight away. I was like that, "Sweet, Dan Ackroyd's here. I'm gonna terrorise him," said Sparrow. 'I'm at least gonna get him smashed, cause I have control of the booth. So I say, "Listen, Dan, anything you need, give us a shout." He said, "Well, I wouldn't mind a drink. But really, I'm just here to see my boy." He was talking about Sasha.'

Bruce Willis came, celebrating his fiftieth birthday. 'His eyes lit up. And the crowd, cause Sasha had not played there for a couple of months, just went mental.' Sparrow also hung out with New York-based Brazilian super-model Alessandra Ambrosio, described by the Brazilian edition of *Rolling Stone* magazine as the most beautiful girl in the world. They stayed in the same house in Ibiza and went to clubs in Los Angeles and Miami. Sparrow described her as a close friend. 'She's a real sweetheart. She's one of the most beautiful women in the world,' said Sparrow. 'I hung out with Sparrow a lot,' Ambrossio, who has a strong American accent, told me. 'We had good times. Good fun. He's nice, it's weird for me, cause with English people, their accents are completely different. It's funny the way that they talk. Sparrow would always, like, call me and I wouldn't understand a word he was saying on the phone.'

Through her friendship with Sparrow, Alessandra met Sasha and became a fan. Her favourite Sasha memory is from just a few years ago, when he played at Warung, in southern Brazil, an open-air club on the coast at the edge of a forest that faces the sunrise. DJs call it the most beautiful club in the world. Alessandra and her friends arrived in a helicopter, which they landed in the dust beside the club. She was a little drunk, she said, but she had a go at flying the thing. As the sunrise steamed into the club, Sasha was at his peak. 'People were like jumping, screaming, it was just a magic moment, you know,' she told me. 'You can look into his eyes and his face and you can see that he's having the best time playing. That's what makes the whole crowd go nuts.'

Sparrow's celebrity-studded life continued, though he still slept on an English photographer friend's sofa when in Los Angeles. He went to the Oscars with the English socialite Lady Victoria Hervey. 'She's a real sweetheart,' he said – another one. 'She quite enjoys me terrorising people, every now and again I get kicked out of somewhere. Usually it's a club we don't have to worry about going back into.'

IN 2004 SASHA released *Involver*, another album through Global Underground. *Involver* is a mix album but one in which he took tracks into his studio, took them apart and completely deconstructed them – remixed them, in effect – and put them back together. *Involver* worked for Sasha. It was a commercial and critical success and sold 125,000 copies around the world.

Like most DJs, by then he had stopped lugging heavy boxes of vinyl around. Most star DJs now carry a neat little canvas satchel of CDs – CD decks are now sophisticated enough for them to use. Sasha uses a computer programme called Ableton that is even more sophisticated. On Ableton, he can remix tracks as he's actually playing them. It is the height of high-tech DJing.

But computers don't have half the glamour or showmanship potential of records. It looked like he was up there with a laptop checking his emails, rather than DJing. So Sasha had a special mixing console built at considerable cost by a hi-fi specialist. It's called 'The Maven' and he has one of only two in the world. It looks like something out of *Star Trek* – a toboggan-sized thing covered in flashing lights. But at least nobody thought he was checking emails any more.

May 2005. Sasha was at Lima airport in Peru, about to board a flight for Brazil, where he was playing the huge Skol Beats rave in São Paulo in just a few hours. They wouldn't let him on the plane. He didn't have a yellow fever vaccination card. He missed the flight. Panic. Sasha went into the car park and bought a fake vaccination card, came back in and managed to get on a flight. The rave was already in full swing when he landed at São Paulo's Garulhos airport.

John Digweed, punctual as usual, had already been playing for two hours. The promoter, Luiz Eurico Klotz, was worried. Sasha hadn't turned up for his set the previous year. He couldn't fail to deliver the star DJ once again. He organised a helicopter to pick Sasha up, at a cost of $3,000 an hour. Sasha was whisked over the giant metropolis. He landed in the middle of the rave and went straight onstage. 'When Sasha arrived,' said Luiz, 'the place went mad because everybody thought he was not coming again. Then Sasha played for two hours and then the last hour him and Digweed played back to back, for a full tent, everybody with their hands in the air, the whole crowd screaming.' Sasha smiled when he remembered this. 'That was fun,' he told me. 'I felt like a rock star that day.'

ELEVEN
WHAT GOES UP MUST COME DOWN

TUNE! ROBERT MILES – 'CHILDREN'

A one-off Italian mega-hit with a driving trance beat and a languidly melodic refrain.

A Dealer's Tale: 'I started to go to the Haçienda in the late eighties, early nineties. Did the classic thing really of starting to supply a few friends with pills. That developed into taking 50 to the Haç, then 100, then selling them on in bulk to some of the dealers in the club and letting them work for me. I was in the fortunate position of having what were widely regarded as the best Es. And I had pretty much exclusive access to them. It got to the stage in the Haçienda alone when I was probably selling up to 600 pills a night, £20 quid a time. We were buying for £6–7 a time. I was also supplying wholesale to most of the north-west of England – probably about 10,000 pills a week, in total. The pills came from Amsterdam, mostly. Three or four people worked for me. As soon as everything came in on a Thursday, you couldn't get it out quickly enough. People had already come down and they were waiting all over the city.

I vividly remember some guy clocking me on the balcony in the Haç one night. I later found out he'd been in prison and he was the main dealer in the area before that. I came out of the club one night and the tyres of my car were slashed. I had my girlfriend and a friend and his girlfriend with me. Three or four guys appeared, put guns in our mouths, told us they wanted all our money, they were going to take us back to the house and take everything, kidnap our girlfriends, whatever. So I gave them whatever I had on me at the time, which wasn't a great deal. And they let me go. The first experience I'd had of anything like that.

On the Wednesday, I came up with about seven or eight lads looking for them to take them to task for it. Luckily we didn't see them, but word got around that I'd done that. I came up the Friday after that, on my own in the car. Three carloads of them followed me into town. I parked up. As I was about to get out the car, they saw me and I saw them and I jumped back in my car and I left as rapidly as I could. A few weeks later I got a phone call from them asking if I could come up and see them. They said that they'd made a mistake, they wanted me to carry on working at the Haçienda. They wanted me to supply them with drugs also. And maybe give them a little kickback. So I naively decided to do that.

Everything was fine for a while. And then, things dried up and I stopped going to the Haç for a while. After about four months I went back up purely on a night out and one of the main guys said, 'Can we have a word with you?' I just saw this flash out the corner of my eye and this huge guy with a knuckleduster basically put my nose across the other side of my eye. I fell down the stairs. I tried to run out the club and they blocked me off and stopped me leaving, then I was on the floor in the middle of the Haçienda, blood pouring out my nose. The doorman then came to me and said, 'Look, you need to go outside, they want to talk to you.' I said, 'I'm not going outside.' And he said, 'If you don't go outside, they'll come in and fetch you. You don't want that. Go outside.' So I went outside and they were threatening my girlfriend, saying they were going to do the same to her, that I'd taken the piss out of them by not contacting them, that I owed them money. One of the guys was really nice to me, he said, 'Just get away from here, because they'll kill you if you don't.' And that was my love affair with the Haçienda over.

In the beginning I would pick up my weekly supply somewhere remote. Later on someone else would do that for me. I had all of the drug dealer toys. Nice car. Lots of hi-fi equipment. The lifestyle thing. You spend it because you've got it. The bigger it got the more I got removed from the process. It makes me shudder thinking about it, the risks that I took. Driving round with thousands of pills in the car. Being followed. You know you're being followed by regional crime squad but almost thinking, 'They'll never get me.' The main guy who worked for me, he used to go off and base himself in different cities each week and pre-arrange meeting points. It was all done on pagers. They'd get paged where to go, but in code, so it never actually told you the place. But he got caught in the end. And they came for me and kicked the door of my house in, took me, didn't find anything in the house, kept me locked up for three days, hoping that he would turn me in. Which he didn't. So they had to let me go.

Strangely enough, I didn't think I was doing anything that wrong. What I was doing was supplying the best I could to people. The twisted way you think. In hindsight it was one of the most unpleasant years of my life, in terms of the stress and the worry. Every night you go to bed, wondering if the door's going to come in. Either the police or maybe someone else, you know. So it was kind of nice – very hard, but nice to leave that behind.'

IT SHOULD HAVE been a perfectly respectable eighteenth birthday party for Leah that Saturday night, 11 November 1995. It was being held at her parents' house where she lived, in Latchendon, Essex. She and her friend Sarah listened to the Oasis album *Definitely Maybe* while they were getting ready. Downstairs there was a buffet. Her mum Janet, a senior staff nurse, and stepfather Paul, a retired police inspector, were going to be there. Nothing too crazy, bar the four ecstasy pills she and her 17-year-old best friend Sarah had bought from a dealer who worked Raquel's nightclub in nearby Basildon. Leah had a Saturday job at Alders in Basildon and the two girls did the deal after work, on their way home. They'd done Doves before, the more common 'brand' of E with its tiny white bird logo, but these were 'Apples', with a tiny stamp of the fruit. Sarah suggested they just do a half. Leah wanted a whole one. At 8.30 p.m. they popped one each and went downstairs.

There were about 30 guests, mostly listening to rock. Generally it was a quiet do. Leah had three sisters and a brother. It was her brother who came and alerted her mother Janet. 'He said, "Leah wants you in the bathroom, she's not feeling very well,"' Janet Betts told *Mixmag* reporter Jane Headon in a later feature. 'I went up to the bathroom and she was bent over the washbasin. I said, "What's the matter, Leah?" and she turned round. I saw her pupils were like saucers – I've never seen pupils like that, not even in neuro-patients.' Janet lectured in schools about drugs. She immediately knew what was wrong. She said: 'Oh my God, Leah, what have you done?' Leah was violently sick. She complained her legs were going numb and she collapsed. Her father Paul came upstairs and her parents put her in the recovery position. 'On the bedroom floor, she kept going stiff,' Janet Betts said. 'She kept jerking and clawing me, I've still got the marks on my arms. She was yelling, "Please help me!" and she kept going on about the pain in her head.'

Then Leah stopped breathing. And though her parents resuscitated her and kept her body organs going, she died in her father's arms ten minutes later. In those ten minutes, Paul Betts asked his daughter what she'd taken and where she had got it. 'She told us who had supplied the tablet, she told us that at least twice she had taken these, that they had never affected her before, that she had taken ones with doves on them before but the one tonight had an apple on it. Her dying declaration, hoping that something she said would enable us to help her, was that she had taken it twice before.'

An ambulance arrived and Leah was taken to hospital where she was put on a life-support machine. But it was already too late. Four days later the life-support machine was switched off. Her organs were donated. Leah Betts was not the first youngster to die from ecstasy, nor will she be the last. But her parents took a decision to release a picture of her in a coma. Months later, another picture of Leah, smiling and healthy, would become a controversial anti-drugs billboard, along with the headline 'Sorted. Just one ecstasy took Leah Betts.' For a week she was to dominate the headlines. That Monday the *Daily Mail* printed a picture of her on her deathbed with the headline: 'The picture her parents want Britain to remember. How ecstasy wrecked girl's 18th birthday'. An ordinary Essex teenager became more famous in death than she could ever have imagined alive.

On Saturday 11 November 1995, I also took ecstasy, at a London club called The Cross with my then girlfriend Janine. On the crowded dance floor we shouted and whooped with the rest of the club. It definitely left me a little hazy when I arrived for work at *Mixmag* that Monday morning. I was the editor and the magazine was becoming high profile, the biggest in the expanding dance market. As the Leah Betts story broke, the phones went mad. The BBC news programme *Newsnight* called up. They wanted me to go on the programme to debate the issue with a Conservative MP, Nigel Evans, on television that night. Terrified, I agreed to do so. I got on the phone to contacts

I had at drugs agencies in the UK and Holland. I wanted to make sure I had my story straight.

At this point nobody really knew what had killed Leah Betts. Nobody knew very much about ecstasy, apart from the fact that a lot of people took it – the much-quoted figure was 500,000 a week – and that sometimes it seemed to kill people. But *Newsnight* had an angle worked out: they wanted me to say that Leah had been killed because she took a poisonous tablet and that ecstasy testing in clubs, as happened in Amsterdam, could have saved her. Early in the evening, the programme's host Peter Snow even called me to check this. But I wasn't so sure. My research with the drugs agencies suggested it wouldn't have, that actually a very small number of users reacted badly to ecstasy with fatal consequences. Live on air, with my heart beating so loud with nerves that I was sure the little lapel microphone would pick it up and broadcast it to the nation, I said as much – she had reacted badly to ecstasy and died and that tragic though her death was, it would not stop hundreds of thousands of people going out and taking ecstasy. Opposite me, the Conservative MP Nigel Evans did his best to score a few predictable political points.

The inquest into Leah's death bore this out. The pathologist said she died from ecstasy poisoning causing brain stem death. Dr John Henry, director of the National Poisons Unit at Guy's Hospital, believed fluid excess was the most likely cause of death in absence of her dancing. 'I think she felt ill, so she took water but she obviously took too much. Water is not an antidote to ecstasy. Water is an antidote to dancing, to cool the body down,' he told *Mixmag*. Her plasma sodium level, a measure of how diluted her blood was, had fallen to 126 illimoles per litre from an average of 135–145.

THE DEATH OF Leah Betts threw ecstasy into the national spotlight. Suddenly Middle England woke up to what was going on in all those clubs. There was a media outcry but no sense of any kind of reasoned national debate. Her death didn't stop people taking it. Nor was she the only victim. In 1996 there were 12 deaths blamed on ecstasy. In 2002, there were 72. Seventeen-year-old Daniel Ashton died a few weeks before Leah Betts. He collapsed in Blackpool's Palace Club on 29 September 1995, after taking ecstasy – a brown 'dove' tablet this time – and speed. His girlfriend Vanessa Watson, with him that night, told his inquest into his death that he had taken ecstasy at least three times previously. Fears that his tablet had too been contaminated were disproved by *Mixmag* who had a similar pill, purchased the day after Daniel died in Blackpool, tested by the National Poisons Unit at London's Guy's Hospital.

In court, Home Office pathologist Dr Edmund Tapp supplied the gruesome details of his death, which were reported in the magazine. 'There were bruises all over Ashton's face and upper body, some three inches across. His left eye was badly bruised, so was the eyelid. His right elbow and upper arm were bruised. Both Ashton's temple muscles were damaged. His brain had swollen from a normal weight of 1,200 grams to 1,650 grams – over one-third heavier. Blood-stained fluid filled his airways. There was the same fluid in his chest cavity… His lungs were grossly heavy, with bruising on the front of his chest. His heart was normal apart from haemorrhaging and fistule on its front. There was also clotted blood in his stomach…Death was due to intravascular coagulation (blood clotting), due to him taking ecstasy.'

But Daniel Ashton didn't become famous. His photo was never used in a billboard campaign. And later, questions would be asked about the billboard campaign that used that smiling image of Leah

Betts and that 'Sorted' slogan – in a *Mixmag* story in February 1996 and later in the 1997 book *Ecstasy Reconsidered* by writer Jim Carey. The billboard space had been given free of charge by media buyers Booth Lockett Makin. The posters were designed by Paul Delaney, then 52, from the advertising company Knight, Leech and Delaney. 'It transpired that the hoardings weren't massively booked over Christmas,' Delaney told *Mixmag*. 'One of the companies who own them, Booth Lockett Makin, told us that if we could come up with a suitable charity poster, we could have them. We were told they would prefer it to be an anti-drugs message.' Mike Mathieson who worked for rave organisation Tribal Gathering and youth marketing consultants FFI helped with the slogan, 'Sorted'. Booth Lockett Makin split the cost of printing the posters with Knight Leache and Delaney. Everybody gave their time and services for free.

There is no suggestion that their motives were anything but altruistic. But by coincidence, Knight Leach and Delaney and FFI worked for Red Bull, then being marketed as an alternative to ecstasy. As Carey pointed out, the drinks industry had been worried about the impact ecstasy and club culture were having on their declining profits ever since an influential report on Leisure Futures by the market analysts the Henley Centre for Forecasting in 1993. This report revealed that between 1987 and 1992, pub attendance in the UK fell by 11 per cent and predicted a further drop of 20 per cent by 1997. The report estimated the percentage of 16–24-year-olds taking any illegal drug doubled to nearly 30 per cent between 1989 and 1992. Estimating that one million people attended licensed raves each week, the Henley Centre reckoned UK ravers were spending £1.8 billion a year on entrance fees, cigarettes and illegal drugs. Money they weren't spending on alcohol.

Over the next decade the industry fought back across the board. Brands like Smirnoff became heavily involved in sponsoring dance and music events. Pubs became female-friendly 'gastro pubs', with wooden floors, wide windows and food and wine, rather than just beer. Designer 'club bars' with DJs opened all over the country – Piers Sanderson was just one promoter who moved into this new market. New drinks like Hooch alcoholic lemonade flooded in. In 1996, the Conservative MP Barry Legg introduced a Private Members Bill, which became law the following year as the Public Entertainments Licences (Drug Misuse) Act, which gave authorities the power to revoke licences from clubs where drugs are known to be dealt.

Meanwhile the drugs issue continued to swirl around Leah Betts. In December 1995, the month after her death, a gangland killing in Rettendon in Essex sent shockwaves through the country. Patrick Tate, Tony Tucker and Craig Rolfe had all been shot in the head at point-blank range, supposedly over a drug deal. All were well-known 'faces' in Essex: Tucker was a gangster and drug dealer who 'ran' the door at Raquel's nightclub in Basildon, where Leah Betts had bought her ecstasy. He was also a friend of Carlton Leach, the former Ministry of Sound head of security discussed in Chapter Eight. Two other drug dealers, Jack Whomes and Michael Steele, are currently serving life sentences for the murders. There are a number of books, including Tony Thompson's *Bloggs 19* and a film, *Essex Boys*, about the murders. Leach wrote extensively about it in his book *Muscle*.

Ian Wardle, chief executive of Manchester drugs agency Lifeline, with whom *Mixmag* frequently collaborated on drugs editorial, told the magazine the 'Sorted' posters had failed to contribute positively towards the drugs debate. 'As a nation we can only have a debate on drugs that's triggered by tragedy,' he said. 'In that environment you can only have a debate from a very emotive point of view.' The tragic death of Leah Betts had no impact on the drug's consumption. Indeed the 'apple'-type ecstasy she took became a popular pill. One clubber was spotted wearing a T-shirt with the billboard's slogan: 'Sorted. Just one ecstasy took Leah Betts.' On the back, his T-shirt read: 'Lightweight.'

As WARDLE POINTED out, drugs are a complicated and emotive issue. But for many young people, then as now, they have a seemingly irresistible allure. And not just in dance music: Kate Moss's *Daily Mirror* cocaine exposure has not harmed her career as a model at all. Quite the opposite: business is booming. Popular mainstream celebrities of all kinds have been caught up in drugs scandals. Even Graham Norton has talked about taking ecstasy – and enjoying it.

Drugs are cool, that is the problem. At least they are when you are 21 and feel indestructible. Just ask Dave Beer, a man who has taken more than most and who is remarkably candid about it. 'It's all down to the lifestyle, being a part of what's going on. With youth culture especially, drugs have always played a massive part. It's like smoking being cool. James Dean with a ciggie in his mouth, Keith Richards with a ciggie in his mouth, it goes with the look, with your leather jacket,' he said. In 1990s clubland drugs were part of the territory. If you were 'on one', you were down. If you weren't, you weren't. 'It's all a part of being a part of something,' said Beer. 'That's when you get dragged into it. It takes a strong person that can actually abstain and still be a part of it.'

Drugs aren't just about highs, about turning up the volume on Saturday night and making a club more intense than it is already. They are about peer group pressure, about belonging, about feeling one of a gang, joining in a secret society where everyone is in on the joke.

There is the jargon of ecstasy: necking a pill, banging the beans, double dipping, coming up, coming down. There would have been no acid house, no superclubs, no superstar DJs without ecstasy. 'I don't think the scene would have happened without it. The music was there, but the music fed off it. It was a two-way street. They went hand in hand,' said Sasha. 'We all know it's part of the culture.'

Smart DJs like him knew how to read the crowd's drug consumption and play up to it. 'As a DJ, you know when you're playing to a drinking crowd. They have a short attention span,' said Sasha. 'I can tell when I'm playing to a room that's got good ecstasy in it. It's a lot less these days. People like much more hallucinogenic, psychedelic drugs now. People like to mix up different things. The music's much more psychedelic now than it was.'

There was with ecstasy a kind of natural curve. In the beginning, clubbers fell in love with it. Everything was natural. Then the glow began to fade. 'Your first two or three years with it when you take ecstasy, you get your hit off it,' said Sasha. 'Then maybe you have a bad experience. Or maybe it doesn't work the way it did. Or maybe the music changes direction and you don't like it. Then cynicism starts to come in. That's something you fight so hard as a DJ that's been around so long.' To stay in the game, he has had to think about where his audience might be on that curve. 'People, they go out, they cane it, then they start to go out not taking ecstasy. "Oh, I don't like this music, it's shit, it used to be so much better three years ago." Three years ago they were on ecstasy! Having their first sex on ecstasy and experiencing those magical nights where everything falls into place.'

But there is a darker side to that curve – even for the vast majority of ecstasy users who don't have that dramatic, fatal reaction that killed Daniel Ashton and Leah Betts. Regular ecstasy users all knew about the temporary depression experienced a few days after taking the drug. It was known as 'Tuesday Blues'. There have been many inconclusive studies into the effect that the drug has on the brain and the supply of serotonin, the 'happiness' chemical the brain produces. But in the last few years, studies have begun to prove potential long-term brain damage to ecstasy users. In 2007, a University of Hertfordshire study found that even small amounts of ecstasy significantly affected both long- and short-term memory. Professor Keith Laws, from the University's School of Psychology, told the *Independent*: 'This meta-analysis confirms that ecstasy users show significantly impaired short-term and long-term memory when compared with non-ecstasy users. The ecstasy users also displayed significantly worse verbal than visual memory.'

In 2005, the BBC reported a Cambridge University study that found that people with a certain genetic make-up showed greater signs of depression after using the drug. Dr Jonathan Roiser told the BBC: 'There is evidence here that ecstasy use can result in depression in some vulnerable people.'

In other words, if you have a tendency towards depression anyway – as many people do – then ecstasy use might make you more likely to run into problems. Given the amount of ecstasy that was being consumed in the 1990s and that is still being consumed today, would that lead to an increase in mental health problems? Here the 2007 NHS Statistics for Drugs Misuse report makes sobering reading. Although we should bear in mind that these statistics cover all kinds of drugs, including crack and heroin, they do show an increase in drug-related mental health problems.

In 1996/7 let's assume the main age group taking drugs like ecstasy and cocaine was 16–24. In that year, the number of Finished Consultant Episodes with a secondary diagnosis of drug-related mental health and behavioural disorders – that is, people spending time as in-patients in hospital for drug-related mental health problems – was 3,706. By 2005/6 that number had doubled to 6,724. Even worse are the figures for 25–34-year-olds. In 1996/7 5,859 of them spent time in hospital. By 2005/6, that number had tripled to a staggering 15,698. Over the last ten years there is a huge increase in people from 25 to 34 having drug-related mental health problems – people who ten years ago would have been in the main drug-taking age range of 16–24 at the peak of the drug-guzzling superclub boom.

That looks very much like a proportion of the generation who consumed drugs on a regular basis is now experiencing problems. That there is a downside to regular recreational use of class A drugs. Is the 1990s generation experiencing a national comedown? Ancedotal evidence bears this out. Amos Pizey is one of a number of people who told me he knew many, many people who had ended up in rehab. He believed at the hardcore, extreme, constrained end of drug taking, that the nineties generation had gone too far. 'You can't take class A drugs like that,' he said. 'You think about how natural it was for us. People were just hammering it, day in, day out and becoming well known for it. You have to get a fallout and that fallout is what you see now, with endless people dropping like flies. And the question is, was it worth it?'

I MET NICKY HOLLOWAY on a Monday night in a big, empty Irish pub up the scraggy end of Turnpike Lane in North London. A pub full of men with red faces full of broken veins and broken dreams. Dust twirled slowly in the air. Nicky had a couple of pints of Guinness and told me he hadn't wanted to meet at his home because he was a bit embarrassed about it. He didn't own a mansion in the Hollywood hills like his old friend Paul Oakenfold. He lived in a one-bedroom flat in

North London, ex-council. I went there for my second interview with him. It was a tidy, concrete block. A normal council flat – but a long, long way away from, for instance, the beautiful hilltop villa in Ibiza where I'd interviewed Pete Tong. Pete Tong used to work for Nicky as a DJ, when Nicky was the biggest club promoter in London.

Nicky Holloway was there right at the genesis of acid house, along with Paul Oakenfold, Johnny Walker and Danny Rampling. He was one of London's first and most successful acid house promoters. He was profiled in the *Observer*. He raced around London with pockets bulging with cash. 'I was just the kid in the brand-new BMW, pilled off his head, having fun, going to warehouse parties with six and a half grand in my pocket,' he said. He ran West End disco the Milk Bar and owned the Velvet Underground club: a cheeky-grinned impresario in a crushed velvet suit. His party trick was stripping naked. He once hired a helicopter and a couple of models to fly to a Chuff Chuff party in a stately home in North Wales.

What happened to Nicky? He was a victim of the other drug, much nastier and more dangerous than ecstasy, that arrived in British clubs in the mid-1990s: cocaine. Danny Rampling became a superstar DJ with his own Radio 1 show. Paul Oakenfold one of the world's most famous and most successful DJs. Johnny Walker worked in record companies, such as the independent dance label Champion, but is now a gardener in Spain. And Nicky Holloway became an alcoholic and a cocaine addict.

Like many people in London in the lottery that is the property market, Nicky had had his highs and lows. He had a flat in Forest Hill and a big house in Putney, South London, but lost both when he defaulted on payments he was making on an outstanding VAT bill. Nicky went bankrupt. His friend Paul Oakenfold, who had visited his Putney place, later bought it at auction. 'He only did what any of us would have done,' said Nicky philosophically. 'I don't hold it against him, it was just very fucking weird going round there one night.' In Oakenfold's biography there is mention of a Putney house: 'the old Victorian place in Putney which was Paul's base in the mid-nineties, which just come on the market for an eye-watering sum'.

By the mid-1990s Nicky had bounced back and was running the West End club Velvet Underground. 'When you have a nightclub, it's perfectly acceptable because everyone that comes down wants to give you a line because they want to go in the office to do it in the first place. When you've got a nightclub, everyone's up your arse,' he said. There were always drinks after the club shut. There were always girls around. 'Just before the end I'd get the doorman to ask a few girls if they wanted to stay behind – haven't spoken a word to these people all night long. And then they all say yes. Right. And you end up with a few groups of friends and a few groups of girls. You're sitting around and you're chatting to them and then the gear comes out. Before you know it it's eight in the morning and it's back to yours,' he said.

Nicky thought about the money he'd spent. In two years, he reckoned he'd spent £45,000 on cocaine. 'While you've all got your nice houses and you're all fucking doing well on the property market and I'm renting, now you know why.' He laughed. 'And I ain't blaming no one, it went up my nose. When you're off your head you'll buy every cunt a drink. You don't give a fuck about how you're getting home, you're lending everyone everything, money ain't the question.'

But the Velvet Underground closed and Nicky's next venture, a club he'd planned to open on Archer Street in Soho, dragged on and then didn't happen. He kept partying. But now he didn't have the club and he didn't have the money. He became 'the bloke to avoid', he said, going out every night, borrowing money. He found his clubland friends weren't his friends any more. Everybody wanted to know Nicky the Winner: lovable Nicky, the cheeky boss of the Velvet Underground, the star DJ. Nobody wanted to know skint Nicky, drunk Nicky, cokehead Nicky, Nicky the Loser. 'It's deep how shallow clubbing is,' he said. 'I'd had seven or eight years of being out every night, drunk every night, coked off me nut every night, I was fucked. My head was scrambled. Gone. Gone to bits. I'd burnt out, you know.'

He decided to go into rehab the morning after he'd broken into a girlfriend's flat, consumed with jealousy, only to find she wasn't there. But he had to wait a fortnight for an available place. For a fortnight Nicky was locked up in Johnny Walker's house, waiting to be admitted to rehab. He drank everything he could find – miniatures of Baileys, Johnny's special whisky, everything and anything. Climbing the walls. Walker rang around Nicky's old DJ mates and they all chipped in: £500 from Pete Tong, £500 from Paul Oakenfold, £500 from Danny Rampling, £500 from DJ agent Lynn Cosgrave.

His records went into storage and he spent a month in Charter Nightingale Hospital in Paddington, London. He described it as 'pure relief'. And he came out clean. Now he talks that AA talk. 'I am bitter about what I've had and lost,' he said, 'but I know it's all my fault.' For seven years he never had a drink. He also never had a girlfriend and that was why he said he started having a few drinks again. 'At the end of the day, if you meet a girl and you go out with them and they go, "Do you want a drink?" And you go, "No, I don't drink." They go, "What?" You go, "Well, I had a bit of a problem." They go, "Weirdo alert, run away, baggage."'

What is it about cocaine that is so addictive? 'I don't know,' he said. 'It ain't good for me.' He talked about a gig he'd just done in Austria, how it was great because no one had any cocaine, so they'd all forgotten about it. 'But if you said to me now, "Do you fancy a line?" I'd have one. So work that one out. Work that one out.'

Nicky told me he had been DJing again that weekend. After seven years of abstinence, he had recently begun to drink again, even to dabble in a little cocaine. He looked a little crumpled. He would have cancelled this interview, he said, but he didn't want to seem unreliable. Then he took me round the corner to a tiny studio he'd just taken on in an industrial unit nearby. His battered hatchback was parked outside. And he played me a track he and Danny Rampling were working on with a local poet. A track Nicky was hoping might be a hit. He needed one, he said, to pay the rent on this place.

COCAINE AND ECSTASY are two very different drugs, but a lot of people in the 1990s found they went well together. There was a perceptible shift as one generation moved slowly from ecstasy to cocaine. Was it that cocaine felt more grown-up, more sophisticated? Was it that the comedown was easier, or that you felt more in control? Was it the free advertising campaign that nineties celebrities like Liam Gallagher gave the drug, the feeling that by 1999 so many celebrities seemed to be using it in their glamorous lives?

Cocaine landed like a smart bomb in 1990s clubbing. And if ecstasy had feminised clubs and the society around them, cocaine made it all masculine again. It was a drug of power and influence, not love and hugs. In the beginning, cocaine separated clubland's insiders from their customers out on the floor. It kept knackered DJs, by then inching into their thirties, going night after night. And it was on offer when they got to clubs. When DJs arrived at each club they were playing that night, cocaine would be offered out. And unlike a pill, which could be slipped into a hand discreetly, the whole complicated business of doing cocaine, which requires a dry flat surface, a note, a credit card, needed to be done in a secret place. Hence the sudden popularity of the manager's office or the fire escape behind the DJ decks. Cocaine made DJs, promoters and clubbers, no longer in the first flush of youth and exhausted by their relentless weekends, feel young again, feel indestructible, at least until the next day.

The punters soon caught on. And like the promoters, they too discovered that cocaine had a lot to do with hierarchy and power games. Who had got the wrap and would they invite you into a secret cubicle for that incredibly intimate process of taking it? The sense of danger – would that bouncer pop his head over the door and boot you out? The thrill of collusion and the way a gram or two of cocaine could divide a group of friends on a night out. Because one person might have it, but there wasn't enough for everyone, so immediately a pecking order was established in those who were getting it and hiding it from the others who weren't. Cocaine bought power and influence. Who would they give it to? Who would they trust not to do the whole gram if they did?

Cocaine didn't have the natural curve that ecstasy had. It travelled easily from the nightclub to the dinner party. It was as at home in a designer bar as it was in a dingy toilet. By 1999 cocaine was in fashion – being taken by lawyers and accountants, builders and plumbers, models and hair stylists. By the millennium city centre bars and pubs all over the country were posting up warnings to drug users, even smearing Vaseline on toilet paper dispensers to stop people chopping out lines. It affected people differently. There were people who dipped in and out of cocaine use for years, people who had a problem, then kicked it and people who spiralled down into terrible addiction problems. Not surprisingly some of them were DJs.

From 1995 to 1996 Judge Jules was a cocaine addict. 'You can get carried away in an environment of DJing where drugs are just everywhere,' he said. 'I'm probably quite a typical drug taker. The classic coke addict tale is you start doing it very occasionally, then it's once a month, then it's every weekend, then you can't enjoy a weekend without it and then you start redefining what the weekend is and the weekend comes Thursday through to Sunday night, then the weekend becomes longer and then it just joins in the fucking middle and it becomes doing it all the time.'

He quit on New Year's Day 1996. He had done three gigs the night before, finishing at London's Camden Palace at 8 a.m. He had a New Year's Day gig at Lush in Northern Ireland, which he missed, sparked out in a post-cocaine coma, his driver hammering on his door. 'I was pretty revolted at myself for not turning up and doing a gig and that was the spur to just say "no".' Since then, said Jules, he has not touched the drug.

Dave Seaman's cocaine problem began more gradually. His use crept up throughout the 1990s, until it got out of control just after 2000. 'I had a problem saying no and once I started I couldn't stop.' His daytime work, his record label, perhaps an innate sense of responsibility kept him together much of the time. He wasn't taking it every day, but for three years he was taking it every week. 'It became like a ritual, where you didn't even have to ask for it,' he said. 'You'd arrive at somewhere and the promoter would be, "Do you want a line before you go on?" And you'd be like, "Yeah, okay." And it's the worst thing in the world to do! You do a line before you go on, so you get in front of a group of people, with a spotlight on you, all facing in your direction, all looking at you with a spotlight on you! Don't ask me why we all did it for so long, why it went on for so long.'

One Sunday, after a long weekend of cocaine, he had a panic attack. He arrived back at his converted church in Henley with some of the drug left in a wrap and finished it off on his own. It was a stormy, rainy night and as usual his chapel was full of creaky noises as old buildings are. 'But I convinced myself somebody had broken in. So rang 999, convinced somebody had broken in downstairs,' he said. 'I'm like, "There's somebody downstairs." I'm gasping for breath. I'm completely paranoid at this point.' The police arrived and found the house devoid of burglars. Had there been one, they pointed out, there would have been wet footprints on the floor. 'You've got to get a bit of control over what's going on here, mate. This is just getting a bit silly,' Seaman said to himself and finally went to sleep.

It got to the point where he was doing it midweek. 'And that whole thing of not really going out to the club any more, just staying at home or in the hotel room, with a few people doing loads of coke. And just keep doing it and keep doing it and once you've started, it's all gone. And then try and get some more at God knows what time in the morning.' Then he'd beat himself up about it for a few days. 'And sometimes to get over the self-loathing, you go and have another drink and the drink leads to doing another night,' he said. Eventually Seaman went to see a drug therapist on London's Harley Street. He kicked the habit. 'Not to say I haven't done it since, cause I have, on occasions, but every now and again and to be honest at the minute I don't really do it at all.'

By the time he reached his Take That! Tour, Peter Cunnah had become a very serious cocaine addict with a six-gram-a-day habit. He got a series of wake-up calls. One was the night his heart jumped suddenly in his chest. Another was a realisation – something he said the Catholic in him might have recognised – that this was wrong. Phoning up girls at two in the morning to come over and do coke. Or just sitting there alone. 'I got into a closed room, windows shut, phone switched off, just didn't want to be with anybody. Just wanted to be with the drug. And I knew that was wrong.' The turning point was a visit to his dealer one night. Cunnah was horrified.

'He'd lost a lot of his teeth. He was emaciated. His gait was low. There was a smell in his room. There was this girl who was his coke whore basically and you could tell she was a lovely girl at one stage, but she was following the same path as him. And it's heroin and crack that they were into and I can only remember them saying, "My God, look at his teeth. Look how white his teeth are." They were looking at me. And I was going, "I had them cleaned last year." Because I'm two years behind them in the queue. I just thought, "This is *dangerous*."'

For Cunnah, the drug was caught up with something else – that compulsive desire he'd had since his childhood for stardom. 'Chasing fame and celebrity is caught up in that stuff as well,' he said. 'So I had to separate both out of my life and kind of go, "No to that."' He ended D:Ream and spent two weeks in rehab at Charter Nightingale. Then he spent months walking his dog on Wormwood Scrubs. 'Just literally staying clean, day by day, white knuckle ride, going to the meetings, staying clean.'

In 1998, according to NHS statistics, 12.1 per cent of adults had used one or more illicit drug in the last year – more than 4,100,000 people. By 2005/06 that had decreased to 10.5 per cent. But this was due to a fall in cannabis use. For class A drugs the trend is upwards. As the report says: 'The use of any class A drug in the last year has increased, from 2.7 per cent in 1998 to 3.4 per cent in 2005/6, mainly due to a rise in the use of cocaine powder.'

In 1998, almost a million people (920,000) had used a class A drug in the last year. The UK has the second highest cocaine consumption in Europe, after Spain.

SOME PEOPLE ARGUE that drugs should be legalised. How could that work? Would that mean the government selling class A's at chemists? Would that be on prescription – or over the counter, like Nurofen? What if multinationals were allowed to sell them? We've seen how seductive Starbucks made coffee; imagine what they could do with cocaine. Will governments ever stop the trade? No. Drug dealers and smugglers are good capitalists and there is too much money to be made. Look at Pablo Escobar. He was so determined to maintain his worldwide business, he even built a mini-submarine in which to smuggle cocaine. We live in a society that is supersaturated in terms of pleasure and experience. We want it all, now. That goes for shopping and materialism as much as it goes for pornography and prostitution. Modern British people expect their desires to be satisfied. Drugs are part of that ride. It is only if they become socially unacceptable that their use will decline. Societies do change. Smoking is going that way, just as drink-driving did 20 years ago.

Judge Jules, Dave Seaman and Peter Cunnah are the lucky ones. They all came through their cocaine addiction. All are now married with children. Nicky Holloway continues to DJ. When I last saw him, at his North London flat, he was on good form. He is enjoying DJing, he'd just split up with a girl, his humour was occasionally black but he was still resolutely cheerful. Like the Nicky of old: one of life's survivors.

Dave Beer is another one. He claims to have never suffered a comedown. 'If you're positive, it's not a comedown, it's just a relax period. You're chilling out. You're on the settee, you make it nice for yourself, get comfy. And smile and think what a good crack you've had,' he said. 'I've had comedowns from life but never from a session. It's self-inflicted. It's your own doing.' Today, as in the 1990s, he is still universally liked. 'Yeah, I'm naughty, I'm mischievous and things like that, but I know I'm a good person and I know that from other people's reactions to me,' he said. 'I'm not wealthy in financial terms as such but I'm very wealthy in love and friends.'

But there is a darker side. For Beer, the end of the 1990s didn't mean the end of the party. He carried on. And in February 2007 the party caught up with him, when he contracted a virulent strain of pneumonia and then pleurisy. He spent two weeks in a coma in hospital. 'I had the immune system of a 70-year-old man. So it was just shocked. Everything just shut down. I was on 100 per cent oxygen for two weeks.'

Beer said doctors told him that his massive narcotic intake over the years had helped him. 'Your body's used to recovering after large amounts of drugs,' they said. But his body was so accustomed to them he couldn't be sedated. 'I wouldn't go down on them. I couldn't go under. I wasn't asleep. I was moving all the time and it was compromising my health and they were going to give me a tracheotomy.' Then another doctor, who had been a Back To Basics regular, said, you can't do that, that's Dave Beer. The doctor spent the night with Beer, lying on top of him, keeping him steady. Beer came round, to the amazement of the doctors. The head doctor couldn't stop laughing. He called Dave Goliath and Beer started planning his escape from the ward. 'I started playing little tricks to get better, I'd nip me cheeks to put colour in me cheeks, I'd practise walking while there was nobody around. Constantly getting out of bed when I shouldn't. Sometimes I'd trip up and fall over with all the apparatus on me and make a bit of a mess, then they'd come and give me a bollocking. It was a bit embarrassing, having to have all the bed pans and all that with the nurses, it was like being an old man.'

Beer put a brave face on it. By April the same year he was at the Snowbombing music and snowboarding event in the Alps. But now he wheezed when he talked and though his famously unintelligible Yorkshire drawl was now, bizarrely, more coherent, he looked skinny and weak. During our interview he smoked half a pack of Marlboro Lights and worked his way through a bottle of wine.

It was late afternoon on a Saturday. Beer told me he had tried to seize the opportunity this wake-up call had given him to straighten out. But after coming out of hospital, his wife Vicki left him. 'The dying bit was easy, that was the hardest to overcome,' he said. The break-up of his marriage hit him harder. Dave knew one way to ease the pain. 'It was straight down the off licence, buy a packet of cigs, bottle of wine, straight on the phone, call the man that can, you know what I mean?' He meant the dealer. Just months after his near-death experience, Beer admitted he was 'partying' again. Would he ever give up?, I asked him. He seemed uncertain.

'Yeah. Definitely, yeah. Well I did and I do. I'm at that transition period, might take five years for it to kick into effect. That's a goal at the end of the day.' But as Beer explained, he still made his living out of clubs and drugs, drink and cigarettes were all part of the game.

I told Beer's story to Norman Cook, a few weeks later, in Brighton. Norman grimaced and said: 'God doesn't write fucking letters, you know. What bit are you not getting?' Perhaps Dave felt he couldn't be nutty, lovable old Dave Beer without all of this. Perhaps his nightclub existence, still running Back To Basics after all these years, doesn't make sense without it.

'It's like a lifestyle thing as well. Again, it's faking it again to an extent in clubs. I need to actually still be a part of it, to be in the game to win the game. Otherwise you just become fat, old and boring.' Dave talked about never knowing when you were going to die, about a woman he'd read about, who'd been killed by a bee sting. 'I actually do want to be clean. But I still I want to…' His voice faded out. Dave will never get fat and he will never get boring. But I sincerely hope he gets to get old.

'Mitsubishi, buy one, get one free. For further details, see local dealer,' says the TV advert. Well, imagine my surprise when I put this to my local dealer last Saturday only to be told to fuck off. Is this a breach of the advertising Codes of Practice?
Scott King, Liverpool, letter to Mixmag, *April 1999*

CLUBLAND IS NOT about the ageing generation. It's about youth. It's about constant flux. At the end of the century, its profile seemingly irretrievably damaged by the low-quality pills that had been available, ecstasy staged a dramatic comeback. In 1997, in Amsterdam, a new 'brand' of ecstasy appeared. These new pills were strong and came stamped with a Mitsubishi logo. By 1999, they were flooding into the UK. In February 1999 Dutch police intercepted a suspicious container on its way to Britain. Inside they found 400,000 ecstasy tablets with the Mitsubishi emblem. In a feature published that year, *Mixmag* journalist Julian Rolfe went on the trail of the new 'Mitsubishi' pills. His journey took him to Amsterdam, where East European scientists were being employed to make ecstasy in isolated laboratories. He also found evidence that the new pills were being manufactured in the UK. The magazine had some tested. 'What's consistent about Mitsubishis is the consistently high quality,' Rolfe wrote. 'Of five Mitsubishis tested this year by toxicologist Dr John Ramsey, all but one contained high, consistent doses of MDMA (the active ingredient in ecstasy). This is in contrast to tests *Mixmag* ran last year, which found less than one in three varieties of pill containing any MDMA at all.'

Mitsubishis arrived just as the Sheffield club Gatecrasher had taken over from Cream, now without Paul Oakenfold, as the country's most high-profile superclub. Gatecrasher's soundtrack was a high-energy, dramatic trance – big on emotional breakdowns. Judge Jules was back in fashion – he was playing a lot of this trance stuff. So was German DJ Paul van Dyk. Gatecrasher and clubs like it, such as Birmingham's Sundissential, had its own new breed of clubbers – the Cyber Kids – who wore fancy dress, sci-fi outfits, Day-Glo hair, studded belts and neck-collars, rubber and fetish wear. Mitsubishis became so popular in this scene that clubbers used to write the name on their arms – or even tattoo the Mitsubishi logo on their bodies. Clubland was booming again and the stage was set for a dramatic millennium. Or so it seemed.

In Holland, on his Mitsubishi trail, Julian Rolfe ended up in an office with a Rotterdam Police chief inspector, Jaap de Vlieger. 'He went to a locker in his room, took out this bag and just emptied it out on the table. It was like the last ten years of my life, just spilt out before my eyes. Love Doves and Callies and White Lightnings and Snowballs and Rhubarb and Custards and all these things, going back to 1989. Just one of each,' Rolfe told me. 'And then he turned his back on me and bumbled away. He seemed a bumbly kind of character. And they were just sitting there – temptation. I just thought, "I'm not going to start pinching pills, in a police station." There's nowhere to run, nowhere to hide, is there? I just sort of stared at them for a while. And then he cleared them up.'

TWELVE
THE MILLENNIUM MELTDOWN

TUNE! ATB – '9 P.M. (TILL I COME)'

The unstoppable Dutch trance hit with one simple killer riff that sold millions.

Gregor, the owner of the ritzy Russian club they'd spent all weekend trying to get out of, finally persuaded the British crew to go to his after party. Rufus Murphy, a dance music PR, didn't usually do the after party and he instantly remembered why and he immediately regretted it. They were in a cheap, nasty brothel somewhere in a Moscow suburb, decorated with flock wallpaper, its only concession to luxury a grubby jacuzzi the size of a bathtub, its only girls three sullen, unattractive teenage hookers who glared at the British lads every time Gregor mentioned them with molten anger. Sex with them would surely have involved taking your life – or at least your family jewels – in your hands. It would, in any case, have been impossible, as the one promise Gregor had delivered on, as he had been doing all weekend, was the cocaine. There was a mound of it on the table in this upstairs room, more cocaine than Murphy had ever seen in one place in his life. 'A whole trough of cocaine,' he said, 'and we all had our noses in it.'

The American superstar DJ came, surveyed the scene – and scarpered.

Instead, there was a Turkish construction magnate in leather trousers. And a beautiful, confused and utterly wasted woman whose only flicker of sexual interest, many hours ago, was in one of the DJs. She was a sommelier, she said. She danced with the photographer, wobbling in her heels. It was 7 a.m., or possibly 10. There was vodka and endless, endless cigarettes. And there was Trevor.

Trevor lived in Moscow. He was English and claimed to be a croupier, though drug dealer might have been a more accurate description. There was something very scary about him. The sudden whoops. The odd, pent-up, shadow-boxing dance he did on his own, in a corner of the club, grinning devilishly while throwing punches to the beat. His wife Valentina was Russian – she had arrived at the club with her plastic surgeon, sporting brand-new breasts. Now she sat on the couch next to Rufus, in front of the coke mountain, and told him a story about trying to fuck Trevor in a car outside a club in Plymouth and him being unable to come because he'd done too many drugs. Trevor cursed her from the window. She cursed him back.

Rufus got into a conversation about Russia, about the problems of the country, the corruption, the violence, the drinking, the strange beauty and roaring hearts of the people. 'I suppose the problem with Russia is,' he said, flushed with the illusion of sudden intimacy the cocaine had given him, 'that there are so many gangsters everywhere.'

Rufus remembered the way the room went creepily quiet and the morning sun streaming in through the dirty net curtains. He remembered realising slowly, through the fog of drugs and alcohol, that Trevor was probably a gangster and that Gregor was running an upmarket club in Moscow, which most likely made him a gangster as well and as for the Turkish bloke... Somebody – the photographer, perhaps – coughed quietly. Trevor, Gregor, Valentina, silently they acknowledged the stupidity of the comment and let it slide away. The Turk in the leather trousers came in and made a joke. Rufus and the lads went downstairs. They sat by the miniature jacuzzi and waited for their taxi.

THIS WAS IT. This, most certainly, was it. The future writ large – right here, right now, as Fatboy Slim put it. The millennium. Science fiction had been focusing on the turning of these most symbolic of centuries since the 1960s: Kubrick's *2001: A Space Odyssey*, 1970s TV show *Space 1999*. The build-up had begun way back when. I remember as a child people talking with awe about 'The Year 2000'. In 1983 Prince sang: 'Tonight we're going to party like it's 1999.' And through the 1990s millennium fever intensified. 'This amplification of things, this move to what everyone felt would be this moment when the millennium would dawn and we'd all be wearing white suits, right, out in space, going, "*Cool*",' said Dave Dorrell. 'The nineties couldn't get any smaller. It had to get bigger. It had to embrace 2000, for God's sake.'

In the countdown to the millennium it seemed the world was going mad in its desire to celebrate in the most outlandish way possible. *Mixmag* reported a computer systems engineer in California who wanted to use out-of-commission cruise missiles for a ballistic fireworks display and an American woman planning to have a Caesarian on the South Pacific island of Kiribati on New Year's Day – first place to get dawn. And it wasn't 'The Year 2000' any more – it was 'Y2K'.

If the world didn't end first, that was. Because there was a new enemy – a virtual one, the Millennium Bug. Like a science-fiction monster, the bug was impossible to detect and could attack anywhere. But in quintessential 1990s style it even had its own logo – an angry little insect in a warning red triangle, a branded nightmare all of its own. This furious little beast was going to send all the computers haywire when 1 January 2000 arrived because systems could only recognise the last two zeroes on numbers and would self-combust in confusion. 'The problem is ticking away simultaneously inside many computers, mainframes and electronic systems all over the world,' said Prime Minister Tony Blair ominously in a speech on 30 March 1998.

And what an apocalyptic vision it was. Jumbo jets were going to fall out of the sky. People believed this: in 1998 a Gallup survey for the *Daily Telegraph* revealed that two-thirds of the British population believed planes would be affected. Nuclear missiles might launch themselves. In 1999 America and Russia agreed on a jointly manned early warning station in case the bug accidentally prompted a nuclear attack. Police forces across Britain cancelled leave over the millennium period because of concern over failing alarm systems and blackouts. Scotland Yard sent an officer to Sydney to provide an early warning system. The Boston mass transit system planned a shutdown. Bristol rapper Tricky had certainly pre-empted the mood when he named his doom-laden 1996 album *Pre-Millennium Tension*.

And what was clubland going to do? Blast into the new century with the biggest parties ever. If anyone knew how to celebrate, it was the superclubs. And they were going to party like – well, like it was 1999. Which it actually was. Luckily, thanks to the Mitsubishis, clubbing was booming again. The cyber kids were everywhere. But this was an oversaturated clubland. The music was poppier than ever: intense, vocal trance records. The fashions were more outlandish than ever – the cyber kids in their sci-fi fancy dress, the Mitsubishi name and logo daubed all over the bodies, even tattooed. Not everybody was enamoured. The doubters were already making noise.

At *Muzik* magazine, Ben Turner was disillusioned running stories about Gatecrasher and its crowd. This was a long way from his beloved techno. 'All this fabulous Detroit-inspired music that we'd been championing for many years became irrelevant. It just all became mainstream,' he said. 'People who went to superclubs were the wrong people.' The cyber kids were dividing clubland. Even Gatecrasher fans such as Miranda Cook started backing off. 'The logo, that was embarrassing. When that cyber fashion, to paint your face with drug logos, spread about the country, a lot of people thought, "This isn't cool. This is *not* cool." I didn't want to be talking to someone with a pill drawn on their face! Who would?'

The people at the top of dance music, the DJs and the promoters, had become increasingly blinded by ego and by greed, the brief flurry of idealism at the beginning of acid house by now completely forgotten. 'The truth is it wasn't stolen, it was sold, everyone knew what they were doing,' said Amos Pizey. 'It was a business.' But with their judgement clouded by money, they forgot about the clubbers who paid their wages. Increasingly these clubbers were being treated with contempt. Everything was being squeezed a little too hard.

The DJs were too caught up in the whirlwind of their superstar lifestyles to notice. 'You're thinking, "This is it." You're at the pinnacle of what's going on,' said Dave Seaman. 'You're getting caught up in how much money you can make, how many places you can go, if you're going to have a private jet here. You're getting caught up in the "bling" of it. And all of us working towards this millennium.'

Dave Dorrell watched his DJ friends with mounting horror – the people he had known since acid house was a cottage industry, since the illegal warehouse party days and the little northern clubs and the parties in caravans, were increasingly behaving like divas. 'If you weren't rolling the red carpet out for the limousine that picked them up from their fucking hotel room, with the champagne in the box and the E and the coke line chopped out and my girlfriend's winking at you,' said Dorrell, 'it was, "Well, I might not come back and DJ." *Whoa*! Calm down, you're only playing records, guys.'

But there was a payday to be had. The superstar DJs and their agents had been hyping up their fees for years. New Year's Eve was always a big-money gig. But this was insane. The millennium turned into the most cynical feeding frenzy that acid house and superclubbing – not exactly a scene renowned for its self-restraint – had ever seen. How much were they going to get paid? Fortunes.

Sonique made £5,000 for Gatecrasher – her six-figure fees would come later, with her pop-stardom. Jon Pleased came out of retirement, donned his drag outfit and got between £8,000 and £12,000 (he can't remember) for playing three Scottish events. 'Yeah I was probably thinking, "Oh, it's more about the money now, tonight."' Nick Warren played home in Sydney for £20,000. Dave Seaman got £30,000 for two Renaissance shows and bought his parents a house in Spain with the money. Danny Rampling pocketed £50,000, playing to 30,000 at the River Club in Cape Town, South Africa. 'Everyone had been offered ridiculous amounts of money, ridiculous, inflated amounts of money, as if it was going to be the last night on earth,' Rampling said. 'That was the last days of Rome, in a sense. It was one last payday of the superstar DJ era.'

The money mounted up. Jeremy Healy flew around the country in a private plane and earned around £80,000. 'It's sinful,' he smirked. 'It was the height of the stupidest money.' Judge Jules got £100,000, for playing Gatecrasher. 'The most that I've ever charged,' he insisted. 'The most I've ever charged by a factor of five.' Pete Tong was on £125,000. 'It was pretty crazy money. The fact it was over six figures,' said Tong. Norman Cook got £140,000. 'But that was four gigs. I absolutely worked my arse off. I did Brixton, Cardiff and the two in Liverpool. It nearly killed me,' he said. And Sasha? He still won't say. But he claimed it was more than anybody else – which, if that were true, would put him at £150,000-plus. 'I made a lot of money. I think I did more parties than anybody else,' he said. 'It was the extreme of everyone getting ripped off, all the DJs making loads of money.'

Jon Pleased summed up the feelings of many. 'It's not bad for a night's work, is it?' he smiled. Not bad for a night's work? It isn't. And in a sense, who could blame them for charging as much as they could get away with? They were meant to have been hairdressers, game-keepers, ad men, shop managers, photocopier salesmen, bass players at best; yet they had ended up celebrities, pop icons, superstar DJs. They simply couldn't believe it had lasted this long. They certainly couldn't believe how much their agents had bullied promoters into paying. They had gone from an average £500 a night to £100,000-plus in just eight years.

As many record company executives who worked with them in the 1990s could tell you, DJs would always choose the shortest route to the largest amount of wedge. Nice guys, great to hang out with. And utterly money driven. They always struggled with a long-term vision. They failed to make albums that would feed the longevity of their careers. Because, short term, there was always somebody waving a wad of cash for a gig next weekend. But the rumours of those astronomical fees were out there. Everybody knew. And the clubs fed this too – they all wanted to stage the biggest event ever. It was a bidding war.

'The real bidding started earlier this year when Gatecrasher sent a fax to the DJ's managers with the prices they were willing to pay for a set. Gatecrasher said the offer would expire in 48 hours, to hurry things up,' ran a *Mixmag* news story. 'Gatecrasher invited one prospective DJ to Sheffield's Don Valley stadium, the site of its party. They stood him slap bang in the middle of the stadium, turned on the floodlights and said, 'Now tell us you don't want to play for 25,000 people.' It worked.

With the clubs out to make a killing too, they were going to have to charge around £100 per ticket just to make it work. Huge, glossy adverts in all the magazines promised quite simply the night of a lifetime. Gatecrasher's adverts for their 25,000-capacity event at Sheffield's Don Valley stadium were typically breathless.

'Imagine the buzz of the Best New Year's Moment ever lasting from 5 p.m. until 8 a.m.,' they frothed. 'Now imagine you are dancing in a huge arena. You're locked into the beat, you're lost in music, your eyes are closed. When you open them, it's hard to believe what you see. There must be tens of thousands of people here, lasers and searchlights strafe the giant room while the DJs are above your head on a massive suspended stage. Massive screens are beaming out images from around the world, people partying in Ibiza, South Africa, Australia, Israel: the global village has come alive and everyone, everywhere, appears to be having it right off. Science fiction? Nah. It's just midnight on 31 December 1999. You're at Gatecrasher 2000GC and parties don't get bigger or better than this.'

Cream too had spectacular plans. There were five events in total under their name. There was an outdoor show at Liverpool's Pier Head (£75 a ticket) with live acts like the Stereophonics and Orbital and DJs like Pete Tong, Fatboy Slim and Sasha. Their club Nation had many of the same DJs, for £99. For the same price there were shows in Cardiff and at London's Brixton Academy. The same star DJs – Tong, Fatboy Slim, Sasha – were racing around the country to play all of them. 'You can't afford to miss this event,' ran Cream's Brixton ad. But in the run-up to New Year's Eve, thousands of Cream regulars, like clubbers all over the country, decided that they could, in fact, afford to miss this event. News began to filter out that ticket sales were pitifully low. A local paper ran a story that Cream had only sold 30 tickets. 'And we were going, "Don't be so fucking stupid. As if we'd be going towards the millennium with only 30 tickets sold,"' said Cream's Jayne Casey. 'And we'd only sold 30 tickets.'

The club was being filmed by a Sky TV crew – Cream had a habit of inviting TV crews in when times were getting rough – and tension was running high. 'We were half a million pounds in and we hadn't sold a ticket,' said Casey. 'James was like, "Look, if we can just hold on in there, these millennium shows will start dropping off. And as one drops, we'll pick up the ticket sales for them." And he hung in and he hung in.' It was a brave move. And slowly, tickets began to sell. Cream's Liverpool shows sold out. But their London night in Brixton was half empty.

Things were worse at Renaissance. A huge spectacular was planned for Nottingham's Trenton Park, with £250,000 spent on production, but poor ticket sales forced Geoff Oakes to cancel. They needed to sell 2,500 tickets at £110 each. They sold just 500. But they still had to pay all their star DJs – big American names such as Frankie Knuckles, who was getting around £30,000. At the last minute, they cancelled the event and shifted everything to their new Nottingham club Media. John Digweed gave some of his fee back. Renaissance lost £200,000 and nearly went under. 'At a time when it was difficult for the businesses to sustain it,' said Geoff Oakes. 'We very nearly lost everything at that point.'

With ticket prices like this, if you added in triple-time taxi charges, drugs, overpriced drinks, a millennium club night out was going to break the bank. Clubbers started planning house parties. They voted with their pockets. They weren't going to buy it. 'For one night, it was the price of a holiday,' said Jon Carter, earning what was for him a bumper £5,000 for playing on Bondi Beach in Sydney. 'It was a sort of crumbling disaster, little pieces falling out of the wall, bit by bit.'

As the millennium inched closer, the air of looming disaster thickened. On 31 December hackers distorted the Railtrack home page with a message that said no trains would run until 3 January because of the Millennium Bug. A three-day barrage from hackers nearly covered the Vatican website with porn. In Hamburg a 1,500 capacity nuclear shelter was to be opened under the railway station in case of a power failure. Lifts in Hong Kong were to stop from 11.45 p.m. to 12.15 a.m. And the Bank of England stockpiled £8billion of banknotes in case the bug stopped cash machines, credit cards and telephone banking systems working. Just after Christmas, 1999, the bug finally struck when thousands of swipe card machines installed by HSBC failed to work because the machines thought the date 1 January 2000 was 1 January 1900.

31 DECEMBER 1999: D-Day. Zero hour. In Sheffield the lowest temperature was below zero. The doors at Gatecrasher opened late. The car parking was a nightmare and cost £5 alone. The venue was freezing: fire officers wouldn't let Gatecrasher put the special heating equipment on because it 'did not live up to their professed standards', the club said later. Promised fairground rides were cancelled by Health and Safety officials due to the potential of temperatures plummeting below freezing. Which must have come as a surprise, in Sheffield, in December. The doors opened late. There were enormous queues at the bar, which was serving vodka and a dribble of Red Bull for an inflated £4.50 or beer for £4. The ladies' toilets overflowed. And just

as midnight approached, the whole thing turned to farce, when one clubber climbed the 'king pole' of the tent and started flashing his buttocks. Everything ground to a halt for five or ten minutes, as the music was switched off. 'Everyone started shouting, "Wanker, wanker,"' remembered Miranda Cook, who was on the dance floor with Gatecrasher boss Simon Raine.

Judge Jules got on the microphone to try and persuade the reveller to descend. 'I was telling him to get down in a chirpy, get-the-crowd-going way,' said Jules. Then another voice came booming in: a police officer, in bluff Yorkshire tones, saying, 'Judge Jules, can you please shut up?' The reveller eventually descended, but midnight had gone and German DJ Paul van Dyk, who had created a track especially for the occasion, was so incensed he punched him. 'It had all fizzled out really badly,' said Miranda Cook. 'The atmosphere had just gone by then.' Despite this, Gatecrasher was judged a success by the end of the night. Though not for Sonique, who was booked, but for once was squeezed out by the boys and didn't get to play. 'I never played that night. Cause everybody was just greedy. I wanna play! I wanna play!' she said. 'I cried my eyes out at that gig.'

Judge Jules was on a private plane by then, with Miranda Cook, his wife Amanda and the DJs Brandon Block and Alex P, flying to another party at Manumission in Ibiza. Tickets for this shindig cost £599 for airport, hotel transfers, hotel parties, welcome drink, transport to and from Manumission at Privilege and back to the hotel in San Antonio or carry on at Space. There was champagne on the plane and Miranda did cocaine. But no toilet, which caused the drunken revellers some discomfort.

Jeremy Healy was on another plane, which took off from Luton airport. He'd played a club called Area in Watford he had a share in and was on his way to shows in Glasgow and Edinburgh. His agents Lynn Cosgrave and Ian Hindmarch were also on board. With that much money involved, said Healy, 'they were making sure I was getting to those gigs'. It was a clear night and from the plane they could see fireworks going off in cities all the way up the country. 'That was the best bit of it,' Healy said. 'Cause when there's a lot of money and you're worried about what's going to go wrong and are you going to get there, it completely takes the fun out of it. Cause it's stressful.'

Cream's Brixton and Cardiff events were half empty. Their star DJs all had mini-disasters. Pete Tong's son fell ill and he couldn't make the Brixton show, which led to a long-running dispute with the club over money. He never got his full fee. Sasha was in a car with four other partygoers – Sparrow included, naturally – hurtling down the M1 at 100mph-plus. Sasha had a brand-new Audi A8 and wanted to push it. 'Sparrow's like, "There's this weird knocking in the back." We pulled over and the back tyre was shredded. If that had been the front tyre, I would not have been sitting here talking to you today,' Sasha said, shuddering at his near miss. 'Idiots. Absolute fucking idiots.'

Norman Cook and Zoë Ball didn't want to risk flying what with the Millennium Bug and had arranged a party bus for themselves and all their friends. But the bus was going too slow, so the couple had to switch mid-journey to a fast Mercedes and leave their friends behind. 'We were driving across the Severn Bridge at midnight, on our own, with a bottle of champagne,' Cook said. 'Like Norman No Mates.' His busload of mates didn't even make it to Liverpool. 'I spent most of it in a car with Zo, driving round England. But if you sell your arse, if you prostitute yourself like that for the dosh, you have to bend over and take it,' said Cook.

Cream's Liverpool shows were judged a success. The Archbishop of Liverpool even turned out at the Pier Head gig. But financially, it was a disaster. They lost £400,000 across all their shows. 'Which nearly wiped us out,' said boss James Barton. But they had their TV series and a new compilation album, effectively the soundtrack to the series, which sold hundreds of thousands. Jayne Casey was to leave soon afterwards. 'It was the end of dance music in its coolest sense and it was dance music going overground, that last six months in the run-up to the millennium,' she said.

In Scotland, promoter Ricky Magowan had been running parties since he started his Streetrave nights in 1989. In 1995, inspired by the superclub boom he launched Colours. He had planned his most ambitious New Year's Eve yet with a five-arena show on in a gigantic industrial unit in Shotts, between Glasgow and Edinburgh. Jeremy Healy flew up on that private plane. It had a capacity of 20,000 at £70 a ticket. It cost Magowan £90,000 to install two fire escapes. His security company, normally around £25,000 for an event like this, charged more than £90,000. Only 6,000 tickets were sold by the night but he decided to go ahead anyway. 'I think your ego always helps you – we worked for a full year on the project,' he said.

It was a disaster. The venue was half empty. Planned live link-ups with the big club events all over the world failed: in the end, all the crowd got was Brandon Block – live from Watford. The cloakroom was absolute chaos, mainly because inexperienced cloakroom staff had used sticky tape to fix numbers to coats, which in the humid heat of the rave had fallen off. At the end of the night, cloakroom staff faced a pile of coats with no tickets and a scrum of angry clubbers who wanted to go home. 'This is the A to Z of how to run an event. Number one, make sure your cloakroom staff know what they're fucking doing,' Magowan said. 'A lesson learnt in business.'

Financially, it was worse. He lost £250,000 on the event and had to remortgage his house to stay in business. 'I didn't have it to lose. Then my dad died three weeks later, you can imagine what a good fucking January I had,' he said. 'But I'm still standing.' Colours and Streetrave are both still running parties. 'We never had any money up here anyway, so it didn't really matter,' said Magowan. 'Recessions don't really hit Scotland.'

The big night had gone off not with a bang, but with a whimper – and not only in clubland. New Labour fared just as badly. The Millennium Bridge between St Paul's Cathedral and Tate Modern opened and closed after a mysterious wobble. The Millennium Eye failed to open on time too due to a 'clutch problem'. Tickets for the party at the Millennium Dome with Tony Blair and the Queen hadn't arrived and thousands of important guests were left queuing for hours to pick up tickets in the freezing cold at Stratford Station. Some people waited over two hours – and then another 90 minutes to get through Dome security. Then the free Tesco pack including a quarter bottle of champagne ran out too. They were later offered free tickets and a £15 voucher in compensation. But at least, bar HSBC, the Millennium Bug didn't strike.

IN THE AFTERMATH, a deluge of letters from furious clubbers poured into the *Mixmag* office. 'Why have I just paid £100 to go in a freezing tent and have a shit night?' asked one. 'Shame on you, Gatecrasher,' raged another. 'What the hell went wrong?' asked a post-mortem feature. 'The world's biggest party turned, in many places, into the world's biggest cock-up.' The promoters bluffed it out. Gatecrasher blamed Health and Safety for not letting them put up the fairground. Cream apologised for a half-empty Brixton Academy. But the damage had been done. And suddenly clubbing wasn't looking quite so golden. The emperor's new clothes had fallen off. And there he was, naked and shivering in a cold January wind.

Over the next couple of years clubland's punctured bubble slowly and surely expired. It started at the top, with Darren Hughes and Ron McCulloch's new superclub, home. The club, which had opened at 9 p.m. on 9 September 1999 in Leicester Square, was Ron McCulloch's brainchild. The Scottish entrepreneur and architect had built up his Big Beat company, which now owned a portfolio of businesses including hotels, restaurants and high profile clubs like Glasgow's Tunnel. Big Beat was reckoned to be worth £40-50 million.

Number Seven Leicester Square was the flagship for McCulloch's most ambitious project yet – a global club brand that would take in venues in Sydney and New York. Darren Hughes had left Cream and brought Cream's star DJ Paul Oakenfold with him. £10 million was invested in Leicester Square alone in a building that spread over eight floors. Amos Pizey was running the top floor VIP with Lisa l'Anson. There was a restaurant. Renaissance's Geoff Oakes and his partner Joanne were running a venue in Nottingham called Media for Big Beat too. And Hughes and Oakes were talking up clubland's brave new world: a shiny, high design fusion of restaurant, hotel and club for 'grown up' clubbers, with places for them to sit down.

'It was never right,' said Darren Hughes. 'It was all wrong from the beginning. Lack of understanding of the beast that London was. Leicester Square. It was a dream for Ron McCulloch.' The problem was nobody wanted to go to Leicester Square, which for Londoners is a no-go tourist zone. Hughes had been determined to win them round and show the Southerners how to party with a proper northern club. But while there was a lot of talk about home's chic, metallic décor, amazing sound system and its amazing design, there wasn't much about who its audience might be.

Home was supposed to represent the future of clubbing. Instead, it represented its past. The club was struggling. 'It was a fucking disaster,' Darren Hughes said. 'McCulloch was starting to drown within it.' Ron McCulloch insisted that the club was beginning to break even and was no longer haemorrhaging money. 'We had budgeted that it would take us a year to get it into profit,' he said, 'but it's not till you actually do a thing that you can see what it's actually going to take get it there.' Then, just 18 months after it had opened, police raided the club on 23 March 2001 and found an ecstasy dealer with 16 tablets.

The police wanted it closed down. At a special hearing, they succeeded in having the club's licence revoked. Chief Inspector Chris Bradford, of Scotland Yard's clubs and vice unit, told the *Independent* newspaper at the time: 'It was necessary to take the unusual course of action in a bid to try and eradicate this serious and open problem.' McCulloch pulled in his London staff to tell them the club was going to shut for a while. A few days later the bank pulled the plug on Big Beat's credit. McCulloch called the staff back in and told them they were all out of work. Big Beat went bust. Seventeen venues closed. Over 300 people in all lost their jobs. The dream was over. McCulloch was devastated. 'Shattered, emotional, bit of a wreck to be honest, that day,' he said. 'George and I lost quite a sum of money. Everything we had in the company was gone. So yeah, it pretty much clobbered us personally as well as the company.' McCulloch moved his wife and young family to Sydney, bought home's Sydney club from the receiver and started again. Hughes had already left.

SLOWLY THE WHOLE house of cards that was the world of superclubs began to collapse. James Barton at Cream sees home's closure as a watershed moment. 'I think home was the straw that broke the camel's back with dance music. I think it contributed to a real change in opinion about what us, Ministry Of Sound and people like that, were all about.' Now the authorities seemed to have it in for all the big clubs. In May 2001 160 police officers raided Gatecrasher. Police described it as 'awash with drugs' and made 13 arrests. In April 2002 the club went monthly, though Gatecrasher survived and today Gatecrasher own venues in Birmingham, Nottingham, Leeds and Sheffield.

Cream was beginning to unravel too. In July 1999, Liz Wood, a 20-year-old tourist officer, had died at the club after taking speed and ecstasy. In May 2000 a massive police raid by 150 officers found £1,000 worth of drugs and arrested nine people. Stringent conditions were imposed on the licence. 'The first thing you had to do was remove all of your personal things and put them into a plastic bag and show them as you walked into a nightclub,' said Barton. 'That's when I realised it was over.'

In March 2001 an article in the *Guardian* attacked Smirnoff for signing a three-year sponsorship deal with Cream the previous year – a deal Barton said was worth £2 million. 'The choice of Cream as the vehicle for this marketing extravaganza is a dubious decision, as the Liverpool-based nightclub has been dogged by controversy over its failure to control its drug problem,' said the *Guardian* piece. The Smirnoff deal didn't go its full term. By 2002, Cream was only pulling in 500 punters a week and losing £50,000 a week. In July, they took a decision to stop running weekly nights.

It made national news. Barton was interviewed for Radio 1. He sat in Cream's London office in Great Portland Street and listened to the story unfold. 'It was something that had been suspected about superclubbing full stop and here was Cream, one of the biggest names, saying we can no longer sustain running our club. It was a massive story,' he said. 'I didn't feel remorse or regret, I think, if anything, I felt happy, in a weird way. Because it had been hard, personally and emotionally, it had been a really difficult ride.' He paused. 'I'll be honest with you, I was tired, I was burnt out.'

On the club's last night, Fatboy Slim and Jon Carter both starred. Carter stage-dived off the DJ booth. Norman Cook followed. Barton was in the booth. The crowd started baying for him to follow. On the last night of his club, he followed, leaping off the DJ booth into the welcoming arms of his audience. The biggest superclub weekly of all was dead. Though like Gatecrasher, a slimmed-down Cream survives, having closed its London office and today runs Creamfields events in the UK, Spain, Portugal, Romania, Czech Republic, Poland, Peru, Chile, Malta, Argentina and Brazil. They also own the Nation venue, which they now rent out to other promoters. Barton now lives in Liverpool full time.

ACID HOUSE WAS standing on shaky ground – the shifting sands of popular culture. DJs, electronic dance music, it was all looking old and tawdry. But rock was back, enjoying a wave of creativity that hadn't been seen for nearly a decade. Plus American R 'n' B – a seductive mix of hip beats, glamour and soul diva attitude – was making waves. Creatively, dance music was no longer competing. Ministry felt the pinch. '2002, 2003, those were the years where it became quite tough,' said current CEO Lohan Presencer. 'That was the time of Eminem. It was the time of the resurgence of rock music.' Ministry of Sound Recordings pre-tax profits plummeted – from £4,166,000 in 1999, to £781,000 in 2002, to £379,000 in 2003.

In 2001, five skinny, handsome private-school boys from New York called The Strokes exploded into the world of pop music. They wore leather jackets and had messy hair and on their debut album, *Is This It*, propagated a sharp, angular, stripped down rock 'n' roll that sounded modern, cool and relevant. It had brio. It had balls. From R 'n' B came Destiny's Child, an all-girl three-piece who combined powerful, sexy images with irresistibly funky pop-soul hits and who suddenly connected on a worldwide level.

The sexual politics had changed. Club bunnies were yesterday's news. So were ladettes like Zoë Ball. Instead the American drama series *Sex and the City* had arrived, sweeping all before it. The show began on America's HBO in 1998 and reached Channel 4 in 1999. Its characters were glamorous, successful, intelligent, sexy and – most important of all – grown-up women to aspire to. In the UK, independent, affluent, single girls didn't want to be ladettes or club bunnies any more. A new breed emerged, dubbed by one female brewing executive 'Cocktail Bird'. Cocktail Bird did not want to paint the name of an ecstasy tablet on her arm and put a flashing light on her head. She wanted to be like Carrie, Charlotte, Miranda or Samantha, wearing Manolo Blahnik shoes, sipping Manhattans, exchanging razor-sharp repartee with her girlfriends in upmarket bars – bars which invariably had their own DJs. Cocktail Bird listened to Destiny's Child singing hits like 'Bills, Bills, Bills' or 'Independent Women Part I', songs about independence, about paying their own way, about dumping useless boyfriends, about how sexy they were.

Not surprisingly, the group's lead singer Beyoncé Knowles became one of the most famous women in the world. Bar Sonique, 15 years of acid house had not thrown up one single female star. Instead, it now offered up Amanda O'Riordan, the wife of Judge Jules. Jules had long ago given up the trumpet. Instead, he featured on a 1999 *Mixmag* cover, riding a white unicorn. Jules's dance act Angelic, with producer Darren Tate, featured his wife on vocals. In their videos, Destiny's Child purveyed a colourful, fun and powerful glamour. On the video to Angelic's 2000 bubblegum-trance hit 'It's My Turn' Amanda O'Riordan lip-synched, dead-eyed, in front of prancing forest nymphs, with all the charisma of a loaf of wet bread. Pale, tepid, limpid pop music, acid house completely disassociated from its black roots, Judge Jules a universe away from rare groove.

In 2004 the Brit Awards recognised the malaise and dropped its annual Dance Act Award. Dance music's vibrant originality had dried up. The grown-up playground of mid-nineties handbag clubs had become institutionalised into a high street disco – with Judge Jules talking on the mike, as he increasingly did at Radio 1 live broadcasts. The wild invention of early British 'progressive' house had evolved into formulaic trance – with the DJ's wife on vocals.

Even DJing itself was no longer something special. DJs had already stopped playing vinyl and started playing CDs. 'It's not really hard,' said Sonique. 'There was something super about having those two vinyls in your hand. It's not cool now.' The Internet meant anybody could find that hot new track that previously only a few DJs had on limited vinyl copy. iPods meant anybody could be their own DJ. Nobody needed DJs any more. By August 2003, Alexis Petridis, a former raver who had worked at *Mixmag* for years, from work experience through to deputy editor, was the *Guardian*'s pop critic. He nailed dance music's demise in a landmark piece. It was in decline and only had itself to blame, he argued. 'It was as if the DJs and club promoters who "ran" dance music simply assumed that audiences were too befuddled by the drug ecstasy to realise they were being ripped off,' he wrote. 'What seemed, ten years ago, to be a sophisticated and stylish alternative to rock and indie music now just looks tawdry and uninviting.'

The DJs took this personally while completely failing to engage with the argument. 'It was horrible to see what the journalists and people did to that scene. It was like watching a group of hoodies kick an old man to death. They really turned on it. "Wicked! Dance music's gone. Thank fuck for that,"' said Sasha. Judge Jules said: 'It's frustrating when you've created your life out of something and the evidence that you can see before your eyes is totally contradictory.' Not that he had actually read the piece, he admitted. 'I didn't read it first hand but it just made me furious.' Jeremy Healy put his hand up. He had spent his career knowing what was hot and what was not and he had long since felt the wind of change. 'DJs went from being the most wanker people to being the coolest persons to being the most wankerest people,' he laughed. 'Maybe we should leave it there.'

IT WAS A crowded cremation, as funerals for people who have died unnecessarily young often are. Gilles Nobbs was just 41 when he killed himself in his Portsmouth flat in 2007. His friends from London crowded uncomfortably close to the coffin as they played Primal Scream's 'Loaded', its introductory sample of excitable American teenagers declaring, with terrible irony: 'We wanna be free to do what we wanna do. And we wanna get loaded and we wanna have a good time.' Later they played Robert Miles's sentimental trance hit 'Children'. On the dance floor, it was a song that created a kind of overwhelming, melancholic euphoria. At the funeral, it was simply too sad to be played all the way through. 'I think everyone would have just collapsed,' said Gilles's friend Julian Rolfe. 'It was a very, very emotional day.'

Gilles Nobbs was a freelance photographer – his byline was just Gilles – who specialised in club work. Julian was the *Mixmag* deputy editor, who worked with Gilles for three seasons in Ibiza on a weekly magazine produced for the island. The humanist preacher at the service talked about those three summers on the White Island. 'He referred to the time we were out in Ibiza as the good times,' said Julian. 'And said that, in recent years that work has dried up and been more hard to come by and Gilles had struggled with that. And there is certainly some truth in that. But Gilles was far more complex a person than that.' I had met Gilles once, on a DJ trip to Iceland, and found a big, burly, friendly guy with a dry humour.

The acid house recession had continued to bite into the new millennium. In 2002 Ministry closed its glossy monthly club magazine. In 2003 *Muzik* magazine closed. Dance music's lucrative industry encompassed more than just clubs – there were PR and advertising companies, DJ agencies, studios. 'In the club world, it attracted a lot of people who weren't particularly good at anything else,' observed Paul Fryer. The former transvestite DJ managed to become the successful artist he always wanted to be. Gilles Nobbs wasn't so lucky. Or perhaps just not as talented.

In just a few short years, the culture disappeared from view. 'The whole thing just spiralled to a level that no one had ever dreamt of,' Pete Tong said. 'Too big and too much infrastructure. There was too much business around not enough money. There were dance departments at every record label, too many magazines, too many record labels, too many DJs probably, too many records, too much everything. After the millennium it didn't collapse, it got punctured. It slowly but surely faded away before your eyes.'

Julian Rolfe had always loved Gilles's company, but had also been aware of a darker side. 'I always thought he had that in him. I wasn't that shocked,' he said. 'There are certain people who are a bit depressed or a bit upset or a bit angry at the world. So maybe you make an extra effort to look after them.' Pre-photography, Gilles had a colourful life. He was in the army. 'Didn't last very long. Bought himself out. Hated it,' said Julian. Gilles was a holiday rep as well, which he'd loved. But like many people who'd found careers in dance music, he was also something of a misfit, somebody who'd found a place to hide away from the realities of the world. Where better to do that than in a disco, particularly if you were getting paid at the same time? 1990s dance music was a fluid place and a lot of people suddenly found themselves in creative careers. As somebody who started as a college dropout, travelled, worked in kitchens and factories and then, with nothing more than a glorified fanzine launch behind them, somehow ended up editor of a major national music magazine, I understood that better than most.

Julian Rolfe remembered his friend Gilles struggling with relationships, watching the work dry up as the post-millennium club recession hit. Nobbs had organised his own death with a military precision, arranging nights out with all his friends in months before that they only realised with bitter hindsight were last suppers, fond farewells. The suicide note Julian received was full of apologies. 'He just wasn't happy any more, wasn't enjoying himself, didn't see a way, didn't see himself in the future,' said Julian. 'Just didn't see himself. Didn't have anything going on romantically. Was just really low.'

For Gilles, the disco dream was over. Clubs have always been a place to escape to, but sometimes after too long they can be difficult to escape from. Gilles found somewhere to hide from it all in his lonely flat. He put his head in the oven and turned the gas on. He didn't need drugs to find this oblivion. It came all by itself. 'He did really love dance music,' said Julian. 'He couldn't dance very well though.'

AT MINISTRY OF SOUND, in 2001, CEO Lohan Presencer decided they didn't need superstar DJs to sell their albums any more. 'The DJs were getting very, very expensive for us to include,' Presencer explained. Ministry now had an impressive repertoire of its own music. But DJs were reluctant to include the tracks Ministry wanted them to. 'It was a case of the tail wagging the dog,' Presencer said. 'We were Ministry of Sound. We got the sense that the DJs were becoming less important than the brand and the music.' He was proved right. Ministry of Sound dance albums continue to sell on the brand name alone.

Premier division DJs like Sasha, John Digweed, Dave Seaman and Nick Warren had already moved into the lucrative foreign market. That was where they were going to stay. 'I don't think any of the people that ran the superclubs in the year 2000 would have envisaged that by 2003 they'd all be fucked,' said Sasha. In the UK, others suffered. Judge Jules saw his fees drop by 20 per cent. '2002, 2003 and 2004 were the lowest points as far as dance music was concerned,' he said. 'There was a legion of DJs who'd just found it easy to get work who suddenly had none.' But he was one of the luckier ones – his reputation was enough to keep him in DJ work. And he was an adept enough broadcaster to keep his Radio 1 show. He still has it. He says he's as busy as ever.

DJs from the lower divisions watched their careers dry up. London's Steve Lee was one of them. Things got 'much harder', he said. Even though he was never a big name, throughout the 1990s he had worked regularly. 'Couple of grand a week. I could do three or four gigs a weekend, five hundred quid each, no problem,' he said.

Inching into his late thirties, watching his income go down, he decided to change his life. Lee became a taxi driver and spent three and a half years driving around London on a scooter, doing the famous 'knowledge' test. He still DJs – but just for fun. 'There was a need for me to do something else in my life,' he said.

Derek Dahlarge also found that his life as a DJ got tougher. No longer was he being flown around the world. Now his regular gigs are at London's Café de Paris – and a local pub. 'It peters off after a while. Dance music's not as popular as it was,' he said. 'That was kind of weird to deal with.' In Birmingham, Phil Gifford's club Wobble had run out of steam in 1999 and closed. By 2001 he had moved to London and was working for the Ultra DJ agency. 'Dealing with DJs who were on their last legs, Z-list DJs, phoning you up saying, "Oh come on, you've got to get me a gig, I can't pay my mortgage,"' Gifford said. 'I was half glad I was in London, so I didn't have to walk down the street. Cause you did have that, "Oh, I'm a fallen star" kind of feeling. It makes me laugh now.' Gifford stuck it out for three years and moved back to Birmingham. He is now a hairdresser again.

Another was Adrian Gent, whose roving Manchester club night LuvDup had given him and DJing partner Mark Van Den Berg, a South African ex-pat, a profitable and enjoyable DJing and remix career. By 2001, the former partners had fallen out and the club finished. His bookings were going down. 'It had thinned out from what it was in '95, '96. I was getting half the bookings from what I was then,' he said. He split up with his partner, who no longer lets him see his young son and who emptied a lock-up of all his possessions: books, records, studio equipment. His life was in turmoil and, worse, he had fallen out of love with DJing. 'I didn't like the music, I didn't like the records. I was like, "What am I doing this for?"' Gent bit the bullet, got a job as a computer programmer for Ticketmaster and now has a new partner and daughter.

Miranda Cook, so enamoured with Gatecrasher and a young cyber kid boyfriend that she had moved to Sheffield and started working for the club, came down to earth with a bump. She lost her flat and ended up sleeping on a mattress in a spare room that Gatecrasher kept for staff. She lay there listening to the staff from the venue below emptying out the rubbish. 'And I felt the last ten years of going out every weekend was catching up with me. Lying there on the mattress, listening to bottles crash into the bins, thinking, "How did it come to this? What have I *done*? What have I done?"' She moved back South, worked in a furniture shop, started doing PR work for Judge Jules and has just written a book about her clubbing experiences. 'Sheffield finished me off,' she said. 'I never thought I'd write anything again. The whole thing was over.'

A REALISATION OF HOW greedy and disassociated from its audience the dance industry got has since hit its major players. 'Things started to get very, very organised and very military and very corporate, then inevitably they're not going to be as good,' said Pete Tong. 'People were just getting away with it,' said Dave Seaman. 'Shitloads of money coming in from sponsors. Loads of people earning a living out of the scene, it became something you could tag along with and get by.' Nick Raphael from Trannies With Attitude echoed the same theme. 'Cocaine and money,' he said. 'Everyone got greedy. We fell into it and had to turn it into a business.'

Somehow Renaissance survived. They still run nights around the world, release mix CDs – though they don't sell a tenth of what *The Mix Collection* did – and stage a music festival near Nottingham called Wild in the Country. 'I think I'm as guilty as anyone of getting caught up in the whole superclub thing and believing it,' said Geoff Oakes. 'Not really thinking where it would really take us in the long term. The millennium was really the straw that broke the camel's back really. That was the point it all came to and then imploded.' Oakes was planning to sell the business. If he got what he was looking for, he said, he could retire.

Sitting outside his villa in Ibiza, finishing his bottle of beer, Pete Tong reflected on where DJs are at now. 'DJing is the ultimate glorified manual labour. It is great – but you have to be there,' he said. 'I'm very preoccupied now, 46 years old, I wanna make more money doing things when I'm asleep –' he laughed here, slightly awkwardly '– than when I'm awake.' That was why Tong was here in Ibiza. He plays Pacha once a week all summer, taking a 'disco nap' before he goes down there. A man of 46 can't just keep going all night without a little rest. The Ministry's decision, the fall in salaries, the fact that there was simply nothing left but the lucrative foreign circuit condemned the superstar DJs to an eternal groundhog day: Tong's 'glorified manual labour'. Having largely never made hit albums of their own music, they had no choice but to keep travelling in order to keep getting paid, to fund the luxurious lifestyles both themselves and their partners had got used to. It was either that, or get out and find something else to do.

'I'M VERY PASSIONATE about personal development. I flood myself with it every day,' said Danny Rampling, confidently addressing a room so full of affluent-looking, fashionably dressed West Londoners that it was standing room only. It was autumn 2007. Sitting next to me was a woman in her late thirties in a Kangol cap called Renata Aly, who had been an executive producer on the clubbing film *Human Traffic*. She was with a group of female friends. They described themselves as 'the naughty corner'. On a nearby table, former DJ Jeremy Newall, who now works at the Apple Mac store on London's Regent Street, sat with his friend Blue Khiroya. It was quite an impressive turnout for a blustery Tuesday night in West London. Danny spoke their language. He got a big laugh early on for suggesting his audience spent less time on Facebook. But he didn't say that he had once been one of the UK's most famous superstar DJs, with his own Radio 1 show. Nor that he had been one of the famous four who brought acid house to Britain. He said he had worked in the music business. And nobody recognised him.

These successful 30-somethings had gathered in this function room above a Pizza Express because, as Jeremy Newall, a friend of Danny's from Facebook, put it, they were 'looking for something else'. Danny hoped he had that 'something else' for them. With a group of salespeople, he was talking up the Success University – an American-based, Internet business that sells business and personal development to subscribers paying a monthly fee who, in turn, earn money by recruiting more 'students'. Selling the Success University is where this former superstar DJ has ended up.

'There's a plethora of subjects. Communication, leadership, health, nutrition, marketing, Internet marketing, property, finance, a wealth of subjects that benefits people's lives,' Danny had explained to me earlier, over a pizza. 'If you're coachable and open to continued learning, it's a great opportunity. And also,' he added, brightening, 'it's another income stream.' When I met up with him at St John's Wood tube station, he was sizzling with positivity. He walked very quickly and talked very precisely about how positive he felt. He marched down the road and I marched alongside, trying to keep up. Phrases like 'amazing opportunity' ricocheted out of his mouth like bullets. The Success University was, he said, something he was very passionate about.

In front of his audience, in his ironed jeans, smart shoes and pink and white striped shirt, the 46-year-old former DJ star looked just the part for this affluent crowd. The name being bandied about was that of self-help business guru Bob Proctor. The book in front of *Human Traffic* producer Aly was called *Think and Grow Rich* by Napoleon Hill. 'If you love people,' added Danny, 'this business is so right for you.'

It would cost £85, he explained to his engrossed audience, for the intro pack, £25 a month the rest. And the more subscribers you recruited, the more commission you would make. Danny explained how one of Success University's other leading lights, Simon Hinton, standing nearby, had sold him the concept in just 30 minutes over lunch. 'Over a very good bottle of wine,' added Simon, to laughter. 'Which he paid for,' Danny shot back, to even bigger laughter.

A woman in a business suit was first to address the meeting. 'Stand up and give yourselves a round of applause for being here,' she said. She talked about the 'beautiful, vibrant' energy in the room. Danny was sandwiched in the middle of the bill. The main event was Prab Paul, director and student of the Success University. Each speaker followed the same theme. If we could seize control of our lives – one phrase used was 'masterminding' – and find a new, lucrative income stream, we would become much happier. Success University was the way to do that.

'I am going to be – and I say this proudly and humbly – an enlightened billionaire,' said Prab. Danny nodded solemnly, leaning against a pillar. Later Prab described to me the way that Danny was changing since he joined the Success University. 'He's a completely different human being to what he was a month ago,' Prab said. 'He has completely come out of his shell. He is a sponge. He is hungry to learn.' But despite his oratorical skills, Prab was unable to explain what seemed a very complicated commission system to me. There were thousands of pounds to be made. If you could only work out how it worked.

There was something odd, something cultish about the gathering. It seemed more a social event, a networking thing, than anything. It turned out the 'naughty corner' were already signed-up subscribers, just here for the crack. 'Most people come for the top totty,' said one of them, Samantha O'Connor, a well-groomed blonde woman, who was sitting next to another blonde, singer-songwriter Prudence Allen. Samantha told me she was a clairvoyant and revealed she had a sixth sense I was a journalist. I didn't say the fact I was writing busily in a notepad may have given the game away. Jeremy Newall seemed unsure about what he'd seen. 'I'm not going to dive in tonight,' he said. 'I've got my trunks on but I'm not stripping down. I need more substance.'

Danny wandered over to chat. He asked Jeremy's friend Blue what she had thought. 'Can I be honest?' she smiled. 'I liked the first 20 minutes. But I lost interest during the money part.' Danny was ready for her. 'If we can just change that attitude,' he said and began to talk about the problem we British had talking about money. Blue mentioned the phrase Pyramid Selling. Danny's smile didn't falter, but a little steel came into his voice. 'Pyramid selling is illegal,' he said. This was something different. On the way out, he introduced me to a 'great nutritionist'.

IN 2005, DANNY had retired from DJing after a six-month farewell tour and a ten-hour goodbye set at London's Turnmills. 'It hasn't been easy since leaving the music behind, it's been pretty challenging at times. And I thrive on challenge,' he said. 'I'm at a major crossroads in my life. I feel that my life, in terms of the music history, I've played in a pretty outstanding way. I've been success driven. And now I've stepped away and created these other opportunities. My game plan is to play part two of my life in a more spectacular fashion. Part one has been the prelude.' His interests, outside of the Success University, also include a property development company on the south coast.

Danny Rampling was a star DJ before anybody even knew what a star DJ was. 'Something I absolutely loved which was a hobby became a career,' he said. 'I didn't care for anything else. That was it, I was just totally intoxicated by the music and the lifestyle that went with it.' By 2005, for him, the shine was wearing off DJing. And so was the money. 'People were far more frugal and there was a lot more negotiating. Everyone had slashed their budgets as a result of the losses that were taken on Millennium Eve.'

Danny had become a father when his second wife gave birth to a son. He was also reeling with the onset of his forties. 'I understand what a mid-life crisis is about because I was pining for the days of my thirties. I couldn't accept it. I could not accept the fact that I'd got into my forties,' he explained. A keen cook, he initially planned to open a restaurant. 'I needed to put my back against the wall,' he said. His wife wasn't so pleased about his decision to turn his back on the lucrative DJing lifestyle – he called it a 'glittering career' – to go into a business as risky as restaurants. 'My wife had gone from this lovely affluent lifestyle, to nothing,' he said. 'She was full of uncertainty and women do not deal with uncertainty well and that's not a sexist comment, that's a fact. That is a fact. And that put pressure on my relationship for quite some time.'

But after 18 months of work, delay and protracted negotiation over a site in London's Spitalfields, Danny gave up on his restaurant idea. He saw this as a positive. 'Uncertainty is very healthy for ambitious people,' he said. But it seemed he wasn't just banking on the Success University. His old friend Nicky Holloway said Danny was 'sneaking' back into DJing. He now has a radio show on the Internet, his name is popping up on club flyers. Nicky and Danny had recorded a track together in Nicky's tiny studio. Danny has written an online book on how to make it as a DJ, which he flogs himself on a YouTube video. 'I don't like to use that word retire,' Danny said firmly. 'Because my view on retirement is you're just too tired to do anything. And I will be doing something until my dying day.'

IF SUPERCLUBBING as a mainstream pastime was dead by 2003, it had certainly left its mark. Today a night-time economy of shiny bars and clubs booms across every city in the UK. The social changes that first showed themselves in superclubs are now entrenched in mainstream society. Primarily, these are about what writer George Monbiot called the 'celebration of the self', which started in clubs in the early 1990s with the idea that anybody could be a star and which have now reached their logical conclusion in programmes like *Big Brother* and the legions of throwaway celebrities they created. Before acid house, people watched bands perform on stage. During the superclub years, they got up on podiums and showed off themselves. Fifteen years later, Britain is like one big superclub and *Big Brother* is its VIP room. Like most VIP rooms, it doesn't have anybody famous in it. Instead, there are a lot of very ordinary people – a little brighter, zippier, prettier or zanier that most, but ultimately nothing special – talking a lot and saying very little. It is a mirror image of the back rooms of the superclubs – only without the drugs.

Twenty-first-century Britain is a different place. After the death of Princess Diana in 1997 and the national outpouring a grief that followed – surely *something* to do with the amount of ecstasy in the water supply at that time, a massive contact comedown – emotions aren't as hidden any more. There are openly gay people on television rather than gay people pretending to be straight and metrosexual, heterosexual icons like David Beckham. And rightly or wrongly, Britain has decided that it's how you get on with people, how you connect, how you network that counts, not where you're from. Or indeed what you actually do.

On *Big Brother*, the success of a contestant depends on the amount of entertainment they provide coupled with how much people warm to them. Exactly what was required to succeed in 1990s clubland. As if a nation had learnt the lesson Dave Seaman wrote in his little black diary: 'be nice to everybody'. It is hardly surprising then that *Big Brother*'s long-time host, Davina McCall, started out as a door picker at Choice, the London club that made Jeremy Healy's name. That Melanie Hill, a contestant on the first series, was a friend of Norman Cook's from the House of Love, or that Norman himself was later a celebrity guest on Brazilian *Big Brother*, DJing to a TV audience of 40-million plus. Or that *Big Brother* winner Kate Lawler is now a successful DJ, proving that anybody can do it. Or indeed that Paul Oakenfold, having spotted the show's potential straight away, wrote the theme tune with Andy Gray – the single sold 250,000, but he got paid a buy-out which means he doesn't get repeat fees every time it's shown.

Outside of the *Big Brother* theme, how will history remember something as ephemeral as the 1990s club revolution? Its memories belong to clubbers – and they are all different, because clubbing was a subjective experience, as well as a collective one. Wasn't that night great? Yeah, what did he play again? No fucking idea but it was funny when that girl put the flashing horns on. And when those clubbers and their memories die, a popular music wave that swept up millions will slip back into the sea, leaving nothing on the beach but a few memories and the flotsam and jotsam of memorabilia – flyers, clothes, photos and CDs. A pair of silver strappy sandals, an empty wrap, licked clean. Memories of a love affair that flashed across a crowded dance floor and didn't even survive the night, missed in the chaos of end of the night lifts and taxis. A glorious night out they remember – just – with a smile. And the records – Underworld, Leftfield, Mo' Wax, Orbital, the Chemical Brothers, the thousands of fantastic one-off hits that flared for a few months across the dance floors, virtually none of them, bar Fatboy Slim's catalogue of hits, made by any of the super-star DJs.

This was a generation that found the friends or the networks or the confidence to get their grown-up lives going in clubs. They got involved, had the time of their lives, lived life on the edge – sometimes, just after dawn, a little too close to the edge – and got out in time. They were the real winners in the superclub wars. Now they are reuniting on Facebook. There is now a nineties club revival going on. Vague, Renaissance and Wobble have active, busy Facebook groups all remembering past glories. Wobble and LuvDup are already staging reunion nights. It's like a twenty-first-century version of the Northern Soul scene, whose adherents today still meet up and dance together. 'Facebook for all its faults might end up the Northern Soul scene of house music,' said Adrian 'LuvDup' Gent, excited about a party he was planning.

The staff of *Mixmag* boomeranged off in different directions. Andy Pemberton edited *Q* magazine, then moved to New York and launched the hugely successful *Blender* magazine. He is now back in the UK. Alexis Petridis is the *Guardian* and *GQ*'s pop critic. Frank Tope is a DJ and has a successful career in music publishing. David Davies is a powerful publishing executive. All four are married with children. Karla

Smith lives in Thailand and has a baby daughter. DJ Stan is a hackney cab driver in Maidstone, planning a university degree. Elsewhere Peter Cunnah and Al Mackenzie have revived D:Ream and are working together and playing gigs again after a chance meeting in a West London park. Sonique and Alessandro have split up. And Nicky Holloway was full of beans when I last spoke to him. The little studio had gone and he was planning to use Facebook to fill up his new venture: Desert Island Disco, a choose-your-own music club for the 30–44 year-old-age group. 'It's nostalgic but we're going to play new records as well,' he enthused. 'I'm hungry again.'

Facebook also means nobody can escape their past any longer. It's out there, waiting for you, so you better hope you were nice to it first time around. Like a virtual Davina, there with her clipboard, waiting to knock you back because you were rude to her ten years ago. But these ex-clubbers don't post up pictures of the DJs heroes. They put up hundreds of pictures of themselves, looking young, gorgeous and wasted. Because ultimately the superclubs were a backdrop onto which clubbers projected their own glories. And they understand that they, not the DJs, were the real stars.

Some DJs will tell you that dance music is thriving and that there are clubs all over the UK and that is true. There is Fabric and the Gallery in London, Shindig in Newcastle and big festivals like Creamfields and Global Gathering every summer and smaller nights all over the country. Ibiza is full as ever. And people will always want to go clubbing. But acid house is just another ripple in the pop-music pool now, not a tidal wave. And pretending anything else is just an avoidance tactic.

How will history remember the superstar DJs? What will their legacy be? There is only one movie about them, that 2004 comedy *It's*

All Gone Pete Tong, in which Paul Kaye plays a DJ who goes deaf, partly inspired by Sasha's eardrum accident. Pete Tong himself appeared briefly in the film as himself, interviewing Kaye the DJ with a tape recorder. He was wooden. Kaye made a convincingly idiotic DJ, but despite a few funny moments, the film wasn't very good. And like the millennium, it was another PR disaster. It made DJs look like ego-centric, cocaine-guzzling idiots, which was unfair, as they were generally much smarter and more likeable that that. Not realising this, some took cameos in the film.

Pete Tong's profit share never materialised because the film never made any money, his one bad business deal. Instead he has been immortalised in the *Penguin Book of Rhyming Slang*, for the phrase 'It's All Gone Pete Tong' – it's all gone wrong. 'Had to explain to my mum years ago that it wasn't meant to be a bad thing,' he said, determined to make the best of it. 'Anything like that, notoriety is a dream, isn't it? To make your name.'

It is a shame that Jeremy Healy and the rest of them never took that picture of them lined up with their flash motors. At least we would have one definitive picture to remember them by. So let's imagine it instead. There is Jeremy in his leather rasta cap with his black Ferrari. Lined up in their Porches are Geoff Oakes, Leftfield's Paul Daley, James Barton (his bought for cash, naturally) and Piers Sanderson. Tong sits in his fastest car of the era, a Mercedes AMG ('0–60 in like five seconds, made a fantastic noise as well'). Sonique leans on her Aston Martin DB9. Norman and Zoë circle in that slow-moving, Millennium Eve party bus. Oakenfold zooms overhead with Bono in a private plane. And there's Sasha, hunting around in the background for a maroon Rover 216 coupe he lost somewhere in a northern town, one lost weekend in 1993.

But even the wildest parties have to end sometime. 'A lot of people got caught up in their own world and had delusions of grandeur,' concluded Derek Dahlarge, that most archetypal of 1990s DJ stars. 'When it stops, the lights go on and everyone's gone home.'

PRESENT DAY

SUMMER 2008. SASHA went back in the studio to finish *Involver 2*. He sourced an interesting, eclectic mix of tracks. There were three of his own, which had started out as remixes of other people's songs. In his New York studio, working with a team of engineers, he spent nearly six months creating *Involver 2*, deconstructing every single piece of music, and remaking them all again. Unfortunately he had to go on tour before it was properly finished and was delivering final instructions regarding the finished mix via mobile phone from his tour bus. Now he was worried he had over-tinkered with it.

Around the world, dance music is back. In the charts, in the clubs, slowly, under the radar, acid house is back in fashion. It is a comeback that started slowly in 2004, with the Ministry of Sound's international house hit 'Call On Me' by Swedish DJ and producer Eric Prydz. There was been a short-lived fad called 'new rave'. Now there are clubs all over London with names like Zombies Ate My Brain and Minimal Hospital. France has a new school of explosive, noisy, punky dance acts like Simian Mobile Disco, Ed Bangers and Justice. A new urban sound has arrived in the UK – 'bassline house' – reaching high into the charts with hits like 'Heartbroken' from hitherto unknown Huddersfield producer T2. Pete Tong is playing this stuff: it is his job. But Sasha isn't. Instead there are rumours that he is losing his all-important credibility. His last 'Emfire' mix CD for Renaissance sold pitifully: just 3,500 in the UK.

Involver 2 doesn't do anything noisy or nasty. Instead it is a pretty, consistent and slightly dull album of polished trance – though he wouldn't call it that. It has peaks and lows. And it all sounds the same. The Son of God is now playing God, remaking everything in his own image. And in this process making everything less interesting than it was in the first place. A crackling, abstract electronic track called 'Arcadia' from Berlin's Apparat politely tidied up, its offbeat rhythm made metronome, its ghostly vocal buried under whooshing noises. An introspective solo number from Radiohead's Thom Yorke called 'The Eraser', reduced to a vocal sample over another politely funky electronic groove.

Sasha still can't manage his own creativity, can't stop impulsively polishing the shine out of his music. He long ago eliminated the random element, the gloriously unlikely clash of opposites that made his name at Shelley's – Leftfield's 'Not Forgotten' mixed with Whitney Houston's voice, singing 'I Wanna Dance With Somebody'. But neither can he be Vangelis, creating grandiose synthesiser symphonies. He is stuck in the middle. And he has forgotten something important. That dance music is pop music and that pop music needs to surprise and entertain. That the 'underground' is an imaginary place that never actually existed, outside of the fantasies of boys in record shops, a throwback to the punk days, a redundant philosophy. What matters now in 2008 is the result, only that.

In spring 2008 Sasha did a short DJ tour of Brazil. The country's upmarket clubs still provide rich pickings for DJs like him, touring the world's circuit of playboy discos, five-star restaurants and boutique hotels. It is a glamorous life. But it is also the acid house equivalent of a bloated Elvis Presley in the white suit playing Vegas. So here he was, the evening after our interview in Guaraja, playing a small party in a beautiful club called Vive La Vie. It is a dramatic place, a spill of wooden terraces on a cliff top in a forest, the waves churning a hundred metres down below. Carnival weekend – a national holiday – and the club was full of women because the promoter decided to charge them a quarter what he charged men. They were young, beautiful, sexily dressed, up for a party. It's unlikely many of them knew much about Sasha apart from his name – and that this name signified something desirable and European.

A rainstorm started just after Sasha went on, which sent the whole crowd inside, jammed together under the club's roof. Now he had a captive dance floor and his designer trance sounded tailor-made for this designer crowd. On a bench in front of the DJ booth, three stunning girls were dancing wildly. Sasha, bent over the Maven's flashing green and red lights like an engineer fixing a fuse box, ignored them. For some reason I thought of the rock comedy *Spinal Tap*. But the superstar DJ didn't smile. He sipped his champagne seriously. He looked like a man with a long night's work ahead of him. He looked utterly bored.

FEBRUARY 2008. Pacha, in São Paulo, Brazil, is a very modern sort of club. Big and shiny, part of an expanding superclub franchise that grew out of the famous Ibiza flagship. There are 23 Pacha clubs worldwide – in London, Marrakech, New York, Buenos Aires, Barcelona, Ischgl in the Alps, Bucharest – even Vilnius in Lithuania. It is the world superclub brand that Ron McCulloch dreamt home could become. Tonight a big crowd was packed in: dressy, affluent, chic – the big spenders of the booming Brazilian economy. They were lined up at the front of the DJ booth but they hadn't come to see a DJ. They had come to see a pop star.

David Guetta didn't disappoint. He entered the DJ booth with his arms outstretched, Jesus-like and the crowd roared like they were greeting a rock icon. He put on a CD – an old house classic, Robin S's 'Show Me Love', updated, punched into 2008, with a flourish and they all started bouncing. His wife Cathy fluttered beside him, filming things on a tiny video camera. Behind him in the booth was a bottle of vintage champagne in an ice bucket. It remained unopened. David and Cathy don't drink, smoke or do drugs. They are far too business-like for that.

Guetta encapsulates the new breed of superstar DJ. His appeal, which spreads worldwide, has captured a new audience – not the druggy clubbers of the 1990s, but a clean, respectable, mainstream crowd who treated him like a rock star. At Pacha, Guetta did things DJs don't do. He got on the mike and talked. He stood on the booth and raised his hands. He turned down the volume and got the crowd to sing along to his hit 'Love Is Gone'. And he played hit after hit – old ones, new ones, his own, reworks. He had no problem being commercial. 'Our music is 20 years old,' said Guetta the next day, over lunch by the rooftop pool at São Paulo's designer Hotel Unique. 'We cannot act like this music is a new music and we want to keep it for ourselves. If we do this, it's going to die.' He smiled. 'Now I think I've really proven my point.'

With his floppy blond hair and skinny jeans, Guetta looks much younger than his 40 years. He had 40 dates lined up in just two months between late July and September. Cathy works as his manager and publicist – together, they make a formidable couple. The club night Fuck Me I'm Famous he and Cathy run at Pacha dominates Ibiza, the point hammered home by its propaganda – giant, beautifully photographed billboards of the pair looking like glamorous models in an ad campaign. Which is just what they are. 'It's my culture against her culture. VIP culture against acid house culture,' said Guetta. 'And together it works.'

Guetta grew up in Paris the son of left-wing intellectuals who ran a small Paris restaurant. He began DJing at 13 and by 17 had a regular gig in a gay club. He met Cathy, whose father was in the military, in a disco in the south of France. She is black and had found in clubs a way to escape the casual racism sometimes found in France. 'In one minute I didn't see any difference between the rest of the people and me,' she said.

Guetta has had an unusual career curve. He ran a wild after-hours night in a strip club, Cathy was a waitress at celebrity hangout Les Bain Douches and used to send VIP clients on to him. The pair opened and ran a string of clubs – they later took over Les Bain Douches, which is the same place that Amos Pizey and Jeremy Healy's Bleachin' weekend finished off – and the club Queen. They had restaurants. Cathy even owned an upmarket strip club, called the Pink Pussycat. Their clubs did what Fuck Me I'm Famous does in Ibiza – mixed celebrities with out-there clubbers. In Ibiza, Kate Moss and P Diddy are just two of the club's faces. In Paris, the Guettas are famous. But three years ago Guetta was unhappy. He didn't get to DJ any more. He spent all his time in the office. 'It was a very successful business. And I was like on TV. And everybody was like, "Oh, your life is so great. And you're friends with Lenny Kravitz." I was like, "'Okay, then what?'"'

Three years ago he persuaded Cathy that they should sell everything so he could concentrate on DJing. 'I was like, "Cathy, we have to stop this."' Cathy was nervous. But she went along with the plan. He realised his plan was going to work when he was at Space in Ibiza. The American DJ Erick Morillo, a friend, put on Guetta's track 'Just

A Little More Love', turned the music off and got everybody singing along. 'And he's like, "Ladies and gentlemen, David Guetta," and everybody's clapping hands. Wow.' Since then Guetta has sold more than three million copies of his three albums (two originals and a mix) and 960,000 of his hit single 'Love Is Gone'. He has a cameo in the video, sitting in a corner of a diner, wearing sunglasses, reading a book entitled *Principles of Trigonometry*. Trainspotter chic.

Guetta first took ecstasy at a young age, while DJing in a college party. He never drank – just smoked a lot of weed. 'I tried cocaine one time, I hated it. Then I met my wife. And she never touched anything. And she was like, "You, you look so stupid."' He gave it all up. That was 15 years ago. 'A lot of the new generation DJs, they're not so much into drugs,' he said. Now, he told me, to be a successful DJ you had to be a producer too. Someone like Carl Cox, the British DJ star who still enjoys a worldwide reputation but who never released more than a couple of minor tracks, wouldn't make it today. Producing makes you more money. 'When you make a hit record, your fees go up,' Guetta said.

Today the superstar DJs are more likely to be European than British. That makes sense – from Boney M to Swedish techno pop star Basshunter, Europeans have always been better at the blandly catchy Euro-disco that is unstoppable on a global stage. Like Dutch trance DJ star Tiesto who sells out stadium-sized gigs, releases hit singles, even opened the last Olympics. 'There's a whole new wave of DJs that have come through that are a lot more focused, organised and they're running it as a business. It's a very well-oiled machine,' observed John Digweed admiringly.

Before São Paulo, in February 2008, Guetta played a float at the carnival in Salvador with Norman 'Fatboy Slim' Cook. Rumours from Salvador whispered that Guetta was the bigger success this year. That he looked more confident, that the crowd responded more positively to him. That Guetta is the star now. Maybe. Fatboy Slim's last studio album, 2004's *Palookaville*, sold just 75,000 in the UK – compared to the 1,173,000 his 1998 album *You've Come A Long Way, Baby* shifted. But Guetta is at his peak.

The Guettas have two children but they don't own anything – no house, no car, no studio. Their enormous Parisian apartment is rented. 'I wanna be free, this is why I do this job,' said David. Cathy was hurrying him along. They had to go. David had a flight to catch, another club to do, another crowd waiting.